SUPERTEACHING

Master Strategies for Building Student Success

Eric Jensen

Copyright © 1988 by Eric Jensen

ISBN 0-8403-4592-5

Printed in the United States of America
10   9   8   7   6   5   4

Contents

Acknowledgments, vii

Introduction, ix

I. Building a Foundation for Success   1

1. The Game Has Changed, 1
    Nine trends that rocked education
    How each of them affects you
    What to do about it

2. Who You Are Makes a Difference, 7
    The quality of your presence is what matters
    Attitudes, beliefs and actions of a winner
    Keys for classroom success

3. Learning—From Theory to Practice, 18
    What's new in brain, mind and learning theory
    How it affects you and how you teach
    What changes are now needed

4. Skills That Make the Magic, 31
    The fundamentals skills of success
    When to use them, how and why
    The dramatic results you can expect

II. Preparation Makes It Possible   41

5. Mastery Lesson Planning, 41
    How the pros make it happen
    Top-notch lesson planning
    Develop a personal and course purpose
    Mind-mapping

6. How to Build a Quality Learning Environment, 53
The power of the non-conscious senses
How your room can do 25% of your teaching
Affective learning—Using all the senses

7. Last Minute Readiness, 61
The medium is still the message
The most important element in your class
Do's and don'ts for super teachers
Rehearsal and finishing touches

III. Delivery and Presentation

71

8. How to Open Your Class, 71
The 6 secrets to know before starting
The four parts to a successful introduction

9. High-performance Teaching Tools, 95
Specific strategies for super-teachers
Motivation boosters, interest builders
How to have your students understand almost anything
Creating active involvement and better feedback systems

10. How to Successfully Close a Class, 126
Qualities most needed and least used
The most powerful tools you can use right away

IV. Student Communication

139

11. Relationships Make It Work, 139
Rapport: Teacher-student relationships
Teamwork: Student-to-student relationships
Attitudes: Student-subject relationships
Self-Esteem: A student's relationship with himself

12. The Lost Art of Listening, 148
Do you make these mistakes?
16 ways to listen more effectively
Three keys to success
Building classroom "safety"
How to empower the listener

13. Successful Classroom Interactions, 160
Why this may be the most important skill
Three simple steps you can do today
New ways to respond more effectively

14. Discipline and Class Management the Easy Way 176
Remediation: First aid for the battle-worn
Rules, guidelines and agreements that work
Prevention: 10 ways to prevent discipline problems

V. The Discovery Process   193

15. *Active Learning Strategies, 193*
>   Four key elements you should know
>   How to do selection and planning
>   Introduction and instructions
>   Operation and maintenance
>   Debrief and closure

16. *Self-esteem: A Way of Being, 203*
>   Five ways to boost self-concept
>   Student appreciation rediscovered
>   How to acknowledge and make sure it lands
>   Direct and indirect appreciation

17. *Successful Evaluations Made Simple, 214*
>   Test varieties: Eight of them
>   New thinking about testing
>   How to grade successfully

VI. The Vision   227

18. *The Return to Aliveness, 227*
>   How to prevent burnout
>   Keys to personal renewal
>   Steps to professional renewal

19. *Making Education Work, 241*
>   Implications of the latest global trends
>   Recommendations for committed educators
>   Step-by-step planning: The blueprint for success

Appendix   251

>   Reader evaluation
>   Strategies
>   Suggested resources

Bibliography and Suggested Reading, 264
Index, 269

Acknowledgments

I was raised in a family of teachers so I acknowledge my mother, Peg, and father, Robert, for their inspiration, love, and support. I've worked with thousands of students and they have all contributed, in some way, to this book. I especially appreciate the loving support from Joelle James and Shannon Murphy who helped make this book possible.

Others who have made contributions to this book or my teaching are: Jeff Alexander, Bill and Carol Baras, Scott Bornstein, Linda Brown, Stephanie Burns, Joe Chapon, Steve Curtis, Bobbi DePorter, Lynn Dhority, Werner Erhard, Buckminister Fuller, Michael Gelb, John Grinder, Jack Hill, Madeline Hunter, Dwight O'Neill, Mona Moon, Ann Nevin, Mark Reynolds, Anthony Robbins, Marshall Thurber and Rebel Williams. In addition, my copy editor Joelle James was instrumental in making this work simpler and more readable.

The contributions of others are endless and what's unfortunate is that many of my contributors I may not meet nor be able to give the recognition due to them. So to you who know you made a difference, thank you.

The purpose of teaching
is to provide for your students
an experience of their own greatness

Introduction

The first Monday of March in 1972 was one of the low points of my life. I had just taught my first class and was being critiqued by my mentor teacher. She did her best to say things in a kind way. She was gentle and told me how much she appreciated the time I had put into preparation. She also mentioned that she knew I was trying very hard and she appreciated that, too. In spite of her kindness, one message came through loud and clear. I was not fit for a classroom! When I was a student it seemed easy to make fun of the teacher or find things that he or she did poorly. Being the one up front was different and my introduction to teaching was not a pleasant one.

Fortunately, I had two things going for me—I was a proud person and I didn't like criticism. So, I had incentives to get better even if only for my ego. Also, I needed a job. Having food on the table was a high priority. Although those two reasons were not the noblest of motives, I did manage to improve enough to keep my job and my students remained reasonably happy. This pattern served my needs for years . . . until one day I was exposed to an entirely new level of teaching quality and it was an eye-opening knockout! I saw another teacher getting results and getting them fast. The best part was that the class was a lot of fun and had virtually no discipline problems!

Being exposed to a true master-teacher did wonders for me. It was also very humbling. I realized that my training as a teacher was out-dated and, in many ways, useless. It was no longer enough to have most of my students reasonably satisfied with a minimum of complaints. Why couldn't my students and I be ecstatic, wanting to come back for more? Before that could happen, I had to admit something that was not easy to swallow: I really didn't know how to teach effectively.

Since that humbling moment, I have dedicated myself to becoming effective in the classroom. I have made untold mistakes and I continue to make them. But now I learn from them instead of trying to cover them up. I ask for evaluations of every class I teach and I make the necessary adjustments. As a student of teaching, I take classes every chance I get and now, years after committing myself to teaching excellence, I'm proud to say I get fabulous results!

My work has been featured nationwide on NBC, UPI, AP and in USA Today. My first two books, *You Can Succeed* and *Student Success Secrets* have become standards in many schools, I co-founded Supercamp, a unique 10-day residential accelerated learning program for teens. I also founded Turning Point, a revolutionary program for training teachers. These successful model programs have attracted students and educators from 50 states and seven countries. Not bad for a kid who spent much of junior high school in the vice principal's office.

Yet what nourishes me is the individual impact made. When a student says to me, "I took your class four years ago and it changed my life," I know I'm on the right path. Chances are, if you are reading this book, you are on that same path. This book will provide you with both the vision of how to create extraordinary results in the classroom as well as the specific tools to make that vision possible. The commitment must come from you and I'm confident that it will. Through simple, useful examples and hundreds of proven classroom tools, you can make education work for you and your students. The larger purpose of this book is:

1. To re-inspire and empower educators to realize the enormous possibilities of public education.
2. To provide the resources necessary to make use of, and transform as needed, our existing systems to actually deliver on the unrealized promise of authentic education.

Mark Twain said, "Don't let your schooling get in the way of your education." My hope is that this book will add much to your education! Some of this book may run counter to what's been traditionally taught. In such case, you may appreciate the thoughts of novelist and philosopher Andre Gide who said, "The only real education comes from what goes counter to you." Consider yourself a trailblazer, a pioneer in the classroom wilderness. By using the tools in this book, your journey will be far easier and much more rewarding.

Before you start, I want to acknowledge you, the reader. You've invested your time, money and attention in this book and I respect you for that. Your time is valuable, you work hard for a living and you parcel out your attention sparingly. You and I share a dream—the dream of making education work for everyone—for educators and for students. Presently, education works for neither and that doesn't sit well with me. Writing this book has been a turning point because I must continually live and teach what's in it. I'm excited that it can be a turning point for you, too. With your vision, your commitment to making a difference in education and the tools from this book, we can make it work. Together. By living the commitment to our vision, we can turn education around so that it works even better than our wildest dreams! Congratulations on taking your first step!

Building a Foundation for Success

T

The Game Has Changed

Objectives

- To identify nine nationwide changes affecting education
- To articulate vision for education

This book is not about the problems facing today's educators. It is about the vision and possibility that we can bring forth to make education work. After all, the problems we face as educators are, to a large degree, merely symptoms. Solving the problems will not change education. New ones appear faster than we can solve the old ones. We are bailing water out of a boat that we already know has holes in it!

We've spent nearly a trillion dollars in education since landing on the moon and most measuring sticks say the quality has remained the same or gotten worse. Teachers experience widespread powerlessness, bitterness and resignation. Teacher strikes have doubled in the last decade. Instead of a conversation about the joys of learning, education has become a conversation about dropouts, low test scores, teenage pregnancy, vandalism, AIDS, teenage drunk driving, violence, drug abuse and suicides. Not that those areas don't deserve attention. They do. But somehow the focus seems to have changed.

What's caused it all? What's putting us on such a treadmill? How can we get at the real source of the frustration? Why do we seem to be constantly behind at making education work? The questions we raise seem to point to something fundamental:

"The Game Has Changed"

It's changed in many profound ways. We cannot play by the old rules and succeed. A return to the basics will not work. Another simple "band-aid" will not work. Nearly anything we've used so far may still be causing the problems. We simply cannot use the old behaviors and expect the same responses as before. Things are different now. Here are some of the more dramatic changes and their corresponding results:

Change 1: *Greater Velocity of Change*

Entire industries start and stop within a single decade. Schools are no longer preparation for a single job or career. Schools now must be a preparation for many careers. The average high school graduate in 1990 will have 3–5 careers compared to 1–2 for his or her parents. Jobs simply become extinct faster nowadays. Students need to learn HOW to learn, not WHAT to learn.

1

Results: Many students recognize that the curriculum is outdated and does not provide them with the real tools for life. More and more students are attending alternative classes, schools, summer programs and taking home study. Classroom enthusiasm is at an all-time low. Dropout rates are staggering: Texas—33%, New York—34%, Chicago—43%, San Diego—35%, inner city schools average 40–60%. Nationwide, one out of four students drops out of school!

Another result of the increasing rate of change is found in staff development programs. Many of the ideas and programs offered as solutions to problems are out of date immediately. Teachers have become tired of having to learn something new only to have it dropped and replaced by something even "newer." This constant "band-aid" approach leaves teachers burned out and cynical about additional teacher training since most programs continue to teach content, the WHAT rather than the HOW. Even if a program is useful, it often trains teachers in an area so specific that they exemplify the saying, "If what you hold is a hammer, you only look for nails."

Change 2: *Information Age Impact Is Increasing*

This creates a widening gap between what's known and what's implemented in schools. The research in psychology, sociology, neuroscience, biology, physics and education has a 2–5 year lag time for individual educator implementation. The lag time for in-the-system innovation is usually 5–8 years for pilot programs and an 8–25 year lag for widespread implementation!

Results: This wide gap creates a sense of hopelessness about staying informed. Teachers stop trying to stay updated. Textbooks are often out of date at print time. Students make an unfortunate distinction between what happens at school and the "real world."

Change 3: *Increasingly Advanced Technology*

The sophistication of the information age means that we have created a new entity—"The electronic authority." Students now turn to computers, television, radio, audio and videotapes as their source of up-to-the-moment information. Perhaps creating an even greater impact is the additional learning students get electronically: trends, values, fashions, manners, customs, or ethics. Historically, this information was taught through the authority of parents, churches, or schools. None of these seem to be today's primary source of authoritative information.

Results: This trend creates fewer positive role model relationships, less sense of community, bonding and responsibility. Results are greater classroom discipline problems, delinquency and crime. There's less development of family relationships because the students don't HAVE to go to their parents for critical information as they did forty years ago.

The power and charisma of the media has changed student standards for communication. The congruency of actors and impact of multi-media electronic presentations spoil students for unrealistic standards. Two generations ago, the classroom teacher was one of the most visible and powerful role models. Now role models come from sports, theater, film and entertainment . . . celebrities made famous and visible by the media. Teachers simply can't compete.

Results: Students bring the mindset of television to class each day. In comparison, students often see teachers as inadequate or boring. Thus, students have less respect for their teachers, daydream more and participate less in class.

Change 4: *The "Provider-User" Relationship Has Changed*

In the past, school was designed as a "provider" of information for students who would be "users" of that information. This created a power structure with the teacher as dispenser of valuable information and the student as powerless receiver of the "pearls of wisdom." In this role, the student was passive, a vessel to be filled.

> In these times of rapid change
> it is the learners who will inherit the future.
> The "Learned," who "know it all" will
> find themselves frustrated by a
> world that has passed them by.

When the teacher controls the information, the student expects the teacher to "do it to him" rather than being in a learning partnership. The old method keeps students from being responsible for their learning. The information age has enabled students to become their own "provider." They are no longer at the mercy of teachers to get information. Hence the old "provider-user" relationship is obsolete.

Years ago, teachers had fewer demands placed on them. Today, the demands are extraordinary and the school structure is not set up to handle these needs. Our educational system simply does not support and nurture the teacher. And, teachers need both, especially now. There are insufficient pathways for teachers to express themselves and be heard. There is a chilling lack of acknowledgment and support for the job teachers do. Most schools are designed to bypass the teacher on some of the most important decisions teachers must live with: teacher-student ratio, class hours, curriculum and classroom design. And to add to the insult, teachers' salaries have lagged behind other comparable professions.

Results: This changing role has left the teacher with little prestige and respect. These factors, the powerlessness, the lack of respect, the lack of support and nurturing have left most teachers in a state of resignation. To survive, they have simply adapted to the problems and circumstances. The evidence is in both conversation and actions. The prevailing conversation in education right now is about problems and circumstances.

Change 5: *Restructuring of the Economic and Social Family*

More and more mothers work outside the home than ever before. More and more children live with just one parent. Parents spend less and less time with their children. In addition, Jerald Bachman of the Survey Research Center in Michigan says two-thirds of all high school students are working part-time. He adds that one-quarter of them work over 20 hours a week! The impact is staggering. We have "latch-key kids" who come home to an empty house in the afternoon . . . child care centers bulging at the seams . . . kids without a sense of belonging and teens spending increased time on the job. There's no one left to give the emotional nurturing, the support, the sharing of values, the discipline and responsibility of our nation's kids. Most parents leave the job up to the schools.

Results: The kids are suffering. Teenagers report experiences of alienation, feelings of separateness and painful aloneness. Suicide, drop-outs, crime and drug abuse rates are at an all-time high. Runaways are increasing and so is teenage pregnancy. Working teenagers are frequently exhausted and unable to stay awake in class.

Change 6: *Drain of Leadership from Education to Business*

Years ago, some of the best and brightest persons provided the vision and leadership for schools. Now, the economic opportunities in business have attracted many of the leaders with vision. Now, schools often set aside "vision", hiring administrators for their ability to solve problems, reduce vandalism, raise test scores and manage disenchanted staffs. The role of principal is often compared to that of a police chief or fire-fighter.

Results: The kinds of roles principals are asked to fill attracts fewer visionary and more of the problem-solver type of person. This creates a school environment that consists of conversations about problems, rather than vision. What most faculties and staff need is a vision empowering them to create the kind of nurturing learning environment they know is possible.

Change 7: *Increased Market-Driven Consumerism*

The power of the media has grown so much that nearly anything or anyone can be the next "hot" item. There's a constant push for being rich, famous, healthy, happy, attractive and successful. Sports and entertainment salaries have become public record and making a million dollars a year seems commonplace.

Results: This emphasis on being one of the "beautiful people" places tremendous pressure on our youth. Stress in children has become commonplace. It's just too difficult for them to keep an even keel in the "go for it" world of glitz and glamour. Unrealistic expectations are demoralizing our nation's youth. Kids don't see any way they can "make it" the way the system has it set up, so they simply give up. They can't win, and they know it. Teen suicides have jumped dramatically—up 83% in the last ten years.

Change 8: *An Increasingly Multi-Cultural Society*

In many cities, the term "majority" or "minority" populations have reversed. For example, in Los Angeles there are more non-whites than whites. This shift in ethnic percentages means that school staffs need to be more sensitive to a wider range of needs. In the Southwest, there's an increasingly greater Mexican-American and Asian population, while in other areas the increase is in Blacks. The old concept of "WASP-based" schools is obsolete.

The effects of this change have been most dramatic in cities like San Diego. The innovative Race and Human Relations Department has been assisting teachers who are wholly unprepared to deal with student populations of three to five ethnic backgrounds and for whom English is a second language.

Results: This diversity has created significant challenges for both faculty and staff. Teachers experience consistent communication failures, mis-diagnose learners and an increase in student tension. Many educators predict the problems will increase with the new immigration policies.

Change 9: *Less Predictability*

The difficulty that education faces is compounded by a supremely complex society that constantly gives mixed messages. While ten trends are increasing, five others are decreasing. We have so many more indicators and statistics available that even the simplest of issues is clouded.

For example, we are nearly paralyzed by the process of creating a responsible and authentic budget. The problem is not that we don't have enough money for education. We do. The problem is not that we don't have enough information. We do. The problem is that we are often unable to sort out the information in a way that tells us what we really need to know in order to spend the money responsibly.

Results: This makes for missed opportunities, cost overruns, wasteful resource allocations and increased difficulty in assessing budget priorities. It means money gets wasted while other deserving programs suffer. We have larger budgets than ever before, yet there's constant conversation about scarcity of money. It's no wonder that teachers experience feelings of resignation about education.

With all these changes occurring, where are we? What do we, as educators, need to do to make some sense out of this world in flux? There are no simple answers. Answers wouldn't help anyway. Answers don't empower people. Answers are deadends and, typically, the too-soon finality of much needed introspection. What's needed is continual inquiry. Who are we as educators and what do we bring to the party? And, we need to keep asking questions about ourselves. Questions such as:

"What is needed right now around me?"
"What am I really trying to do?"
"What do I really know about learning?"
"What's right about the role of schools today?"
"Who do I need to be to truly make a difference?"
"How can I get the skills that are most needed?"
"Where is my own level of commitment in the matter of education?"

It's clear that as a whole, we have not yet contemplated answers to these questions. Certainly many individuals do ponder, but as a profession we have much introspection to do. The education of our children is a critical job of staggering importance. Success will require that we be more than "who we are" right now. We will have to be all we are capable of becoming. And, we will need a powerful vision.

The Power of Our Vision

The late Senator Robert F. Kennedy said, "Some men see things that are and ask 'Why?' and others see things the way they could be and ask 'Why not?'" This book is born from the vision of "Why not?" It's a vision of possibility about what education could be, not how it is. One where students run TO school instead of FROM school. One where students ask for homework instead of complain about it. It's a vision where teachers are heard, appreciated and respected. It's one where teachers have the power to affect decisions about the curriculum, their classroom, their students, and school policies. It's also a vision about partnership—where teachers work with students, not teach "at" them and where teachers, students and administrators work as a team, sharing ideas, supporting each other and enjoying the privilege (not the burden) of being co-responsible for education in America.

Sound like a dream? It's not. A dream is a vision without a plan. There is a plan and you are the most important part of it. The plan is almost too simple. Start right now, with yourself . . . start figuring out where you "are" with your role in education, what is needed and what you can do next to make education work around you. Begin to make small changes at first. Build your confidence in new areas. Get comfortable with change. Then begin to network and support others in growing. And what will support you as you continue to impact education? You have your hands on it! This book is designed to be your companion, your traveler's aid and owner's manual for the educator with more than just a dream. It is for you with a vision. You with a commitment to "make it happen." As partners, you and I can "break the back" of mediocrity in education. One by one we can make it happen. It's inspiring what one person can do. Gandhi said, "In a gentle way, you can shake the world." The "you" he spoke of is the "you" holding this book. Turn the page, you are about to begin!

☑ **Check These Key Points**

1. The rate of change is accelerating.
2. The impact of the information age is increasing.
3. Technology has created a new "electronic authority".
4. Schools are no longer the sole provider of information.
5. The restructuring of social roles affects schools and learning.
6. Many visionary leaders are being attracted to business, rather than education.
7. The power of the media creates unrealistic expectations and stress for today's children.
8. Our society is increasingly multi-cultural.
9. Our complex society gives mixed messages to people causing less predictability and certainty.

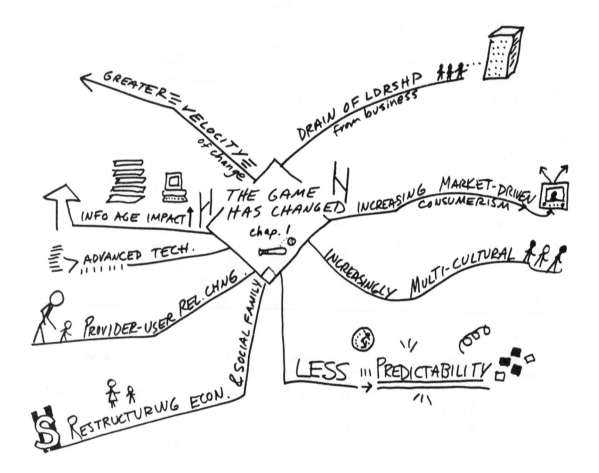

Chapter Two

Who You Are Makes a Difference

Objectives

- To describe specific beliefs and attitudes of successful teachers
- To illustrate the impact an individual teacher makes
- To establish values as the foundation for all successful teachers

The potential impact of a teacher on students is enormous and lifelong. Results reported in *Harvard Educational Review* discussed students educated in a poor neighborhood of Montreal. Despite the likelihood to the contrary, two-thirds of the former pupils of "Miss A" achieved the highest level of adult status, while the remaining third were classified as "medium status." None of her former students fell into the "low" group. Years later, the students remembered her unshakable faith in their ability to learn and the extra time and attention she gave. Both the students and the teacher remembered one another well and their special times together.

To have that kind of long lasting influence, a teacher needs even more than subject mastery and well polished presentation skills. Recently, Turning Point for Teachers completed a study using a nationwide cross section of teachers. The goal was to describe values, beliefs, attitudes and their correlation (if any) to results in the classroom. The study demonstrated conclusively that teachers with better classroom results had a certain set of attitudes about themselves, learning and their students. These values or underlying premises are literally HOW top teachers think of themsleves, their job and their students.

Remember a time when you thought someone was prowling around your house. You probably felt fear. Then, later, you discovered that it was only the wind or the neighbor's pet. The "prowler" caused your reaction of fear, even though he didn't actually exist! Although it was an illusion, your mind and body reacted as if the prowler was real. You responded "as if" it were true. This could be called the "As If" principle: act as if something is true and you will get the same effect as if it is true. Accordingly, whether any of the following premises are provable is of minimal importance. It is not necessary for something to be true to produce results. Each person's mind creates its own "reality" of the outer world based on what it imagines to be true. The invitation here is to try these out for yourself and discover whether or not they work. The result will speak for itself.

Premise: *Know You Make a Difference in the World*

It's easy to have the attitude that only CERTAIN people really matter, and that the rest are simply pawns in the checkerboard of life. But on closer inspection, every so-called important person has many others who support and make possible what he or she does. Every one of us does matter and because of that, everything we do, small or large, adds to the sum total of all the effects and nationwide contributions.

Because you do make a difference, every part of your life is worth attention. For example, does it matter if you say "hello" to the student in the back of the room? Absolutely! And it does matter if you take the extra moment to prepare your presentation better. Everything you do, in some way, contributes to your students, as well as to the educational system. This attitude also says that the value you add to the lives of your students will also enrich your own life.

Here's an example. As a teacher, if you excite and inspire just ten students from your class, and each of those kids relates their enthusiasm to ten other kids, how many have you actually affected? The answer is obviously ten times ten or 100 students! Can you imagine the cumulative effect over a period of years? That's why every student is valuable, unique and important. And each student is deserving of both your time and respect.

Premise: *You Are a Free-Willed Being*

Top teachers have the attitude (whether true or not) that they have free choice to feel and experience exactly what they choose. After all, if you're not in charge of your own thoughts and experiences, who is? There are those who believe that someone or something else made them feel a certain way. It's easy to tell by their expressions: "You make me so happy!" "You make me mad." "You frustrate me!" "The way you do that makes me nervous." All of these statements are borne out of a belief that someone else can force you to have certain feelings or experiences. A super-teacher chooses his or her own feelings, and chooses the appropriate ones for the situation. Instead of "you make me so frustrated," a super teacher accepts responsibility by saying "I feel so frustrated." In order to be able to manage your student's behavior and learning in class, you must have control over your own attitudes and responses.

Premise: *You Are the Cause of Your Own Experience*

If you are indeed free-willed, then you can choose how things go in your life. And if you choose how things go, then the result is your responsibility. It means you also have a choice over both what you experience externally and internally. It means you can choose how to feel regardless of whether you are in a traffic jam, a rainstorm or a class of so-called problem students. It is your choice to feel frustrated, happy, sad or peaceful—you have the power to run your own life. You are choosing your job, your friends, your spouse, your foods, your activities, what you read, and the T.V. programs you watch. It's all up to you and you are not a helpless victim. It means that, at any point on life's merry-go-round, you can change horses, enjoy the one you've got or get off the ride.

An interesting corollary of this belief is it can allow you to make the shift from considering yourself responsible-guilty (as in "Who's to blame?") to being responsible-accountable (as in "You can count on me"). Being accountable as a teacher means that you are the one who makes the choices that lead to the results. When there is credit to be given out, give it to others—especially your students. When there is accountability to be considered, raise your hand high.

If every year you have lazy unmotivated students, and every school or grade level you teach at has lazy unmotivated students, guess what the common element is in all those situations? It's you! You are the one that is making it possible (creating the opportunities) for motivation and high energy to be present in your students OR making it impossible for those qualities to manifest in your presence. Truly, accontability is one of the most important qualities a teacher can have.

Premise: *Reality Is Personal*

If all of us are creatively constructing our own world, then it's bound to be very different for each of us. Super-teachers believe that each person experiences life a bit differently from one another and that each person's reality is as valid as another's. This means they can allow another person's experience to be honored and respected even if it's very different from that of another. Each person's construction of the world, each person's model of how the world works is equally valid, TO THEM. In other words, while YOUR world may be totally different, their world still deserves to be respected. Because to them, it is as real as the nose on your face.

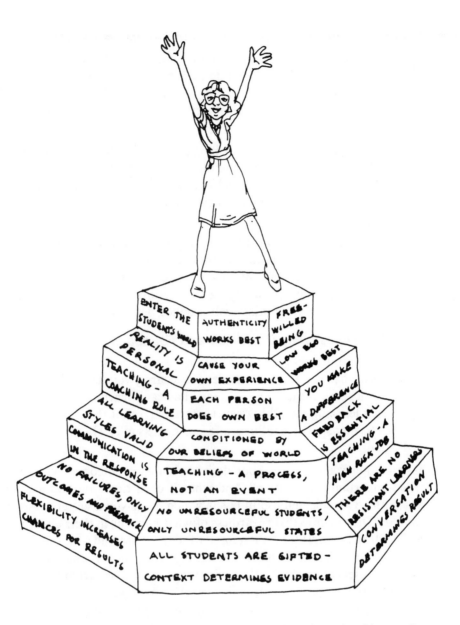

Because of this, the best teacher does not tell others what they should experience, or to discount someone's expression, thoughts, feelings or recollection of an experience. The classic example of many varying personal realities is the six blind men and the elephant. Each, feeling a different part, claimed that what they felt was the nature of the whole animal. Who was right? They all were; reality is very personal.

Premise: *It's Your Job to Enter the Student's World*

Successful teachers approach the student from the student's point of view. If a student's interest is motorcycles, the teacher would relate the course materials, in some way, to motorcycles. And what's more, if the student does not understand the material, the teacher adjusts the approach. Does this sound like more work? Initially, it is. Does it work? Dramatically well. It should be added that the students also need to know how to teach themselves so that the teacher's job, in the long run, gets easier.

9

Premise: *The Meaning of Your Communication Is the Response You Get*

If you explain photosynthesis to your students and they don't understand it, you have several choices. You could assume that they are a bit slow or didn't do their homework. You could assume that the topic is too tough for their understanding, or that it's an off day because of the weather. The problem with any of those choices is that none will accomplish the objective of insuring that your students understand photosynthesis.

The solution? Acknowledge that regardless of how clearly you THINK you explained it, the students didn't understand. And remember, your commitment is to do what will make the students successful. Then choose to "re-package" or re-format what you just said until they get it. If you say "green" and they hear "red," simply try something else until they receive what you mean to put out. That's flexible teaching!

The only problem with this belief is that it means that you will be constantly re-formulating what you say because you have ceased to blame it on the students. Yet something exciting happens when you adopt this belief: the quality of your communication and success in class goes up dramatically. The shift to make here is that from blaming others or justifying poor results to being accountable for them. It's a much more exciting way to teach and it certainly will produce better results.

Premise: *There Are No Failures: Only Outcomes and Feedback*

If you accept responsibility for your communications as well as what goes on in the rest of your class, you could begin to feel that you fail a lot. Unless, of course, you had a belief that each time you "fail" at something that you learn something . . . and that each learning experience is valuable and needed. If your belief is that learning something new is more important than "looking good" or avoiding failure, you begin to enjoy former so-called failures and see them as gifts. Or, at worst, see them as simply a result to be learned from.

What's a failure? When you don't get your desired results or outcome? What if each time that happened, you learned important information? And what if each time you had a so-called failure, it actually provided you with a valuable and useful lesson which made you a better person? That's exactly what top teachers believe. They believe that regardless of what happens in their classroom, that they can learn, grow and excel from the experience—therefore, a failure is as good as a success. Each and every happening builds successes; it adds to the knowledge necessary for success and increases the chances of the next event being more closely aligned with the desired results. Are we turning lemons into lemonade? Absolutely! It's highly effective in gaining personal excellence because it forces you to learn and find a lesson in every so-called failure. There's nothing wrong with failures—it's only when you don't learn from them that a result is truly a failure.

Could you imagine how much fun you'd have in life if this was a belief of yours: every adversity carries with it the seeds of an equal or greater gift! It's a well-worn cliche, but it's as true as ever: what you look for, you shall find. Look for the negative and you'll find it. Look for a gift in your mistakes, and you'll find it, too. Welcome mistakes because any person who doesn't make mistakes certainly is risking very little.

Premise: *Feedback Is Critical to Successful Teaching*

What follows from the previous belief is that feedback and correction are absolutely essential to classroom mastery. Your progress towards mastery could be measured by your willingness to allow yourself to be coached. To the degree that you allow input from qualified others and you do something about it, you'll improve. Teaching means you must be willing to be a student yourself. In fact, your students will learn from you at the rate you learn from them.

Once in the classroom, if you're trying new things, you can expect to have lots of learning experiences. You begin each class knowing very little about how each student thinks and organize their "reality." The only way you'll find out is to ask, or try something and risk making mistakes at it. Due to the unlikely odds of successfully hitting every student's communication and learning strategy the first time, you're going to have many unsuccessful outcomes.

Yet, failure is a label put on an event in which you don't get your outcome. You might as well put on another more useful label: feedback. Now success comes easier knowing that failure is no longer possible, only outcomes. Failures and mistakes are simply feedback you need to be successful; hence they are valuable and useful. Correction, without invalidation, is indeed, one of the real keys to mastery. Masters use such phrases as "Wow, I learned how *not* to do it that time!" or, "Boy, is this an *apparent* mess. What can I learn from this?" You can re-frame the meaning of the word failure, and replace it with the word lesson or gift.

Premise: *Flexibility Increases Chances for Results*

With many types of students in your classroom, you'll need many different techniques and that requires plenty of flexibility. Each so-called failure gets you closer to your outcome, so the greater your flexibility, the greater your chance of success. It means a complete and total detachment from any method you use. After all, you may need to abandon it in seconds. It also means that you'll be doing more thinking on-the-spot than ever before.

Premise: *There Are No Resistant or Learning Disabled Students*

You may be saying "That's going too far. I know some students who really are disabled!" Remember, whether this belief is or is not true is not the issue. The real question is: If you act as if this belief were true, will your results go up? There is much evidence that they will. In other words, if you believe it is *your* responsibility to get through to the students, you will become a better teacher. If you claim that it's the student's responsibility to get the material, you might as well just mail a book to him. If, on the other hand, you accept that you have something to do with how the student performs, then it will allow you to use the students successes and so-called failures to learn from and become a far superior teacher. It means a total suspension of any unresourceful or negative judgments about your students. After all, they are simply responding to your level of teaching skills.

As a corollary to this, there are also no resistant students, only inflexible teachers. No student gets up in the morning and says to himself, "I think I'll resist learning today." The natural tendency is to want to learn, since most learning occurs non-consciously. Our job is to make learning as much fun for our students as it was in kindergarten. With greater flexibility in teaching strategies, there would be no more tracking, grouping, or hierarchies of so-called intelligence. Bellamy's experiments at the University of Oregon discovered that it was inflexible teaching that led to the labelling of mentally retarded as "untrainable." His results proved that with FLEXIBLE teaching strategies, you could not only teach, but job-train students with IQs below 50. That's super-teaching!

Premise: *All Learning Styles Are Equally Valid*

One of the most common teaching tendencies is to teach in the way that you like to be taught. That way is guaranteed to please at least one person: you. Unfortunately, most students know very little about learning strategies and when they don't learn quickly, begin to draw damaging conclusions about their ability to learn. How could any one single learning style be "more valid" than another? It's impossible. Each student is unique, special and worthy of your time and attention. Simply because of the sheer numbers of students you have, you'll encounter a wide variety of student personalities, background and stories. Those individual histories have created vastly different learning strategies—every one of them as valid as the next.

Premise: *All Students Are Gifted: The Context Determines the Evidence*

The same student who flunks the math test at school may be a top surfer, socialite or car mechanic. The student who writes poorly may be a good video game player, actress or cook. The student who is doing poorly in all of his classes may be the most creative, resourceful and powerful neighborhood gang leader. Treat your students as if they were gifted—you'll make discoveries about their resources; creativity, flexibility, social skills, leadership and problem-solving abilities.

All of your students have talents and gifts; it's your job to find useful application in the classroom. Create opportunities for responsibility and success in the classroom for students so they can use "street skills" in an academic setting. Soon they'll begin to re-assess their potential to succeed scholastically. Students want to succeed. Give them the chance by letting them use, inside the classroom, what they already do well outside school. The rural student who does home chores and looks after his siblings has developed the attributes of perseverance, commitment, dedication and loyalty. Enhance those qualities in the classroom. Top teachers assume that every student is gifted. They simply act "as if" it was true to get better performance from the student. The result is a student who enjoys learning and has self-esteem.

Premise: *We Are Conditioned by Our Beliefs about Our World*

Over time, each of us has learned what can be done and what cannot be done. Yet each person seems to produce different results. This tells us that our beliefs and attitudes, which have conditioned us very powerfully, vary widely from person to person. That variance of beliefs about what can and cannot be done is subtle, but easily measured in the classroom. Translated into teacher expectations of student performance, those beliefs can dramatically affect behavior. When you believe your students will do better, they usually do. This simple cause and effect was documented by Rosenthal in *Pygmalion in the Classroom*. Rosenthal even claimed that IQ scores could rise if students were treated as if they were gifted.

In an exhaustive 1975 review of teacher expectation studies, Carl Braun agreed that teacher expectations do influence student behavior. But he also added many other interactive variables such as sex, ethnic background, socioeconomic status, parent impressions, physical characteristics, prior test results, student input, name and family background. In addition, four other teacher mechanisms contribute to a subjective bias which, in turn, affects student performance:

- Unconscious reactions. You may dislike or like a student simply because he unconsciously reminds you of your own child or a neighbor's. All it takes is an action, a comment or look that you associate with another child, and the instant association is made.
- Cognitive Dissonance. We often have a tendency to ignore evidence which is inconsistent with our expectations or prior experience. Your least-liked student can make a brilliant deduction and you're much more likely to ingore it than if it was from your class "genius."
- Halo Effect. We often allow one characteristic to overshadow others as an umbrella or behavioral "halo." If your favorite student has a small annoying habit, you are more likely to discount it and be more forgiving.
- Projection. One tendency is to see in others the things we like or dislike the most about ourselves. This creates a strong subjective "filter" through which you evaluate behaviors.

These other factors make it difficult to single out any one variable as the reason for student changes in performance. As a top teacher, your goal is to reduce your bias and subjectivity as much as possible. Although many factors are present, at least start with the awareness that you are likely to be biased! The bottom line is that teacher subjectivity is a dominant influence in student performance.

Premise: *Your Conversation Affects Your Results*

It's both interesting and exciting to discover the distinctions between average and true master-level teachers. Once key difference is in the conversations, both internal (what do you say to yourself?) and external (what are you saying to others?). The single greatest difference is that the great teachers have conversations about possibilities and the less effective teachers have conversations about complaints, problems and limitations. In other words, top teachers talk about how they want things to be, what could happen, openings for success, student breakthroughs, new ideas, potential within students and the opportunities for their work. The less effective teachers have conversations about the limitations of their students, how bad things are, how no one listens to them, how they were right all along, what's wrong with education and who is to blame for the problems at their school.

Possibility or Complaint? That's the distinction to be made in your conversations. What's the possibility that your students could actually be twice as smart than they appear to be, but you are actually stunting their growth? What's the possibility that homework could be a joy instead of a punishment. What's the possibility that learning could be fun instead of a routine? If you think about these things as a dialogue, your conversations will put you on the path to success in the classroom. Teaching well is a conversation with students about their possibilities, not complaining that they are not meeting them. As a conversation, teaching needs to be empowering and exciting. Very few people get empowered out of complaints or limitations. Beginning now, begin to monitor your conversations about education and teaching. You may be surprised to discover that you will get in your life, the result of your conversations. They are THAT powerful!

Premise: *There Are No Unresourceful Students, Only Unresourceful States*

Every teacher has encountered the student who appears slow, unmotivated or incapable. Yet that same student can rebuild a motorcycle from scratch or write magnificent love letters to a friend. A key principle, one that super teachers know and live by is this: all behavior is state-related. What your students do has more to do with the momentary state that they are in than their abilities or capacity. All of us go through moments when we are exhausted, tired, depressed or doubting. In those moments, even the most well-trained and professional educator can be unresourceful. Obviously, students have unresourceful moments, too. To change behavior, change the state. Some of the most effective are presented in later chapters.

The teacher's job is to
Re-discover the childhood joys of learning
With students as their partners

Premise: *Each Person Does His Best*

Evidence shows that successful teachers are compassionate and understanding. But how can you teach another teacher those traits? The answer is simple. It's a matter of whether or not you believe that every student is doing his best. Super-teachers, those who teach with compassion, understanding and care have a different belief about people than average or below-average teachers. The belief is this: Each person's behavior makes total and perfect sense when understood from the context of that individual's reality.

Since each student has had a different upbringing, different parents, different information, experiences and in fact, lives in a different world from you, the behavior he exhibits is totally appropriate—regardless of how illogical, bizarre, stupid, crazy or sick it seems. If you had the exact same everything (parents, home, history, etc.) as your students, your behavior would have to be the same as theirs. In reality, we'll never know if this belief is true or not. We don't have a control group to study. But if you follow this belief and its implications, you'll be much more successful.

When using the expression "doing their best," it refers to the best for that student, not for you. And there should be something more added: "everyone is always doing the best GIVEN (1) the context, (2) their perceived choices available and (3) their intended outcome. Given those three qualifiers, people are always trying to, meaning to, and actually doing the best that they can. YOU might be able to do better, but your students are not you. If you keep reminding yourself of this, you'll gain much peace of mind and compassion for others in a world of seemingly whacky behavior.

Because each student is always doing the best, there's a positive intent to all behavior. You may ask, "But what about the student who defaces materials, assaults others, destroys property?" The answer is the same: the intent is positive, even though the method used to achieve that outcome is deplorable. When a student assaults another, the positive intent may be to clear out his anger, resolve a feud, gain peer acceptance or build a sense of importance. When defacing property, the positive intent is to release anger or feel important. When you ask why a person exhibits delinquent behavior, there's always a good reason, to that person. Because of this, super teachers are constantly trying to create outlets, avenues and alternative methods for the positive intents to get the positive behaviors they really want.

Premise: *A Low Ego Works Best*

Your teaching can take many different paths and options. The difference between having a low ego and a high ego is enormous and shows up many ways. One of the ways could be described as having these actions:

- Wanting to let students know when they make a mistake
- Resisting picking up the trash on the floor in your room
- Wanting students to remember you at the end of the year
- Wanting to be right about something in debate or discussion
- Hoping students will like you and think highly of you
- Having it be important to look smart, witty or charming
- Making students wrong for forgetting something
- Having your own life be more important than your student's
- Keeping things the same, protecting status quo

The above actions all radiate from a point of view: that of high ego. The ego is the part of us that tries to protect us from looking bad, being wrong or to blame. High ego is not high self-esteem or self-confidence. It is a concern for what will others think and operating from a basis of "How can I cover my act?" There is a better way.

Having a low ego means that you are more concerned about what is true to yourself and your own integrity instead of what others think. Low ego means others come first, not in the sense of harming yourself, but in the sense of allowing others to be "the star." If we re-did the list from above, a low ego person might take actions like these:

- Letting your own humility and mistakes set an example
- Never being too proud to do whatever it takes to be of service
- Wanting students to remember the material at the end of the year
- Wanting to allow others to be heard and acknowledged
- Wanting students to experience how great they are themselves
- Having it be important to make others look good
- Making it safe for students to admit their own mistakes
- Getting satisfaction by helping others make their life a success
- Encouraging change and exploring new possibilities daily

One of the easiest ways to determine where your ego is at is to ask a simple question: "What am I committed to, getting credit or having my students get credit?" The person with a low ego will answer that the commitment is to his or her students. Another simple way to measure ego is by the amount of change you are comfortable with in your life. The ego wants to protect status quo and resists new ideas and changes. The ego wants you to be comfortable with no upsets, changes or threats to your teaching. But quality teaching requires risk and change. And that means a low ego.

Premise: *Authenticity Works Better Than "Acts"*

All of us have our "acts." These are roles that we play, hats that we wear and personalities that we have. The good part of our acts is that it can provide us with great flexibility in our behaviors. It is also convenient because if someone rejects us, they are not really rejecting us, it's just our act. The bad part comes when we start believing our acts and think that we "are" our acts. Often we have acts as a protective device to protect our ego against the attacks and criticism that life brings us. Other times our act is an attempt to be interesting, cute or theatrical instead of being genuinely interested in others. In either case, acts can present problems.

As an example, if you act aloof or "cool" when it's time to admit a mistake (that's the act called "I'm so perfect, I don't make mistakes, I just change my mind"), the risk is that students will never get to know who you really are. That's because they are responding to your act and not who you are underneath the act. Many teachers think they are friends with their students when, in fact, they are not. Their students don't even know who you are, just the act. Don't try to be perfect or totally "together" for your students. If you do, your students will feel uncomfortable around you and will be afraid to make mistakes of their own. Your students will miss out on really knowing who you are if you take your acts too far. The solution is to be authentic. Always let your students in on what is your act and what isn't. And never believe your own act.

Premise: *Teaching Is a Process of Learning, Not an Event*

One does not "become" a great teacher—one simply commits to it as a path. There's no big "ta-da" or end point of skill level to celebrate. This means that it's an on-going and expanding path of growth and "becoming." One of the best ways to stay on the path of commitment and growth is to reinforce your philosophy with the writings of Lao Tzu. Translated, Lao Tzu's *Tao Te Ching* means "the book of how things work." Written in the fifth century B.C., it has long been a classic in both Chinese and world literature. Its much-loved wisdom has withstood the test of time well. In fact, many of its sayings are familiar to you: "The journey of a thousand miles begins with a single step." Not surprisingly, the best teachers seem to include ancient wisdom as well as modern tools in their teaching. The best updated version to study is *The Tao of Leadership* by John Heider. Here are some variations on its philosophy:

> A wise teacher lets others have the floor. A good teacher is better than a spectacular teacher. Otherwise, the teacher outshines the teachings. Be a mid-wife to learning—facilitate what is happening, rather than what you think ought to be the happening. Silence says more than words, pay much attention to it. Continual classroom drama clouds inner work. Allow time for genuine insight. A good reputation arises naturally from doing good work. But do not nourish the reputation, the anxiety will be endless; rather nourish the work. To know what is happening, relax and do not try to figure things out. Listen quietly, be calm and use reflection. Let go of selfishness; it only blocks your universality.
>
> Let go of your ego, and you will receive what you need. Give away credit, and you get more. When you feel most destroyed, you are most ready to grow. When you desire nothing, much comes to you. The less you make of yourself, the more you are. Instead of trying hard, be easy: teach by example, and more will happen. Trying to appear brilliant is not enlightened. The gift of a great teacher is creating an awareness of greatness in others. Because the teacher can see clearly, light is shed on others. Teach as both a warrior and a healer; both a leader and a yielder. Constant force and intervention will backfire as will constant yielding. One cannot push the river; a leader's touch is light. Making others do what you want them to do can become a failure. While they may momentarily comply, their revenge may come in many forms. That is why your victory may be a loss. To manage other lives takes strength, to manage your own life is real power. Be happy, content and at peace with yourself.

The Tao for teachers is really more of a way of being more in tune with the way things naturally work. Once you discover that the way things are is "the way they actually are" instead of "why aren't things different?" then you gain peace of mind. Much of an ineffective teacher's time is spent trying to MAKE things go differently or DISPUTING what actually is occurring. An unwise teacher is PUSHING or FORCING and ANNOYED at the processes of life. For you to grow as a master teacher, you must know what teaching really is about. It is about serving others, discovery of each person's highest self, humility, acknowledgment and allowing others the respect and love they need to grow.

Premise: *Great Teaching Requires a Coaching Role*

The old model of a classroom teacher "filling up" students with knowledge is obsolete and damaging. The role which works in today's world is that of a coach—that is "one who instructs or directs in the fundamentals." It's a delicate shift, but it may be the most important one a teacher can make. In sports, the top names and biggest winners in sports coaching history all taught much more than the sport. The legends, Vince Lombardi, Don Schula, Red Aurbach, Jerry Tarkanian, "Bear" Bryant and John Wooden all built character and had a powerful affect on the personal lives of their athletes. Coaching means that the teacher is more interested in providing direction in learning than the learning itself. It means the teacher is a guide, not an authority. It means that the personal, philosophic and emotional part of the learner is coached and directed as much as the intellectual part. Yet, in order to do it, the teacher must have his or her own life in order. That's a tall order for any occupation, much less one that puts personal growth at the bottom of budgetary priorities.

Premise: *Teaching Is an Inherently High-Risk Job*

The notion of teaching as a safe, comfortable easy-going job is changing. Many years ago, elementary education teachers needed mainly a lot of love, secondary and college teachers needed lecture skills. Elementary teachers still need a lot of love, but that's about all that's the same. Teaching is far more rigorous than it ever has been. It's a front-lines position for courageous and committed learners willing to take risks and make mistakes. It's a dangerous job because teachers must confront whatever ideas, systems or relationships not working in their personal or professional lives and change them. It's a place where consistent performance breakthroughs are needed just for survival. It's an intense on-the-edge line of work which requires that you set a public example of integrity, love, commitment and awareness for up to six hours a day with your "dirty laundry" on display.

It also requires an extraordinary commitment to change, learning and being coached. Just as teaching is a coaching job, it is also critical to have a willingness to being coached yourself. One of the greatest baseball players who ever lived was the Japanese legend Sadahara Oh. In spite of his unparalleled success, Sadahara was so committed to growth, that he went to his teacher to get coaching after each ballgame. This meant being up, after a day's workout and a nightgame, from midnight until two in the morning to get tutored!

Ask yourself what you do that acts as a stand for your commitment to being coached and learning new things. How do you respond to suggestions, changes and new policies? When was the last time you tried out (and committed to mastery) an entirely new teaching methodology? It takes that kind of openness in order to be effective. It takes that kind of role modeling for your students—the more they find you being willing to being coached, the easier it is for them.

There is no other occupation which requires such rigor and such exemplary behavior. There is also no other occupation which has provided such possibility to our children and the planet as a whole. In your classroom, you can break the back of classroom "deadness." You can put an end to the boredom of learning and make it into a real joy. You can build nurturing relationships that can last a lifetime. You can break the back of any of your own limitations in life, using the classroom as your own education. Learn to live with more love, more integrity and more vitality by being the very embodiment of it in the classroom. Accordingly consider very strongly whether or not you want to play by the game one hundred percent. Because once you call yourself a "teacher," you must, out of fairness to yourself and your students, play the game as if it mattered. Because it does. Your students may become a success or failure in life dependent on not how you teach, but who you are in the classroom.

This chapter has included many ways of thinking about yourself, others and teaching. If any of these ways are new to you, you may want to review to be sure you understand them. Check to see if you agree with them. If you don't, gather evidence to support the possibility that they may be true. Or, simply "act as if" they are true. Have the desire and faith necessary to make them a part of you. You might repeat them to yourself or write them up on 3″ × 5″ cards and put them in plain view for daily review. Use mental pictures to rehearse the actual activity, allowing you to become more comfortable with them.

And finally, the most important step: use them. Integrate these patterns of success in your behavior and you'll be pleased with the results. You can begin the path to mastery with these successful ways. Now is a good time to start.

☑ Check These Key Points

1. Know that you make a difference in the world.
2. You are a free-willed being.
3. You are the cause of your own experience.
4. Reality is personal.
5. It's the teacher's job to enter the student's reality.
6. The meaning of your communication is the response you get.
7. There are no failures: only outcomes and feedback.
8. Feedback is critical to successful teaching.
9. Flexibility increases chances for successful results.
10. There are no resistant or learning-disabled students.
11. All learning styles are equally valid.
12. All students are gifted: the context determines the evidence.
13. We are conditioned by our beliefs about our world.
14. Your conversation affects your results.
15. There are no unresourceful students, only unresourceful states.
16. Each person does his best.
17. A low ego works best.
18. Authenticity works better than "acts".
19. Teaching is a process of learning, not an event.
20. Great teaching requires a coaching role.
21. Teaching well is a high-risk job.

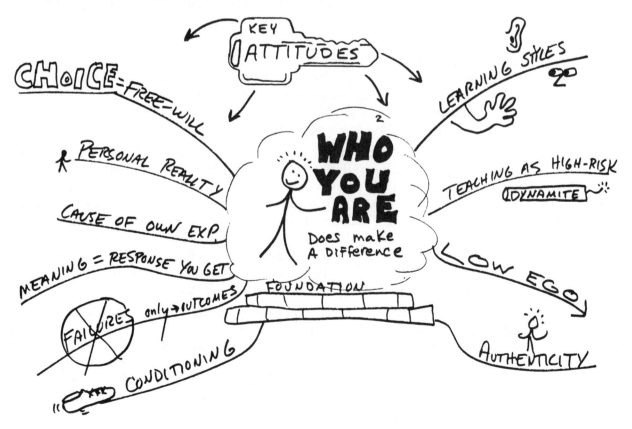

17

Chapter Three

Learning—From Theory to Practice

Objectives

- To explain learning theory
- To describe six primary learning styles
- To list additional learning strategies
- To give examples of how to determine a student's learning style

So much attention has been focused on the teacher and the teaching process that we often forget something: we are all in the business of having our students learn, not in the business of teaching curriculum. The difference is best characterized by the car salesman story. The new salesman said, "I was great today. I made ten perfect sales presentations today . . . and boy, were the customers impressed!" His boss says, "Wow, that's something. How many cars did you sell?" "None," answered the car salesman. "I guess they just weren't motivated buyers." It reminds us of the difference between selling and buying. As teachers, we often sell. But our job is to create "buyers," not complain that our students aren't motivated enough.

Getting students to "buy into" our teaching or to become "buyers" of our material is becoming increasingly difficult. The world is more complex and the contexts for behavior, values and learning are getting wider, deeper and more overlapping. Somehow we need to find a way to sort out all the information about learning and make some sense out of it. As teachers, it may be our most important role—to discover how our students learn and to know what to do about it.

There are many ways to characterize learning. In *No Limits to Learning* by James Botkin, two major types of learning are presented: innovative and maintenance. Innovative learning is the ability to find, create and absorb new contexts. It's an active participatory event that explores, challenges and anticipates. It is also a must for society because it works at all levels from social planning to the intellectual breakthrough. It's a learning that's accountable and responsible because it must include the needs of a growing and complex society. Innovative learning requires critical judgements of why and how. It's the journey into what's NOT known using society's values as the stimulating enzyme of action. It certainly asks for cooperation—the kind of wholistic thinking that implies an integration of many ideas and values. In an exciting class with a top teacher, much of the learning is innovative.

Maintenance learning, on the other hand, relies on existing structures and rules. It's what you do after you understand the principles of addition and are solving many problems for practice. It needs normative values, fixed rules and societal approval for continued operation. It needs the boundaries of science, authority, schools and business to work. It is essential for growth, but limited in its scope. There is no room for change or possibilities for breakthroughs. Unfortunately, it characterizes much of the so-called educational process. The good teachers seem to use it merely as support, the less effective ones seem to embrace it.

One of the skills that seems to distinguish ordinary teaching from the extraordinary is an uncanny ability to get at the heart of the appropriate learning and to present material in a way that invites learning. If you are like most teachers, you have done it successfully many times. And, if you are like most teachers, you have successfully failed at it many times, too. To reduce the hit-or-miss approach, you need to have a better idea of what's going on inside your student's heads. The best book on this topic is *Human Brain & Human Learning* by Leslie Hart. Knowing how students learn is fundamental to making the appropriate adjustments in your teaching styles.

LEARNING IS:

1. *Multi-leveled experience*
2. *Mostly NON-conscious*
3. *Possible with NO new information*
4. *A result of two variables: state and strategy*
5. *Highly personal*

What Is Learning?

The end product of learning, from the brain's point of view, is a distinctively categorized and long-term stored visual, auditory or kinesthetic representation (picture, sound or feeling) of the process, experience, conclusion, fact or feeling. Ideally, it is one that can be retrieved and acted upon when needed at a later time. As a teacher, that's *all* you are really trying to do—create representations in the brain.

1. Multi-level Learning

Learning affects our intellect, emotions and actions. To insure complete and thorough learning, we must teach our classes with attention on the desired attitudes and feelings as well as the information and behaviors. Since your sensory input (eyes, ears, touch, taste, smell and digital thinking) is connected by a central processing unit (your brain), each form of input affects another. For example, if you hate math, it's likely you have minimal math skill competency. If suddenly you became a math wizard, those feelings of dislike or hatred are likely to disappear.

In other words, learning includes all three (affective, behavioral and cognitive) patterns. The most commonly measured classroom learning is cognitive yet each learning style important and equally valuable. If the material (the "what") you teach is up to you, your job is to teach not only HOW to learn it, but to teach the values and experience of what's learned. In other words, if your students score high in your math class, but lack the know-how (alternative cognitive or behavioral learning strategies) and the way to deal with upsets, wrong answers, or frustration (affective experiences), they may go on to the next math course and do surprisingly poorly.

The greatest gift you can give to your students is a lifelong love of learning and feeling of self-worth. While the content of your course may become outdated, the strategies, the feelings, and experiences of curiosity, wonder and enjoyment can remain. These may become the most valuable and precious experience of your student's education.

2. Non-Conscious Learning

The greatest percentage of what your students learn is NOT in your lesson plan; it is in your attitudes, feelings, dialogues, actions and the classroom set-up. In this area lies the greatest potential for change.

It's entirely possible to learn something without knowing you know it—infant modeling or accidental mimicking of a skill occurs quite often. In fact, MOST of what you have learned has been through non-direct, non-classroom instruction. It's been by the natural process of living. A common experience is learning something while your attention is focused on something else. For example, think of all the information you casually, almost accidentally pick up while driving your car. While the attention to the radio or the road may have been your CONSCIOUS learning, the greatest tomes of information was what you casually picked up about the scenery, your passenger, your car or your inner thoughts. That's NON-conscious learning. A surprising corollary of that fact is this: most of the learning that your students will get in your classroom is from other sources than the content you are teaching. If your subject matter is math, students are getting more messages about math from your voice, your actions and personal presentation than from the curriculum. The reason why many of the best teachers are also the wonderful, loving human beings is that the students pick up on and unconsciously model the human qualities more easily and often than the professional skills or subject knowledge.

3. Learning without Any New Information

Some of the most profound learning occurs by simply changing the meaning of yours or another's existing experience. It's the self-discovery process, the creative, self-directed introspective learning. One of the more important ways you can influence your students is by providing them with the skills to learn this way—and on their own. By emphasizing critical thinking and self-discovery, your students can learn to grow simply by altering their own perceptions, feelings and behaviors. This change in meaning of their own experiences is a powerful tool which can improve attitudes and shape behaviors. It's also a very freeing experience—to discover that each of us can learn anywhere, anytime.

Learning takes no time at all
It's not learning that
takes all the time

Here's an example: let's say a student gets a low score on a math test. If his experience is that of lost self-confidence, you may want to counsel him about it. How much better for him if you could allow him to see the failure as: (1) part of a larger context of succeeding . . . or (2) as an improvement over his last one . . . (3) as great feedback on his lack of studying—it was a way to wake him up to the realities of the studying required by that subject. Then instead of being depressed over a score, he learned something from it.

Stop your class and ask your students what was the meaning of their recent learning experience. Create an open-ended discussion about what it means to each of your students and why. Ask students to share the process of their conclusions and you'll encourage self-confidence, more consistent thought and critical thinking.

4. Learning Variables: State and Strategy

Learning is dependent upon only two variables: state and strategy. If you learn how to master both your physiological, emotional and psychological state as well as that of your students, you can create the necessary receptivity. Then if you are flexible enough, you can find and use the strategies necessary to meet the needs of the student.

Learning Variable 1: State

State is a momentary personal condition denoted by a specific combination of breathing, emotion, posture, expressions and eye patterns. Each physiology also carries with it corresponding emotions and thoughts. For example, if your breathing is in your upper chest, your shoulders are back, your posture is upright and your eyes are looking upward, it is impossible to feel depressed. Try it. The behavior of any person is dependent on physiological factors which in turn effect the emotions and the intellect. When a person's state is anger, he doesn't write love letters. When a person's in love, he usually doesn't rob banks. The importance of understanding state in regards to learning is simple but profound: all behavior is state-related. If you want to begin to affect the behavior of your students, learn to first identify, then next, affect their state.

Understanding state means that you will be able to drop judgements about your students such as whether or not they are motivated, or good or bad students. A more useful question than "Why isn't Johnny motivated?" is "How can I positively affect Johnny's state so that he can best learn?" You don't need motivated students to be effective; some students may never like your subject matter their whole life. Some students may not like you nor be a goal-oriented accomplishment-driven person. In spite of that, you do need to be able to put your students in a resourceful and alert state for the length of your class. State is the equivalent of a snapshot in time and is relatively easy to affect. Character traits such as drive, motivation and purposefulness are a long-running movie and are more difficult to change. Focus your attention on just the momentary state, and the longer term benefits of love of learning, motivation and curiosity will come about as a by-product.

The three most-distinguishable states are visual, auditory and kinesthetic. Students in a visual state will breathe shallower; it's usually a higher, upper-chest breath. They tend to speak more quickly, with a higher monotone tonality. Their shoulders are often back and eyes are up. When in a visual state, students are more "hyper," process pictures, charts, print, movies, slides, sights and spell better.

The auditory state is characterized by a moderate, mid-chest breathing rate and moderate paced speaking, with a wider range of tonality and timbre. Eye movements are from side to side. When in this state, students listen better and talk more.

The kinesthetic state is characterized by slower, more abdominal breathing. The speech pattern is slowest of the three. The shoulders are often dropped lower or rolled slightly forward. The eye patterns are simple; down and to the left for right-handed person. In this mode, students are in touch with how they feel about things as well as being more responsive to the kinesthetics of the environment. They'll feel the room temperature more fully, the discomfort of the chair and often adjust their posture accordingly. The kinesthetic learner is usually interested in physically doing things, touching, handling and holding.

There are many other possible states besides visual, auditory and kinesthetic. Those are the ones most commonly found in your classroom, and easiest to recognize. Students could also be in a state of confusion, anxiety, excitement, joy, fear, hunger, pain or love. Each of those states will determine to a large degree how much or how little your students learn. In general, you'll want your students in a state most typically characterized by restful, resourceful, curious alertness. But even that will vary depending on what's effective at the moment. When you see a student in an unresourceful state, your first job is to change the state; then the behavior will automatically change. This simple principle has countless implications from learning new skills to classroom discipline. THE EASIEST WAY TO CHANGE YOUR STUDENT'S BEHAVIOR IS TO CHANGE THEIR STATE. A later chapter will tell you how to do that. Learn to quickly and accurately distinguish which state your students are in and you'll be able to make the corrections necessary for maximum learning.

Learning Variable 2: Strategy

A learning strategy is simply the sensory-specific steps needed by an individual to grasp the learning. It's the individualized content (the method) and sequence (the order) for that student's brain to learn. It has often been called "the numbers of the combination lock." Student's strategies vary immensely from subject to subject, skill to skill and person to person. If you could put each student in an optimal learning state and customize your material based on the individual's appropriate learning strategy, every student would be successful at learning as fast as you could deliver the material. When both state and strategy are met, each student appears as a genius.

We expose students to months and years of math, grammar and foreign languages. Yet, colleges still have to offer "bonehead" English, remedial math (you must know by now, there's no such thing as "math-phobia", there's only unskilled teaching) and many cannot carry on a simple conversation in a foreign language. The answer is both state and strategy. Students are usually exposed to a teacher's single strategy, and if it happens to fit theirs, presto, you have success. By and large, it's a mismatch. Consequently, many students begin thinking they are dumb, slow and stupid because they take years to learn something that they could learn in hours . . . IF it was presented in their particular learning strategy.

Many normal learners are labelled as "learning disabled" because the teacher failed to understand and correct the existing mismatch. For example, students who have trouble following directions are often talking to themselves (auditory learners) as directions are being given. This creates an internal "interference pattern" which blocks the processing of the external information. In the same way, an auditory learner will appear to be "stupid" when it comes to spelling because spelling needs a more visual strategy. Learn a variety of strategies, so you can offer any of them as the situation dictates. These strategies are necessary to customize and personalize the learning process.

5. Learning Is Highly Personal

As teachers, we must customize, adapt and change what we do from student to student, culture to culture, age to age and day to day. Learning is a living process, in flux and requiring constant re-reading and adjusting to individual needs. The way you can be most effective as a learning facilitator is to first, understand the different strategies needed for different kinds of learners and second, have the flexibility to keep changing what you are doing until it works.

How We Learn: Learning Styles

Representational Systems

Most learners will favor learning and their own processing through just one of the five senses. Our brains consistently "represent" the outer world to us in a favorite way. This predominate representation is fairly consistent within each person. For example, when hungry, one person may be PICTURING himself starved, then with a big sumptuous plate of his favorite food (that's visual). But another, in that same moment, would HEAR himself saying how good food would taste (that's auditory), while another might FEEL excited about eating (that's kinesthetic). Naturally, one might also combine SMELLING it or TASTING it. This simple discovery has significant implementations: a student who has a dominant pattern as "visual" needs to imagine and picture what you are saying in order to learn it. And, of course, others have to talk to themselves, while to others, it must feel right.

Approximately 40% of the general population prefers to learn visually (seeing, reading, being shown, etc.). Another 40% prefers to learn auditorally (listening, talking to others, being told, etc.). The remaining 20% learns best kinesthetically (physically, with feelings, moving the body, etc.) or in rare cases, gustatorally (by taste) or olfactorally (by smell). This preferred mode of learning seems to remain consistent based on early learning experiences. And, naturally, persons tend to teach others in their own predominate learning mode. The result? Most teachers are "missing" part of their audience in each of their presentations. Here's an example of how you can better appeal to them:

> Visual learners: like to look at charts, graphs, pictures. Likes puzzles, neat surroundings, likes to read to himself, can find things quickly. Likes hearing visually related predicates such as "Picture this . . . How does this look to you? See what I mean?"
> Auditory learners: talks often, would rather read out loud, like stories, songs, knows words to songs, tuned in to your voice tempo, volume and rhythm. Prefers auditorally related predicates such as "Listen here . . . How does this sound? Hear what I'm saying?"
> Kinesthetic-tactile learners: wants to touch and feel to learn, likes physical movement, object manipulation and is sensitive to his own body sensations, feelings, physical environment. Prefers kinesthetic predicates such as, "How does that feel? Can you get a sense of this? I need more grasp of the subject."

The particular representational system a student uses to learn either information or a skill will determine his success. For example, a good speller uses a primarily visual strategy while a poor speller uses either an auditory (sounds the words or letters out) or kinesthetic (spells by how the word or letters feel) strategy. Use of the visual strategy insures perfect spelling as long as the student follows the pattern. A strategy can easily be shortened as the student becomes more confident and familiar with it. There are similar strategies for learning math, writing, music, speeches, etc. You can teach any student to spell perfectly if you use the visual strategy listed in the appendix. In addition, *Master Teaching Techniques* by Bernard Cleveland is an excellent source and it is listed in the bibliography.

Hemispheric Dominance

Dr. Roger Sperry of the California Institute of Technology discovered that the left and right side of our brain have specialized functions. Subsequently, educators Gregorac, Butler and Hermann have made two further distinctions within each hemisphere, the upper and lower.

1. *The Cerebral Right* (Abstract Random). The creative, holistic, synthesizing person. Prefers abstract concepts, patterns, spatial data and is better at processing wholes instead of parts. Also fills gaps, uses intuition, leaps of faith, spontaneity and non-linear thinking. This learner wants the material in one big package all at once; hold up a large globe first before you teach the geography of a single continent, country or city. Prefers to work independently. This learning style is characterized as thematic, emotional and interpretative. Very common of artists.

2. *The Lower Right* (Concrete Random). Lives in the kinesthetic-auditory world of music, feelings, relationships and physical movement. Detects more easily tonality, tempo, inflection in speech; but less of the content of the words. Relies more on hands-on experience, their own sensations and feelings about what they are doing. This learner gets "antsy" easily and wants to touch, feel, taste, construct, handle, manipulate and listen to the material. In addition, they like more fun and surprises in class. Prefers to work with others. They are original, experimental, investigative, option-oriented and risk-taking. They need challenges, like to dream, investigate and like concrete problems that can be solved with random, non-linear means.

3. *Cerebral Left* (Abstract Sequential). The counterpart, the left-side, processes parts better than wholes. It works sequentially, processes words, grammar, syntax, and linear data. It is logical, orderly and proceeds step-by-step. This learner measures, memorizes, organizes, names, compartmentalizes, compares and watches clocks. This learner wants schedules, predictability, organization, precision work and problems to solve. Prefers to work independently. Their style is both intellectual and rational; they need a sequential and structured approach.

4. *Lower Left* (Concrete Sequential). This learner is best characterized by steadiness, reliability and organization. Prefers words over shapes, concepts and general ideas. Likes specifics, has patience, can stay in one place, is loyal, a good listener and great at following directions. This learner dislikes change or surprises, needs careful directions and substantial encouragement. Prefers to work with others. They are practical, predictable, to the point and structured.

As you can tell, each of these learning styles is very different. Yet they are equally valid. You're most likely to teach in the style that matches how you learn. This means that part of your student audience's will be left out each time. The solution is two-fold: first, make sure that you build relationships and rapport with your students so that when you are teaching a different style, you can still keep their attention. Secondly, begin to include components of their styles so that you can also be reaching other kinds of learners.

For many years, the focus in education was on the teacher and the question: "How can we get the teacher to teach better?" Maybe more appropriate questions are "Who is the learner?" "What do we know about how students learn?" And finally, "If we did know how students learn, would we change what we are doing?" These questions are important because our next section is on the learner and how to make the presentations more brain-compatible for him or her.

The Triune Brain

Since your student's brain is responsible for the learning, you are really teaching "brains" in your classroom, not students. By knowing the basic structure, function, possibilities and limitations of the brain, you can modify your teaching approaches to get big results and have more fun in the process. Building on the work of James Papez, Paul MacLean has identified three areas of our brain to know about and some important conclusions.

Part of our brain (the brainstem) is designed to process non-conscious information: breathing and heartrate. This is the oldest, most reptilian part of our brain. It's the top end of our spinal cord and enters the opening at the bottom of the skull. It includes the reticular formation (the "doorbell" for information) and the cerebellum which is a motor, balance, position and memory structure for rich symbolic experience.

The significance of this information for learning is that we have an enormous untapped possibility and are missing out. To tap into this part of brain, include more and better-designed symbolic classroom rituals. Include the use of archetypes, the heroes and characters which influence our values. To affect our brainstem processing, we can "unsettle the set" by putting more attention on deep and rhythmic breathing.

The second part of our brain is the mid-brain (the limbic system). It's function is maintaining homeostasis in the body for emotions, eating, sleeping, drinking, sexuality and hormones. It includes:

- the hypothalamus (our "brain" within our brain)
- the pituitary (the master gland and hormone releaser)
- the hippocampus (memory and associations)
- the amygdala (comparison of visual and tactile memories)
- the thalamus (there's 2 of them and they are responsible for consciousness and preliminary information appraisal
- the basal ganglia (there's 2 of them and they are responsible for fine motor movements

This is part of the brain that is most responsible for whether or not you feel good, have a good day or are happy. It includes your daily routines, your feelings, memories and associations. The significance of this information for learning is simple. For information to be learned powerfully, stored in long-term memory and available for recall, it must be *emotionally charged*. The memory part of our brain works directly with emotions. Put feeling into your class materials, put emotions in the learning process and create suspense, excitement, joy and ecstasy in each class day. That's where music, love and celebration come into the picture.

The third part of the brain is the cortex, stuffed into the skull around the midbrain and brainstem, filling in the corners like a blanket. It's your "thinking cap" and its function is information processing. It does have the well-publicized lateral specialization (a left and right side). The sides have lobes or territories and each lobe handles a different kind of sensory information:

- Occipital—visual information
- Temporal—auditory and nascent
- Parietal—kinesthetic and motion
- Frontal—adaptation, plans and decisions based on current sensory information

This is the part of your brain that does the thinking. It's what you use to plan, organize, create, problem-solve or do the homework. It handles the conscious information—or rather the information consciously. There's always information being processed that you are not aware of at all.

The implication here is that we need to be as or more aware of the non-conscious information being processed by our students as we have of the more traditionally presented information. A sparse or depressing physical environment can affect the moods of the learner's limbic system and decrease receptivity of the cerebellum to process. Your non-verbal gestures, positioning, expressions are important to improve. Your tonality, pitch, tempo and volume all are processed. Take presentation classes, theater, Check These acting and voice lessons. Get background in music. This part of the brain (under command from the limbic system) literally shuts down and "downshifts" when under ANY threat at all. Remove any and all threats on your students—especially psychological, emotional and moral-ethical ones.

A perfect model for creating a broad-based classroom success is our own early learning experiences. It is said that from ages two through five, the human child learns proportionally more per day than during any other time of life. The components of a child's environment should tell us something about how we might better teach to the brain. In other words, what seems to speed up the learning process in students from ages five to ninety are the same things that we quit doing for them because the student supposedly had outgrown them all. It means an artful teacher (or a great parent!) is one whose personal style is:

1. congruent
2. optimistic
3. flexible in approach
4. committed to results
5. holds high expectations
6. highly supportive

As a baby growing up from birth to kindergarten, you were a fabulous learning organism. No wonder you learned an entire language, gained control of your body and discovered much of your world in a few short years. The specific teaching and learning methodologies used were:

- Lots of emotion and celebration
- Multi-sensory experiences
- Lots of play
- Relaxation and restful periods
- Humor
- Use of music and singing
- Fantasy and imagination
- A rich visually stimulating environment
- Positive suggestive language
- Supportive group dynamics
- Games and physical activity
- Tireless support, love and adulation

The same methods that worked for you as a child, will work today. If you are overwhelmed by the volume or complexity of adapting learning strategies, use the simple model above. Make your classroom fun, use games, singing, relaxation, fantasy and humor. This kind of unstressed, child-like environment is the safest, surest bet for meeting your specific course outcomes. To make your class work better, play more, especially with teens and adults.

Additional Learning Strategies

It would seem that the only way a teacher could hope to fulfill the infinite number of student strategies is to teach in an endless variety of styles. Obviously, even a super-teacher cannot possibly present information in every one of these styles. The key is to learn to recognize a strategy as quickly as possible so that you can make the appropriate individual variances necessary for success. It makes sense to teach your students how they learn and how to meet their own learning strategies so they can begin to teach themselves. Here are some additional learning strategies:

Comparison/Match. Many students learn by finding sameness. They learn things by asking themselves what is similar to something else. For example, by looking at four cars, or four rugs, they can learn about them by discovering that all four cars have headlights or all four rugs have the same red-green-red color sequence. This student is often more sociable because he finds similarities between himself and friends very easily.

Contrast/Mis-match. Other students learn by finding differences. They discover things about the world by finding disparities, flaws and what is unusual. This student is often criticized by others as being negative or fault-finding when in fact, that's his primary learning strategy. As you might guess, this student either socializes less or has more antagonistic or sarcastic relationships. Treat this student with respect, their ability to find what's different about something is both useful and necessary to his survival.

Process Oriented. This student is interested in HOW things work and WHY we are doing this and HOW we got from a to z. He is interested in the journey, not the destination. Less time oriented, more interested in how people are treated and maintaining relationships. In your class, this student likes explanations of why you are doing things and enjoys personal stories.

Result Oriented. This orientation is the bottom line. This student wants to know the end of the story first, the final score, the conclusion and the numbers first. In your class, give the answer first, then tell how you got there second.

"Prove It to Me First". This framework of learning requires not only the logical facts and numbers, but also wants to know who else has done it first. In your class, be methodical and set a personal example to reach the student using this line of thinking.

Time Tests. For better or for worse, Westerners have a unique cultural sense of time. We find it useful to distinguish between the past, present and future. Interestingly, that distinction has created a format or reference framing for learners. The best way to describe it is as a "coupling" . . . we are "coupled" to time the way your car is "coupled to the road" by tires. The tires determine much of the car's performance—it's the relationship. Several researchers assert quite persuasively that learning is highly dependent on the time "test" given.

In other words, a "past test" will evaluate what is being presented against what was said or happened before. A "present test" will evaluate the experience in terms of "How well am I getting this at the moment?" A "future test" may cause a student to ask, "How will I use this information in the future?" Obviously, an appropriate strategy for learning could include all three time tests. But right in the moment of a particularly important segment, you are more likely to get the best results if your students use the present test. In your classroom, this means satisfy time concerns by presenting a brief background and a brief glimpse into the future with the material. For further details, read *The Emprint Method,* by Cameron-Bandler, Gordon and LeBeau. It's listed in the bibliography.

Motivation: Intrinsic. The students who appear to be self-starters and effective learners are able to use the time tests effectively. While one might recall how he did poorly in the past and work harder to avoid future failures, others may envision a good grade on the report card and the subsequent good feelings.

Authenticity. Many students cannot learn effectively with a constructed or created reference. ("Imagine this," "for instance" or "let's pretend as if"). They need actual real-life references and examples. Others can learn quite easily with their constructed references. As long as the student is willing to adjust the constructed references to reality, it can be a very successful learning strategy. Be sure to offer both of these in your class.

Anchors: Fully Associated References. Can you remember your graduation, an assassination, the first moon landing or an exciting first date? Chances are, you recall not only the incident, but have a full sensory memory of it—the sights, sounds, smells and feelings you had about it. Each of these incidents can be re-evoked with a certain stimulus, and POOF! Suddenly, you are drifting off into memory lane. The interesting thing is that there are thousands of other past events (and the associated sensations) which can be triggered by the slightest reference. For example, a student's traumatic near-fatal bicycle accident with a red-haired driver with glasses may re-trigger feelings of fear or anger the next time he sees a red-haired teacher with glasses. These re-triggered experiences can impair or enhance new learning depending on the triggered experience. An astute teacher pays close attention to students so that when a student is triggered into another state, corrective action can be taken.

Student Discovery:

MATCH THE LEARNING STYLES LISTED BELOW WITH THE STUDENTS_

(A) Linear
(B) Right Brain
(C) Mismatch
(D) Temporal
(E) AUDITORY
(F) Kinesthetic
(G) Match
(H) Visual

Answer: (1-H, 2-E, 3-B, 4-F, 5-A, 6-G, 7-C, 8-D)

There's an interesting paradox about the learning environment. Some research indicates the optimal learning situation should be as stress-free and relaxed. Yet, other students will prefer and perform better with long-term pressure (they use the positive future time test). In addition, one of the strongest motivators for all students, especially teens, is peer pressure. The difference between paralyzing pressure and a "benign stress" is both subtle and enormous. While the first is usually self-induced and healthy, the second can create a stifling of the creative energies.

Chunking. G. Thomas Bellamy of the University of Oregon has pioneered work with severely mentally retarded persons. Bellamy's success has been in his meticulous behavioral analysis and modification. He discovered that when any task is broken into sufficiently minute steps, ANYONE can learn the activity. A task as simple as stuffing envelopes may be broken into three steps for most learners, but Bellamy might break it into fifty steps for the mentally retarded student. The result is success. Especially in sports and subjects with near-phobic reactions, chunk down the steps to make is easier to master.

Chunking can take other forms, more conceptual. Many students need items "chunked up" to larger, more generic categories before they can grasp them. For example, cars can be chunked "up" into transportation, pleasure or status. They could be "chunked down" into metal, rubber, glass, plastic. Or even into a 1977 light-blue 4-door Buick Skylark. Literature can be chunked "up" to communication, or chunked "down" to e. e. cummings. In your class, simply make sure that you are chunking up or down constantly to assist in the understanding of your material. Chunking is discussed in detail in the chapter on presentation.

Relational. This style of learning means that the student can understand that which mirrors or matches his own world. The student fails to make the necessary leaps from what you are saying to his own world, so you must do it for him. To reach this student, you must continually relate what you are saying to his world. "This is much like the example you raised earlier, John." Or, "You know how your notebook has three clasp rings? This tool also has a mechanical clasp."

27

Options and Procedures. A student is likely to take action and be motivated to learn based on either a set of procedures or a choice of options. The way to find out whether a person is "options-oriented" or "procedures-oriented" is simple. Ask a "why" question. "Why did you choose . . . ? (to wear a hat, have juice for lunch, go ice skating, etc.)

A procedures-oriented student will answer with a story or tell you the procedures they went through. They'll talk about the "right" way and discuss facts. "I wore this hat because I was at this party with my friend Jim and everyone was goofing around with props from his dad's garage. . . . I saw this hat and tried it on . . ."

An options-oriented student will talk about possibilities, new ways and options. They'll give you criteria, values and choices. They are interested in comparing more, better, etc. "I was shopping for a hat that would both be a sun-shade and look good. I tried on several and each had something I liked. But one of them had it all . . ."

Multi-Cultural Diversity

One of the things teachers in ethnically mixed areas have discovered is that students may learn great cultural diversity. For example, you might discover that (as an example only) Asians are likelier to be a more "visual, future-referenced" learner. This implies the use of strategies such as reading and other visual, and the use of future-based motivation ("If we do this today, what we can get tomorrow is . . .").

As another example (and only just an example), you might find Hispanics or Blacks to be more "present-referenced and kinesthetic learners." Often a culture will encourage certain styles and have subtle reinforcements such as the "manana attitude" ("take it easy, we can always do it tomorrow"). This infers the need for more immediate value in the classroom, not long-term benefits. It also infers more "hands-on" learning with a chance to learn by doing with less lecture.

Some cultures, such as the American Indians, are more likely to be "past-referenced, right hemisphere learners." In the classroom, this translates to a teaching strategy which builds heavily on tradition, our past and what we have learned from our ancestors. It is also important to deal in wholes, not parts, feelings, not facts, music and ideas, not texts and lists.

Putting It All Together

With so many learning strategies mentioned, and so many others still unrecognized, it could seem fruitless to pursue them all. Yet it's much easier than it seems. Any time you get the least frustrated with an individual student, take a moment to learn what their learning strategy is. A few simple questions will uncover it:

- What is trying to be learned? (a skill, a concept, a value? etc.)
- What are the essential components of it? (each of the micro-steps)
- What is a similar or parallel activity to the learning activity being attempted? One that the student has already done successfully?
- Discover the strategy that the student used before to succeed in the new activity at hand.
- Utilize the same resources from the earlier success to the new one.

In an outdoor adventure program a student was afraid to climb up a tall tree as part of a group activity. Even though the climbing was done in a double safety harness, he was too afraid to leave the ground and to do the activity. The teacher solved the problem like this:

TEACHER: "Is there any reason you don't want to climb the tree?" (information gathering)
STUDENT: "Yes, it's too dangerous."

TEACHER: "But you'll be in a safety harness." (attempts an obvious rebuttal to gather more data)

STUDENT: "It's still too dangerous." (Discovers it's not a matter of logic, it's something else. Teacher needs more data.)

TEACHER: "Have you ever done anything else that was dangerous?" (notice that the teacher has quit insisting that it's not dangerous. It is, to the student. Now the teacher attempts to find a parallel activity which included danger, but ended up fun)

STUDENT: "Sure, I ride my skateboard pretty fast." (just the reference the teacher had hoped for)

TEACHER: "So what. Lots of kids say fast, but HOW FAST?" (teacher challenges student's activity, attempts to elicit risk-taking braggart part of student)

STUDENT: "Sometimes, forty or forty-five miles per hour." (strategy worked)

TEACHER: "YOU'RE NUTS! That's so dangerous, how in the world did you ever do that?" (teacher affirms student as a dangerous risk-taker in another context, then asks for the strategy)

STUDENT: "It was no big deal. I just started out at lower speeds and worked my way up." (jackpot! Student has given you the learning strategy, but teacher elects to verify)

TEACHER: "You mean you learned how to do something that scary by breaking it into small chunks and working your way up?" (is it chunking, teacher asks?)

STUDENT: "Sure, it's easier that way." (strategy verified)

TEACHER: "Take a look at the tree once again. Since you seem to learn best in chunks, if you were to climb up just part of the tree, how far could YOU GO (emphasis on these two words) and still feel safe?" (teacher asks student to participate in selecting chunk size)

STUDENT: "About ten or twelve steps. But that's all, no more." (chunk given)

TEACHER: "OK, but do you have enough nerve to do even that much?" (challenge issued to complete first chunk)

STUDENT: "Sure, anybody could do that." (student now completes the first part of the climb and returns to the ground.)

TEACHER: "You did great! Now that you've conquered that, how far could you get on your next time?" (reinforcement, further challenge issued)

STUDENT: "Well, about to there." (Student points to new goal, and this process continues until student successfully reaches top of tree in four chunks)

Detection and Diagnosis

One of the most often-asked questions is "How can I discover a student's learning strategy?" Read the book listed in the appendix as *Learning and Teaching Styles* by Susan Butler. It gives several self-administered surveys and ones you can use with your students. The model that it uses is very helpful; it was the one referred to above created by Gregorac. Try it out—it's very useful!

Once you know what style you are presenting with, you can begin to include other styles. The most common behavior is that teachers use the teaching style that fits their own learning style. In order to reach more students, you will need to present in a full multi-dimensional, multi-sensory mode that includes many of the major strategies. This comes with practice. When any of the most common ones fail, your experience will guide you to try some of the other possibilities. There are students which will elude your diagnosis. A key part of the process is making sure that you work as a team with your students in discovering and eliciting the strategy. You'll learn the kinds of questions to ask and how to draw conclusions from them. Always check out your conclusions and recommendations with actual experience. Then make sure the student knows which strategy is best for him. Not only will you be more successful by cooperating with the student, but you are doing a long-term favor for the student when you teach him how to teach himself. The next time he is having trouble in a similar situation, chances are, he'll be able to do it on his own. Discovering your students' learning strategies and fulfilling them is both exciting and gratifying. That empowerment is the mark of a real super teacher.

☑ Check These Key Points

1. Learning may be innovative or maintenance.
2. Learning is a multi-leveled experience.
3. Most of learning is non-conscious.
4. Learning can occur with no new information.
5. The keys to learning are strategy and state.
6. Learning is highly personal.
7. The 4 distinctions in hemispheric dominance theory are: Ideas/Right, Hands-on/Right, Ideas/Left, Hands-on/Left.
8. The triune brain theory designates 3 areas: the reptilian (brainstem), the limbic (midbrain) and the cortex.
9. Additional learning strategies are comparison, contrast, process or result orientation, past-present-future orientation, relational options and procedures.
10. There are cultural differences in learning strategies.

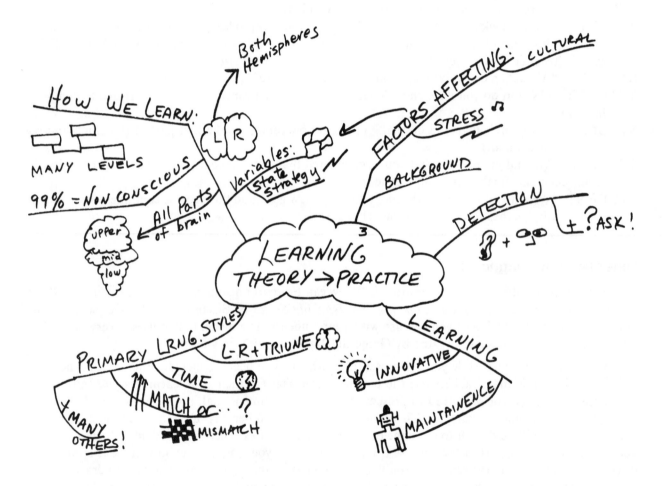

Chapter Four

Skills That Make the Magic

Objectives

- To identify myths
- To describe recent findings and their implications for teachers
- To provide a model for meta-teaching

Theory and positive attitudes are useful to a point. The real world of teaching also requires skills. Today's teachers need hundreds of sophisticated, tested and useful skills to be successful. Some of the skills are simple and most teachers have many of them. Other skills require much knowledge and training and very few teachers have them. Top teachers were not born with a natural gift to teach well, but were self-made. Each committed to the "work" of self-discovery, informed trial-and-error and choreographed himself to mastery. The orchestration and daily usage of these teaching skills in action is real artwork. It is exciting to know that these skills are available to all teachers today if they are willing to work at them. But first, let's uncover a few myths.

Myth: Teacher Skills Are of Primary Importance

Surprisingly, the skills of the top teachers are secondary. What's primary is the person behind the skills. Many skillful teachers fail with their students because they forgot that 99% of what the students learn is NOT in the curriculum. Students learn about life not by what you teach, but by who you are. Your students need, more than anything else, your love, your integrity and your commitment to their potential. If you teach out of a conviction that every one of your students is a "possibility" awaiting the discovery of their gifts, brilliance and humanity, they'll show up for you.

Myth: The Focus Should Be on How to Teach

For years, the focus has been on updating teaching skills and tips on how to teach better. But what about the learner? Do we really know how people learn? If we did know, would we be willing to change anything? The answer is that we DO know more about how learners learn. They learn in a playful, relaxed environment. They learn with rhymes, activities, songs, play and mostly through modeling of behaviors. Most of what is learned is "imprinted" upon students through teacher modeling. Therefore, what are you doing to be a role model? Are you fun to be with, joyful and happy to be at work? Do you keep your word, your promises, no matter what? Are you willing to take risks, to make mistakes and to be different? Are you learning something new and significant every day? All of those are things that students are asked to do. Yet, where's the model for it? For the most part it is non-existent. We as teachers must make an important shift: from focusing on what we are doing as teacher to focusing on what's the effect on our students.

Myth: Teachers Are Unlikely to Make Major Changes

"You can't teach an old dog new tricks." For many years, there has been great reason to believe that statement is true. The field of human behavior is relatively new, especially in the area of training. For many years, people didn't know how to change life-long patterns. Psychologist Abraham Maslow says that "History is a record of how we have sold the potential of humanity short." We've all heard stories of persons spending years in therapy to make modest changes. Recent breakthroughs in training include the "immersion" effect, neurolinguistic programming, accelerated learning and the body-mind effect which now make it possible for any person who is truly committed to make life-long changes quickly and easily.

Myth: Major Changes Must Be Painful

One of the disservices that our society has accidentally done is to perpetuate the belief that for change to occur, one must suffer or go through withdrawals of teary-eyed misery. Another is that one must bring up the past and "work through" it all so that you can start over. Those two beliefs have created suffering and misery for millions over the last few decades and worse yet, many teachers (who are of course, in the healing profession) have begun to believe them also. Change can and should be joyful or at least, painless. The whole nature of the human organism is designed to evolve, grow and change; just for survival, if nothing else.

A polarity of this is also true. Although change may be exciting and joyful it may also be difficult. The ego wants to protect us from change. The nature of humanity is to create more complexity, more challenge, diversity and awareness. Things get more complex at the same time that our perception becomes clearer. Translated, this means that your path as a super-teacher will only get more detailed, more in-depth, more rigorous and more demanding. Prepare yourself well for this journey, it will take greater character to reap its rewards.

Myth: That Excellence in Teaching is Reserved for the Gifted

One of the fads that is passing through education is the whole notion of labelling people as "gifted" or "learning disabled." There is really no such thing as a gifted person, and that statement applies to teachers, too. Labels are indicators of our response to *our* ability and *our* track record with that person, not a statement about the person himself. In other words, if a teacher is successful in teaching a student to read well, we say the student is smart. If the teacher is unsuccessful, the student is labelled as a "slow" or "learning handicapped." Why is it that we don't label the teacher "teaching disabled?" It makes just as much sense, yet it is, of course, not done nor should it be done.

To label someone as gifted is a vast generalization and disservice to the rest of us. It is as if the gifted person had something others couldn't possibly have. Nothing could be further than the truth. You have within yourself the ability to do anything anyone else does IF you are trained properly. When you were a baby, you had your own language of squeals, grunts, cries and giggles. Yet you learned a complex new language from your parents without taking a single class. Yet when students in a foreign language class don't do well, we say they don't have the knack for learning a language!

The recently-developed science of neuro-linguistic programming (NLP) offers the physiological distinctions necessary for anyone to duplicate another's excellence. Author, researcher and communications specialist Anthony Robbins says, "We are all wired up the same. What any one human being can do, any other human being can do." Nobel prize-winning engineer and futurist R. B. ("Bucky") Fuller (of whom there is the largest single listing of personal contributions and credits in the prestigious publication of Who's Who in the World) said, "The only important thing about me is that I'm an average, healthy human being. All the things I've been able to do, any human being, or you, could do equally well or better . . ." Recent research findings indicate that giftedness, creativity and talent can be cultivated, enhanced and even taught.

Myth: The Brain Capacity is Fixed and Limited

In *Use Both Sides of Your Brain,* Buzan suggests that the number of connections that our brain can make is far greater than the number of known atoms in the universe! Our brain processes thousands of bits of information per minute, both analytically and holographically. This means we may have dramatically underestimated the classroom input our students can handle. Our notion of a fixed I.Q. is out-of-date. Recent data indicates that intelligence can be taught and that there are many different types. Dr. Howard Gardner of Harvard suggests at least six kinds of intelligence including musical intelligence and social intelligence which are equally valid as our prior model. In addition, we have discovered that intelligence is very fluid and involves not only emotions, but the state of consciousness of the individual.

Myth: There's One Best Way to Learn or Teach

Recent discoveries have shown us that learning is highly individual and that the success of a student has more to do with the teaching or learning strategies used than any other factor. For example, many top teachers are highly effective when using a fun, playful and light manner. Yet other students may never have experienced a teacher who uses this strategy and comes to the erroneous conclusion that learning is hard or their potential is limited. In worst case, teachers fail to tap a student's learning strategy and the student learns so slowly, he is falsely categorized as "learning disabled" and ridiculed and depressed for years. The ability of the teacher to use a nearly countless variety of teaching styles will bring up student results dramatically.

Commitment to Teaching

Becoming a super-teacher means that you may need to re-examine long-held attitudes and beliefs about using certain skills. Once you become convinced that you want to acquire the necessary teaching skills, you must pursue the acquisition of them like a detective. You must practice and use them to build the unconscious success patterns. It's not enough to know the information, it must become ingrained in you. Your skills must proceed from the level of conscious competency to unconscious competency. This means more than being interested or involved with trying new things. Mastery only comes through a commitment to use the discoveries you have made until they become second nature. Using the analogy of ham and eggs, we could say that the chicken was involved, but the pig was committed.

Change Your "Coupling"

All of us live our lives doing the work that we do based on the relationships we have with our surroundings. This relationship is known as our "coupling." Boats have a relationship with the surface of the water that defines their speed and turning radius. From tugboat to a hydrofoil, that relationship has stayed the same for centuries. That's why the speed record for boats remains near 200 miles per hour. In the same way, cars are "coupled" to the road by tires. The tires "define" the speed of a car as well as its turning radius. A car can only go as fast as a motor can get the wheels to rotate. The land speed record for a car with tires is about 800 miles per hour. That's fast until you change the "coupling" from rubber tires to air—as in the case of a jet. The top speed for jets is several thousand miles per hour. That speed is quite high until you change the coupling again and get rid of the air. In outer space, our vehicles have traveled up to 25,000 miles per hour.

Similarly, you are coupled to your current level of teaching performance. The factors which affect your coupling include your relationships with other teachers, your classroom environment, your promises, your professional organizations, your health, your family life, your interest in learning and others. Notice that all of those factors are possible for you to alter. Also notice that it would take quite a bit of effort or energy to alter them. That's why breakthroughs are so rare. Most teachers are unwilling to "do damage" to their existing coupling—and that's the very thing that keeps them from growing. Changing your coupling is another way of saying breaking the unhealthy bonds you have to the way you are as a human being as well as a teacher. Most persons would rather be comfortable and take things easy. That's human nature. But combine that trait with the coupling mechanisms currently in place, and you can see how it protects the status quo in education.

For you to grow, for you to make a real breakthrough in your teaching and the learning going on in your classroom, you must be willing to assault the things that keep you coupled to your present state or skill level. Otherwise, you have too much "glue" that keeps things in place. Put real briefly, for things to change, *YOU* must change. Not just your skills, but your relationships with others, your ideas, your associations, your promises, your use of free time, your interests and your investment in having things stay the same. No one has a formula or a list of "to do's" for you in achieving a breakthrough in your teaching. It's not an event, it's a process. But a good place to start is to figure out where you want to end up and begin to ask questions and look for places that open up possibilities instead of looking for answers and solutions that end the discussion. And one more thing. You will know that you are changing your existing coupling and breaking out of the glue-like bonds of status quo if new things begin to fall apart in your life. Remember, to have a breakthrough, you need a breakdown. Accept the breakdowns with joy—they are the healthiest thing that could happen to you right now.

There's no such thing
as learning disabled students . . .
There are, however, inflexible teachers

Study What's Really Important

Becoming a master teacher means not only becoming a student of teaching all over again, it means studying the things that really matter. One of the best teachers on the West Coast has never gotten a college degree, a teaching credential or been a student teacher. Yet his skills are so effective he is consistently hired by parents, organizations and businesses, for over $1,000 an HOUR to teach. One of the best teachers on the East Coast has a Ph.D. from Harvard, speaks three languages and has never gotten a teaching credential. What do these two have in common? They both studied what was truly important to learn as a teacher. Follow in their steps; otherwise, you'll be like the professor in this Sufi tale:

> Nasrudin is ferrying a professor across a stretch of rough water and says something ungrammatical to him. "Have you never studied grammar?" the professor asks.
> "No," Nasrudin replies.
> "Then half your life has been wasted."
> A few minutes later, the storm grew fiercer.
> Nasrudin turns to his passenger to speak. "Have you ever learned to swim?"
> "No," says the professor.
> "Then all of your life has been wasted, for we are sinking!"

Recent Findings and Implications for Teachers

The last twenty years have rewarded us with dozens of discoveries which have the capacity to revolutionize education. Whether or not these discoveries are in fact implemented is up to you. Most of them will don't fit in a textbook or a mandated curriculum. Rather, they are a way of being and style of working that is sorely needed. The findings suggest that teachers will need to develop many new skills—ones which were unnecessary, overlooked or literally unheard of a few short years ago. As an example:

FINDING: Following a survey of 124,000 students at 315 schools, the single greatest recommendation that researcher Robert Bills makes is that teachers must improve the quality of the relationships they have at school—both with the students and the administration.

IMPLICATION: Teachers may want to develop whole new skill areas in rapport skills and communications—and be willing to alter attitudes about "the system" as the problem.

FINDING: Great educational potential exists in voluntary self-regulation of physiological states. They include states of consciousness, arousal, attention and volition.

IMPLICATION: Teachers may want to develop these skills themselves and learn how to instruct students in the acquisition and development of them to tap vast learning reserves.

FINDING: Great potential exists discovery of the subjective experience, modes of thinking, learning styles, perception, memory and decision-making.

IMPLICATION: Teachers need to include more information about HOW we learn and less about WHAT we learn. Also teachers may need to become more accountable for the experiences which they evoke in their students.

FINDING: Humans have far more untapped potential than previously thought possible. Peak performance has been better defined and is available to all of us.

CONCLUSION: Teachers need to cease making judgments about which student has what kind of potential. All of them have enormous untapped possibilities and should be considered gifted regardless of their scores.

FINDING: We are all whole persons and our feeling, thinking, and doing is all related and connected. The social, psychological, physical, emotional and spiritual aspects affect learning, self-perception and chances for success.

CONCLUSION: Teachers must begin to treat students as people, not vessels to fill up with information. Teachers may need to develop wider background in social skills.

FINDING: That students are dramatically affected by their belief systems, guiding images, peer pressure and media.

CONCLUSION: Teacher's presentation must include elements which deal with and positively affect student's beliefs, thoughts, pressures and personal life.

FINDING: Most students know very little about how their brain works, their memory functions or their potential. Most students know nothing about how to think, how to create or conclude.

CONCLUSION: Teachers can provide valuable information by learning about this key area and sharing it with their students. Teach students how to run their brain.

FINDING: Most students know very little about study skills, mnemonic devices and note-taking.

CONCLUSION: Teachers should be teaching **how** to learn as well as **what** to learn.

FINDING: The brain is an immense pattern-detecting and record-keeping mechanism which is largely underestimated.

CONCLUSION: Basic instructional design ignores this, add far more multi-sensory input, both in quality and quantity. Increase the quantity and more importantly the diversity of your content. Put music, games, thinking skills and movement into your instruction.

FINDING: Your students are piloted far more than you ever thought possible by their automatic nonconscious mind. Emanuel Donchin, director of the Laboratory for Cognitive Psychophysiology at the University of Illinois claims that 99 per cent of all behavior may be nonconscious.

CONCLUSION: Teachers must educate themselves in nonconscious behavior. Teachers need to find out what messages their students are receiving and learn how to insure they are the ones which meet their outcomes. As an example, nearly 90% of your communication may be nonconscious messages; your gestures, facial expressions, posture, tonality, tempo, volume and breathing.

FINDING: The triune brain model developed by Paul MacLean suggests part of our brain, the neocortex shuts down when threatened. The split brain model of Dr. Roger Sperry suggests we process information in two totally diverse ways.

CONCLUSION: Educators must update classroom activities to insure they are brain compatible. Never threaten a student with the loss of "face" by putting him on the spot with a tough question while his classmates listen. Employ more diverse methodologies in the classroom. As an example, the less traditional right column now needs to be included with the more traditional left.

Traditional	More Appropriate
right answers honored	individual perspective
rote, memorized learning	experiential, reflective
authoritative teaching	coaching, managing
competitive	synergy, cooperation
learning as work	learning as joyful
linear learning only	Gestalt (whole) learning
teacher directed	self-directed
system boundaries	unlimited thinking
quiet classrooms	full of music, discussion
manipulative	shared outcomes
reinforces status quo	moves toward vision and possibility
verbal instructions	additional visual and kinesthetic
logical, systematic	added use of humor, leaps of thought
fixed material	added use of metaphor, stories
discipline based on power	dependence on integrity and relationship
following a lesson plan	teaching people not curriculum
serious, adultlike	playful, childlike

META-TEACHING MODEL

The term "Meta-Teaching" is exactly that—beyond teaching. It refers to the areas of teaching which traditional teacher training has by-passed. The model is simple, but powerful. It has three parts: your input of information, your processing of it and your output. The input is your skills in sensory activity and empathy. The processing part is really the thinking skills and the decision-making mechanisms. The output part is your classroom and communication skills—both the conscious and non-conscious.

Most of the topics in the model are ones of communication—it's the single most significant skill. It could certainly be sub-divided into thinking, planning, speaking, listening and sharing. Although all skills are useful and important, these skills seem to be the ones that set apart average teaching from real master-level teaching. The basic model looks like this:

Input

The input section deals with your ability to gather a wide range of both visible information and the usually "invisible" data. The information could be grouped as follows:

1. Auditory

Conscious signals	Non-conscious messages
what's being said	how it's being said
substance/content	style/delivery
what's presented	what's left out
content	tonality/tempo/volume/pitch

Primary Skills Needed: No "ego" involved while listening, able to listen for meaning behind the content, able to listen without own agendas

2. Visual

what's being seen	how it's being presented
the obvious	the inferences
what's presented	body language
the presenter	dress standard/environment

Primary Skill Needed: Awareness, ability to make fine distinctions and to be able to detect the usually non-conscious information

3. Kinesthetic

what's being done	how it's being done
what's being felt	what it means
love for others	love for yourself

Primary Skill Needed: Compassion, lack of pre-judgements, ability to be ruthless on integrity, yet still loving and understanding

---

Process

The thinking and processing skills required for being a top teacher are really the mechanics of how you think what you think. It includes the ability to make fine distinctions, to determine clear, well-defined outcomes and decisions based on your values.

1. Making Distinctions

attentive awareness	analyzing circumstances
	discovering context, trends

Primary Skills Needed: the ability to make finer and more useful distinctions, the skills to create powerful conditions and contexts for success

2. Knowing Outcomes

setting goals	having vision, ideals
	living out of your commitment

Primary Skills Needed: the will to live your life out of the commitments to your ideals, the ability to create clear, well-defined outcomes and the vision from which to operate and draw strength

3. Decision Making

being courageous	creating values
	living with integrity

Primary Skills Needed: the ability to create decisions consistent with your values and the courage to follow through on your decisions

---

Output

This is the most seen, heard and felt part of the teacher's roles. The top teachers have mastered the non-conscious as well as the conscious elements to great communication. Out of the six categories mentioned, most teachers have been trained in only three of them.

1. Visible Content

the subject matter   process/strategies
                                      methods/styles/tools
                                      mastery of "state"
your actions   your congruency, compassion

Primary Area for Focus: Learn more strategies, especially how to control the "state" of your students and yourself. Also develop your congruency of actions.

2. Auditory Presentation

word choice   voice fluctuations
                                      tonality/tempo/volume
                                      use of music, etc.
                                      congruency

Primary Area of Focus: Develop more range and flexibility in your voice, use it as an instrument and tool for communication instead of a "ticker-tape." Become more powerful in the choice of your words.

3. Visual Presentation

your dress   your actions
                                      gestures, posture, expressions
                                      positioning, congruency
the environment   its sounds, the feel, the temperature
materials used   their quality, their meta-messages

Primary Area to Focus: Dress up for class more, videotape your class and check for congruency of motions. Set up the environment more purposefully, use music, upgrade the materials.

Now that we have the three major distinctions, here's how they would fit into the planning of a lesson:

Planning

Plan lessons from the student's point of view. Can create well-defined sensory-specific outcomes. Knows how to orchestrate the planning process. Includes emotional and physical aspects of every classroom experience as well as the intellectual. Knows how to build a safe and playful learning environment. Saves past lesson plans and makes notes on them of own learning experiences.

State

Has consistent control over own attitudes, feelings and state. Knows how to elicit own state of confidence, flexibility, compassion, excitement, commitment, awareness and resourcefulness. Can successfully elicit from students a state of curiosity, interest, excitement and resourcefulness. Know how the students learn and can plan strategies to meet it.

Relationship

Provides an exemplary role model for the students. Is highly respectful of students and their potential. Creates strong rapport easily with any group of students. Establishes a favorable student-subject relationship. Knows how to and is willing to enter a student's world. Creates subject matter relevancy, motivation, student benefits.

Presentation

Focuses on the learner, not the material. Communicates at the level of the student. Establishes subject matter relevancy to student's world. Builds student self-confidence and self-worth. Orchestrates learning in physical, emotional and intellectual package. Uses the students unconscious capacity to learn. Uses students existing resources to build upon. Is fully congruent in delivery. Elicits and installs learning patterns. Knows how to maintain appropriate student state.

Feedback

Has well-trained sensory activity for unconscious signals. Has developed conscious student signal system in three senses. Insures that all student's needs are acknowledged. Responds quickly to student feedback.

Flexible Intervention

Reframes all mistakes as useful feedback, outcomes or results. Welcomes corrections and appreciates contributor. Has endless teaching flexibility; more than the students. Accepts responsibility for student's learning. Can re-package any material differently based on student's feedback. Recognizes and fulfills learning strategies immediately. Knows how to change the meaning of experiences and empower students to do the same.

Inquiry and Discussion

Listens with no agendas, has many kinds of listening styles. Opens discussion, sharing, thinking out loud and evaluation. Knows whether the students are competent long before any tests are given. Provides students with sense of self-determination and choice. Shapes and draws out the experience, generalizes the appropriate results.

Completion

Prepares the student for the next future application of the topic through visualization or role-play. Offers congruent congratulations to audience. Meets or exceeds both institutional and student-teacher goals.

Your reaction may be "how could anyone do ALL those things at once?" Surprisingly, many do. Most of the top teachers pick a specific area and work on it until it became second nature. Then they went to a different area and worked on that. In time, all of the skills became automatic, as they will for you. Once you are comfortable with your new skills, you can pay attention to the really important parts—your own growth. It is only by first mastering yourself that you can begin to master the teaching process. By itself, learning the teaching process has only superficial value—it comes across as phony and nongenuine. In each of the upcoming chapters, the details will be presented along with the specifics of how to master them. Prepare yourself for an exciting journey!

☑ Check These Key Points

1. Teachers may want to re-examine attitudes and attitudes about skills needed for mastery.
2. Teachers must update classroom activities to insure they are brain compatible.
3. The meta-teaching model consists of input of information, processing of information and output of information.

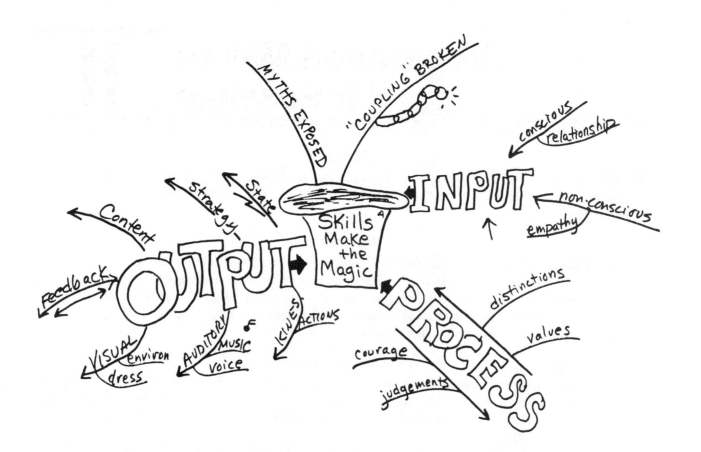

Preparation Makes It Possible

Chapter Five

Mastery Lesson Planning

Objectives

- To identify misconceptions about the planning process
- To introduce 4 new parts for a "world core" curriculum
- To provide specific examples of powerful lesson-planning formats
- To list criteria for evaluation of lesson plans
- To introduce mind mapping

Most teachers are aware of the usefulness of planning for a presentation. One could also say that very few teachers agree on the style, method, or function of lesson planning. Yet there's something new here—a powerful new lesson-planning format. It's one that will dramatically expand your ability to successfully plan a class with respect to content, process and context.

Myth: Every Teacher is Sold on the Value of Planning

An erroneous assumption that could be made is that every teacher is sold on the benefits of creating lesson plans. Contrary to a popular notion of "the better you are, the fewer notes you need," most highly competent teachers plan well. Creating the lesson plan provides clarity, and clarity leads to better classes. Masters can fail successfully, but the master always plans to succeed. "If I fail to plan, I am planning to fail."

Benefits of Strong Lesson Plans:

- Allows you to stay focused on your outcome
- Gives you added confidence
- Allows for creative ideas to surface
- Gives you a place to make corrections and additions

In addition, strong lesson plans can also dramatically increase your chances:

1. To increase class structure and coherence
2. To have a concrete visual with which to 'mentally walk through'
3. To experience satisfaction and a sense of completion
4. To create a permanent record of what's presented, when and how

Myth: Comprehensive Lesson Plans Lead to a Better Class

Good lesson plans by themselves mean nothing. Some of the best designed lesson plans are guaranteed to fail unless the teacher has the resources with which to make them succeed. In fact, the more comprehensive, the more detailed the lesson plan is, and the greater the adherence to that plan, the greater your chances of failure. Why? A great teacher navigates the course of learning. This means that

41

you are ready, at every moment, to make changes, deletions or additions. Your students may respond in a way that prompts you to choose a totally different path. The course objectives are important, how you get there should allow for infinite possibilities.

The lesson plan is like the menu at a restaurant—it's a useful planning tool, but it's not the meal. In many ways, the process of planning is more important than the resulting physical piece of paper. The process insures you have thought out the salient points and how to present them. The lesson plan must get translated through you to the students. Translation and delivery are critical. The success of your lesson plans have more to do with the way you deliver them (the rapport, presentation skills and learning environment) than what's in them.

Myth: Lesson Planning Is Only for Yourself

The 'why' of a lesson plan may be considered from the teacher's point of view and from the administrator's view. Earlier are given reasons for planning from the teacher's point of view. Some of the key reasons from an administrator's viewpoint are:

1. To have an advance notice of the class's content and processes
2. To note the disparity, if any, between lesson plans and the actual class
3. To provide clarity and continuity for substitutes
4. To gain evidence of teacher planning capabilities
5. To reduce extemporaneous and unplanned teaching
6. To insure that classes are fulfilling legal requirements

The additions that need to be made are the items which meet the student's criteria. In other words, let's have our student's concerns be met also. From the student's point of view, wouldn't we want to include such items as:

1. To know that something was learned each day
2. To have gained self-esteem and self-confidence
3. To learn how to apply what was learned in life
4. To gain communication skills, sense of integrity
5. To learn HOW to learn, not just WHAT to learn

Myth: That Lesson Plans Will Destroy Spontaneity

What master teachers have discovered is that there is always room for the spur of the moment story, activity, sharing, or inquiry if, and this is a big if . . . you have successfully taught your class all along. The structure is what makes the time and appropriateness for spontaneity. No one way of doing class is better than another, so your ability as a teacher to move flexibly with what is needed will create more time than it uses. A class could be both planned and spontaneous, for there is value which can come from each.

Curriculum Content

One of the marks of super-teachers is their ability to recognize and be responsible to trends and needs in education. Many teachers already include parts of the new "world core curriculum." Robert Muller, assistant secretary-general of the United Nations, proposes four sections to add for a more global curriculum:

1. Our planetary home. Studies of the earth, sun, space, with special attention to preserving plant life, animal forms and our ecosystem.
2. The human family. A review of the total human population. Its changes, growth, sexes, living standards, geography, races, health and children.
3. Our place in time. The history of our planet, and the connections and interweavings of history. Also what lessons we may have learned from history.
4. The miracle of individual life. Discovery of the inner self. Time and attention on the human condition and how to develop mentally, physically, spiritually and emotionally.

In addition, the curriculum must include the knowledge and lessons of the past, with the awareness and vision to deal with the future. It must deal with trends in education such as critical thinking, communication and learning how to learn. Include learning for sheer joy, awe, satisfaction and curiosity. In doing so, four variables must be balanced:

1. *Intention:* purpose, goals, values and philosophy
2. *Assessment:* tests, observations, results and conclusions
3. *Circumstance:* the existing and surrounding conditions
4. *Implementation:* instructional methods, teacher and materials

Start with a Purpose

A useful place to start is with a clear purpose of the class or course. The dictionary defines 'purpose' as intention; what is it that you intend to have happen? Purpose is different from a goal or objective. A purpose is something that usually has no end to it. It is more of a direction than a goal post. Here's an example:

Purpose: to contribute to the personal and academic development of my students.

Goal: to successfully complete 4 chapters by next Friday and to have an average class competency score of 80% of all my students.

For your class to have purpose, you, the teacher, must have one. What is your life's direction? The purpose you have will affect the purpose you express in the classroom. Also know the importance of not being at cross-purposes, meaning inner conflicts. Many teachers intend to do this, then intend to do that, only to discover that they are getting nowhere. Often at the cause of frustration is the discovery that you have conflicting purposes which create inadequate results. Only you can determine the purpose of your life, your teachings, or even that for the course you teach.

Sample Life Purpose: To discover my gifts and contribute them in a meaningful and satisfying manner.

Sample Teaching Purpose: To create an environment where students can discover who they are and how to function successfully in their world.

(OR) To provide an opportunity to successfully master the course requirements while experiencing a great sense of personal worth.

(OR) To impart a love of learning, of the subject matter and of themselves.

Sample Course Purpose: To expand each students understanding and experience of world history in a way that is joyful, meaningful and empowering.

Address Student Beliefs

All of your curriculum is likely to fall upon deaf ears unless you address important student beliefs and myths about that subject you are teaching. As an example, many students have "mathphobia" which undermines their ability to understand additional math. Think of all the student concerns and likely beliefs in your subject matter and make sure that you address each of those in your curriculum planning. Here's an example for math:

"I can't learn it."
"It's too hard."
"It is too boring."
"It is for geniuses or nerds."
"It goes in one ear and out the other."
"I'll forget it in no time."

Once you have identified the likely beliefs that are common underminers for your subject, plan short pieces to address each of them. For example, on the last belief listed above, set up some simple mnemonic device to insure that students remember each of the key points from the day's class.

Clarify Your Outcomes

The next part of lesson planning is creating your intended results. This is often the easiest part for teachers since much training is directed in this area. Intended results are the behavioral objectives which should be specified in each area of the class or course. You need to have outcomes for your entire course, as well as for every one-to-one interaction, each activity and every talk. If you don't know what your goal is, how will you know when you've accomplished it? And how do you know if your outcome is even a worthwhile one? Here are eight useful criteria with which to evaluate your outcomes.

A) Does it have integrity? Is the outcome you want consistent with the beliefs, values and attitudes that are necessary for the success of everyone? Is it consistent with the school policies? If outcome has integrity, it's success is more likely.

B) Does your outcome 'dovetail' with others? Is it a 'win-win?' Does it also include others in getting what they want? Have you included the wants and needs of the other person? This simple step increases dramatically our chances of achieving your outcome.

C) Have you designated a time for completion? Is your outcome for the next ten minutes or ten years? Is your short-term outcome consistent with your long-term one?

D) Is your outcome stated in the positive? Have you said what you do want to happen, not what you don't want?

E) Do you have an evidence procedure? How will you know when your outcome is reached? Do you have the resources to check it out? Will it be near you, possible to notice, etc.

F) Is your outcome sensory specific? Use the senses to make fine distinctions which will clarify the intended outcome. An example is this: what would be the sounds, feelings and actions of a successful class? How would it look, what would the expressions be on the student's faces, how about the body language, breathing rates and eye movements?

G) Is the outcome of added value to your students? Is it a new breakthrough, a challenge, a growing experience or a 'stretch?'

H) In what context is the outcome preferable? Always? When up for academic review? When students applaud? When your supervisor is near? When you are short on time?

As an experiment, think of something that you tried and it failed to get the impact you wanted. You'll discover it failed in several of the criteria. Get used to running each outcome you want through these questions until they become automatic. In a short time, you'll be easily, quickly and confidently evaluating and choosing outcomes more effectively. For example:

Course: Biology

Outcomes: students will be able to:

1. Identify the major steps of photosynthesis
2. Explain the role of chlorophyll
3. Write the chemical formula accurately for photosynthesis
4. Identify the accessory pigments and their function

The previous outcomes are common for most teachers. However, there are many additional outcomes you may want to consider. Some may be not-so easily measured, yet could be of equal or greater value. For example, it may be useful if your students also got these items:

1. A good relationship with that subject, so that they have a continuing curiosity in it, know the relevancy of it and how it is related to their lives. A love of learning and an appreciation of that subject. Encouraging learning as a lifelong endeavor.
2. An understanding and awareness of, their own particular success strategies for that subject, and have some alternative ones for the future. In other words, do your students know how to learn it again? Are you teaching them the traditional WHAT to learn or the more useful HOW to learn it?
3. Personal peripheral values of honesty, responsibility, humility and love. Greater skills in cooperation, and loyalty as global citizens.
4. An enlarged sense of interconnectedness. Sensitivity to the human condition and our planet's ecosystem. Greater care for the needs of others.

To accomplish these student needs, it means a balance of the intellectual, emotional, physical, social, aesthetic and spiritual in your classroom. The easiest way to begin to include the above elements in your courses is through personal example and discussion. You must provide these; your students will have no other place to get them.

It is suggested that you create intended results for both a single class and the entire course. There is also the benefit of having clearly stated objectives by which to measure your progress. It is also important to understand that the purpose of the course should have precedent over the intended results. In other words, if you feel you have to sacrifice a student's self-esteem in order to meet an objective, don't do it. The purpose is the very reason and intention of the entire course and the intended results are set up more for clarity and for providing a vehicle with which to measure progress.

The first step in creating the intended results is to identify the completed behavior. For example, in the sample objectives above, we stated "To be able to write the chemical formula accurately for photosynthesis." Notice that we said nothing about the teacher's opinions, interests, or judgements. It did not say, "To be able to understand photosynthesis well." This is because that objective is stated in teacher's terms—to be able to understand it according to who's terms . . . and what does "well" mean? To be able to write an article on it? Examples of clear and unclear objectives are below:

UNCLEAR: to create a valuable classroom experience
CLEAR: for each student to role-play two characters, then submit a one paragraph summary conclusion on the experience by next Tuesday at 2 P.M.
UNCLEAR: to be able to remember better
CLEAR: to achieve a minimum of 80% on 4 part recall quiz offered at the end of the class period.
UNCLEAR: to know the U.S. role in the Arab-Israeli war
CLEAR: to orally list 5 ways the U.S. aided Israel.

Avoid giving your students responsibility . . .
it cannot be given away, anyways . . .
It can, however, be taken on and accepted
By an individual as an act of courage . . .
So, be a courageous and responsible
role model and accept all the responsibility
you can handle.

Three Major Learning Areas

Most commonly, the three major learning areas are cognitive (primarily mental), psychomotor (what we do) and affective (what we feel). Because there are many types of learners, you want to insure each class has components which appeal to a broad base of learners. As you know, some learners learn best visually, others auditorally, and others kinesthetically. Here are some of the processes you might use in class to bring across your curriculum objectives and the related learning modalities. (V=visual, A=auditory, K=kinesthetic).

Include a variety of these processes:

1. Cognitive: commonly known as what we know, but better defined as:
   A. Knowledge—(A), being able to recall and define
   B. Comprehension—(A), to translate into his own words
   C. Application—(A, K), using tools outside original context
   D. Analysis—(A, V), to note strong and weak points
   E. Synthesis—(AK), to create from other parts
   F. Evaluation—(AK), to compare and contrast
2. Psychomotor: commonly known as physical skills, also:
   A. Accuracy—(V,K), to be able to hit a target
   B. Coordination—(K), to be able to move within parameters
   C. Manipulation—(K), to create cause and effect
3. Affective: known as values, feelings and attitudes:
   A. Attending—(A,K), participation and commitment
   B. Responding—(A,K), intensity and quantity of response
   C. Valuing—(A,K), importance and worth
   D. Values expression—(A), to be willing to share freely

You may be surprised to see that many of the most common activities are ones which are highly visual or auditory. Students who are highly kinesthetic generally lack a medium to express themselves. As a result, the visual students appear brighter, more active and alert. The more kinesthetic students are soon labelled as "slow learners" because they don't fit the mold. Yet the irony is that many of the so-called "higher" level or "real world" activities such as synthesis and application are the preferred mode of kinesthetic learners. No wonder many students feel like a square peg trying to fit a round hole!

Once you have constructed the processes of your curriculum with the variety of modes which will reach the greatest number of students, you are ready for the format. There are many possible styles and two of the more successful will be presented here as a model.

The first one is for primarily content-oriented subjects such as reading, geography, history, grammar and social studies. The second format is for skill-oriented subjects such as lab experiments, math, note-taking, dancing, sports, music and woodshop. Using them, many of the country's best teachers have successfully increased the rate of both absorption and retention of their coursework. The major differences between these two kinds of lesson plans and a traditional format will be obvious. By using them, you'll discover why you're much more likely to succeed.

Model for Presentation
Content Format

1. *Create proper "state."* The teacher must first evoke from within an excited physiological state of flexibility, enthusiasm, care, positivity and love. Only in this state can a teacher have access to their own range of resources and only in this "electric" state can a teacher even hope to get the students excited over the class.
Next, the teacher must elicit a resourceful learning state from the students themselves. Students must be accessing their best self for optimal learning. This means the teacher takes responsibility for putting the student "in state" before teaching anything.

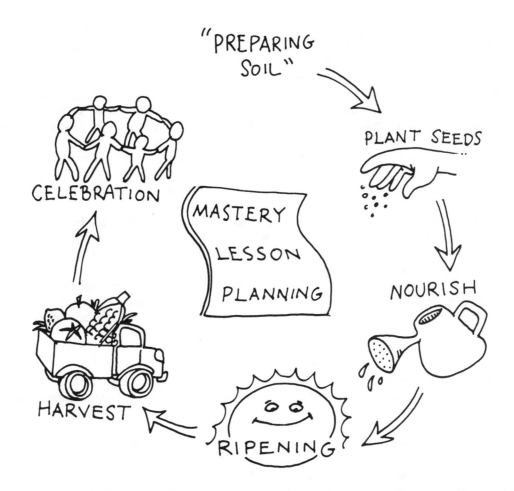

"PREPARING SOIL"

PLANT SEEDS

CELEBRATION

MASTERY LESSON PLANNING

NOURISH

HARVEST

RIPENING

2. *Relationship developed*. First the teachers must establish rapport with the students. It should be done on a conscious level by finding common ground and sharing the ways they are like their students. Also, and more importantly, rapport must be developed unconsciously with the use of artful matching and mirroring of your student's body language, gestures, and voice quality.

In addition, the teacher must create a favorable relationship in the student's mind with the subject you are about to teach. In order for the student to want to learn it, he needs to be curious and understand the relevancy and global nature of the subject.

3. *Outcomes established*. Put them in measurable, behavioral terms. Make sure that they offer value and benefits to the students. Make sure that they are ethical, moral and emotionally comfortable for the students. Then, most importantly, secure student agreement on the outcomes. In some cases, it may be useful merely to secure a commitment to work towards the outcome, while with others it may be to have the students co-create them.

4. *Reality bridge established*. This is a key area. By using the "As if" frame, you will have the students "act as if" they have already mastered the material, and they are at the end of your class. Describe it as a "future party" and have students get up and walk around and talk to other students. Have them brag to or congratulate others (with congruency and emotion) about the success they just had learning in your class. This role-playing insures that the students accept the new material as part of their self-image and become comfortable with it as well.

5. *Presentation delivered*. The purpose of a presentation is to build or change internal representations in a student with sufficient skill to elicit a corresponding behavioral change. This means that you are presenting your information with such congruency, staying in state, so that your students picture, hear or feel the same things you do on that subject. Plus, they'll be able to take the appropriate actions, if necessary.

6. *Feedback received*. First, a good presenter needs alert, well-trained sensory acuity skills. It's critical to be able to recognize the subtle unconscious messages that students are giving constantly. Secondly,

set up an easy-to-use signal response system for on the spot feedback during lecture time. This includes hand, body or sound signals with pre-arranged meaning. Then, an auditory, kinesthetic and visual feedback system for later quizzes and tests.

7. *Flexible intervention.* If what you are presenting does not meet with immediate success, your feedback should tell you to be flexible and change what you're doing. You must re-group, re-package and re-format your presentation in another way. Change styles, use metaphor, quotes, change representational systems, or try any other tool until successful. Teachers need, in order to be successful, more flexibility than their students.

8. *Dialogues and discussion.* Inquiry and questioning. The Socratic method combined with good listening skills. Ask about values, decisions and conclusions. Discover the processes that led to them. Appreciate and respect all points of view. Ask students to tell why and how they think and learn as they do.

9. *Completion experienced.* Once you get the feedback that your presentation has been successful, it's time for closure. This means a teacher or student evaluation, time for questions, review, clarification and affirmation of what was learned. It's also useful to generalize the information to other areas, globalize its importance and review its relevancy. Then take your students into a successful future experience with it in a "future-party." Allow them to get up and circulate among other students as if it was a celebration. Put on party music and have the students congratulate each other on using the information successfully in life. Close with a visualization, give congruent congratulations to them and acknowledge their success.

Model for Psycho-motor Skills

1. *Create proper "state."* The teacher must evoke a personal peak physiological state of enthusiasm, excitement, flexibility, love and caring. Then the teacher must elicit from the students a state of interest, curiosity, confidence, attentiveness, joy and relaxation.

2. *Relationship developed.* Teacher establishes rapport with the students on both conscious level and non-conscious level. Then teacher creates a student-subject or skill relationship by making it global and relevant.

3. *Outcomes established.* They must be measurable, in directly observable behavioral terms. They must be benefit and value-oriented so that the students know "what's in it for me?" Outcomes must also be ecological and be in alignment with the students personal morals, ethics, emotions or personal history. Both teacher and student must agree upon them.

4. *Give historical or literary metaphor.* Make sure that the students have accessed internally a model of the parts and the "whole" of what the skill is like when used, or some similar skill.

5. *Reality bridge established.* Create "Future Party" to celebrate in advance, the successful mastery of the skills. Have the students get up and walk around the room as in a party atmosphere. Have them congruently congratulate others, with emotion, on their success in learning the new skill. This "bride" activity allows students to begin to integrate the new skill with their personality and self-image.

6. *Demonstration.* Give an accurate demonstration after showing and telling the students what to look for first.

7. *Digitalization of the demonstration.* Next, re-do the activity in micro-steps so that each step is understood and repeated by the group. Elicit the steps from the students (have them SHOW you visually, TELL you auditorially, and DO it kinesthetically) to insure that they know each of the steps precisely.

8. *Instructions for the structured experience.* Tell and show the students how to practice the skill, whether it's with partners or in small groups. It is crucial that they do it with others to get the feedback, correction and reinforcement. The directions must be very specific and clear. Make them easy to understand, and present them in all three modes; visually, auditorially and kinesthetically.

9. *Closely supervised experience.* Make sure that you have adequate supervision to insure that the skills are learned. Discover the class leaders and have them help monitor others if you are unable to do it alone.

10. *Clean-up.* As soon as it's over, ask how it went, and ask for questions. Make sure that the entire experience is well understood and integrated. Also make sure that the students feel good about their experience of it with their self-worth intact. Then, make sure that the skill is generalized by the students and you to other areas of their life. This gives relevancy and greater value to the exercise.

11. *Completion.* Do a short visualization with the students in the form of "future pacing" their new skill. Have them go into the future in their imagination, then successfully use the skills. Makes sure they see, hear and feel themselves use the skills and get reinforcement for it. Once the imaginary part is complete, have them get up and physically act out the same part in a "future party." Let the students tell others how much they have used their new skills, how good they are at them, and how easy they are to maintain. Have students shake hands, laugh, and have fun. Then, end the party, and congruently congratulate them for learning a new skill and wish them well.

A Thematic Approach to Curriculum

One of the more successful formats to curriculum development is the theme approach. The underlying principle is that our world is an integrated whole, and that one of the greatest gifts you can offer your students is the connectedness of classroom education to the real world. The thematic approach urges you to follow threads that weave throughout your student's world instead of a single subject or textbook. Textbooks are not only often out of date, but more importantly, they are a single viewpoint or approach which the authors have chosen. In this fast-moving information age, your preferred sources of information should be the student's real life experience, magazines, computers, videos, television, journals and libraries.

The theme approach is well presented by master teacher Susan Kovalik in *Teachers Make the Difference,* listed in the bibliography. Here are the steps, in its most simplified form:

1. *Select an annual theme.* You might list several possibilities, and let your students vote on them. Vary the complexity of the theme depending on your grade level. Examples: nature, courage, people, color, sound, communication or thousands of other broad-based themes.

2. *Select focusing areas for the theme.* Use ones which can connect well to practically any theme. Example: Kovalik suggests using ones such as: past, present, future, music, art, literature, drama, careers and politics.

3. *Select special themes for mini-focuses:* These may include topics which are specifically relevant to your students such as science, language, math, or world economics. Each of these can be delved into at a level consistent with the time available. Example: under science, use machines, medicine, energy, people, discoveries, relationships and values.

An Example:

The color red as a monthly theme can be related to red plants, red fruits, and red vegetables. It can be related to red tides, Red Skelton, Red Barber, Red Cross, redheads, Red Square in Moscow. It can be related to Mars, clothing, cars, paint, emotions, eyes, blood, tulips, stop signs, cosmetics, hearts and Valentines. Think of the classroom possibilities for discussion, projects, plays and writing. Give your students a list of at least ten addresses where students can write to for free information including U.S. Government agencies, the Chamber of Commerce as well as state agencies. Then let your students experience the power of results from their own writing. This teaches students how to learn, how to communicate, how to research, problem-solving skills and persuasive writing. Many students will begin to ask you how to take better notes, how to study, analyze and classify. Out of this project, many will become an expert on something—a real boost to self-confidence. It also trains the mind to search for and identify patterns in life. And the bottom line is improved long-term self-esteem and a better grasp of how the real world works.

What to Look for in Your Own Lesson Planning

Recognize the areas of course planning. Below are each of them, followed by a brief description. Be aware that many times others will have a different name for the same ingredient. Each of these areas will be discussed in detail at some point in later chapters.

1. Pre-class . . . The environment. What negative-suggestive factors could be eliminated from the learning environment? What positive ones can we build into it? Includes all wall posters, decorations, assignments, notices, etc. on the walls, includes temperature, lighting, room neatness, circulation, set-up, and general impression created. Also includes pre-lesson set, the clues and tools to start the learning before the class actually starts. Also includes the personal, emotional, and psychological readiness of the teacher plus appearance.

2. Introduction . . . known as set induction to some . . . includes getting attention, putting yourself and students in "state," introducing the topic, exciting the students, making it relevant, clearing expectations, giving positive learning suggestions, imbedded commands, opening ritual, relaxation, early learning re-stimulation, selling the benefits of the material to the students, building teams, conveying interest in and care for, the students, physical stretching, building trust, establishing credibility, ground rules, etc. Also a good time for "as if" frame where students go into the future and congratulate themselves on learning so easily and use it confidently.

3. Active Dynamic Presentation . . . the body of the class . . . includes content of lecture, the tools, processes, and procedures for achieving the objectives. Also includes puppets, flipcharts or other dramatic aids, such as slides, video, sounds, chalkboard, plus time for discussion, inquiry and questions and continual review.

4. Passive Presentation. This is a relaxed re-delivery of the same material using music as a background. The purpose is to use it to "carry" the material in a relaxed way, while you add the content as a secondary backstage addition. In other words, focus the attention on the relaxation, so that the material becomes secondary—hence easier learned.

5. Interplay . . . the part of the class which allows the students to integrate the content into the affective domain, the right hemisphere and the unconscious mind. For example if they learned your original material visually, now present it auditorally and kinesthetically. Especially use role-play, simulations, skits, etc. Could include group discussions, interviews, games, physical movements, a dance or a quiz show. Primary focus is on the activity, not the material.

6. Review Process. Can be either active or passive. Active review might include group unison oral recall, use of lap boards for visual recall or hand signals for kinesthetic recall. Passive review would mean an eyes-closed process with soft music in the background while you recount the key ideas.

7. Evaluation . . . the time traditionally saved for tests. In this case, make it an ungraded quiz, self-corrected and uncollected. Students work together, usually in pairs, continually changing partners from one day to the next.

8. Completion . . . the time saved for review and wrap-up. Also an excellent time to help students feel confident and competent with the material presented, to integrate it into the rest of what they know. To preview the next class, offer congruent congratulations and future pace them to using the material. Includes closing ritual.

Format Your Lesson Plans

Every teacher needs to find the format that works best for him or her. What's important, as master teachers know, is to be sensitive to the results. For a moment, visualize, or even bring out a copy of the lesson or presentation format that you are currently using. Next, read over the following questions, and answer them as best you can:

1. Rate the quality of your last few classes?
2. Do you often run out of time, or have time to spare?

3. Is your lesson plan something that you can use as an example for the students to learn from?
4. How long does it take to make your lesson plan?
5. Does your format give you the flexibility to go back and change, delete or add new material? Or is it full of correction marks?
6. Can you read your class notes from several feet away?
7. Do you ever get confused or lost while teaching?
8. Do the actual notes you use in class provide you with insights and fresh ways of thinking?

Mind Mapping

If you have discovered some dissatisfaction in your actual physical layout of your lesson plans or class notes, you may want to experiment with a different format. May I recommend mind mapping?

A mind map is a creative pattern of connected ideas. It emerged in its current form in the mid 1950's and was popularized by Evelyn Wood and Tony Buzan who has written several good books on it. It is similar to a sentence diagram, a road map, a blueprint, a recall pattern, a schematic or clustering. The purpose of a mind map is for clarity and recall. At its best, a mind map may generate refreshing ideas, great recall and more creativity. At a minimum, it stores information, is relaxing and fun. You might use mind maps for lecture notes, organizing your thoughts or study notes.

To do them, use colored pens and start in the middle of the paper. The rest is simple: (1) decide on a main topic or idea. (2) print the topic in the center of your paper and enclose it (3) add branches to hold the important points (4) add details and key words on to the branches (5) then add symbols and pictures for better recall.

As a planning tool, it's perfect for meetings and lesson plans. You might label the branches for the parts of your class. In studying textbooks, articles and other non-fiction, the branches could be titled from the bold-face print, chapter headings, or simply labelled what, how, why, who, and when. If there are no clues, make up labels such as purpose, methods and result. In fiction, use branch labels such as chapter titles, character names, places, events, problems, conclusions. Then attach the details to those branches. Samples of mind-maps are provided in this book as chapter reviews.

Additional tips are: Use pictures, arrows, symbols, cartoons, illustrations and abbreviations. Put your words on the top of lines, be brief and simple. Turn the paper sideways and use medium to thick colored pens. Printing is more easily recalled than longhand. Change the size of your words; the more important they are, the bigger they might be made. Use a different color for each of the branches. Be outrageous! Put in action, creativity and your own personality. With some practice, your mind maps will become eee-zzz. Results? Better use of your material, plus more ease and satisfaction in learning. When done well, you'll be able to read your class lesson plans from a distance because each topic is color-coded. The flexible and easily-recalled style makes teaching much easier and a lot more fun. With more sophisticated organization of content and a more readable format, you're now ready for the personal preparation.

☑ Check These Key Points

1. Strong lesson plans have many benefits including: allows the teacher to stay focused on outcome, creates record of presentation, provides structure for coherence and corrections.
2. Curriculum must include understandings of our planetary home, the human family, the history of our planet and our place in it, attention on the human condition.
3. Start with your own unique, individual purpose.
4. Address prior limiting student beliefs about your subject.
5. Clarify lesson outcomes and evaluate using the 8 criteria listed.
6. Plans may use content format, psycho-motor skills format, thematic approach.
7. Lesson planning includes the learning environment, introduction, presentation, interplay, review, evaluation and closure.

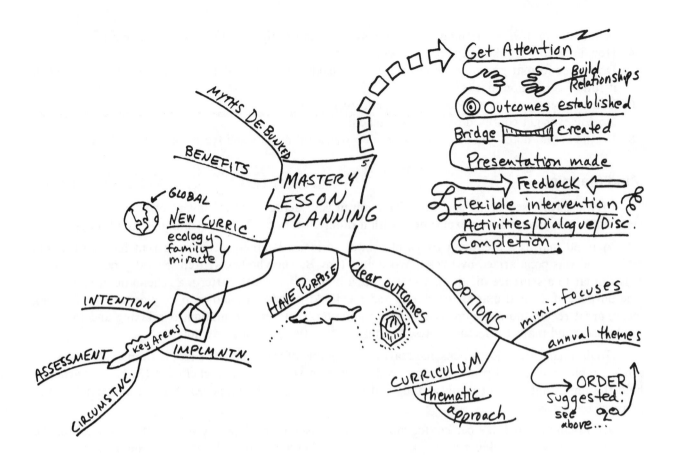

MASTERY LESSON PLANNING

Get Attention
Build Relationships
Outcomes established
Bridge created
Presentation made
Feedback
Flexible intervention
Activities/Dialogue/Disc.
Completion.

MYTHS DE-BUNKED

BENEFITS

GLOBAL
NEW CURRIC.
ecology
family
miracle

INTENTION
key Areas
ASSESSMENT
IMPLMNTN.
CIRCUMSTNC.

HAVE PURPOSE
clear outcomes

OPTIONS
mini-focuses
annual themes
ORDER
suggested:
see
above...

CURRICULUM
thematic
approach

Chapter Six

How to Build a Quality Learning Environment

Objectives

- To identify myths about classroom environment
- To describe key aspects of a quality environment

With all the hours spent in a classroom, the cumulative effects on both students and teacher are tremendous. Leslie Hart, who pioneered the brain-based approach to learning, refers to the traditional classroom as a "prime obstacle" to learning. What can be done to change the negative associations that many students have about classrooms? A lot. An artfully designed and carefully planned positive-suggestive environment can do 25% of your teaching for you. Conversely, a poorly-designed learning environment can significantly detract from the learning process.

Every moment the student's eyes are not on you, they are taking in the classroom—sometimes in parts, sometimes as a whole. The environment they take in must reflect your end purposes or you risk results.

A Note about This Chapter

This chapter includes some generalities about classrooms. You, as a teacher, may be in the sciences, humanities, elementary, college level, metaphysics, business or artwork. By their very nature, these teaching environments will be very different from one another. Make any distinctions, deletions, and modifications in order to make the information in this chapter useful for you. In spite of that, it's likely that you'll find this information to be extremely valuable. It's about how can you set up a classroom which will make better that which you are already doing. But first, let's examine the myths.

Myth: The Classroom Isn't All That Important

At least that's the conclusion one would draw by mere observation of many of the nation's classrooms. There is so much emphasis put on other areas, the quality of the classroom often falls by the wayside. When the priority of the teacher is on course content each class, it's easy to miss giving attention to the classroom itself. However, it's critical that you make sure you set aside the time for that the physical environment can be managed properly. Although a master teacher can teach well in any environment, experience says that master teachers take the time to put together an optimum learning atmosphere because they know it ultimately matters.

Myth: You're Stuck with What You've Got

Another assumption is that creating an optimum classroom environment is hopeless. Regardless of the room assigned, the possibility exists to make it work well. Teachers cannot always turn their classroom into a Better Homes and Gardens award winner or an Architectural Digest showcase, but it can be made bright, nurturing, expressive, useful, and humane.

Myth: Classroom Fix-Up Is Expensive

Another false belief is that to make a classroom look right, it takes money. Most of the time, this is true, and most of the time, the amounts we are talking about are $50 or less. There are more ways to decorate a classroom for free than there are stores to shop in. There are major sources of paper, art objects, plants, and other classroom items that cost nothing or next-to-nothing. Most beautiful classroom environments are put together with a combination of donated, borrowed, budget-bought items and spontaneous creations. Having no or low classroom budgets cannot justify an ineffective classroom.

Great Environments Produce Results

A well-designed learning environment can do many things. At its best, it can create a favorable relationship between the student and the subject matter. It can also create rapport between the teacher and the student. It can stimulate thought, creativity and curiosity. It can build self-esteem, confidence and self-worth. At its best, it can inform, influence, persuade and excite. It can add to your student's level of responsibility, sense of justice and positive feelings about school. It can definitely do part of the job for you and much to make your classroom "the" place to be. Nobel Prize winner Buckminster Fuller said that "If you change the environment, you change the people." If this possibility intrigues you, then get ready for some big changes and even bigger results.

A city had no concert hall for opera and the performing arts. The bond issue was consistently turned down by the voters because they thought the city would not support it with sufficient paying customers. And, in fact, when small-time concerts and operas were performed in rented school auditoriums, the attendance was poor. Then a group of investors financed the building of a beautiful and stunning concert hall for the performing arts. Major attractions were booked, and promotion was done. Amazingly enough, the new concert hall was sold out for the entire season! What does this have to do with your classroom? Have you ever thought your students didn't want to learn?

We could draw the conclusion that the city did not have sufficient clientele to support the arts. In that same way, it is easy to say that students in a classroom have no interest in learning or growing. But when the new concert hall was completed, the customers appeared practically out of nowhere. In that same way the student, as a "customer of learning", may appear in your classroom just as the concert-goers appeared in the new concert hall. It wasn't that there were no wealthy or cultured clientele in that city. It was that those wealthy or cultured clientele appeared only when the conditions were sufficient. You will know what those sufficient conditions are for your group when your true-blue 'learning customers' have shown up. Until then, you have not built the necessary 'concert hall'. This chapter is a blueprint for that beautiful classroom environment.

Start with Knowing the Traditional Classroom Doesn't Work

Educational pioneer Leslie Hart says we must do everything we can to "unsettle the set" and change the traditional associations that students have in the classroom. He suggests making the classroom as different as possible every day. Change where you have the front of the room often—at least once a week! Change where you have the back of the room. Have the students sit on the floor (yes, even secondary and college level students). Have them sit on tables, on the backs of chairs, on pillows, ANYTHING to keep changing the formalized lecture-theater style seating arrangement. Everything that he has discovered about the brain in the last twenty years suggests that we need more stimulus, more change, more movement and more points of view in the classroom. The most unproductive arrangement possible is the standard, rigid sit-still format that is driving most kids and teachers crazy. Of course, whenever weather or finances permit, work with your students in the less traditional environments: take field trips, teach science in a nearby field and use the rest of the school or neighborhood as a place to learn.

How to Get Others to Help

To get help, be helpful. Help other teachers with their classes. Do things in your own class that may not be your responsibility. Most teachers find themselves doing things that are actually the responsibility of others. The solution is to support those others in them doing their job more effectively, or be willing to do the jobs yourself, without resentment. Those last two words are important. The best way to do any job is with a song in your heart.

For example, if something is the responsibility of the janitor and it didn't get done, stop for a moment. Recall how many times last month you complimented or left a thank-you note for the janitor? Remember, too, that sometimes we must do what is necessary for the result we want, regardless of our job description! Winston Churchill said, "It is not enough that we do our best; sometimes we have to do what's required."

Most of the more successful teachers have developed a system which works with the students and custodian to get the job done. When the task is done within a context of meaningfulness and contribution, students are more than willing to support the teacher in the creation of a successful classroom environment. In an institutional classroom, the room is an on-going project and a system can be implemented where the students have their own team that rotates and is responsible for the looks of the room. They are allowed to create, input and contribute the things which they are good at, whether it is drawing, painting, synthesizing, giving advice, or scavenging for useful items. In this spirit, it is possible to have a beautiful and functional classroom which is being constantly kept up by your own students. The appropriate time to set that up may not be right now, but something which is woven into the curriculum at a later time as the mastery within you expands.

MENU FOR CLASSROOM ENVIRONMENT

VISUAL:
- LIGHTING
- PLANTS
- CLEANLINESS
- WALLS
- FLOWERS
- ORDER

KINESTHETIC:
- TEMPERATURE
- FLOORING
- SAFETY
- SIZING
- TEXTURE
- SURFACE

AUDITORY:
- MUSIC
- WHITE NOISE
- DISTRACTIONS

Is Your Classroom Safe?

Safety is a primary consideration for teachers, above all else. Each teacher should be familiar with how to prevent and deal with any type of physical emergency. Teachers must know where the fire extinguisher is and the nearest phone. In addition, you should have for easy access, a listing of doctor, police and fire numbers. In addition, make sure you know who to call in case of other emergencies such as a nervous breakdown, epilepsy, or psychiatric problems. You should have a first aid kit on hand which includes plenty of gauze, tape and band-aids. Also have access to a broom for cleaning up glass, plus cloths and rags for spilled items. Teachers should also know how to contact the building administrator or manager. Other necessary information includes knowing emergency procedures for fire escape, earthquakes, floods, hurricanes, windstorm, power failure, or blizzards. These are all part of the overall safety of your students and they are just as important as anything else a teacher does or knows about.

Temperature Is Number One

It is often overlooked and always important. The first thing a person will notice when they enter the room is the temperature of the room. Classrooms kept between 68 and 72 degrees Fahrenheit seem to feel most comfortable for the largest majority of students. Often a teacher becomes so engrossed in what they are doing that they are insensitive to the temperature. For this reason it is suggested that teachers leave their class after each break to get a sense of the outside temperatures. If at all possible, a teacher should find a way to provide good air circulation—windows are easiest if the weather and building design permits. Many teachers have found it helpful to attach a small indicator piece of cloth next to a window or air conditioner so that they can tell at a glance if the air is circulating. For teachers who are interested and have access to them, ionizers and humidifiers have been found valuable for student and teacher comfort. About 20% of the population is affected adversely by atmospheric electrical charges. Many experience great discomfort when the weather turns super-dry and static electricity is everywhere. A negative ion generator can be useful in those cases.

Open Space

Room size is also a critical factor for first impressions. For those teachers who have no other choice about room size, it is suggested that they use any resources available to create the illusion of the room being the size they want it. The apparent size of rooms can be enlarged or shrunk with dividers or enlarged with mirrors or room arranging. In a standard classroom, students at desks need 10–15 square feet each and about 5–8 square feet without desks.

The chairs and desks that are used in most classrooms are an unfortunate compromise of price and quality. Most of the chairs used promote lethargy, back aches, poor breathing, neck pain and sore bottoms. Learn about anatomy so you can support the postures which are physically healthy. Dr. Shorbe and Dr. Ishmael of Oklahoma City have three valuable suggestions:

1. Do keep the knees higher than the hips
2. Do support the arms and shoulders
3. Do get up and stretch often

   I would like to add:

4. If you HAVE to have desks—have a desk or table which is 3″ or less from your belly button
5. Do have a chair with a seat from 16–22″ from the floor, depending on your height.
6. Do make sure that your chair or a pillow provides lumbar (lower back) support.

Is Your Classroom Happy, Strikingly Pleasant?

The walls of the classroom can be a real support to the effects in your classroom. One of the ways the walls can add to the environment is in color. The shades, tones and hues on the walls are so important that entire businesses have been created to do color consulting for optimum working environments. If your walls are not a pastel blue, light green, or aqua, find out about the possibility of painting them. Some teachers have found certain yellows to work well also. Other colors create reactions, whether conscious or subconscious within many of the students. A wood paneling or brick-face can create a warm, home-like feeling in many cases, and the cost of paneling is reasonable.

The positioning of visuals on the wall can make a major difference in how they impact on the student. The direction your eyes look indicates an access to a certain physiological mode such as visual, auditory or kinesthetic. If you want the item to evoke good feelings, put it below eye level for the students. When the eyes are looking down and to the right, the body can most easily access the kinesthetic mode. Items at this level would be past items of student work, and other things you want them to feel good about. If you want kids to talk about an item on the wall, put it at eye level, since your body accesses constructed or created sounds with the eyes looking to the left or the right. This area is for communications and upcoming events. If you want them to simply notice the information, just process it visually as in the form of review material, put it above eye level, because that puts the student in the visual mode for recalling the information. In the area of content, they can be used at least three valuable ways:

You can nearly teach
anything to anyone.
Start by providing
Favorable conditions for learning

---

1. As a communication board. (Eye level for auditory mode) . . . to post assignments, messages, lost and found, resources, and other pertinent bits of information.
2. As a results report. (Shoulder-high or lower for kinesthetic) . . . has been found to be more useful to chart the progress of the class as a whole than to post individual test scores or well-written papers. Possibilities include putting up collective mind-maps of the week in review, group art projects, or presentations or even a large graph or thermometer showing the progress of the entire class as a team.
3. As an inspirational area. (High up for visual recall mode) An example is a large, bright colored poster saying, 'Life is wonderful!'

In the class of a teacher of learning disabled students, the teacher (an excellent one in every other way!) had a poster with a nature scene and the message, "Things take time." What was coming across to the students might actually be the message "you learn slowly, so don't expect too much, too soon." In another classroom the poster was seen which said "School is something we sandwich between weekends." Here the message is that school "is something which gets in the way of things, and that weekends are what living is really for." Posters which inspire, challenge or enliven with joyous and supportive messages will add much to the class environment. A poster which says "You Can Do It" is much more useful than "Hang In There, Baby."

In the rear of the classroom, put a trash can by the exit. This increases the odds of trash going in the right place and saves clean-up work. If there is a clock in the room, the rear of the class is the best place. And of course, there should be a clear-cut policy about when the class is out—is it when the clock says so or the teacher says so? On the door at the rear of the classroom, there should be a note which tells visitors, intruders, messengers and observers exactly what to do before or upon entering.

What Does the Front of the Room Say?

The front of the room is generally seen the most and accordingly, deserves the most attention. If it's possible a mini-stage or mini-risers should be built to elevate the teacher two to six inches above the floor. This allows for maximum visibility and enhances the teachers 'on stage' awareness. The front of the room should be impeccably clean and orderly; not because being clean and orderly is valuable by itself, but because of the impression it creates in the student's minds. Students are more likely to give credibility and veracity to the instructor who is well-prepared and orderly. Get plants put in at least four corners of the room, especially the front. And make sure that they are kept up; pruned, watered and loved. There's something pathetic about a dying and withered plant! In addition, make sure that all the papers, notes, and books at the front of the classroom are orderly.

How to Use Peripheral Stimuli

While the front of room is best kept aesthetic, simple and happy, the sides of the room are also important. How often do you see your student's eyes wandering around the room? In most cases, very often! Put your most important instructional visual stimuli on the sides and up high. Then draw no attention to it—the students will find it and learn it quite well from it accidently. In fact, the peripheral messages are often more powerful than the standard front-of-the-room ones. Be sure to make all of your messages positive and done with quality and simplicity.

Student Reinforcement

Your room should be a fertile source of confidence, information and good feelings for your students. One of the best ways is to put 5–15 posterboards up, each a 16″ × 20″ up to 22″ × 28″ size. Use light colored boards such as white, natural, canary, pink, powder blue or light gray. Then in simple, easy-to-read letters, paint or print in reminders for your students. Put them in the first person so that the student reading them know that they apply directly. Put these signs up high, on the sides and back of the room. One above the door is especially potent. Change them often, and use them to refer to or repeat in class. These are useful, regardless of whether your students are four or forty. Here are some suggested affirmations:

"I am a bright and capable learner"
"Learning is fun, easy and creative"
"I do things simply, easily and playfully"
"I am healthy, happy and wise"
"I am the change I want to see"
"For things to change, I must change"
"I am a unique and precious being"
"I can do magic"
"I enjoy reading and using affirmations"
"For things to change, I must change"
"I love myself just the way I am"
"Every problem offers a gift"
"I am a resourceful learner of many choices"

How to Use Markers

Most teachers find it useful to have a chalkboard with colored chalk in addition to white. It allows for more choice of expression, in addition to being aesthetically pleasing and easier to recall. There is an extra-fat brand of chalk-stick gaining rapid acceptance. Many teachers wrap the base of the chalk with masking tape to prevent breakage and reduce chalk dust, while others use the metal chalk-holders.

The ceramic boards with the quick-dry markers are a great improvement if you can get them. One of the great benefits of using a flip-chart with large sheets of paper is that you can save what you write, and put them up on the walls. This is in contrast to the disappearing act that chalkboard material does each day. With the flip-chart, use several different colors of pens so that the visual impact is stronger. In making lists, alternate colors to increase visibility. Print legibly, keep the messages simple and useful. Then you'll have more interest in wanting to save the most useful ones.

Lighting

Lighting is one of the most controversial areas of classroom environment. It may be that each teacher has such different needs that it is difficult to obtain consensus. Some areas which most agree on are that indirect lighting, natural daylight is best. It is certain that some areas of the room have greater needs for light than others. The front of the room—both on you and the chalkboard and flip charts are critical. Some have cited studies which indicate that full-spectrum lighting (natural or incandescent) is better than the florescent style. In many cases, you are not given much of a choice, so whether one kind of lighting is better than another is a moot issue unless you have a choice.

Room Arrangement

Another area of physical environment is the arrangement of the room itself. Include unattached chairs and moveable desks for maximum comfort and flexibility. If possible have carpet all over or at least a throw rug at the front of the classroom. The room needs to meet the needs of the subject matter, the student and the teacher. To accomplish this, first notice what the course content demands are. They are obviously different in a woodworking class than in a speech class. In general, position yourself at the front of the room in a way which puts the least depth from front to back with your students. In a rectangular-shaped room, be at the center of the longest side. Far better to move from left to right across the stage than front to back. Then decide what kinds of student-to-student interactions will be needed. Most teachers have carefully set of the class to avoid exactly this. But in the classroom of a master, student disruption and behavior problems are at a minimum. A big need is for teacher-student contact and this one will again, depend on what the situation calls for. One of the most useful rules for seating require that the students do the following:

1. Be sure to sit more than one chair away (in any direction) from someone that you knew prior to the first class.
2. Be sure to sit next to a different person (on all sides) than who you sat next to in the last class.
3. Switch sides of the room and front to back in the room to freshen up your approach every half hour. Where you sit DOES change your perception.

Make Your Room Spic'n Span

An important area of classroom environment is that of cleanliness. Your classroom should be straightened each time a group of students leave so that the next group will come into an aesthetically pleasing environment. Sound crazy? It has been said that an oriental master will not sleep if there is a single straw out of place on his grass mat. What is the importance of making something perfect so that it can get messed up again? The reason is because everything is important . . . the wad of trash paper in the corner is important, the pencil on the floor is important, the chairs out of line in their row is important. The masters take, when needed, the ten seconds necessary to pick up a piece of trash before a class starts.

What Does Your Class Sound Like?

The amount of stimulation that the human brain can accept and integrate is astonishing. And while you may have your room visually attractive, 40% of your students learn best by sounds. Students love music and it can be used very effectively to enhance the classroom atmosphere by affecting attitudes. You can use music extensively in the classroom to create and evoke specific desirable mood changes. For example, many play lively classical music at the outset, slower music during moments of relaxation or test-taking and up-beat music during activities. There are some specific suggestions in the chapter on presentation tools and a special music orientation tape you can order in the back of the book.

For the set-up, keep it simple. Do use stereo and position the two speakers as high as possible in the room and secure them to the walls or ceiling. Then be sure to mask the speaker wire so that it is invisible and out of reach. The tape cassette player should be cheap but dependable; keep it in a desk drawer which is either locked or off limits.

You may have noticed that the effective classroom is an affective one which appeals to all of the senses. It looks bright, playful and happy. It feels comfortable. It sounds joyous and enticing. It even smells great. When you maximize your environment, your teaching will be just that much easier because your students will be put into a more resourceful and receptive state for learning. And that's the whole point!

☑ Check These Key Points

1. Classroom environment can create an optimum learning atmosphere.
2. A beautiful environment can be created with little money.
3. If you change the environment, you change the people.
4. Be willing to do whatever it takes to get the job done.
5. An effective classroom looks, sounds, and feels comfortable.
6. Student/teacher safety is most important.
7. Use the walls of your classroom to communicate information, to show team or class progress, to inspire.

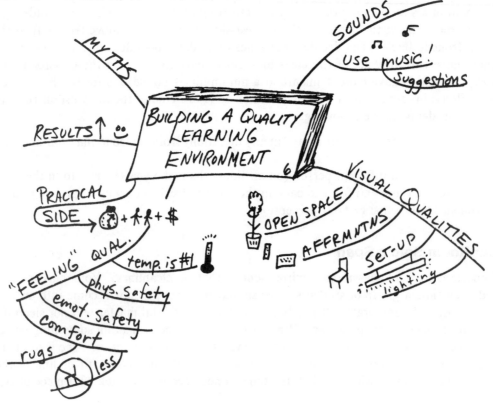

Chapter Seven

Last-Minute Readiness

Objectives

- To emphasize the importance of pre-class readiness
- To identify the one most important element in the classroom
- To describe specific last-minute details

In the moments before class begins, many details require your last-minute attention. These can make the difference between an average class and a great one. Top teachers take the time to make sure they have done their homework, just as they ask their students to do. For teachers, as with students, the payoff is enormous.

Myth: Last Minute Preparations Are Useless

Some critics say if you aren't ready by five minutes before "showtime" you'll never be ready. This is false because some of the most important things must be done in the final five minutes before class. Right before each class you'll want to clear your mind, relax, and put yourself in a resourceful and effective physiological state.

Myth: Teachers Already Do the Right Last-Minute Things

Many teachers do. Many have a mental or written checklist of their last-minute items. But many don't and most begin their classes in the same way they end: in chaos. It takes a distinct purposefulness to prepare your class in a way that includes all the necessary elements for super-results. When your class starts chaotically, students are put into a confused, disjointed state of mind and the learning effectiveness drops.

Myth: A Teacher's Content Is the Main Message

Various percentages are used to describe how little the content of words affect your audience. The one most-often quoted is from communication specialist Mehrabian who says only 7% of your influence is from words! Thirty-eight percent is from voice patterns and the remaining 55% is body language. Another way to interpret this is that your students are getting an awful lot of information from what you are *not* verbally saying! All your gestures, postures, faces, changes in tonality, tempo, volume and rhythm form the bulk of the information your students receive. If just 7% is words, imagine the possibilities for learning in your classroom if you could learn to effectively use the other 93% available resources for teaching.

Myth: Your Students Will Notice Changes

When it comes to packaging yourself as a medium of expression, you may be concerned about what your students will think of your new attention to the non-verbal messages you give. Won't your students get suspicious or ignore any effects you try to create? The surprising answer is "rarely." Students know that their role is to learn the material you present. As a result, their conscious attention is on the content of the material, not on the medium. Although a few of your students may notice some of the changes you make in your presentation, the majority of them won't have the slightest idea. Most of the time they are paying attention to the words *consciously* not the other *unconscious* messages. Until you get to the end of this sentence, you are likely unaware of the room temperature. In your class, the effect is the same. Unless it is pointed out, it's unlikely that your students will know that you use gestures, posture or grooming standards more potently now than ever before.

Myth: A Teacher is Hired to Teach, not Grow

Today's super-teacher is a far cry from the lecturer style of years ago. There was a time when a teacher would show up for class, lecture, assign homework, and go home. A virtual robot, a mechanical device probably could have done as well, maybe better. Today's teacher deals with discipline problems, absenteeism, a wide range of learners, classroom overcrowding and more. These challenges require specific people-skills with a high level of competency. They require being able to play the role of mother, father, disciplinarian, therapist, cheerleader, coach, friend and authority figure. To be successful in those roles, train yourself through courses, reading, thinking, sharing, practicing and risking.

The Most Important Element in Your Class

Can you think of another professional who has more prolonged contact with his clients? No doctor, lawyer, dentist, grocer, repairman, priest, minister, rabbi, best friend, or mechanic spends as much time as teachers do with students. Because of that, the three most important keys to producing better students are:

> Set an example.
> Set an example.
> Set an example.

In a survey reported by Marilyn Ferguson in *Aquarian Conspiracy,* nation-wide leaders were asked to rate the most important instruments for social change. The one mentioned more than any other? Personal example. Teachers are observed, heard, felt and interacted with hour after hour. Every facet of a teacher's personality has an opportunity to surface and it usually does. Why pay attention to such detail about your personality? Because you, the teacher, are the single greatest determiner of your student's success. You are so much more important than the textbooks, the video, the classroom or the lesson plans.

In the late 60's, Marshall McLuhan popularized the expression, "The medium is the message." It may apply better to the teaching profession than any other. Although ultimately technology will augment or replace much of your impact, today you are the carrier of the classroom message. Because you have your own personality with attitudes, feelings and opinions, you will "package" your message uniquely. In short, there is no objective teacher. You are as much or more of a packager of information as a television set or videocassette player. Because of this enormous influence, your own beliefs and values in education will filter and flavor your teaching. Take this as an opportunity to re-examine your "medium" more closely and make sure it represents you in the best possible way.

Your Health

Are you in your best health? You can be sure your students are getting subtle messages about your care for yourself, how you treat your self and your overall self-esteem. Make sure you have an overall health and fitness program that includes stress reduction, relaxation, nutrition, aerobics (breathing), stretching and muscle toning. It sets a good example of participation, aliveness and self-esteem. Plus, you'll feel better, act better and teach better.

Physical Messages

Your actions . . . where you stand . . . your gestures . . . where you put books . . . what you do, where you move, it all matters. The question to be asking at all times is, "Can this action create better results if done differently? Can I do it differently, slower, faster, more efficiently, more graceful, more forceful, with more flair? Would a hand here, or touch on a shoulder make a difference?" As you become increasingly convinced of your influence and suggestive impact on student behavior, your observations and distinctions will increase. And with them, your results.

Posture is another powerful part of your presentation. Your posture gives an uninterrupted stream of messages about your joy, self-confidence and energy level. You may be pleased or surprised to know that you are not permanently stuck with your posture. There are qualified physical therapists and health practitioners who can do wonders with your back and shoulders.

A recent article in *Psychology Today* talked about the "mugger susceptibility" profile. It was discovered that persons whose posture was tentative, stooped and tired-looking invited attackers. In that same way, your classroom posture can often invite student attacks—whether physical, verbal or mental. This does not mean to walk as if there is a steel rod going up your back . . . it does mean to present yourself with pride, dignity and energy.

Dress Standards

Your dress and grooming are the most visible and easily altered part of your presentation. Starting in the late 60's, a new permission moved through the ranks of teachers nation-wide. It was a permission to be yourself without pretense or show, without the stuffiness that had characterized teacher grooming standards for years. Yet, for many teachers it was a wide swing of the pendulum which has not come back to middle ground. Many teachers were and are wearing clothes that create a too-casual reaction in their students. The original idea was to be comfortable, genuine and relaxing but for many it has turned into permission to look unprofessional.

John Malloy, author of *Dress For Success* and top nation-wide clothing consultant, used to be a teacher. As part of a research project, he did a study on the effects of clothing on learning in the classroom. The results are a powerful argument for the careful choice of classroom clothing. Malloy summarized it this way:

> "The outcome . . . proved that the clothing worn by the teachers substantially affected the work and attitude of pupils . . . a breakthrough in education! Clothing had a significant effect on discipline, work habits and attitudes in the classroom."

Malloy claims that he has run surveys, experiments and tests which "would run several thousand pages" to find out the exact effects of clothing on people. In his teacher's experiments, he had two different teachers work with the same groups and tested them separately. The teachers were matched for style, delivery and course content. The teacher who dressed more professionally and conservatively had students who out-produced the casually dressed teacher. His specifics include:

- Neatness counts—even the tiniest speck on your clothing can be source for an unwanted judgement
- See yourself through your audiences' eyes. What looks great at 2–3 feet away may be quite ineffective at 10–20 feet away.
- Avoid strong patterns. They distract your audience—studies showed increased audience blink rates when exposed to loud patterns.
- Always be a contrast to your background. Make your outfit stand out just enough to be noticed easily.
- Keep your outfit quiet. Avoid things which jingle, crackle or scrape unless you're teaching pre-school. Let your message be the noise.

In general, dress one level "up" from your students. For men, may I suggest strongly that you read *Dress For Success* by Malloy? And for women, may I respectfully suggest Emily Cho's *Looking Terrific?*

Complete body hygiene is important. Check yourself for the following things. Are your clothes clean and pressed? Is your hair clean and combed? Are your shoes clean and shined? Are your face and hands clean and smelling good? Are your teeth brushed and breath smelling fresh? These all have the capacity to create or destroy that all-important rapport with your students.

What about Self-Expression?

Your language is a powerful medium of expression and the master teacher is very aware both in front of the classroom and in the informal settings. As a role-model, it is inappropriate for teachers to use foul or abusive language, even when provoked. It is unprofessional (and not useful) to criticize (ever!) or make critical value judgements about your students. By the way, a 'judgement' is different than an observation. Here's an example:

JUDGEMENT: "Johnnie is a real jerk—he doesn't want to learn."
OBSERVATION: Johnnie is talking in a raised voice and is not completing his assignment.
JUDGEMENT: "Susie, the brightest kid in the class . . ."
OBSERVATION: Susie has gotten the highest test score twice.
JUDGEMENT: "That stupid assembly was a waste of my time."
OBSERVATION: "I don't recognize any immediate value from the assembly."
(Notice the shift from "it's out there" to it's "in my power")

Affirm the Positive

At the beginning of reading, writing, math or other skill class, it's common for students to say, "I'm awful at this." We hear ourselves when we affirm such thoughts and the effect of our words can be powerful. There is much truth to the self-fulfilling prophecy idea. Politely correct the statement made so the student would now say, "I used to do poorly in this," or "So far, my skills have not met my expectations." If that does not sound as if it is very different, or if the difference in the two phrases sounds trivial, please go back and re-read them. There is a universe of difference between saying, "I am . . ." versus "in the past I was . . ."

There's also a big difference between saying, "I'm awful at this" versus "I'm not good at it." Your mind reacts strongest to the dominant influential words in the sentence. The mind hears "awful" in the first example and "good" in the second example. Which influencing words would you rather your students hear? Obviously the one that will build self-esteem.

Take Acting Lessons

It's amazing how much "star" is bottled up inside every teacher. You have your own kind of charisma and electricity which are possible to bring out. Acting is a form of self-expression and one of the best things about acting classes is that they encourage the forms of self-expression which can ultimately serve you well in the classroom. For example, you can learn a simple facial expression which will create suspense, another which creates surprise, another which expresses appreciation and so on. From an acting class you have the opportunity to gain two important teaching tools:

1. You will be able to get your intended communication aligned with what actually 'lands.' Many teachers will say how much they care about their students, yet their body language shows otherwise. Or, a teacher may be really interested in the material and yet his presentation leaves the students bored to tears. This is one of the most common problems and a good acting coach can help you learn to get your communication across more effectively.

2. You will be able to utilize a wider range of expression in your presentation. Many teachers consider certain expressions and emotions taboo in the classroom. The only question to ask is, "How's your class?" If your class is terrific, you don't need much more flexibility. For most teachers, acting expands your choices and gives new possibilities for getting the results you want. If you have three ways to respond in class, you are likely to be less effective than someone who has ten ways. Behavioral flexibility is one of the biggest keys to classroom mastery and acting can bring it to you.

Rehearse for Super Results

How much should you rehearse a presentation? Many factors will help you decide: the importance of the presentation, your current skill level, available time, the difficulty or familiarity you have with the material and your comfort level. So the question is not, "Should I rehearse, but rather, how much?" The steps for rehearsal vary. Each person seems to have a different strategy. The most widely used ones include the self-directed and the other-directed feedback.

The self directed rehearsal could happen several ways. You might sit down and talk it through, occasionally visualizing a key point or gesture. Use a mirror to check physical presentation and make sure that it carries the non-verbal messages as well as the verbal ones. The other-directed methods include the use of video feedback which is one of the best ways to see yourself objectively. You may also want to work in peer groups to get some live, direct feedback on your performance. The main thing is to learn from others and keep your self-confidence up.

Once you have prepared yourself sufficiently, you should have a clear picture of yourself as a powerful and effective presenter. You should be able to hear yourself saying exactly what you want to say, in the way you want to say it. Visualize yourself as an exciting, successful and congruent teacher. Then visualize the students responding positively with joy and confidence. Make it so real in your imagination that you can almost feel and taste it.

These internal pictures and sounds that you create and carry as a presenter will, to a large degree, determine the success of your efforts. Your pictures, when accessed by you at class time, will cause you to feel confident and powerful or, if they are unresourceful, cause you to feel scared and ineffective. It is critical that you create and choose confident images of yourself and your students. This is the time to create the future the way you want it. You can predict the success of yourself and your class if you create it first by your attentive preparation.

With the kind of preparation suggested so far, your chances for classroom excellence are great. You, as the medium for the message, are a carrier of hundreds of subtle, as well as obvious, messages. Which messages are being picked up and ingrained by your students? Which are being discarded? Who knows for sure. The real question is, "Can any teacher afford *not* to cover all the bases?"

Do Your Market Research

The more you research your students, the better prepared you are to 'reach' them. Ask yourself the following questions before going into the classroom:

1. Why are these students in this particular class?
   (forced to be there, a job, reputation, etc.)
2. What do they already know about it?
   (who has told them, what have they read or seen?)
3. Where did they come from?
   (ideas, philosophy, geographic area?)
4. What do they expect from this class?
   (How can you meet or adjust their expectations?)
5. What's going on in their lives at the moment?
   (tired, sick, happy, just ate, world news, problems?)

How would you learn this information about your students? Some possibilities include asking questions before class, asking others who know the students or even sending a survey questionnaire beforehand. Once the class starts, it's simple to ask for information though it does require some real on-the-spot modifications if you discover a major discrepancy between your plans and students needs. Regardless of the method used to get the data, make sure that it's done. Most every teacher has had the experience of walking into a class 'cold' and feeling out of time and place, having virtually no rapport. Worse yet is misjudging the knowledge or skill level of the students. That hurts your credibility. Being prepared with background information will greatly increase your effectiveness.

In addition to background information, a teacher must be aware of learning styles. How does each student think? Does he need to process information by seeing it, hearing it or feeling it? Use your sensory acuity to learn about differences, then have the behavioral flexibility to make the necessary adjustments.

Notice any kind of difference, from language to politics to cultural differences. For example, what's appropriate for Chicanos may be inappropriate for Indians which may be inappropriate for Blacks which may be inappropriate for whites which may be inappropriate for ghetto students which may not be . . . well, you get the message. Be aware of language barriers. The problem is not that people speak different languages. Usually, the problem is when people speak the same language and still don't communicate. Learn the slang, the qualifiers, expletives, and other common words of your students. Learn what's not appropriate to say or who's in low favor at the time. Learn the metaphors of individuals or groups. For example, there are different word associations for the following groups:

music lovers	senior citizens
ghetto residents	farmers
surfers	sports fans
athletes	wealthy persons
military	business persons
teens	nature lovers
rural students	dancers/performers

Also be aware of preferred listening styles. If you have a class of machinists, mechanics, wood workers, or athletes (who came to you by choice) you could already know that much of your language may need to be kinesthetic metaphors. You'll be using expressions as: "This will feel better," "stay in touch," "come to grips with . . ." "get a handle on . . ." and others. Mostly, it's important to stay sensitive to exactly who your students are. The measure of your success as a teacher is largely due to your ability to go to their world or have them come easily and willingly to yours. In one word, it's rapport.

It may seem like quite a bit of preparation to make for a single class, but the preparation diminishes with student familiarity. As your skills in lesson planning, rehearsal and market research increase, you'll find yourself doing these things automatically. Best of all, your results will go up dramatically because you have sowed the seeds for success and you are now ready for harvest.

Classroom Preparation

As part of your pre-class preparation, the physical classroom must be checked out quickly. Run through your check list to confirm all is ready:

1. Is the room neat and organized?
2. Is all the trash put away, chairs neat?
3. Are all chairs arranged the way they're needed?
4. Are all the books or handouts counted and readied?
5. Are the materials spot checked?
6. How's the room temperature, breeze, humidity?
7. Are your lesson plans out and ready?
8. What's on the chalkboard? There should be a greeting and any pre-class directions the students need.
9. How about the peripheral walls? Have you put up happy, thought-provoking posters? Have you rotated the ones you've had up for a while to keep the atmosphere fresh?

Arrange Seating for Success

It's important to maintain a lively and varied set of stimuli and seating is an excellent way to do that. Where a student sits in the class affects his or her learning experiences, so the solution is 'fluid seating'. This means that students must choose a different seat each time they enter the room and make sure that they are in a different part of the room, too. Remind the students that the room looks different from each section and that they can gain additional insights and experiences by changing their viewing points. It's true in a sports situation and true in a classroom. The whole notion of switching seats helps students find fresh, unconditioned situations, leaving old fixed, limiting patterns behind. If at all possible, set up the seating so students can see and interact with each other. The novelty of it will wear off soon and the effectiveness will far outweigh any conversational distractions.

Have Background Music Ready

In the chapter on learning environments, we were reminded of the importance of including auditory stimulus in a full-range and balanced classroom. The sounds of your classroom are just as important as the looks and feel of it. Begin playing your tape-deck music about five minutes before the start of class. The best way to decide which kind of music to put on is to observe the state of your incoming students. If they are lethargic or kinesthetic and you want them upbeat, put on faster-paced music such as exciting movie themes. If they are over-active and restless, put on slower-paced music with 40–60 beats per minute. The music will set the stage and tone for the way you want to start class.

Check Yourself Out

As usual, make a last check on yourself. You are the most visible part of a classroom and your appearance is as important as your demeanor. Check your hair, clothing, and for a smile on your face. Do you look professional and confident? Are you ready to be observed as a role model for all your students? If not, make some quick corrections.

How do you feel? Are you upset by any problems? Now is the time for you to clear those thoughts out of your mind with this simple technique. Close your eyes and visualize any problems or concern you have as a simple round ball. If the ball is glowing or bright, use your imagination to make it dark and dimmer. If the ball is dark, make it faded and colorless. Then listen to the ball—if it could make a sound, what would it be? Then change the sounds to a tune you like and turn the volume down low. Is the ball moving? Make the ball move away from you slowly . . . further and further. Finally, shrink the ball into a dot and let it evaporate into a sunset. Now ask yourself: How do I feel? Chances are, you'll feel great! By the way, this exercise works with your students, too. You can use it any time during class when they seem overwhelmed by any problem. Yes, it's possible for you to change how you feel anytime you want!

Rehearsal

You may also want to quickly rehearse your material or key points for the upcoming class. Simply see yourself making the presentation confidently, hear yourself speaking with clarity and flexibility, then feel your self-confidence to assure success. If you are not ordinarily satisfied with the quick, on-the-spot rehearsal, then more advance planning the night before might be appropriate. Your self-confidence is essential to your student's success because they are continually picking up non-verbal messages. In addition, make sure that your pre-class attitude is that of acceptance and respect for all students and high expectations of their results.

Ice-Breaking

Some teachers reduce pre-stage jitters or nervousness by socializing with their students. If you do talk with them before a class starts, be on your best behavior. You may want to start parts of the course beforehand. You could be preparing their mind with bits and pieces about how easy the school will be. This is a good time to notice any prejudgements about the students, then just let them go. Be sure to make good eye contact, set them at ease and create positive expectations about the class. Pre-class mingling is also a good time to enjoy students and learn what common interests you have.

Your biggest challenge may be
to fight the daily anesthesia
of mediocrity . . . .

Going into State

The other part of your readiness to start a class is to be "fully present." This means having all of your senses and attention turned outward and on high. Psychologist Abraham Maslow says:

> "This is the state in which you are doing whatever you are doing with a total wholeheartedness, without thinking of anything else, without any hesitation, without any criticism or doubt or inhibition of any kind whatsoever. It is a pure and perfect and total spontaneous acting without any blocks of any kind. . . ."

This is "going into state". It's a distinct physiological state of excitement, energy and attention on the audience. If you are in the proper state, your teaching will be interesting, exciting and creative. Your state controls your behavior—hence more possibilities for excellence in teaching arise out of a powerful, electric state. In addition, you must be able to put all of your attention on your students and *their* needs. If you're worried about how you look, what you are saying or what you are feeling, you are not really 'with' your audience. Block out all useless self-originated sensory information while you are in front of the room and save that mode for special circumstances. You must look, sound and feel inspired about what you are teaching if you want your students to do the same. It also means that you have rehearsed your presentation in your mind and have a clear picture of success for your upcoming class.

In the moment before class starts, be sure you are ready to give your students your full attention. This means that the front of the room is ready and all your notes and papers are organized. Make sure that your posture, facial expressions, dress and gestures are ready to convey the exact messages you want them to. Be confident and ready for a great class.

The Grand Entry

Does it matter how you walk up to the front of the room? Social psychologist Roger Drake of Western State College of Colorado has done experiments in which students oriented their eyes toward their left or their right side to hear instructions and write responses. The result? Students asked to orient toward their left (using their right persuasive hemisphere of the brain) had more positive first impressions than when oriented toward the right (using their left analytical hemisphere) side. A more favorable impression is created among your students when you enter the room and open your class so that your students are looking to their left.

Always Start on Time

Always open the class and introduce yourself on time, even if you don't actually start any teaching. Do this whether everyone is there or not. Your time, as well as that of the other students is valuable and deserves to be respected. Fortunately, you can always have time for an introduction even if you are very rushed and have to say to your group, "I'll be with you in a moment . . . here's something you can begin with . . ." Starting on time is one of the ways you show that you respect the audience and their time. Being on time is also a way that you keep your agreements about when class starts and honor those who are on time.

Being on time is one of the ways that you create a context of class as "worth being on time for". In the remote chance that you are late, never give excuses, regardless of the sincerity and severity of your rationale. What's appropriate if you are late is to say, "I apologize for being late. You and your time are both important to me just as this class is, too. Let's get started right away so we can still finish on time." Here are some other suggested openers:

1. Situation: Many students missing, first class, it's time to start.
   Opening: "Good morning and thank you for being here. I appreciate very much your being on time, and in the next couple of minutes, the remaining students who are looking for this room should arrive. We'll give them until five after, then start. Right now, I'd like you to find out five things about your neighbor."
2. Situation: Many students missing, time to start, not the first class.
   Opening: "Good morning and thank you for being on time. Obviously some students are not here, but it's time to start. Today we'll be discussing . . ."
3. Situation: Time to start, everyone on time.
   Opening: "Good morning and thanks for being on time! Give your classmates a hand! Today we'll be discussing . . ."

As you can tell, everything you do in some way sets the stage for the upcoming class. You are always teaching something, even if it's not subject matter, it is your values, attitudes and background. These form, even on the unconscious level, the mind set of your students which, in turn, affects their performance. Yet, once you have set up your students properly, you'll have your class half-taught because you'll have the soil prepared. There are quite a lot of things to do before the moment of truth. Yet, it's the little things which add up to make a great class. One of the best parts about teaching is that with practice, all of the little things quickly become second-nature and you'll be doing them effortlessly.

☑ Check These Key Points

1. Last minute attention to yourself and your classroom does matter.
2. The most important element is YOU.
3. Use a personal checklist to see that your dress and self-expression are up to par.
4. Rehearse for super results.
5. Do your market research.
6. Use a checklist to be sure the classroom is ready.
7. Always start on time.

Delivery and Presentation ▌▌▌

Chapter Eight

How to Open Your Class

Objectives

- To identify myths about introductions.
- To list the four keys to powerful introductions.
- To identify learning barriers and provide solutions for them.

There is enormous potential for creating classroom magic during the first moments of class, when students are in a distinctive, first-time state of mind. The opening of a presentation has many purposes including to orient the audience, preview material, motivate, inspire and gain rapport. Your students begin class with their own "mental set." Your job is to unsettle their existing mindset and create a new more resourceful one. A carefully designed and artfully orchestrated introduction can make possible a significantly better class. Therefore, the purpose of an introduction or "set induction" as it is often called, is to maximize the effectiveness of the following presentation. Regarding introductions, many erroneous myths persist:

Myth: Prepared introductions Are Not Necessary

An introduction may appear to be an added burden placed on lesson planning. However, a strong introduction has the capacity to make a real difference in what becomes possible during the presentation itself. An excellent teacher, Mona Moon, reminded me of two common student attitudes. First, a student wants to know, "What's in it for me?" Second, many students have a "ho-hum, why-bring-that-up," attitude. A quick introduction can satisfy the needs underlying such attitudes and may be the factor that determines whether or not your students learn the material.

Myth: The Effects Don't Last Long

Another assumption is that the effects of a good introduction wear off quickly, so the value is minimal. No one really knows how long an introduction lasts because each is different. In this chapter, we will define what is needed to create a strong first impression each and every time you begin a presentation. Lifelong impressions can and have been made in just 30 seconds.

Myth: There's Not Enough Time for an Introduction

Many times a class session lasts 50 minutes or less. In such a short class is an introduction worth the time? The answer is an emphatic "Yes!" During the introduction you create a new 'mental set', making it possible to actually save time overall.

The length of an introduction, in general, is proportional to the entire presentation. For example, a ten minute speech might need only a one or two minute introduction. In a 55 minute class, the introduction might be five to eight minutes. In a two day workshop or seminar, the first one to two hours may be needed for the introduction.

Myth: That You Have No Say-so Over Student Listening Habits

You may have had the experience of presenting material one day when it seemed as if everyone was on a different wavelength and almost no one was listening. Other days, all ears on you. In the first case, one could say that the audience didn't have "a listening" for you, and in the other, they did. Some teachers say that students don't listen to the first few minutes of class. If true, all the more reason for an attention-getting introduction! One of the major functions of your introduction is to create student receptiveness.

FOUR KEYS TO A POWERFUL INTRODUCTION

The parts of a good introduction vary a great deal, depending on whether it's the first time you've ever been with this group of students, the length of the class, and a dozen other factors. However, these four keys are essential regardless of the circumstances: (1) Get attention. If you don't have it, you are wasting your time. Usually this means you need to create a state-change to a more powerful psycho-physiological condition of excitement, curiosity and confidence in your audience. (2) Develop rapport. With rapport, you can lead students almost anywhere. (3) Provide clear information. Your students need to know what they can expect, what the rules are and how to operate in the situation you have set up. (4) Establish a receptive learning environment. You'll use a specific set of actions which will dramatically increase student response to class material.

Part 1—Getting Attention

It all starts with getting and bringing attention to you. That's really two tasks: first, to change the physiological state of your students to a more resourceful and receptive learning state and secondly, to direct the attention towards you. There is no one best method. Through experimentation and commitment to the results you seek, you'll find attention-getting combinations that work well for you.

"Inviting" Your Students to Begin

Be generous with your eye contact. Enjoy "taking in" all of your students for a moment, so they know you have personally seen them and acknowledged their presence. Let them know by your facial expressions and body language that you are happy to have them in class and that you are excited about the upcoming lesson. Make sure your posture and positioning say you are open to your students. Avoid starting out behind a desk or table. This softer, gentler manner "invites" student attention instead of other more direct ways which "scream" for attention or "insist" upon it. Try this one first.

In many cases, non-verbal behavior is sufficient to create an association or a 'trigger' signaling it's time for the class to begin. Then, when the class is fully attentive, a verbal opener is used. Be sure the words are appropriate. For example, under the conditions of election time, a heat wave, cold war tensions, world series, snow, high winds, or room temperature discomfort, your first words would vary greatly. What's important to keep in mind is that your first words carry a lasting impact and influence the flavor of the class so choose your words well. This magic moment is open to immense creativity, surprise and results. Plus, it's also a great way to set the tone of the class for the day.

Non-verbal Attention Getters

Bring a tape player and play exciting upbeat music such as a movie theme from a big hit: Top Gun, Star Wars, Rocky, Raiders, etc. (If a movie production company has already spent millions creating a favorable impression on the American public, you may as well take advantage of it.) Get eye contact . . . begin clapping . . . raise your hand . . . hold up an interesting object . . . motion towards the clock . . . use the director's signal for 'cut' by drawing a finger horizontally across your throat . . . stand fully straight and attentive . . . open your mouth and pause . . . have a student get the attention of others for you . . . move to the center of the room . . . stand in a designated spot . . . be in an unusual spot . . . look anxious and ready to start . . . hold up your finger to your lips vertically . . . have an event occur which signifies that class is ready to start . . . play an instrument, a drum . . . putting on a special hat . . . pass out a book, handout, or class item . . . noisemakers . . . try to avoid getting attention . . . do charades or mime . . . do magic tricks . . . say "my next statement will affect our grade" . . . give coded messages . . . use puppets, finger plays . . . announce good news . . . hold up an unusual object or picture . . . have a science experiment set up . . . use unusual lighting . . .

The Greeting

The first few words can be a greeting, a story, a question or an event. You are the best judge of what's appropriate. Each of these must be presented with your own style and flavor.

Whatever the greeting, put energy into it! It could be "Good morning" or "Hello, how are you?" "Hi, and welcome to. . ." Congruence is critical at this time. Make sure your verbal message is also conveyed by your body language and gestures. Project your voice and make sure you are talking to each and every student. Here are two simple openers:

- A question. It immediately invites participation and like a good joke, must be worded well. Design a question that plants thoughts and gets hands raised. "How many of you would like an extra day to study for the test?" "How many of you would like something unusual today?" . . . How many of you don't even want to raise your hand?" The idea is to get everyone engaged right from the start—one question or another, so that the early message is that everyone participates.
- A command—a call to action can be appropriate at times. The most common kinds are those which ask for attention, or to start a process. Possibilities include: "Everybody take a deep breath, please." "Listen up" "Your attention please!" "Eyes and ears up front, please." "Please stand up!" "Please find the best colored pen you can from the tray in the back." Any command is best started with a tone of respect, support and expectancy that it'll be followed.

Your Name

If it's the first time with that particular group of students, your name and a brief biography (very brief) is next. It's important for them to know your name and what you are most comfortable being called. For example: "My name's Eric Jensen and I prefer to be called Mr. Jensen."

Be Positively Positive

Use words in their positive form! Make sure that what you are saying is exactly what you want to occur. Words have a powerful impact on your audience so for the sake of clarity and overall effectiveness, use the positive form. Here are two openings. Pick the most powerful one.

1. "Good morning! My name's Eric Jensen and I'm pleased to be here. In this unusual new kind of class, we'll be discovering fun, relaxed and effective ways to learn with total comfort and ease. And although you may not be thrilled yet, you may soon agree with the other successful students who have done well in this course while practically falling in love with learning."

2. "Not a bad day, is it! In case you have forgotten my name, it's Eric Jensen. For me, teaching this class isn't bad at all, so I hope it's not a waste for you either. This class isn't like the other kinds at all. Here there'll be no tension, no effort, no struggle or anxiety. I'll make sure of that. Also, we'll go past old limitations and totally destroy our negative attitudes about learning."

With each word we hear or read, our brain does a search to find its meaning from our memory of past experiences. Consider the statement, "Don't think of the color red, think of any color but red." What color must you think of to understand the sentence? Red, of course! In the case of "no struggle" the mind must first think of struggle in order to consider "no struggle". Obviously, we don't want students to think they'll struggle in our class! In your classes, and especially your openings, avoid the use of negations and negatively-referenced words. Use the positive! Now, go back to the two introductions and compare the kinds of words used.

From Intro #1:

Pleased, unusual, new, discover, fun, relax, efficiency, total comfort, ease, thrilled, join, successful, easily, learned, falling in love.

From Intro #2:

Bad, forgotten, bad, hopes, waste, like other kinds, tension, effort, struggle, anxiety, old, limitations, destroy, negative.

Is there any doubt in your mind which introduction is likely to produce a more favorable outcome? Both attempt to say the same thing. One of them is stated in the positive (with the purposeful exception of "not thrilled") and the other in the negative. The difference is enormous.

Putting Your Students in State

A critical piece of teaching is to make sure that your students are in a resourceful, receptive learning state before you begin teaching. There are many ways to do this. If you have read of the experiments that Pavlov did in stimulus-response research, you'll realize how simple it is to create a target state (a salivating hungry dog), create an associated stimulus (a bell), then repeat until the stimulus and response become linked unconsciously (bell rings, dog salivates).

1. Have students recall an excited resourceful state from some positive past experience
2. Have them fully access the state, making sure that they are actually re-experiencing it.
3. At the peak of that state, create a new stimulus for it, such as a visual signal, word or touch
4. Later on, re-check the stimulus to insure that it re-evokes the desired state
5. If needed repeat stimulus until fully linked

For step one, simply ask your students to play a learning or memory game: "Find a time in the past when you felt totally confident, excited and happy (a birthday, Christmas, a vacation, sports event, an award or celebration) . . . put yourself right there in the moment . . . feel how it felt . . . hear the same sounds . . . what did you say to yourself? . . . what were you seeing? Now go back to a time you were curious and interested in learning something new . . . allow yourself to re-experience the same positive feelings now . . . and what did you see . . . what did you hear or say to yourself?" You want to have the students really re-experience that positive state.

Once you have made sure that your students have fully accessed that state, then "anchor it." Use a particular expression (such as raised eyebrows, O-shaped mouth) with a particular gesture (such as hand held up high) with a particular sound (such as snapping fingers) with a particular word (such as "brain-ready!") with a particular tonality (such as strong whisper) to line (a la Pavlov) the desired state with your associated stimulus. For reference with your students, you may want to call that state "the R-zone" (R for resourceful and receptive). You may need to do this anchoring process several times.

Later, during class or on another day, check your "anchor." Re-trigger the stimulus and you should hear, see and feel many distinct physiological changes in the students. Once the students have re-accessed the R-zone easily, you can simply refer to it and ask them to go to it on command. In fact, you may have some fun in your class by playing a fanfare music selection when you want students to take on that receptive state!

Other ways to get students into state are to simple give them polite commands to change their physiology. Behavior is state-related and states are determined by either the outward physiology or the internal thoughts and representations of your students. To change their physiology, ask students to stand and do something, or you can clap your hands, switch their seats, or do any other auditory, kinesthetic switch.

For example, use class unison affirmations to open each class: "I am a quick and happy learner!" Or, "I am a good and worthwhile person who grows every day." Or, try "I am a unique and precious being who is compassionate and resourceful." Students will grow to love these (especially if you use, "I enjoy using and benefitting from class affirmations every day!"), and even miss them if you don't remember them someday. And once students are in a positive state, maintain that state through use of periodic state-change activities or reminders throughout the class. State change is so important that you should teach only those students who demonstrate the proper state change necessary for your particular class.

Part 2—Develop Rapport

Rapport is a mysterious "chemistry" that tells you if your students are "with you." More technically, it is a distinct physiological state of positive responsiveness. With rapport, you can lead your students nearly anywhere. Without it, you're like to be ineffective and frustrated. As a teacher, it's critical to have your audience continually responding to you. Only then can you insure your students will get the appropriate learning experiences. Your students do not need to like you for you to have rapport with them. Rapport equals responsiveness, not affection. As a teacher, you can do just fine if others dislike you. But you must have responsiveness.

The relationship you develop with your students will be *the single most important* thing you do to encourage learning. Rapport gives you the continual responsiveness *based on your relating,* not threats or promises of better grades. Your effectiveness in using power, control and threats on students will continually decrease over time. And your ability to use the positive favorable relationship you have developed with your students only increases.

Many times you have established rapport unconsciously. As a professional educator, a teacher must be able to develop rapport with nearly anyone almost anytime! In a way, rapport is the ability to enter a student's world to see things the way he does, hear what he hears and feel what he feels. A class with good rapport consists of students who feel validated and important.

To consistently build rapport, you'll need to know when you are in rapport with a student. This is called calibration and means that you have something with which to gauge your actions. You'll also need excellent sensory acuity to notice changes in skin color, movements of micro muscles, breathing, physiology and posture as well as tonality, sensory predicates, tempo, pitch and volume of vocal expression. *Influencing With Integrity* by LaBorde is an excellent book on this subject. Good rapport building also includes the flexibility to respond appropriately. If any one strategy is not successful, do another and keep changing strategies until you succeed.

Establishing Group Rapport

The simplest and easiest way to develop rapport with your students is to love and care about them. Be interested in them instead of trying to be an interesting teacher. Greet your students at the door with a smile, handshake or hug, whichever is appropriate. Give warm, sincere and authentic greetings that convey real caring and interest in every student. Repeat the dose daily throughout the year. More than anything else you can do, being a caring and loving teacher will build relationships.

Once you have begun teaching to a group, you'll need a variety of personalities to cater to in gaining rapport. Here are several strategies you can use successfully. Even before you start, smile and show your students you like them. Establish individual rapport with key persons before the class starts. Second, while teaching you can identify leaders in your class, singling them out to develop rapport with. Once you have developed rapport with the class leaders, other students will follow the leader's behavior and attitudes. Since you will mirror many subtle gestures, you can actually gain rapport with several "leaders" at once. If the class has two "leaders," match a gesture of one and a different gesture of the other.

1. Discover the breathing rate of another by watching for the rise and fall of the shoulders. Match that rate with your own breathing.

2. Notice gestures such as a tapping foot, a flicking pencil, a rocking posture or similar methodical movements. Then begin your own gestures of a different type, using the identical tempo.
3. Notice posture such as slumped over, tilted, or strongly upright. Then match it exactly. Also notice if the legs are crossed or arms are folded and do the same.
4. You can easily match or mirror facial expressions along with eye movemens and patterns.

How do you know when you have established rapport through non-verbal means? Two ways. First, become the "leader" instead of the follower and notice if the student soon follows your behavior. For example, if you are tapping your foot to match a student's pencil tap, quicken the pace and notice if the student follows suit. If so, you have established strong non-verbal rapport. If not, try another method, or do the same one a bit longer or differently. Second, you'll know if you have established non-verbal rapport by the responses to your teachings. Is the student responsive? If so, you have succeeded.

Verbal Rapport Strategies

In establishing rapport verbally, there are both content and style messages. Content is word selection and style is how the content is said. Both of these are powerful and can be used to augment the non-verbal rapport-building.

Content

1. Be happy to see your students daily and tell them. Say, "Hi, I'm glad you're here. It's great to see you again!"
2. Use the same kinds of words. If a student uses the superlatives "cool" or "great," you'll build rapport using those same descriptive words.
3. Use an appropriate metaphor. When talking to mechanics, relate to things mechanistically. When talking to rural groups, use nature metaphors.

4. Use matching predicates. Students tend to favor certain predicates which relate to the physiological state they're in (how they are at the moment) or their primary representational system (favored thinking style: in either pictures, words or feelings). Occasionally, you'll encounter a student who represents his world gustatorally (by taste), olfactorally (by smell) or digitally (no preferred sense).

Students in a visual mode will often say, "I see what you mean. The picture is clear to me now." (note references to visual mode: see, picture, clear). Students in an auditory mode will often say, "Listen, this sounds good to me." (note auditory references: listen, sounds) Students in a kinesthetic mode may say, "I feel like I'm up against a wall; this is rough!" (note kinesthetic references: feel, up against, rough). Students in a gustatory or olfactory mode may say, "That's a tasty idea. Here's a yummy solution to what could have been sour grapes." (note references: tasty, yummy, sour). Students in a digital mode use unspecified predicated such as: "From what I know, this makes sense to me. I believe it's a reasonable, thought-out solution." (note generalized references: know, sense, reasonable, thought-out).

If a student says, "I'm feel stuck," you might reply "relax and let's try to get a handle on it." Or, a student may say, "This doesn't ring a bell at all. I can't tell what it says." You might reply, "You sound as if you're not quite tuned into this. Here's something that will make it click." These simple replies impact the student in a subtle but important rapport-building way.

Verbal Style
1. Listen to the pace, tempo and rate of delivery. If it's fast, then you can gain rapport by also speaking quickly.
2. Listen for the tonality, intonation and range. Is it treble, nasal, bass, gruff, whining, sing-song or monotone?
3. Listen for volume variances and talk at approximately the same volume.

Stable Datum
By definition, a "stable datum" refers to information that does not fluctuate or change. Using a stable datum in class creates rapport through a common or comfortable experience and provides students with a sense of sameness and comfort about you as a person. After an epic event such as an election, moonwalk, a catastrophe, we experience a commality and talking about it gives us a common base of communication.

For example, in a class of pre-teens through teens, play up-to-the-minute music during breaks or before and after class. Make it your job to know what music is 'hot', what TV shows and heroes are popular. Refer to that information in class. Using a symbol from the students' out-of-class world creates powerful rapport. When the 'Star Wars' trilogy was popular, teachers used a Yoda doll in class. You don't have to be like or have your students like you. Do let them know that you share much of the same world.

In a class for older students, find out about their interests and take to class hobby items, nostalgia, magazines or trade journals. Many students like puzzles, creative games or posters and plants. Again, use whatever necessary to show the students you relate to their out-of-class world.

Acknowledgments
Acknowledging your students is an excellent way to build rapport. Students give their time and attention and deserve to be acknowledged and appreciated. Few teachers do this, and those who do often give a perfunctory "thanks" to the students. Say it with your heart, being congruent with your body. An acknowledgement may simply be, "Good morning, and thank you for being here. I appreciate your time and attention and plan to make today worthwhile." This is critical—be sure to sincerely acknowledge your students every single time—it is *truly* a gift to have the privilege of being able to learn and grow together.

Keep It Personal

When students feel close to you, they are more likely to like you and be in greater rapport with you. There are many ways to increase closeness with your students. You can disclose:

1. Observations ("what a beautiful day!")
2. Opinions and beliefs ("politics is ruthless!")
3. Information sharing (For example, telling your students something you read about which relates to class)
4. Feelings ("I feel real nervous about something")
5. Dreams, goals, needs, wishes ("someday I'd like to write the great American Novel"). Give your vision or dream for education. Share your goals or accomplishments.
6. Activities (disclosure about personal hobbies, pets, trips, interests, shopping, concerts or learnings).
7. Relate your life to classes:
   • in an English class, tell students about some writing you may have done.
   • in a physical education program, tell your students about how you are doing on your own fitness program.
   • in a geography class tell about how on your drive to class you noticed ways the earth ages.
8. Relate your past, especially if it can be useful to your students. For example, in a math class, you can tell (if it was true) about when you were a kid and disliked math because you were ineffective at it. Then after getting unstuck and learning some simple principles, you were able to master it easily and go on to become a successful math teacher.
9. Relationship sharing. Talk about important people in your life—those who have influenced you the most and more importantly, why.
10. Ask what's going on in your student's lives—and care enough to listen without interrupting.

Student Respect and Trust

One of your highest priorities in opening a class is to develop an atmosphere of mutual trust and respect. When students feel trusted and respected, they are more likely to respond to you in class. These are developed many ways, primarily by having an attitude that each student is valuable, worthwhile and a unique precious being. Respond to each as if he or she was a generous heir deciding if you're worthy of a major monetary bequest.

Another simple way to develop respect is to honor each student's contributions, thoughts and ideas. Let your students help generate curriculum ideas. They'll feel empowered by being included.

Relate to your students
out of who they could or might be
Not out of who they appear to be
You may be pleasantly surprised
At the difference it makes. . . .

Keep your word with your students. Your integrity is a cornerstone of the relationship and every promise kept is important. If a student shares something with you, keep it confidential unless you have permission otherwise. If you ever have to break a promise, negotiate it by telling the truth and asking how you plan to make it up to the other party. Be on time. Be count on-able to deliver what you say you will. Acknowledge the other students who keep their word and participate with integrity.

Gradient

Be sure to respect the emotional, psychological, physical, and spiritual mood of the students. Be sure to respect the beliefs, opinions, prejudices, attitudes and experiences of the audience. The way to do this best is to meet and match them at the start and slowly "pace" and "lead" them to the place you want them to go. If you want to do anything which is out of the group's experience or simply new and risky, build up slowly to it. Do intermediate steps, set an example and prepare them for it gradually. Be sure to ask permission of the group for anything you need that requires the trust of the group.

Part 3: Provide Information

Each student comes into your class with a lot of questions, "What's coming up," or "What do I do if this happens?" or the most common one, "What's in it for me?" You must answer those immediately, plus allay the most common fears.

Student Fears Addressed

The three biggest fears are that the class will be boring, that they won't learn anything, and that they won't be treated fairly. Let's take a closer look at student fears and what to do about them:

1. Are you interesting? . . . One of the biggest fears of students is boredom. Regardless of the value of the course, students want to know right up front if you are interesting, fun, and can make class go quickly. Every student has had the misfortune of suffering through a slow and boring class and the last thing they want is another slow, boring class. As an instructor, assure them either verbally (you can say, "What I've found is that students learn more when they enjoy what they are doing. This class will be a lot of fun.") or non-verbally: use plenty of expressions and show lots of aliveness.

2. Are you competent? . . . Maybe the second greatest fear is that they won't learn anything. Some high school students complain that they know more than their teachers, therefore the class was a waste of time. Whether that's true or not isn't the question. Students want to know that you have something to offer. It's important to establish credibility and professionalism so students have confidence in your knowledge. Here are some possible ways to say it:

A new teacher: "My name's Eric Jensen and I've been interested in business for over six years. I did successful graduate work in business administration with an emphasis in marketing. You'll find I know my subject well, teach it in a fun and new way, and I love sharing as well as learning with you."

A veteran or tenured teacher: "My name's Eric Jensen and I'm pleased to have you in class. I've worked successfully with over 10,000 students in the last 15 years and am confident you'll do well, too. Because of the new way this class is set up, you'll not only learn a lot, but have fun doing it.

3. Are you fair and trustworthy? This question is prompted by the thought of being evaluated and the fear of failure or, just as bad, not getting what is deserved. It's important for a teacher to give the students some assurances or sense of fairness. A possibility is: "In the past, other students have found me easy to talk to, my evaluation methods to be fair, and I'm sure you will too."

Authority versus Credibility

Students also need to have a clear sense of your competency and credibility. Let them know who you are and what you can do for them. Emphasize credibility, not authority. Authority actually undermines the capacity of others to really hear you. When you stake an inappropriate claim to authority with people, they immediately create a barrier. Master teachers build bridges, not walls. What your students need is a teacher who has power and empowers others. Then they have no fear of you and can get down to the business of learning.

If they are afraid that you will misuse your power or that they don't have as much as you, they will try to gain it, often at your expense. Your authority in the classroom is a direct function of the value you have to the students. The more useful you are to them, the more value they perceive that you provide, the more respectful they will be to you. In short, authority cannot be insisted upon, only given willingly.

The more you provide them with what they want—such as power, confidence, security, and relationships, the more they will allow you to do what you like to do. Let them know who to check with if there's a problem, and is there anyone else in charge? Early in your introduction, students need to know what is the likely relationship they will have with you and what roles each of you will play. With this information, students can feel more comfortable and be able to learn easier.

Use This Marketing Secret

Studies from sales and marketing surveys show that newspaper-type headline openers create immediate attention. Using words like "you" instead of "I" or "Here's why you can remember names better after listening to music. . . ." People like to know who, what, how and why, so use those kinds of phrases. "Here's how we can understand history in half the time." Use "this" item, not "the" item. Use "now" we are ready, not "are we nearly ready?" Prefer immediacy and proximity to alert the senses.

You can get the attention of the whole group by addressing part of the group. Do you want your "lower-performing" students to listen carefully? Simply say, "The next thing I'm going to talk about is only for those who consider themselves in the top 15% of this class." Or say, "I only want those with green eyes to listen to what I'm going to say next. . . ." By creating exclusivity, you elicit the interest of others not in the group.

Preview Coming Attractions

Have you ever noticed the catchy headlines of the publication *The National Enquirer?* . . . 'Five Ways to Improve Your Marriage.' 'Why Single People Are Less Lonely,' 'New Diet Reduces Grocery Bill' and others. As much as people criticize tabloids, people buy them! In the same way, you can preview your class material to your students:

Biology Class: 'Today we'll be learning about DNA. We'll find out how nature has put enough information in your genes to fill 10,000 volumes of encyclopedia Britannica."

Ancient history: "How would you like to have 20 slaves working for you? Today we're going to talk about a civilization that had 20 slaves per citizen."

Health class: "In a few moments we'll learn why you couldn't catch a cold at the North Pole during the winter."

Geography: "Next we'll be talking about the formation of the earth and how there are pieces of matter on our earth that are older than the earth itself."
or, "We'll discover which country has sand dunes as high as a 35-story building." (France, by the way!)

Literature: "One of the things we'll find out today is what author wrote a 6,000 word poem when he was twelve years old.

How to Fail Successfully and Succeed

Make sure you give the all-important information on how to succeed. It will vary from group to group, but it may be as simple and general as:

1. Participate
2. Take notes
3. Review notes twice a week
4. Follow directions
5. Know what you want to learn
6. Ask questions

The important thing for students to know is that they have choice in how the course will turn out. These choices include learning responsibility, commitment and clarity. Ideally, every part of your course will add value to you and your student's lives.

Pre-testing

In nearly every subject, students like to know that they made a gain from the start to the finish. It doesn't always have to be a significant jump, but improvement is the key. One of the challenges is that improvement is not always easy to measure.

Sometimes you can simply have students rate their attitude at the beginning of a course. Use a scale of 1–10, asking students how they feel about a certain subject. There's not an easy way to measure starting positions but this simple 1–10 scale is better than nothing! What's also not easily measured is whether a shift has taken place which moves the student from an attitude of "I can't" to "I can." Sometimes that is not easily quantified, but it's the most important shift of all. For a specific subject, do a word association quiz and evaluate the answers. At the beginning of your class, you might find a simple way to evaluate, such as listing five topics, key words, or vocabulary terms up, then asking their meaning. At the end of class, re-test. The form is unimportant. What is important is that it's done. Demonstrated improvement can be a useful tool for increasing self-confidence.

Clear Up Expectations

The introduction of a class is the time to discuss your expectations and to be sure the students share those same expectations. For example, if your students thought you were going to cover subject "xyz" but you had actually planned to cover "abc", you have a public relations problem. The first thing to decide is which of the topics you will cover. Are you obligated to cover certain content because of what's legislated or published material about the course? If so, obviously you must teach it.

If there is a difference between what was expected by the students and what you want to do, you must ask their permission to make the change. It could sound like this: "Your expectations are that I teach xyz, but I had planned to do abc. I'm required to do abc by law. Could I have your permission to do abc? Is there anyone for whom that is a problem?" Be sure to make it safe for them to express their concerns and expectations in class as an early part of their participation. This is really a way of creating an oral contract that signifies each party has both input and agreement on the matters at hand.

In addition to students sharing expectations, you need to share yours. They should know what you expect them to learn, by when and in what form they will be required to demonstrate competency. In other words, give them your evidence procedure for determining if they have met your evaluation criteria. If it's appropriate, be sure to put the expectations in writing if they affect the evaluation process. Once in writing, the students may refer to them later, giving certainty, peace of mind and predictability.

What Are the Rules

Students also need to know the ground rules. Can they talk in class, move around, go to the bathroom or sleep? What happens if they're late, chew gum, eat in class or disrupt it? In an adult class, can they smoke? What about listening to pocket stereos? Is there a dress standard? Any area which is the least bit uncertain needs to be taken care of in the introduction. Each student brings expectations into a learning situation and the more you handle ahead of time, the fewer problems you'll have later.

Introduce Guests

Anyone who is new or different in the classroom needs to be introduced to your students. One of the keys to creating an emotionally and psychologically safe environment for your students is to insure that they have trust and comfort with the adults in the room. When you introduce your guests, make sure you also let them speak so that students can get a feel for who they are and why they are visiting for the class.

Questions Answered

It's also valuable to ask the students if there are any questions. If you've done your introduction well, there will be few, if any questions. If there are any questions, they will usually be about a part of the introduction that you left out. Accordingly, you'll get a chance to see what part of the introduction you need in your next classes. The results will give you the perfect feedback, either in terms of how the students do in class, or the questions they have. Welcome questions as the information you need to build a more successful introduction.

Course Purpose Defined

As part of every opening of a class for the first time, let the students know the purpose. Know your purpose. It's just as important as your goals. A goal is an endpoint. A purpose is a direction, usually something that goes on and on. There's not a direct goal to shoot for, it's more of a direction, a vector, a territory within which to operate. Here are some possible purposes for other classes:

Speech: "My purpose is to provide the tools and experiences necessary for you to increase your speaking effectiveness."

Math: "My purpose is to insure that you have the strategies to be successful in math and enjoy it as well."

Geography: "My intention is to expand your knowledge of the earth by exploring its geography."

Business: "Our purpose is to increase your understanding of standard business operating procedures and provide the foundation for further study."

Notice the purposes are open-ended and non-specific. A purpose gives the dimensions of the playing field and goals are the way to score. Once students know the purpose of the course, there are criteria with which to evaluate the appropriateness of activities, lectures, guest speakers or exams.

Logistics

Webster's definition of logistics in this context is "the procurement, maintenance and transportation of materials, facilities and personnel." It is, "the handling of the details of the operation." In the classroom, logistics include supplies, administrative tasks, and student needs. Students need to know the location of the pencil sharpener, the bathroom, the trashcan, the books, the drinking fountain and the clock. They also want to know what time breaks are, where they are allowed to go on breaks, what they are allowed to bring back into the classroom and what time to return from a break. Make sure students know what forms to turn in, where to put them, and the deadline. Usually there are a dozen bits of data that students need to know the first time they are in your classroom. Having logistical information allows students to relax and become involved with the process of learning itself.

Part 4: Creating a Learning Environment

So far, we have gotten the student's attention, developed rapport and provided pertinent information. As a result, students pay attention, are informed and feel comfortable in your classroom. Those are important first steps in the creation of a learning environment. This final section is designed to motivate students and open up their learning receptiveness.

Oral Contracts

Once you have proposed the content of the lesson or you have elicited your student's needs, it's time for a contract. Make an oral contract that basically says, "This is what you asked for, this is what's needed and this is what I'm doing. If I do this, will it meet your needs?" You need to get a verbal agreement that what you are doing is useful, relevant and needed. Otherwise, you risk the possibility of failure to meet the needs of your students. All you need is a simple "Yea" or "Nay" from the group and you can proceed with confidence and the support of your audience.

Share Your Qualities

The meeting of you and your students is really an occasion or an event. Tell the students what you bring to "the party". Share the qualities within yourself that you bring to the class. Examples are commitment, enthusiasm or love of learning. Ask what it is that your students are willing to bring to the "party". Let students share the qualities they bring that will make the event worthwhile. Usually this begins the process of students learning to develop and accept responsibility for the success of the class.

Establish Needs, Provide Solution

Students need to know the benefits of taking your class. What will a student "get" by being in your class? Benefits are especially attractive to someone who has needs so spend a few moments learning about student needs. The more a student perceives need for your material, the greater the motivation. Build on student needs to "sell" your course! Here is a sample interaction:

1. *Establish needs* . . . ask one or more questions:
"How many of you think your studying takes too long?"
"How many of you fall asleep sometimes while doing your reading?"
"How many of you have had the experience of studying for a test, thinking that you know it, then blowing it at test time?
2. *Suggest possible benefits* to your audience:
"Who would like to know 3 ways to cut study time in half?"
"Is there anyone who'd like to be better at _____ ?"
"How many would like to have a choice of colleges to go to?"
"Who in here would like to learn more ways to earn a living?"

This quick activity creates immediate recognition of students' needs and offers benefits for taking your class. It can also create a feeling of commonality among students. By hearing responses to these questions, students get a sense of the needs of their classmates, know that others are in the same "boat" and can lessen fears of "looking stupid".

What's the Price Paid for Failure or Success?

Depending on the course, it might be appropriate for students to know what results from not learning the material you'll cover in your class. It is also important for students to know what is likely to occur if they don't accomplish the purpose or intended results of the course. Ask for student suggestions of what the consequences might be. They may suggest the following self-motivators:

1. Be behind in their class
2. Often feel uninformed or ignorant
3. Possible peer or family pressure
4. Feel incomplete or badly about failing
5. Lack information for important decisions
6. Get a poor grade
7. Ruin chances for scholarships

Part of your strategy to evoke motivation might be to build a desire to succeed in your class by making sure your students perceive that the rewards of success are great and the price for failure is high. Many students don't relate classroom behavior directly to the real world. Help students understand that if they don't participate, they will learn less and that may translate to lower grades, fewer chances for graduation or scholarships.

Discover What's at Risk

When a gambler bets $100 on a game, his risk is not $100. On even odds, if he wins, he gets an additional $100, if he loses, he loses his $100. This makes the risk of the game $200—that's the difference between winning and losing. That's formidable stakes, so it's likely his attention would be quite focused on the game.

Your students in class have a stake in it, too. Your students have something to gain by being in your class (experience, discovery, relationship, self-esteem, etc.) and something to lose if they don't get much out of it (time, self-esteem, etc.). But there's more. There's always some kind of other agendas that are up for risk: a prejudice or bias about a subject or teacher is one of the more common ones. Here's the challenge for you. . . . Ask your students what is their stake in your class today. What is it that they are willing to risk in order to "win" something. In other words, what is it that they are "bringing to the party" called your class? Get students thinking about what you bring daily (your commitment, your desire, your flexibility, etc.), then ask them what they bring.

Student Benefits Translated

Students also need to be informed clearly on the potential benefits of the course. Tell them what they can expect to learn, or be able to do as a result of your class. If you can't think of benefits other than knowing the material well, you can be sure the students won't see the benefits either! Find a benefit for your students so they know what's possible to learn from your class. For example:

English: write resume, get better job, interview better, make strong first impressions, improve communication

Geography: increases knowledge of the earth and its life, understand the news programs, discover great places to travel

Business: can get better job, make more money, have more independence, satisfaction, security, etc.

Speech: present self better, gain personal confidence, speak comfortably in front of groups, communicate clearly

The easiest way to promote these benefits is to "enroll" your students in the idea of participating in class and getting a lot out of it. Ask leading questions that induce a "yes" and get students interested in what's next:

"How many of you would like an easier way to study?"
"Who wants a shortcut for next week's homework assignment?"
"How many of you want some ideas for your paper due on Friday?"

Student Commitments

Both you and your class need a foundation of integrity, a system of "wholeness" that includes actions that are congruent with stated values. If the stated values include honesty and keeping one's word, use those values as a structure to build workability into your class. Long-term workability in relationships is based upon people keeping their promises and commitments.

It's often useful to include in your introduction a request for student commitment to the outcome or intended results of the course. Once you and the students agree on the outcome, it's important for students to choose what they are willing or intend to do toward that outcome. Sometimes the only commitment a student is willing to make is simply to show up and participate. Another student may make a commitment to do a project or a paper. There is value in allowing students to choose a level of commmitment to work with during your course. The main thing you need, as teacher, is student commmitment to the "workability" of class, meaning students' actions constructively add to class results, rather than detract or sabotage them.

Say to your class, "Now you know what it takes to fail, and what it takes to succeed. How many of you are interested in succeeding, raise your hand or say 'aye'?" Sometimes students are afraid to make a commitment because of the consequences of failure. A fundamental ability of a successful teacher is to make it safe for students to fail by re-framing failure as simply feedback needed for success. Failure gives as much information as success, sometimes more. This is not to trumpet the merits of failure, but to remind you that failure is okay in the larger context of succeeding. Taken by itself in a microcosm, it can appear bad. When viewed as part of the larger whole of success, failure becomes part of the success-building process.

The format for creating a commitment is really dependent on you. Sometimes it is uncomfortable for students to make a commitment in the first few minutes of a new class. If you have had the students before, it's probably comfortable for them to create commitments at the beginning of the class. Otherwise, "check out" the atmosphere of the class and then decide when it's appropriate to discuss commitments. The actual form can be written and kept by the student, written and given to the teacher, or shared verbally with a partner or the entire group.

The values of students' commitments are: (1) They can experience the process of making a promise and keeping it (2) They experience the risk and success of commitments (3) They increase the chances of getting the outcome. The process of keeping a commitment helps a student feel more powerful and causal in life by giving the opportunity to experience constant creation and results.

Vision Established

At some point, share your vision for education with your students. If you have no vision, discover or create one. A vision is basically your dream, your end product of how education would be if everyone cared as you do. It's your "grand plan" of how the world would be if each student's education was successful. By sharing your vision AND eliciting your student's vision for their own lives, there's more to class than just academic learning. Being in class can become fulfilling, 175purposeful and meaningful. It can be what enriches and puts joyfulness in one's day. Tasks without vision are drudgery. Vision without tasks is but a dream. Both are necessary.

Certainty Affirmation

A similar tool that can work, depending on your audience, is the certainty affirmation. Tell your students, with certainty and congruency, that they will learn and remember the subject you teach. It might be something as simpe as: "I've taught this course hundreds of times and my students *always* get it. I am absolutely certain that each of you will totally master this subject." It's easy for them to feel like they'll succeed in the midst of certainty.

Team Building

If you have set up your students to work in teams, this is the time to allow them to share what's working and what isn't. It's the time for them to express any promises or requests to each other. Let them clean up any past broken promises or damaged integrity. Then move the focus to the positive nature of team-building. Allow the group leaders to focus the attention of the group on each member to make sure that their concerns are heard and accomplishments are acknowledged. This allows your students to feel a real part of the team, to feel important and to create a safe environment for growth and the risks necessary for learning.

Relate the Global Picture

Make sure your students know how the rest of the world relates and operates with your topic. Tell them the forces at play and the mega-trends affecting it. Talk to them about trends, both global and local. Let students know what's involved from the start in your class, from your point of view as well as from the world "out there".

Globalize the learning. Your class, regardless of the subject matter, has the capacity to make a real difference in the student's lives. The more you relate your subject to the "real world", the more interest the student will have.

Here are examples of how you can globalize a class.

Geography—How our local area is a part of the world's history, and the way the earth evolves and changes is much like us—we all have our personal valleys, deserts, jungle days, etc.

History—We are now history in the making, we are in the newspapers, someday people will study our civilization.

Art—Notice how all of us create artistic expressions one way or another, whether we are a gardener, secretary or doctor.

Business—Notice how our private financial lives are like running a small business.

Ask for a Breakthrough

If you asked your students if they came to class today planning on a breakthrough, chances are they would say "No." That's part of the problem. We have conditioned our students for sustained mediocrity. They don't plan on a breakthrough, they don't expect one, and by and large, they don't get one. Your challenge is to wake up your students to the possibility that they are. Tell them what the possibilities are in your class in terms of how great it could be and what kind of breakthroughs are possible. Tell them you expect for them to have a breakthrough in either how they learn, their attitude about learning or what they learn. Tell them you'll provide any coaching that might be necessary. Then follow through on your promises.

Use a Variety of Motivators

Eugene Lang, a wealthy benefactor, gave a startling speech to his Harlem alma mater, Harlem Public School 121. He said that he would provide full college scholarships for every single student who graduated; an offer which could cost him a small fortune. The results were even more amazing. Nearly every student from that school's class has now graduated. Most of them said, "I couldn't pass up an offer like that!" Those students, with marginal study skills and a track record of 50% dropout simply needed to perceive a benefit that far outweighed the cost. They performed well. It is ironic that many of them did well enough to earn scholarships from other sources! The labeling of students as low achievers, un-motivated or slow learners is damaging and wrong. All it took in this case was to provide some hope. Sometimes, students need a different kind of motivation than what you're using.

Clear the Emotions

Many times students can not really "hear" your class because their problems or emotions are re-ceiving all their attention. If there has been a school or major public issue (fight out in the hallways, a school election, a big game coming up, a national disaster) or, a private issue (death in the family, fights at home, parents breaking up), you need to do some preliminary work before teaching your course con-tent. Use your sensory acuity skills each and every class opening to listen, feel and watch for clues as to the condition of your students. If they need a few moments to share their grief, discuss a concern or share their joy, allow for it. It honors the student and clears the path for a more productive class. Even if your students are simply extra-talkative, consider giving them a two minute break at the outset called a "buzz-break." This allows any student to talk with any other student in class and talk all he or she wants for two minutes. Once that's done, you can get to the business at hand.

Physical Stimulation

The relationship between the physical and intellectual was demonstrated by surgeon Dr. William Penfield. In his experiments, he discovered that different parts of our physical body have corresponding parts in the sensory and motor cortex of our brain. For instance, one part would correspond to our fingers, another part to our thumbs, another part to our palms and wrists, etc. He also discovered that the number of nerve fibers running from each part of our body to our brain was not proportional to the size of the limb, organ or skin area, but rather to the need for fine coordination in movement. Hence, there is a huge part of the sensory cortex which is taken up by lips, fingers, face, tongue, while the trunk, arms and legs are vastly under-represented.

The brilliant researcher, author and teacher Dr. Jean Houston, takes the research to the classroom. She says that if a part of the brain controls a part of the body, why not activate the brain by moving the corresponding part of the body? In other words, do the reverse of what Dr. Penfield described. Dr. Houston developed a series of 'brain-activating' movements and exercises designed to stimulate various parts of the brain. To stimulate the "brains" in your classroom, have students use their hands, faces and feet in active ways!

Dr. Paul Dennison and Gail Hargrove have also developed a specific series of exercises which include crawling, cross-crawling and other repatterning. These proponents of the right-left brain behavior model have demonstrated that moving opposite sides of the body increases the neurological traffic through the corups collosum, encouraging better and more balanced thinking. Their exercises have specific appli-cation for reading, writing, listening, memory, math and spelling. Each of those skills requires specific brain functions which are served best by an integrated 'switched-on' approach. The book *E-K for Kids* is an excellent source of these exercises. It is listed in the bibliography.

So what does all this mean to the teacher in the classroom? That the notion of the classroom for intellectual activity only is out-of-date. Think of simple physical activities that can be done in your classroom to encourage better performance and student participation. Some teachers have stretch breaks every 20 minutes, some plan a minute of movement, while others do games such as "Simon Says."

If you see your students
as possibilities instead of an
interruption or a complaint,
you may discover you have
awakened a sleeping genius.

Most activities can be done at a level appropriate for your group. Sell students on the function of these movements by asking, "What does an animal do when it wakes up? What do you do when you wake up? Of course, both you and the animal stretch. Here are some simple physical stimulation activities which encourage better circulation, oxygen and relax the body:

1. Apple picking, Give verbal encouragement while you lead the class in reaching for the ceiling with alternate hands. Then have them picture it as a money tree and reach for money. (The higher denomination bills need a bit more stretching.)
2. Bend-overs. Stand and bend over and stretch for the floor. Then play touch game: first alternating hands to opposite kneecaps, ears, and shoulders. Play upbeat music.
3. Creative Games. Have students invent three new ways to shake hands with their partners. Have the ways include some isometrics such as pushing and pulling. They'll usually come up with excellent stretching movements.
4. Or, simply do fingers, joints, elbow and hand massages, cross-crawl activities (left hand to right knee, vice versa), clasping hands together (then visualize both sides of the brain working together), and making lazy figure eights in the air; first with just one hand, then with two of them.

Use These Learning Suggestions

A pioneer in the field of suggestology, Dr. Georgi Lozanov of Bulgaria, stresses the importance of suggesting to your students that they will be able to learn the material easily with full mastery and recall. This is very different from the old-school philosophy of "no pain, no gain, so you'd better bear down and get it."

Lozanov says there are three kinds of learning barriers which you, as a teacher must handle to maintain or increase effectiveness. The first of these barriers is the critical-logical barrier. It is the negative reaction in the student such as "I have never learned things easy in my life. That's why I'll fail with this stuff." The student is using a prior negative association or experience or even a cause and effect deduction to challenge the possibility of learning the subject.

The next learning barrier is called the intuitive emotional. This one includes emotional reactions to learning. There are some strong feelings associated with fear of failure, fear of success, fear of being the only one to not get it, or not doing well in class. These may have been generated out of some past experience where an authoritarian teacher or parent used threats or attached negative labels to the learning process. The most common area these fears occur in is psychomotor skills such as reading, writing, and arithmetic. Those skills involve such a balance of the body-mind that any paralyzing emotion can shut down the process altogether. You'll also notice these near-phobic fears occurring in other subjects such as math, foreign language, sports, art, music, speech and computers.

The third type of learning barrier is the ethical-moral barrier. There's a cultural bias about the Puritan work ethic and it shows up in the classroom. Its form is often the notion that if you learn things quickly and easily you are either a genius or a cheater. This damaging notion is carried out in subtle slow learning suggestions by classroom teachers who make comments such as: "Take your time and do it well." In actuality, there is little correlation between time spent on a project and the quality of the project. A student can make mistakes slowly or make them quickly.

Solutions for Barriers

At first, the way to handle a barrier is to simply acknowledge it. This step is imperative because it lowers defensive responses and creates an opportunity to build rapport between student and teacher. The most appropriate response is one that assures the student you heard him and you understand. Often, the teacher's response can be a paraphrase of the student's comment. Or, you might tell a success story of how another student you once taught handled a similar situation. Another idea is to give an example of a way this situation might be different from the student's past experience.

EXAMPLE: "I can see how you came to that conclusion given what you've experienced."
EXAMPLE: "In the past you may have felt you worked hard just to get so-so results."
EXAMPLE: "Last year I had a student just like you. In fact, he even looked a lot like you. At first, he thought he couldn't learn this subject either!
EXAMPLE: "In the past you may have had blocks in this subject. It's common and certainly no fun.

Another excellent response to a barrier is to provide a solution and, if appropriate, even ask for a commitment.

EXAMPLE: You'll discover that this course is broken into easy parts that any person, including you, can easily master. What's more, we won't go on until you feel comfortable with each section. After a short period of time, you'll have enough confidence in your ability to learn quickly and successfully. Are you willing to give it a try?"
EXAMPLE: "Remember that student I was telling you about? You know what? He eventually made a breakthrough. Even though he was sure he wouldn't do well, he wound up earning an A. Would you be willing to give 100% for today?"
EXAMPLE: "What I like is to have my students learn efficiently, so I'm going to teach it differently. In this course you'll learn quickly with less effort. You'll still need your concentration and effort, but it'll be worth it."

The second technique to lower barriers is to suggest your students give the best effort possible. Make a statement or suggestion to your students such as, "Do your best to really stay with this lecture. In the past, the students who did were surprised at how well they learned. If you run into a block, as some students have, re-group and relax. You'll get it next time." One easy way to do this is to ask for a "best effort" for just a short time—maybe ten minutes. Then ask for it again and again, depending on results. Shorter commitments work better than long ones.

Another way to implement a suggestive learning affirmation is to make it an auditory group ritual as part of the day. Pick a favorite, easy-learning suggestion and make it a class theme, a promo or unison proclamation. Write the particular saying on a banner and have the whole group say the theme out loud twice a day, with enthusiasm! Suggested themes are: "It's EEE-ZZZ," or "Learning is fun, easy and creative." Or how about "You can do magic," or "Anything is possible—many choices!" Make it fun, full of drama, theatrical and use the same cue each time so the activity can be anticipated.

Truisms are statements best used as an "aside," almost a time-filler, taking only a few seconds. These statements are virtually nonsense, but they provide powerful messages to the student's unconscious mind. Here are several examples of obvious statements that can have a positive cumulative effect on your students:

"At one time or another soon, you have become a great learner."
"Sooner or later you'll absorb this material easily."
"Learning this subject will come easier as you are more ready."
"Either now or later, you'll remember this presentation today."

"Yes Sets" are another way to elicit a cooperative frame of mind. Ask several questions to which the obvious answer is, "Yes." By the last question, students are thinking and feeling more cooperative.

"Would you like an easy day today?"
"Are you interested in having more fun today?"
"Is it going to be easy to learn more today?"

Clear up Expectations

During the introduction of your class, find out just what your class expects will be taught. For example, if your students thought you were going to cover subject area "xyz" but you had actually planned to cover "abc", you have a public relations problem. The first thing to decide is what topic to cover. Are you obligated to cover certain content because of what's legislated or what was published about the course? If there is a difference between what was expected by the students and what you plan to do, ask for student agreement on the subject.

Assign Student Learning Specialists

An excellent theater teacher, Jack Barnard, gives students specific roles to provide a source of on-going course correction. Students who volunteer for these roles have permission to spontaneously stand up and announce the need for their item at any time. It's fun and useful. Here are four student roles that work well:

"Stretch"—This person yells out the word "stretch" anytime the class energy is low or students need to stretch and move around in a more energized state.

"Godspeed"—This person's role is to make sure the class moves along at a rate which keeps everyone interested. If the class slows down too much, this person signals "godspeed" with a director's signal for "speed up" and the teacher knows that he or she could quicken the pace.

"Clarity"—This person's role is to make sure that what you say makes sense. Sometimes teachers explain things so that they are C.O.I.P.U.—clear only if previously understood. In this case, a student might point to his or her eyes as a signal.

Any Other—It's up to you to discover any other regulators that you have the students do for you to insure that what you are doing is interesting, fun, fast-paced and useful. When you empower the students to participate in the way the class is run, they become better students in the long run.

Each of these roles can be done tastefully, with the intention to support the instructor and the course purpose. Roles can be rotated throughout the course. It's a fun and useful addition to your class structure. The students enjoy it and it'll improve your teaching.

Discover What Students Already Know

Two big problems for students are frustration from being unable to understand the subject and boredom from already knowing the material. You can reduce both those problems with a simple activity during opening moments of class. Give students an opportunity to put down on paper or to discuss in groups that which they already know about a topic. Then, have students share with you. Students need to recognize what they already know so they have a solid starting point and feel good about themselves. Having this information, you can accurately respond in your teaching and move into new material.

De-Mystify Vocabulary

A surprising number of students perform poorly in subjects simply because the terminology is a barrier to their understanding of the material. For example, in math many students have problems with quadratic equations, cosines and irrational numbers. In addition, many of those students couldn't give a working definition of those terms. Even when students know the vocabulary, they often have a whole range of fears associated with the terms. To "de-fuse" terms, create a mnemonic with a positive emotional impact. Sometimes, simply letting students come up with a distorted picture, guttural sound or activity associated with a specific term will work wonders.

Establish Transfer from Past Learning

Many times a students will be unaware that your material is simple. By presenting information as it relates to previously learned material, it will be easier. This related-ness from the past could be from yesterday's class, from the student's personal history or it could be metaphorical. The key is to create a sense of connectedness from prior learning to higher level future learnings.

Yesterday's Class: "Remember in yesterday's conversation we talked about the purpose of learning new writing skills?"

Student's Personal History: "Do you remember what it was like learning to ride a bicycle? First our parents helped us and some of used training wheels before we made it on our own."

Metaphorical: "I remember a trip to the zoo once and how much I liked the marsupials, especially the kangaroos. It struck me as so wonderfully efficient how they took care of babies in their pouch for months. Then, it was time for the baby to become responsible and make it on its own."

Re-Establish New Meaning to Subjects

Some subjects create a near-phobic response such as math or a foreign language. By using the tools presented in this book, those responses will diminish. The secret is in preparing the soil. To breed beautiful roses, you need to invest many hours in developing the soil and providing the proper nutrients. Likewise in your classroom, when your student's imagination is prepared, you will reap a crop of interest, self-esteem and joy in learning.

Two simple ways to re-establish meaning are re-framing and anchoring. To re-frame is to leave the content the same, but change your conclusion or circumstances about it. Let's say that you're teaching German. To re-frame German from a foreign language to a domestic language, you might point out the evidences of German in our culture. From food, to rock groups, to movies, to stars, cars and language, our culture is rich with positive German influences. Students are likely to have a favorable association with a German luxury sports car, so use that as the link to classwork. Instead of German being "foreign," it has a new "frame" around it and is representative of everyday experiences.

Challenges

Another tool which some have used successfully is a challenge. This is one of the riskiest, and can be one of the most powerful. Be very sensitive to the student before you use one and challenge with great care.

An example of a challenge is this story: While having my income taxes prepared, I chatted with my accountant. He had just completed his second college degree and was considering getting a doctorate. I asked why he wanted the letters 'Ph.D.' beside his name when it was not necessary for his career. He told me the story of his high school principal who was so convinced that he was not fit for school that he told him he would never graduate and never amount to anything in his life. Guess what happened? The accountant did graduate, then has spent the next twenty years proving that he can succeed and do well in school. That was quite a motivational talk the principal gave. You can't argue with those results!

The secret to finding out if a challenge is right for any particular student or even the whole class is to try a simple one first. You might say, "I'm not sure if you'll be able to complete this text by the end of our course. The last group of students did it, but they were really determined to do well." Then see what happens.

Mind-Calming

There are times when your students are under particular stress. The weather may be unusual or your group is just plain restless. Under stressful circumstances a mind-calming process is a perfect part of a class opening. You simply must sense the need and implement a calming process on the spot. Documented many times is the fact that students learn better when their heartbeat is 60–80 beats per minute. Dr. Brown, In *New Mind, New Body,* says, "With a slower heartbeat, mind efficiency takes a great leap forward." Studies reveal that when the body is at rest, the mind performs better because there is certain relaxation and mental state only available in the alpha rhythm (7–14 cycles per second). The problem is that the body cannot be too at rest. A sleeping student doesn't have a lot of conscious memory available! So how do you get your student's body to idle at the right rate while the mind races? The three senses most used are visual, auditory and kinesthetic. To calm the mind use imagery, music, breathing and movement.

A well-done imagery can lead the student in his or her imagination to a peaceful restful scene where feelings of relaxation and inner joy are restimulated. This resourceful state can be used during class that day or anchored for future use. Slow background music is helpful, though not necessary. Here are the steps for a successful imagery:

1. Have the students gently close their eyes
2. Ask them to relax their body, uncrossing legs and arms
3. Then begin slower, longer breaths
4. Then muscle tensing, then relaxing from head to toe
5. Then go on a short (1–2 minutes) journey to a beautiful place
6. Let them fill in the detail in their imaginations.
7. Remind them to include sights, sounds, feelings and smells.
8. Let them momentarily experience peaceful sensation in their body
9. Fill in the content you want (could be suggestions about it being a joyful and easy day or that they'll understand and like the subject)
10. Tell them that those same feelings of peacefulness and joy are available for him or her right now, and at any time in the future.
11. Bring them back to waking consciousness by asking students to gently open their eyes

Here's a sample imagery. Notice how it uses many of the senses and pauses enough for the students to allow themselves to actually experience it fully.

> "As you relax . . . and take in another full, deep breath . . . and exhale . . . that's it, excellent . . . allow all the tension of the day to drift away . . . now allow your imagination to help you recall a full and satisfying learning experience . . . it may have occurred recently or many years ago . . . alone, or with others . . . a time when you learned something important to you . . . .go ahead and recall the setting now . . . put yourself in that moment . . . what do you see? . . . what do you hear? . . . can you remember if you said anything to yourself at the time? what was it? . . . now . . . allow yourself to experience those same feelings just as you did before . . . and if you haven't thought of a positive learning experience, go ahead and make one up right now . . . what special qualities does the experience have? . . . is it curiosity, joy, or wonder? . . . maybe it's delight or even confidence and laughter . . . fully allow yourself to re-experience those qualities now . . . that's it . . . excellent . . . if you're right there in the moment let me know with a gentle nod of the head . . . good, excellent . . . and now, as you gradually shift back to the present moment, allow those positive and special qualities to remain alive as a part of you . . . knowing that you can draw upon them as a resource any time you choose . . . notice that your breathing is now becoming stronger as you gently open your eyes, feeling perfect, in every way."

There are two important points about guiding an imagery. First, notice that you ask for a sign so you know that the students are right there in the moment, following your voice. If some students do not signal, continue the imagery, giving more sensory stimulation until they all find that moment from the past. Second, be sure to create an "anchor" (reminder) for the experience, such as your tone of voice, a song or a gesture (such as hands on knees) that you have them make during the imagery. Repeating the anchor several times assures students of future access to the feelings of learning success. It also saves the time of having to re-do the imagery if you just re-trigger the whole experience with a pre-set stimulus.

An imagery is best done by watching and listening as others do them, using a prepared script, or writing one yourself. You will learn much each time you do, and your students will be put into a positive and relaxed state in just two to five minutes, alert and ready to learn.

Specialized Myth-busting

Nearly every kind of student brings with him or her many misconceptions and myths that can hinder the learning process. As this book does at the outset of each chapter, you, too, must de-bunk any myths you know or discover that the students have. For example, reading, writing and math share some fallacies:

- that they are hard to learn
- that one must be a near-genius to learn them
- that it takes years to get good at them

The time you spend countering unresourceful myths is time well invested for it will save time later in the course. It is also important to handle definitions of words which could affect the learnings of your students. In certain subjects, like math, the vocabulary is a big part of the phobia surrounding it. Prepare for and anticipate each topic as if you had the same biases, fears, misapprehensions and knowledge gaps as your students. Using their point of view as a guide, you'll be more effective in opening up your classes.

Learning Names and Using Them

When beginning a class for the first time, assist students to learn the names of their classmates. It's a chance for the teacher to get to know the students quickly and it's a way to recognize each student as an individual. As a general rule of thumb, if you have 15 or less students, have them share names, goals and expectations with the entire group. Be sure to learn each name yourself and make a point to learn something about each individual. With 16–30 students, shorten the sharing to just name and goal. When class size is over 30, as it often is, break the students into groups of four or five, having students learn just those few names at first.

If your class is in a phobic-response subject (math, writing, language, etc.), you may want to have students assume a new name until they build confidence in their new skills. In a math class students might pick names like Einstein, Russell, Pascal or Boole. By using another name, any mistakes they make are often discounted and de-personalized and the name itself lends an impetus to improve.

Whether it's a real or concocted name, students appreciate being listened to, heard and recognized. It raises student's self-image, reduces barriers, and creates rapport. You can also use their names later that same class, either in reply to a comment they made, or part of a class recall exercise. Having students learn other students' names quickly opens up the feeling of connectedness in the classroom right at the outset.

Building Community

A key part of a powerful introduction is the bonding or sense of community that students feel. The quicker you build support, allegiance to another, and feelings of comradery, the quicker the learning will begin. Students who feel part of a community usually help each other with classwork and homework, enjoy class more and are reluctant to miss class because of the friendships built. The relationships you build during the first few minutes of class will be the building blocks and support structure you need to carry out the learning. Some of the ways to build a sense of community include having the whole group aligned behind a common goal, having strong communication and sharing fun, celebration and challenges together.

Group Safety

Class "safety" is a descriptive word which characterizes an environment in which students feel "safe" to take risks in learning and disclose themselves without fear of ridicule. There are many ways you can increase the safety level including (1) setting an example with personal disclosure, (2) allowing students time to share with each other and (3) listening empathetically and responding compassionately to students. At first, you may need to structure the sharing to insure its effectiveness. Have students share such things as why they are the way they are, things about their family, values, dreams, needs and fears. In time, the quality of the sharing will increase as you continue to take personal risks and encourage students to do the same. In a safe environment, students of all ages enjoy the chance to become better known and know others better.

Ritual

Rituals form an important part of American life. We have birth, marriage and death rituals, but there are actually thousands of mini-rituals that structure our lives. To a great extent, it is ritual that provides a comforting sense of safety, belonging, predictability and satisfaction. We have rituals for what we do when we first get up, how we eat, work, park our car, and nearly every other function in life. Many successful organizations use ritual. Boy Scouts, Girl Scouts, City Councils, Governments, Kiwanis, the military, Rotary, Foresters, Lion's club are a few examples of groups using specific rituals within each meeting.

In your classroom, a ritual might be a special saying you use to open and close each class. You may develop a class song, group of songs, or set of affirmations. It could be a physical ritual such as a clap. Whatever you choose, be sensitive to how it works for your class and when you find one that works well, keep using it!

Build a "Reality Bridge"

For most students, past performance and future expectations create a "mold" out of which their behavior originates. One of the most important functions of the introduction is to begin to make the skill improvement or subject mastery "real". Unless a student perceives improvement is possible, he may learn the material, yet fail to recognize his new knowledge or may lack the confidence to use it. For example, if a student lacks skill in math, he probably also lacks a good math self-image. Help that student improve self-image by doing a two or three minute role-play activity called a "Reality Bridge" or a "Future Party."

First, begin to build the reality of a changed attitude and skill level of math with role play into the near future. It needs to be done with the emotions, the sensations and the same physical gestures that might accompany the new math level. Have the students "act as if" they have already done well on class problems or homework. Have your students stand up and relate enthusiastically to other students about math. Have them be congratulated by others on how much they've improved. Have them celebrate imaginary new higher scores on math exams. Make sure students do it with excitement and congruency. This begins to make them comfortable with the role change they must face if they're going to improve skills and confidence levels dramatically. It is a key integrating process which will enable rapid long-lasting changes.

A Closing Note on Introductions

There's no doubt that to use even half of these introductory tools in a single class would be a major overkill! Each piece of the introduction has its function and the purpose of this chapter was to provide many choices. Try them out. Use the ones that feel custom-made for your class. Your introduction has the capacity to open up your class, creating a wonderful electricity, a vibrancy in students guaranteed to increase their receptivity to learning!

☑ Check These Key Points

1. The 4 parts of an introduction are to get attention, develop rapport, provide clear information, and establish receptive learning environment.
2. "Invite" your students to begin.
3. Use non-verbal attention getters.
4. For your greeting use a question or a command, be positive.
5. Put your students in a resourceful "state".
6. Establish group rapport—verbally and non-verbally.
7. Acknowledge students by making the statement personal, showing respect and trust.
8. Address students fears, create credibility rather than a dominate authority.
9. Preview coming attractions for your next class.
10. Pre-testing students helps students gauge improvement.
11. Discuss expectations—yours as well as the students'.
12. Be sure students understand the rules.
13. Make sure students know the logistics of your classroom and school.
14. Create the learning environment by creating a contract with students.
15. Share yourself with your students.
16. Establish the benefits of taking your class.
17. Three learning barriers are: the critical-logical, the intuitive-emotional, and the ethical-moral.
18. Tell success stories, clear up expectations, discover what students already know, de-mystify vocabulary, use challenges.
19. Use the technique of mind calming to alleviate stress.

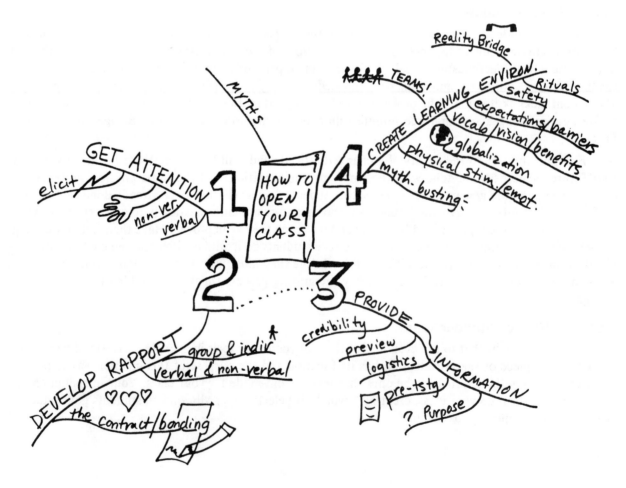

Chapter Nine

High Performance Teaching Tools

Objectives

- To identify misconceptions about communications
- To specify the parts of the communication process
- To describe ways to change a student's "state"
- To provide a model for accurate feedback
- To provide specific teaching tools for communication
- To present the teaching of thinking skills
- To list support tools for the classroom

If you categorize teacher's activities into groups, you might come up with ones such as planning, writing, lecturing, grading, coordinating activities, testing, etc. Yet, if you had to come up with one category which all of the groups would fall into, it would not be teaching—it would clearly be communication.

Communication is not like the proverbial arrow shot into the air, but more accurately the quality of understanding between two persons. The definition of communication? It's simple: "The transfer of meaning". Put more specifically, the meaning of your communication is the response you get! Here are some of the false beliefs and myths that exist about communication.

Myth: That You Already Communicate Effectively

Probably the easiest assumption to have is that you already communicate effectively. Effective means to produce a decided and desired outcome. Only you can know what the outcomes are in your classroom but if you are not reaching the students, chances are it's related to your communication skills. A good communicator creates excited and motivated students who want to learn and enjoy class. And yet, when attending another teacher's class who is a poor communicator, those same students may appear bored and unmotivated.

Myth: It's Up to the Students to Get the Message

This myth is dangerous because it is easy to misinterpret. If you want to be effective, you must pretend and believe that it is all up to you. Otherwise it creates lessened responsibility on your part. It is the responsibility of the sender to make sure that the meaning of the message is received. This means that the sender must do whatever it takes to get through to the receiver. The only way that the sender will know whether or not the message got through is from the reaction of the receiver.

If your classroom is burning down, and you yell "fire" and nobody got up and left because they thought you were kidding, you had better change your communication strategy. It's not enough that you do what works for most people most of the time. What's "enough" is determined by your resources and commitment to the outcome. If 90% of the students get your message about the fire and leave, are you committed to the outcome (safety) of the other 10%? In that same way, it is not enough that you teach a class in which 90% of the students get your message. The other 10% are getting "burned"!

This does not mean that you will always get the 100%, but it does mean that your commitment must be 100%. If you think about it, that's a drastically different message from what we grew up with. All our lives we are taught that if someone else didn't get the meaning of what we say, it's the other person's fault. But there's a better way. Believe that the meaning of your communication is the response that you get. Your classroom results will go up dramatically.

Myth: Paying Attention Equals Understanding

Another assumption is that all a person has to do to get your meaning is just pay attention. However, each listener can only get a certain kind of message delivered in a certain way. Your students have a built-in "mono-frequency radio receiver." And so do you—it's a filtering mechanism. We can only pick up a certain frequency and most of the time you won't know what that frequency is. This does not mean that the ears do not pick up the sounds, or that the words received are not comprehensible. Each person has a model of how the world works, including an elaborate system of how and what to listen to. Each person's central nervous system cooperates in such a way that only information which fits his or her model is accepted. Shortly you'll learn how to tailor your communications so that your students can better tune into them.

Now let's address the receiver's dilemma. Since the receiver can only get certain messages at any given time, he must recognize that responsibility for receiving exists also. Therefore any time that the receiver is the least bit unclear, it is his responsibility to ask the sender to 're-package' the meaning so that it can be received. At the same time, the sender must watch carefully to see if the meaning of the message was received. What we have now is responsibility on both parts. If both parts assume 100% responsibility for the communication, it can occur successfully. Otherwise, it turns into a case of "I thought that was your responsibility," which creates mis-communications.

Myth: Communication Is Primarily with Words

Another troublesome assumption says that communication is primarily with words. It often seems that way, given the emphasis on speaking and language. And indeed, language is incredibly powerful. But if you simply measured the total amount of time that messages were being received by a student, then divided that by what percentage of the time that the teacher was actually talking, you would find that most of the communication is non-verbal. And in fact, if you examined that same phenomenon in your own household, you might be surprised at how much of the time you are receiving information from another without any talking. Communication specialist Albert Mehrabian claims that the total impact of a message is:

7% verbal (words)
38% vocal (volume, pitch, tonality, rhythm)
55% body movements (posture, gestures, face)

Two other factors make non-verbal communication worth studying. First, it's often more believable than verbal. For example, you ask a student, "What's wrong?" He shrugs his shoulders and in a cracked voice says, "Nothing really. . . . I'm okay." You don't believe his words, but you do believe his non-verbal message. The second factor is that many of the impressions we form are made before the sender has even opened his mouth. And first impressions are usually the most lasting.

Myth: Communication is a Natural Process

One of the greatest assumptions teachers have about communication is that many assume that it is a natural process which requires little or no training. Successful communication is a very complex process which requires accurate skills—whether natural and intuitive or trained, that many teachers may not have. But we all have the internal resources with which to learn the necessary tools. What will be presented in this chapter are tools any teacher can learn, and with practice, master.

Of What Do Our Communications Consist?

Your messages could be broken into three parts: content, delivery and context. ALL three are part of the process of communication. The effects of any of the three can be destroyed or magnified by the other two. Any time the result of your communications is below expectations, ask yourself the questions on the checklist below:

- "Is it WHAT I am saying?" . . . Change it!
- "Is it HOW I am saying it?" . . . Change that, too!
- "Is it the circumstances?" . . . Change them!

The focus of communication needs to be on the other party. In your classroom, focus on what's going on for the learner. Ask questions such as, "Could you re-phrase what I just said?" "What's not clear to you?" "How do you know you don't understand?" "What would it take for you to really understand this topic?" "When you say you're not sure, what parts are you sure about already?" Just by asking useful questions, you'll begin to understand how your students think, learn, and draw conclusions. Top teachers are curious learners, too. They are curious about what makes their students learn, how they learn and how they could learn better. Here are three areas of influence you have:

1. Your content
WHAT you are saying

This, obviously, includes your subject matter. But as or more importantly, includes your ability to build relationships, add value, create motivation, elicit promises and requests.

2. Your delivery
HOW you are saying it

This includes your posture, eye contact, positioning, expressions and gestures. It also includes the school's dress code, grooming and, especially, your voice qualities: tonality, volume, pitch, tempo and rhythm.

3. The context
The CONDITIONS and CIRCUMSTANCES involved

This area includes class mood, rules in effect, what's happened prior, etc. You have within you, at any time, in any place, both the ability and the responsibility to create the conditions and circumstances favorable to the learning process.

One last thought, maybe the most important one. When you teach with an emphasis on people, rather than on curriculum, your communications are all student-based. This means that the focus is on the *effects* of the communication on your students, not the generation or creation of the communication. Communication is a two-way conversation with your students. The meaning of your communication is not what you intended, but rather the response you get. To succeed at the game of communication it takes the following:

1. Clear, well-defined *outcomes* for the interaction, presentation or conversation
2. Well-developed perception and *sensory acuity* skills to be able to know what responses you are getting
3. Enormous *flexibility* so you can keep changing what you are doing, if needed
4. A personal *commitment* to the listener and your outcomes such that you are willing to keep trying until you are successful

Maybe the most important thing about your presentation is this: you need to bring all of you—your best self each time. And, being mindful of your intention, caring and vision for your students, bring what is known as "purposeful presence" to your work. This means that you are awake, clear and "fully present". It means you are doing what you are supposed to be doing. Listening, speaking, being "in the moment". Most of all, it means integrity, the embodiment of honesty, truthfulness and commitment to your values.

General Presentation Guidelines

Realize that you have many kinds of learners in your audience and each has a lifetime of attitudes, beliefs, values and prejudices. Make your presentation a multi-media one—always. Use changes in your voice tonality, tempo, volume and pitch. Use visual aids—the flip chart is one of the best. Use bright colored pens when writing. Write as much on flip charts ahead of time as possible. Write key ideas before talking about them to keep interest strong. Tell people to write things down. Take up a lot of space in the front of the room. Walk from side to side and front to back to include everyone. Use congruent and appropriate body language. Express yourself more than you think you need to do so. Make every day a challenge—stretch and try to grow to a new level. Be yourself and let your good qualities come through so that the audience can relate to you as a real human being, not a "teacher."

Part 1. An Accurate Feedback System

Most teachers will say they like audience participation. And with an understanding of the learning process and good student rapport, you're ready for the most useful form of audience participation—feedback. It's just as critical as any other teaching tool and maybe more so. The feedback you get will give you the information you need to be a super-teacher and consistently succeed on-the-spot. Getting feedback that there are gaps in your student's learning two weeks later is too late. Your students have already formed often permanent decisions based on their performance or lack of it. By the time you give a test, you should have already made the learning corrections and the test should merely be a written confirmation of it. By giving and receiving constant feedback on student performance, you'll increase certainty and reduce learning stress.

Sensory Acuity

There are two types of feedback, the conscious and the unconscious. For now, we'll deal with the unconscious. These are the messages which are given without thinking awareness. Mehrabian says that 93% of your communications are non-conscious. Based on that, you may want to pay increased attention to your student's usual form of classroom feedback. You may have had a student in class one day who told you without saying a word, that he or she was having a bad day. Your sensory acuity was able to provide clues about him or her which could make your communications with that person far more successful. That student was undoubtedly giving you information which he or she was not consciously aware of.

Increasing sensory acuity is different from reading body language. Sensory acuity is enormously valuable when calibrated—that is, checked out to make sure it is accurate. For example, if you notice that someone smiles and you draw the conclusion that he or she is happy, you could be in trouble. That person may smile out of nervousness, smugness or fear and you'd be making some blatant errors in communication with him or her if you didn't check out your conclusions. You cannot accurately use your own experience to decide what actions mean to another. Each person has such a different idea of how their world works, you must continually observe, then calibrate. The best way is to notice when they confirm that they are happy, and remember the clues. Then notice when they are sad and remember the clues. This way is more time-consuming, yes, but far more accurate than trying to second-guess.

Sensory Acuity for Non-Conscious Behavior

The first thing to notice is that changes occur on many levels. When you are communicating, the unconscious mind creates both obvious and subtle body changes which indicate a change of state. For example, if you ask students to open their books to page 42, you are likely to witness some changes in your students' physiology. The change of state indicates that you have elicited a new response. If the person was bored, now he or she might be excited. If the person was interested or curious, he or she might now be frustrated or angry. Or if the person was in a feelings-mode, you may have changed it to a visual mode. As soon as you have noticed that a change has taken place, remember what you did, and what the response was. This will give you valuable information for both the present and future in communicating with others.

Five Ways You Can Improve Your Sensory Acuity

1. *Body Movements.* Notice shifts in body weight, gestures changed, angle of positioning and tilts of head, shoulders, neck stretched, or movement in arms and legs. Also included are more gross movements such as posture.
2. *The Subtle Extremities.* Notice movements from fingers tapping, crossing or uncrossing of legs, tapping of feet, clenching of fists, rubbing or rolling of hands or feet. You may even learn to detect the pulse on the wrist!
3. *Facial Expressions.* Notice skin color changes, how different areas of the face have their own colors, how they change, note curvature of mouth, flaring of nostrils, ear movements, lower lip movements, eye patterns of looking up, to the side, or down. the muscles at the outer corners of the eyes and mouth are great indicators.
4. *Voice Patterns.* Learn to distinguish the rate from the tempo and rhythm. Listen for changes in tonality, the pauses, and word emphasis. Notice which modality (visual, auditory or kinesthetic) the speaker is in.
5. *Breathing.* Persons can breathe high in the chest, medium or lower, towards the abdomen. The breathing can be deep and rhythmical or shallow and fast. Learn to watch the chest or the tops of the shoulders.

What this whole section on sensory acuity has been about is simple: students are always communicating. They cannot *not* communicate. To the extent that you can discover what they are saying, you can understand their world better, know what their strategies are, build rapport and gather the needed information to respond more accurately to their needs. Super teachers have developed the ability to respond to the constant flood of information coming to them from their students and use that data as an on-going feedback and correction mechanism.

The following three forms of signal-systems are to be used in addition to your usage of sensory acuity, not as a replacement for it. It is critical that you continue to pay attention to eye movements, skin color changes, posture, breathing, head tilts and sounds of your students. While many on-going conscious-level feedback systems have been created including the ones upcoming, people-to-people feedback is the most useful, accurate and powerful. Use both of them and you'll create powerful results.

Conscious Level Feedback

There are several forms of immediate feedback you can use. One is auditory, meaning what students say, sing or respond to with sounds. Another is kinesthetic where students physically respond or act out and the third is a visual signal where students show a response. There are also combinations which add to the diversity of signal-systems. Dr. Madeline Hunter at UCLA has pioneered many successful systems you can use including a kinesthetic one.

1. *Kinesthetic Response.* We all know of the "thumbs up" response, but for most questions you have for your group, you'll need something more sophisticated. In math, your students can use their hands and arms to create all the numbers from 1–10 the signs of multiply, divide, add and subtract, plus many others. In history, you can use number signals for dates, pantomimes for historical figures, or letters for response to multiple answer questions. In other subjects, ask the students to come up with some ideas; some that are in the signing language for the deaf are excellent.

The way to use them is simple: Every two to five minutes of lecture, ask a question which allows you to know whether or not your students have grasped the fundamentals of what you're saying. Then check the response you get to decide whether or not you can continue or you need to back up and re-cover a confusing point. Here's an example:

"Give me a signal to tell me how many key areas there are in a presentation." (Four is the answer). "Now, give me a signal which demonstrates you understood the topic we just finished discussing."

(Students demonstrate a signal system, since we just finished talking about it.) You may also want to give students a signal for "don't call on me" or "I don't know".

Using this system, you'll be able to sweep the entire class in five seconds and know exactly where you are at with your students. The beauty of this system is that it reduces your uncertainty, helps students learn more quickly, and it stops students from pretending they understood something but were too embarrassed to say so. Will students cheat using this system? Sometimes, but does it really matter whether students learn from the teacher or from other students? Probably not. If you are really concerned, you can always have students close their eyes when they respond.

Another simple expression is "If you're with me so far, raise your hands." Then you can watch for nodding heads, or a show of hands. You might also want to give them the consequences if they aren't with you. For example, "If you're not with me, it's OK. I just want to clear up everything before we go on to the next point so that you can be successful Friday's test."

2. *Auditory.* Master teacher Jean Houston simply says boldly to her students, "Talk to me!" And for the most part, they do. But if you don't yet have that level of rapport, there are many ways to get feedback and class interaction from your students while they learn. Dr. Hunter suggests several successful ways of encouraging learning.

Great teachers rely not on charisma
Instead they rely on the inner qualities
of love, integrity and commitment

The old way was to call on a student: "Bob, how much is ten times twelve?" In this case, the teacher has singled out one student and put much pressure on him. The other students are disengaged from the interactive learning. The solution is to say, "Everyone get ready to answer this question: how much is ten times twelve?" This way, all of the class is thinking, learning and preparing to respond. Now, the teacher can call on Bob (or any student) with less pressure because Bob's had time to think.

If the answer given is not accurate, then find a way to keep the student's dignity and pride intact. Let's say Bob answers "110". Say, "You'd be right if I said ten times eleven. Since we want ten times twelve, we need to add one more _____ ?" This gives the student a chance to answer again and be correct. You might make a game out of it: "No, that's not correct, but I'll let you ask me one question to give you a clue—as long as you don't ask me for the answer. Now what question could you ask that would help you get the correct answer?" In an upcoming chapter on dialogues, there's more on this.

Another way to get feedback is to ask each row or section of the room, "Who in this row has something they'd like to add, or something they're not sure of?" Then move from section to section so that students have a greater opportunity to participate.

Another way to solicit feedback is to ask, "How many of you like what you're hearing so far?" You can also make a statement, then end it with a question; if you are prepared to pick up and have the sensory acuity to notice any type of response. "The U.S. is getting awfully deep into international debt, yes or no?"

In general, avoid the phrase "Who needs help?" For many students it is difficult to admit that they need help—it's almost an admission that they are dumb, slow or stupid. It is much better to say, "Is anyone not sure of the answer?" Or, "Is anyone not sure they'd like their answer published in the morning paper?" When you finish making a point, say to your students, "All of you that understand it, say 'aye,' and after a pause, all of you that are unsure, say 'nay'."

Use the four-box method for feedback. Explain to your students that their level of understanding could be loosely described as fitting in one of four boxes:

lost   hazy   clear   ownership

1. LOST. You are so lost you don't even know what questions to ask to get out of the darkness.
2. HAZY. You are confused, but you know enough to ask the questions to get the information you need to understand it well.
3. CLEAR. You understand what is being said. It makes sense to you right now, though you wouldn't want to have to teach it to another a week from now.
4. OWNERSHIP. You *know* the material cold. You understand what it means well enough to explain or teach it to another—even a week from now!

The easiest way to use these boxes is to explain them at the beginning of class and either post up on the wall samples of them or refer to them often enough so that your students will really know and use them. After five or ten minutes of lecture, simply point to the boxes and say "How many of you are in BOX #1? . . . BOX #2?" . . . etc. The students usually love them and it's a quick way to get feedback on your own communications.

Use Unfinished Sentences. Include the students more and invite participation by using unfinished sentence to hook them into your line of thinking. Here's an example: "The tool that I just mentioned is called unfinished _____ ." Did you notice that your mind had an urge to fill the blank quickly with the word 'sentences'? It's easy, with some practice, to have your students so aligned with you that you are saying the first half of the sentences, and your students are saying out loud in unison the second _____ .

A note of caution about that: don't expect your students to mind-read. Leave open an end of the sentence which has just one likely answer. It's unlikely that you're going to increase student participation if you give your students sentences to finish such as: "The nineteenth century was full of _____ ." That one's too vague, too much of a set-up for failure. By the way, you usually don't even need to tell your students you are looking for the answers to the questions, the natural response of a student is to complete the sentence.

3. *Visual*. This system includes the visual "show" of hand signs which are also kinesthetic, plus several display systems. Naturally, raising hands is both kinesthetic and visual just as the preceding signal-system is, too. One of the quickest and most fun ways to get immediate feedback is with the use of lap boards. These are usually standard notebook sized (8 ½″ × 11″) and made of plastic, cardboard or synthetic products. They are like a mini-chalkboard and every student in class gets one and a marker. The way to use them is as an instant learning feedback tool. It gives your students a fun vehicle to be able to respond to your class questions. Each individual board gives the student room to solve a problem, work out an answer, or even draw something. When you are ready for the answers, you can have the students all hold up their answers at once. You can see in an instant who has the correct ones, and who needs more assistance. Lap boards are especially useful in mathematics, chemistry, biology, engineering and other of the more exact sciences. If you don't have lap boards, a simple piece of paper will do, just have lots of them on hand!

Part 2. Support Tools

Could You Use the Chalkboard Better?

The traditional chalkboard is one of the most difficult tools to use well. On one hand, it can enliven an otherwise difficult-to-understand lecture, and on the other hand, it can put students to sleep. When using a chalkboard, make sure you have an excellent eraser—one that's quiet, large, and effective. Make sure that you have colored chalk. At the minimum, have white and yellow. If possible, get some of the other bright colors such as orange, pink, or bright blue or green. Make sure that all of your students can see well from every corner of the room.

Make sure that you stay out of the way when you write on it. Use big letters, and print. Put less on, but put more important information on it. Ensure that your words are legible, and face the group when you talk. Tell your students first what you are going to put on the board, then write as simply and succinctly as possible. Finally, be sure to show relationships between items if there are any (use arrows and circles). Leave lots of blank space around each item you put up.

Use symbols, arrows, faces and cartoons . . . they increase understanding and recall. Ask before you erase if anyone needs more time to jot down what's been done. Use it only to clarify, or reinforce; at its best, it can simplify the difficult. Put your material on it when students are engaged in something else so that they don't have to wait for you. Keep the board clean and well-erased when not in use.

Would You Be Better Off with Flip Charts?

A flip chart consists of a white drawing pad or newsprint attached to an easel-like stand. The flip chart's advantages are that you can use more colors, brighter ones, and that the message can be stored easily. It's often very useful to put major points (each one in different colors) on the paper, tear it off, then post it up on the walls for easy review and reference. They can serve as unconscious reminders for your students and also serve as a conscious reinforcement of the quality and quantity of material which has been covered. Again, as with chalkboards, print legibly, use colors, and keep it simple.

Are You Using Colors Well?

There's a great deal of research out now on the effects of color on our attitudes and non-conscious reactions. When making murals, posters, signs or writing simple messages on the flip chart, be aware of the impact of how you use colors. Here are the results of the research and some suggestions with how to use each color:

Red—"urgent, present time oriented, feelings, heart, important"
(limited usage keeps impact high)
Blue—"strong, past-oriented, tradition, factual, cold, impersonal"
(use when presenting controversial information)
Green—"soothing, future-oriented, relaxing, growth, positive"
(has widespread uses)
Orange—"active, playful, communications, assertive"
(could be used much more often)
Black—"dominant, dying, serious, intrusive, cold"
(limit usage as much as possible)

How about Presentation Cards?

Many successful teachers are using presentation cards, or p-cards as they are known. These are cardboard-backed visuals on 8½″ × 11″ paper which illustrate key lecture points. A teacher might have a whole stack of them with a kind of associated test question on the back. That way, you can hold up these 'cue-cards' and ask the students what they represent. It's a good, quick and fun way to make visual associations with the information about the topic. For example, you could hold up a math problem, and ask what theorem it represents (question and answer on the back). You could hold up the cover of a book and ask what else that author wrote. You could hold up a symbol from your lecture and ask what concept it represents. All of these are ways to increase audience participation, while at the same time, increasing the actual learning going on.

Definitely Use Posters, Signs and Banners

Your students are going to spend many hours in your classroom. It's unrealistic to think that their eyes will be on you every single moment. Since their eyes will wander around the room, take advantage of that. Make every part of the room a learning experience for them and a reminder of the principles you are teaching. Use large signs made on poster board which have simple and powerful messages on them. If the eyes of a student look above me, they may find a message such as "If you can dream it, you can become it", "Learning is fun, Easy and Creative", or "Miracles as Usual." How about "I learn quickly, easily and playfully", or "You Can do Magic"? It doesn't matter whether you actually refer to the signs or not. The ideas will affect your students positively—especially over time.

Are You Using Audio-Visual-Tactile Sources?

When is the best time to use a filmstrip, a slideshow, a video, a film or computer? Only you can know. Each one of them has the potential, when used with the appropriate audience at the right time, to create a powerful learning experience not available through ordinary lecturing. There's no need to balance your teachings so that you have a certain number of hours which are for lecture, and a certain number that are for multi-media presentations. Your question should be "What's most powerful?" Or "What's the ideal for this time?" Then do whatever works! One of my favorites is to double input to students by lecturing to them on topic at the same time as showing a film or video. This way, the students not only have a choice, but usually end up by understanding both of them. It simply turns into a game and their concentration is better than ever!

Should You Use Guest Speakers?

One of the best and the worst experiences for students is to have a guest speaker take over the class. When it is the worst experience for the students, it is usually because the classroom teacher: (1) did not actually observe and pre-select the guest in a teaching situation first (2) did not prepare the guest properly for the audience (3) did not prepare the audience properly for the guest (4) the subject matter was inappropriate (5) does not have sufficient criteria by which to pick guests. It is very important to make sure that the guest can add something that you cannot add to the audience. Students become familiar with and attached to a teacher quickly and can resent outsiders.

When it works well, it can be magic. Some of the important steps are: (1) go over with the guest what he or she wants to say (2) go over with the guest what you'd like them to say and get an agreement on what will be said (3) tell them about the audience and their needs (4) prepare the audience by giving the guest a gracious introduction (5) tell the audience how to respond to the guest, both during and at the end of the presentation. Do they ask questions, applaud, or stand up? Make sure that you have anticipated many possible scenarios and planned your responses. Good preparation can make things run smoothly and insure that it provides the value you wanted.

Help Out Their Note-Taking

To encourage more and better note-taking, teach your students mind-mapping or other forms of creative note-taking. Make available a box of colored pens for your students. Buy the ones with a nylon or felt tip that are thinner than a magic marker, but fatter than a pencil. The first thing that happens is that the students open up to a more playful learning mood. There's some kind of magic in colored pens that lightens up a group of students and gets them to take creative, expressive and functional notes. Then constantly remind them to write it down; it helps them understand and recall better.

There is strong evidence to suggest that colored pens make information easier to recall than what's recorded by a standard thin-lined ball-point pen or pencil. Tested and proven with thousands of students over many years, they do work. The ways that they can be used in class as a form of participation are simple. After each point that you make, ask the students for a quick and simple symbol that they can use to represent it on their own mind maps. This unleashes creativity and builds recall and understanding.

Music as an Educational Tool

Music is an exciting and useful addition to the classroom. Why use music in an educational environment? Quite simply, it works. So let's get specific. What can music really do?

- Energize
- Align groups
- Induce relaxation
- Restimulate prior experiences
- Develop rapport with another
- Set the theme or the tone of the day
- Preach
- Be sheer fun
- Appreciate
- Inspire

Music can also stimulate the right hemisphere to increase better attentiveness, build concentration and focus creativity. It can activate more of the brain, it can take the pressure off you as a presenter, it can help create sound curtains to isolate classes or groups and can bring forth qualities of the music that reside within each of your listeners. It can help create bonding and closeness, too.

For most students, school is a hostile and alien environment. They're being told what to do, in cold, uncarpeted rooms that someone else decorated. The one thing kids relate to the most, besides their friends, is music and it's missing from most classrooms. The first thing most kids (and many adults) do when they get in a car or arrive home is turn on music. Why, you ask? To relax, to energize, to change moods, to feel good. . . . So why a taboo against it in schools? It's just out-dated thinking. We decorate the walls visually, why not appeal to and utilize the other senses such as auditory and kinesthetic? You can make your learning environment much more user-friendly, build rapport with kids and enhance the learning process with music. Do you need any other reasons to use music in education?

If so, here are two more: it's likely your students will love it, they'll perform better and feel better. Plus, you will too. One of the great side benefits of using music in the classroom is that it affects you, too. It will make your work more fun, keep you activated, interested and creating more in the moment than ever before.

Nature has provided us with such a rich array of sounds on our planet earth, it was only natural for humanity to copy them and use them. Most of our musical instruments are, of course, variations of animal or other natural sounds. So, the use of music as a learning aid is an old and quite ancient idea. Primitive man used it in many ways.

More recently, research has been done by Manfred Clives of Australia, Georgi Lozanov of Bulgaria, Don Campbell of Texas, Steven Halpern of California, Don Schuster of Iowa, as well as by others, to measure the effects of music on the nervous system.

Results show that music affects the emotions, the respiratory system, the heartrate, the posture and mental images of the listener. These effects can dramatically alter the composite mood, state, and physiology of a person. Here's the key: when you change the state of the listener, you get direct access to behavioral change. Simply stated, music can change the behavior of your students. The effects are documented in many books including the *Musical Brain, The Healing Powers of Music, SuperLearning* and in Journals of the Society for Accelerative Learning and Teaching.

Although it certainly helps to be a musicologist, you can still get great results with knowing just the fundamentals about music. The tape and books I recommended earlier are a good start. You may find a renewed interest in taking a music class and I suggest that very much. Here are the key things to know.

First and foremost, all music has some sort of pace with which to measure beats per minute. The single most important question to ask about classroom music is, what's the tempo, the pacing or the beat of the music? . . . Meaning, . . . is it slow, medium or fast? The beat of the music affects both heartrate and breathing—the two most important determiners of mood, feelings and state. So remember, the beat is the number one distinction you need to be able to make.

One more thing about general selection of music. In general, your selections will be instrumentals. The exceptions will include some popular music, but them only for breaks or special effects, outside the lecture time.

Learning to use music is an on-going process. Plan to invest some time and money to make a quality presentation package. Expect to pay from $60–150 for a new, low-cost portable classroom music system. Get a medium quality stereo tape player with separate detachable speakers.

As a starter kit, expect to pay about $75–100 for your first 6-tape starter kit and tape cassette holder box. Include 2 Baroque, 2 new-age relaxation tapes and 2 more popular upbeat ones. Use them for awhile as you become comfortable experimenting when, what and how to use them. When you are ready, you can expand your tape collection. A more complete and advanced tape collection might have 24 tapes in it. My suggestion is to include:

- 6 Baroque tapes (2 of them from the later romantic time)
- 2 jazz tapes
- 6 special effects tapes including comedy, fanfare stretch music, TV tunes and others
- 3 focused slower tapes
- 3 New Age upbeat
- 2 popular rock n' roll
- 2 custom-tailord to your audience

Some of the music you may want is unavailable by ordinary means. The special effects ones are an example. If you need to get recordings of them, ask a student to do it for you, do it yourself or find someone who has already pre-recorded all the sounds you need.

Before you take your tapes to class, make sure that you have tested them and labelled them according to the situation in which they might be most useful. Try color-coding them with multi-colored peel-off dots to make for quicker in-class identification. The dots might signify classical, popular, new age or special effects. Set up your tape player in the front of the room and lay out all your cued tapes.

Think about what's being taught so you know what kinds of specific music can be used and when. Prepare ahead with several tape options so you can make sure that you are totally ready. Use music as a partner, an aid in the learning process. Always be sensitive to the existing mood in the classroom and respect it. If a sensitive, troubling or emotional process just took place, avoid music or use low-volume, low-key music that matches the mood. If a high-energy activity just took place, be ready with up-beat high-energy music to match it. Music should serenade, romance and invite the audience—and maybe provide an occasional nudge. Obviously, it should never intrude. In short, use music to lead and entice.

First, Cue up all your tapes by either rewinding them or fast-forwarding them to the spots where the music of your specific choice begins.

Secondly, get all of the tapes out of their boxes or cases and have them easily accessible for quick usage.

Thirdly, place them in either in the order of projected usage or by category. You might label the categories as follows:

1. *Classical music*—(this is for the lecture presentation) include primarily baroque, (naturally, this includes Bach, Corelli, Tartini, Vivaldi, Albinoni, Handel, Fausch and Pachelbel) but have available music from other classical eras for dramatics, special imaging and storytelling such as Mozart, Satie and Rachmanioff. This can be used as a low background . . . almost a "white noise" . . . or IF the instructor is trained in concert readings using the music as a carrier of dual-plane suggestion.

2. *Slower Music*—(this is for Imagery and Relaxation) include New Age artists such as Steven Halpern, Georgia Kelly, Adam Geiger, Daniel Kobialka, Zamfir, Ron Dexter, George Winston, and the long-time classic canon in D by Johann Pachebel.

3. *Popular Music*—(this is for break time or high activity) include a variety of upbeat popular music that has both an active, fun beat to it and has positive lyrics. You'll really need to be selective, picking the music more by individual case, than by an artist. Examples of upbeat positive music for adults include I'm So Excited by Pointer Sisters, We are Family by Sister Sledge, Do You Believe in Magic by Lovin Spoonful and You Can Do Magic by America. For an older group you can play older music and the audience will still relate to it.

For elementary through teenage, remember that none of the audience was born BEFORE 1970, so be careful of the age of your music selections. Only a few have been revived as classics. Use more up-to-date music such as "Respect Yourself" by Bruce Willis, "It's a Miracle by Culture Club", "Hold Me Now" or "King for a Day" by Thompson Twins, "Tenderness" by General Public, "Se La" by Lionel Ritchey or "The Future's So Bright, I Gotta Wear Shades" by Timbuck 3.

For more inspirational popular music, try using "That's What Friends are For" by Dionne Warwick, "What One Man Can Do" by John Denver, "You Are So Beautiful" by Joe Cocker, "We are the World" by Lionel Richey, "Greatest Love of All" by Whitney Houston.

4. *For Background Music*(this is during an activity, such as small group discussions, used as a mellow, upbeat filler). Select light positive ones such as "Sunshine Reggae" by Laid Back, "You are the Sunshine of my Life" by Stevie Wonder, "Jammin and Positive Vibration" by Bob Marley and the Wailers.

5. *Upbeat Popular Instrumentals*—these are for Stretch Breaks or even a welcome back to the room—Use exciting, fun or adventurous tunes such as movie themes (if you do, tailor them to your audience's age) or TV show themes. For your younger audience, try Top Gun anthem and Beverly Hills Cop Theme Axel F by Harold Faltermeyer. Try Miami Vice theme by Jan Hammer, the Love Theme from St. Elmo's Fire by David Foster and Somebody's Watching me by Rockwell.

For your older audience, try themes from Star Wars, Raiders of the Lost Ark by John Wiliams, O-Bla-Di-O-Bla-Da by the Beatles and Hooked on Classics.

6. *Special Effects*—(use these for those moments when you need a song that says it all) Try theme from Twilight Zone, Mission Impossible, Rocky by Bill Conti, TV Cartoon themes, Chariots of Fire, Eye of the Tiger by Survivor, Break on Through by the Doors, Mickey's Monkey by Smokey Robinson & the Miracles, the Curly Shuffle by Jump'n Saddle. You can set the tone of hurry up, slow down, have fun, get confident, etc. You can also use the more standard special effects such as trumpet fanfare, applause and others.

What and when you tell your audience that you use music as a part of your presentation depends on the length of time with your audience and extent of the relationship you have with them. In general, and especially for shorter presentations, let the audience know right away why you are using music. With more long-term audiences, you can tell them as their curiosity grows.

Be careful of the gradient of expectations in your audience. With some audiences, you might be able to start off very strong with all gun barrels blasting and music all the time. With other more sensitive audiences, start slower and build up. In other words, do some research on your audience ahead of time. And above all, whatever you start out with, be congruent and positive about it.

In general, turn up volume slowly (2–4″) and turn it down slowly when you use it. This makes it easier on the ear—it's just like the eye's sensitivity to lighting—do it gradually. The exception is after a final good-bye or "let it go" when there's been no music on beforehand, start the music volume up high because it matches the high volume of the group's vocal completion crescendo.

It's possible you'll get complaints about the volume of the music. If you do, then (while that person is watching) go over to the music and turn it down just a bit. Thank them for their input. This is your cue to do a couple of things. First, make sure that you explain, sometime soon, more about music, why you use it and how it can assist learning. Then, make sure you have everyone switch seats soon, too. The complainer may have been sitting too close to it or may be especially sensitive.

In general, your audience will love music. Experiment, try recording your own. You are a pioneer in this field. Use music with purpose. Allow for quiet times for your students to breathe . . . avoid saturation . . . the effects of music are far more powerful when the freshness and newness of it is retained. Avoid rigidity with it. Be flexible, listen to your students. For example, many folk tunes and jazz pieces make a perfect compliment to the classroom.

If students want to bring their own tapes, make two requirements. First, that you can preview the tape to insure that it fits in with the messages and values that are consistent with your course. Secondly, that you decide the timing of when and how to use it. In general, avoid heavy metal music—but appreciate the contributor and ask for other choices. Sometimes they'll have a second choice. The key is to stay in relationship with your students—use music as a bridge, not as a way to emphasize differences in taste. And finally, have fun with it. Music is a real joy, make sure that you are saying that with all your self-expression as well as having it be in the music you play.

Part 3. Teaching Tools

The super-teachers, the master teachers who can teach nearly anything to anybody, need a vast array of specialized communication tools. When these tools are used as part of a presentation, the result is magic—a special kind of charisma. Yet, if you are willing to get beyond the "wow stage" of observing great super-teachers, you can discover the magic is actually many small things done well. Charisma is great, but long-term results are what's really needed. This means taking the time to practice and learn many small things; maybe just one a week until they are all a part of you. Then believe in yourself as a good and worthy person and let that self-confidence come across. Be yourself, don't emulate another. Who you are is fine enough. Let that show through without any "acts."

Congruency as Key to a Powerful Presentation

Super-teachers are powerful because their gestures are congruent with their message. When your non-verbal message is the same as your verbal message, your effectiveness is multiplied. While the content of your verbal message is usually weighted at about 10% of the total impact of your presentation, that leaves 90% of the impact to your non-content areas such as gestures, positioning, expressions, voice range, tempo, pitch and volume. The best ways for you to discover your own level of congruency are: (1) tape record your class and listen to the audiotape. (2) video-tape your class and watch it. (3) get some feedback from students and other teachers. (4) put a mirror in the back of your class for a day.

The use of your body as a communication tool is probably one of the most powerful areas left open for improvement. It's also an area which often takes significant coaching to bring out the best in you. The best ways to improve the range and depth of non-verbal expression are to take acting lessons from a local junior college or university. In addition, voice training is excellent if you can find a good coach. A third option is dance, mime or movement workshops. Each of these has the capacity to bring you out, allow you to express yourself and take up much more of the space in the front of the room for expression so needed to communicate effectively.

Use High-Quality Information

Research your data to insure that you are providing information which is (1) relevant (2) useful (3) up-to-date, timely (4) accurate and reliable (5) consistent with the trends that are shaping society. As an example, different trends occurred during the industrial age from those which occurred during the information age. By knowing some of the trends, you can include them in your presentation.

Make sure that you distinguish between what is your opinion and what is fact. Distinguish between what you have personally experienced and what someone told you or you read about. This simple act will add to the critical thinking awareness in your students. Be sure to quote sources and give credit where credit is due.

Use Sensory-Rich Language

The human brain craves high-level input and can make sense out of far greater input than any traditional classroom offers. Auditorally, use classical music as background for speaking or popular music for background during activities. Use sensory-rich language when speaking. Dr. Jean Houston, author of *The Possible Human,* is a master of this skill. She uses different dialects and accents to get the point across. It may be California, Bronx, Shakespearean, Yiddish or German. She wears textured clothing, rich in history and peppers her language with words like salubrious, invidious, surly or yeasting. She uses music, tambourines and a wide vocal range combined with a full range of gestures. Effective? Absolutely!

Another key in sensory rich language is to make sure that you address the visual, auditory and tactile senses. You'll notice it appears, from many perspectives, that some students get the picture better if you show them visually. Talking to others, what sounds good and really rings a bell is the symphony of harmony and vibrations created by a really tuned-in speaker. But what it all boils down to . . . if you get the drift . . . is that a firm foundation and a real sense of good feelings . . . can allow you to come to grips . . . with the person who . . . needs to get a handle on learning . . . in a more kinesthetic way. In the previous three sentences, the sensory language varied from visual ("notice, appears. . .") to auditory ("talking, sounds. . .") to kinesthetic ("firm, sense, feelings. . ."). All of these are ways to reach different kinds of listeners.

Use Analogy

Analogy is one of the most useful of all communication tools. It can be the perfect vehicle by which your students understand in 10 seconds something which might ordinarily take 60 seconds or even 60 minutes. Good analogies say a lot without having to say a lot: "Like trying to sneak a sunrise past a rooster", or "Like taking candy from a baby." It causes a feeling of "Ahh-Ha!" not "Huh?"

For example, you could take ten minutes to explain how a carburetor works to a car novice. Or, you could use analogy and make it easy. Let's say that the person uses perfume—just say: "You know what a perfume atomizer is . . . a carburetor does the same thing, except it mixes air and gas." In this case, you just took a potentially lengthy explanation and compressed it into a metaphor which explains it just as well. In order to explain the theory of relativity to lay persons, Einstein had a great analogy: "When you sit with a nice girl for two hours, it seems like two minutes; if you sat on a hot stove for two seconds, it'd seem like two hours."

Dramatize Your Point

Dale Carnegie devotes an entire chapter in *How to Win Friends and Influence People* to the idea of dramatization. For example, many teachers use special costumes on certain days to make a point more real. Some teachers have the students dress up like the subject they are studying. Others bring in special objects, posters, recordings, props or guests. Could your students dress up like Aristotle, Queen Elizabeth, Einstein, a Middle Ages peasant, a slave, Mark Twain, Florence Nightingale, Churchill, or Newton? If so, it might be a good way to dramatize a particular point some time. Even in your own presentation, you can dramatize a point with greater theatrics, gusto and aliveness. To dramatize is to make bigger-than-life, to parade it, and to be bold and flashy about it. Bring objects to class for students to feel, investigate and ask questions about.

Teaching well is a high-risk career
If you're not risking, you're not growing
And if you're not growing, neither are your students . . .

Appeal to the Auditory Senses

Learning increases when you present material with classical music in the background. The music seems to be a carrier or medium for the material, provides an engaging activity for the right hemisphere, and helps to maintain a physical state of restful awareness. A simple cassette player will suffice, though the better the quality of the equipment, the better the overall effect. Use music from the baroque era at a pacing of 60 beats per minute and adjust the volume so that it is slightly lower than your speaking voice.

In addition, adjust your speaking voice so that it has dramatic variances. Build suspense, make comic relief and imitate others. Here's an example of how to introduce ten amino acids for a chemistry course: "Our first word is (normal volume) lysine . . . lye-scene. Next is (louder) methionine . . . meh-thigh-oh-nine. Next is (soft voice) cystine . . . sis-teen. Then we have (normal volume) threonine . . . three-oh-nine. Next is (loud volume) leucine . . . loo-scene. Next is (softer volume) isoleucine . . . eye-saw-loo-scene. Then we have (normal) phenylalanine . . . fee-nah-lal-la-neen. Next is (loud) tyrosine . . . tie-roh-scene. Then we have (softly) valine . . . vay-leen. Finally we have tryptophan . . . trip-toh-fan. The diversity, distinctiveness and changing pattern of volume and tempo makes it easier for your students to remember the material.

Build the Reality Bridge

To most students, the idea of learning a lot in a short length of time is unreal. They are used to steady mirco increments of trivia which make little impact on their lives. If you want to make dramatic jumps in student skills or attitudinal levels, you'll need to weave into your classtime "bridges" to the new reality you are trying to create. By and large, the likeliness of your students to grow in large leaps is due to your ability to make it real and believable to them.

There are several ways to accomplish this. First, pre, mid and post class testing can help make the improvement more real. Secondly, have the students get the approval and agreement of others that they are indeed learning new skills. After each small increase in knowledge or skill level, have each student get up, walk around and tell 5–10 others of their recent success, regardless of how small. Have them say to others, "Hey, I just learned how to _____." Or, "I just got ten right on today's quiz!" Then instruct others to receive the comments in a receptive and congratulatory manner. The listening student might say: "Wow, that's great, you're a fast learner!" When students hear themselves telling others how they just advanced to the next level and hear others telling them that they are a great learner (you might average one or two per hour; it's a great break), they begin to believe it. It makes their new skills and confidence levels much more real to them. This speeds up progress dramatically.

Use The Principle of Round-Up

The principle of round-up is that most material needs continual 'rounding-up', or contextualization and review. Within each lecture, remind students of where you started, where you are now, and where you are taking them. There's a strength to that process of 'anchoring' their learning in something they know and are familiar with. You can use phrases such as: "Earlier, when we learned about A and B. . ." or, "You may recall that we said that. . ." "Given that we have covered the area of . . . and. . ." Master teachers are constantly including what they have already taught in what they are currently teaching. It's surprising how much better students understand when they have the overview to support the detail. Constant review and recycling of information means that students feel more confident, and teachers know that students have gotten the 'big picture.'

Keep Sentences Brief

If you can say a paragraph in a sentence, do it. If you can say a sentence in a word, do it. It is often more powerful to say a shorter phrase, then pause . . . let it be with them for a moment, then continue on. Long-winded sentences lose audiences. If you have a list of items to read off, make sure that you read only a few items at a time before stopping. Then break the pattern and continue. Here's a great way of delivering lists—interrupt yourself to remind the audience to focus. Say: "You need to know there's A,

B, C, . . . wow, get this! D,E,F, . . .focus . . .G,H,I,J. . . ." This keeps the audience from simply 'checking out' because they know a long list is coming up.

German linguist and cyberneticist Siegfried Lehrl says that half of all adults are incapable of following carefully a spoken sentence of more than 13 words. For a seven year-old student, the limit for ordinary spoken sentences is eight words. And how about recall? Lehrl's studies showed that one-third of all adults forgot the beginning of a sentence after the 11th word. And what about really long sentences? With sentences of 18 or more words, only 15% could understand any subject of complexity. It is usually the teacher who is the most impressed with her information, not the students. Here's a useful slogan from the advertising business regarding the attitude of the consumer towards information:

"Tell me quick
tell me true
or else my love
to #@%$ with you."

Powerful Presentation Words

Top teachers use the words "you, we and I" extensively. They include the audience in what they talk about. For example, "You and I together can accomplish our dream!" Their words 'enroll' the audience in their dream—it's like a call to action. They put in sufficient speaking pauses to allow the audience to process the information in their own way. News broadcaster Paul Harvey is an excellent example of how to use pauses effectively. Top speakers use one level up from the audience's vocabulary. They use a variety of sensory words such as visual, auditory and kinesthetic. Also used: greater volume and wider variety of intonation.

A Yale University study declared that the most powerful words in the English language are words which affect us most directly. These words are said to be powerful because everyone is concerned about health, safety, relationships, and security. Here's their list: "you, easy, love, free, save, discover, health, success, proven, guaranteed, results, new." It's very powerful to phrase a sentence so that you include the word 'you' in it. "As you can see. . ." To those words, you can add the list of "how, how to, announcing, now, I wonder if, most, greatest, best, why, who, when, where and what." How can you be guaranteed you'll discover the best results? With this new list, you've got proven success tips that are easy to use, safe for any class and ones you'll almost fall in love with. Most important, you can use the reaction of your audience as your best source of word clues.

Anchoring Parts of the Room

An anchor is a powerful stimulus-response mechanism. For example, some persons get hungry just by wandering into their kitchen. The physical association of being in the kitchen actually causes salivation (not unlike Pavlov's dog). You can use this powerful tool in your classroom to increase understanding with your students. You wear many 'hats' as a teacher—for example you may be a disciplinarian, authority figure, friend, source of information, etc. You might categorize various parts into opinions, hardline facts, humor, common sense, announcements, or interactions. When you are talking common-sense, go to a part of the front of the room and talk from there in a specific tonality and tempo. When you are getting unusually serious or disciplining, go to another part of the room and speak from there. This strategy 'anchors' the spot to what you are saying. You have created an association, a stimulus-response with the location and type of message. In the future, because of the repetition, you can simply walk to that part of the room and get the outcome you want.

Chunk Up or Chunk Down

To chunk is a computer term which means bundles of information. To chunk up is to find the next larger bundle of a similar kind. To chunk down, you break the same bundle into smaller units. This process enables you to communicate better with your students by putting your information into the language they can understand better. This can open up learning channels because sometimes information is too generalized or too specific to work with. Here's an example: a student says "I don't understand math." In this case, chunk down—say, "I'm pretty sure you understand addition, so what specific part of math do you not understand?"

Here's another example: a student says, "I've got to do all this work on a term paper for just 20 lousy points? It's not worth it." In this case, you could chunk up from the level of the assignment to the benefits in life it could bring. Say, "You're right, that is a lot of work for 20 points. Yet, doing it can bring you pride in yourself and better grades. Then, when you get accepted at a good university for your extra effort, you'll be glad you did it." In your classes, any time a student does not understand something, chunk it—either up or down until the desired outcome results.

Positive Wording

A common pattern of ineffective teachers is the use of negation—they spend more time telling their students what *not* to do, than what *to* do. Communication masters, Richard Bandler and John Grinder say, "No single pattern . . . gets in the way of communication more often than the use of negation." That's a pretty strong statement! The best teachers are putting most of what they say in the positive form. Negation exists only in our language, not in our experience. If you say, "Don't do that!", it doesn't tell the person what *to* do, it only says what to avoid. Therefore it creates no action, involvement or empowerment.

If someone says, "Don't think of the color purple, think of any color as long as it's not purple", you are likely to think of purple! In the same way, if you say to your students, "Don't be late", they have to think of what lateness is like in order to understand the sentence. And why would you want to remind them of what lateness is like if what you really want to do is remind them of "on-time-ness?" It makes more sense to say, "Be sure to be on time." Simply word your sentences so that students know what you want.

Old way: "Don't forget, I said don't turn in your papers late!"
New way: "Please remember to turn in your papers on time."

There's an exception to the rule of negation. There are times that a negation can serve you and your students. If a student needs correction, it's better to use the negation to soften the message.

Old way: "This paper is sloppy, incoherent and illegible."
New way: "This paper is not neat, tightly-worded and readable."

In that same way, you can use a negation ("don't" or "not" etc.) to plant a positive thought in your students:

"Don't begin to relax or use your greater powers of concentration and creativity."
"Don't think of getting better scores on your next test unless you are ready for more fun and confidence."
"Do not participate in this lesson or have a great deal of fun by cooperating with others and respecting your enormous untapped potential."

Compound or contingent suggestions can be given to assist in improving attitudes and enhancing the unconscious learning:

"We're going to have fun today because it is going to be so much easier and different."
"The ideas from this book will become a permanent part of your teaching whether you finish this chapter confidently or not."
"Only relax if you are ready to take your seat."
"As you stand and stretch, your mind is ready to do more for you than ever before."
"If you know that you can learn anything, write this down, right now."
"Sharpen your mind while you are using the pencil sharpener."
"As you clean up your trash and put it away, leave any old or limited thoughts there, too."

Personalize Your Material

Use common experiences that the students have had or know about to refer to as part of your discussion. For example, "Julius Caesar was an epileptic. How many of you know of someone who is also an epileptic?" Here's another, "In making speeches, an introduction is important. How many of you have had someone come up to you and start talking and you didn't have the slightest idea of what they were talking about?" Most people are interested in other people, especially as they can relate them to themselves. Initially, what student truly cares about poet John Keats? But if you asked your students "How many of you ever liked someone so much you wished you had some clever poetry to send to them? Then you might want to know more about John Keats!" In this way, you're reaching down into a bank of common experiences that can evoke some sense of being related. Relate things in your presentation to what's popular on TV, what's popular on the radio and what's the latest in your city at the time. Relate, relate, relate. It's their world you need to enter, not the reverse.

Learning with Riddles

A doctor is summoned to treat a patient in the emergency room. Upon seeing the patient the doctor exclaims, "My God, I can't operate on that boy, he's my son!" That is so, but the doctor is not the boy's father. How could this be? A very simple solution. The doctor is a woman, the mother of the patient. A simple solution, but a good pattern-interrupter and thought raiser. One book which is excellent for classroom riddles is *Creative Growth Games* by Eugene Raudsepp.

Riddles, puzzles and brain teasers have been used for thousands of years in the learning situation. They have a way of encouraging thinking, creating interest and if solved, a sense of accomplishment. One way to use them is to open the class with a riddle, then let students sit with it for awhile. Near the middle or the end of the class, ask for solutions and discussions.

Be Sure to Use Tasking

One of the perennial problems in a class is that the material is often too easy for some students and too difficult for others. If students already have mastery of what you are teaching, have them raise their hands and let you know. You can then give them another task to do so that they are using their class time wisely. The new task would be one that you have already created (or ask what their interest is!) and is more challenging for them. It is entirely inappropriate for you to have students who are bored or lost with your presentation, if you plan properly.

Reinforcement with Recall

One of the ways to encourage participation is to continually review with your students in the form of a unison pattern. Your entire class can have fun while getting reinforcement. For example you can say, "Good, now that we've just finished point D, I want to review the earlier ones. Point A was about ＿ . . . point B was about ＿＿＿＿＿＿＿＿＿＿ . . . Point C was about ＿＿＿＿＿＿＿＿＿＿ . . . And just for fun, point D was about ＿＿＿＿＿＿＿＿＿ ." Let your students fill in the blanks orally. They like to know that they know the material, and naturally, you do, too. It gives you a good reading on how much they've been with you so far. And it's all done by making it snappy, to the point and fun.

Provide Associations

Take the time to insure that your students have the skills to learn the material you are presenting. No one else will teach them how to learn it; its up to you. There are many ways to develop student memories. Learn some of the methods yourself from books such as *The Memory Book* by Lucas and Lorayne or *Total Recall* by Markof. Included in these books are many useful systems such as chunking, location, mnemonics, pegwords, linking, key words, imagery, association and synesthesia. Using these, you can make class much more fun, increase student confidence and build big results.

For example, "Today we just learned about the five great lakes: Huron, Ontario, Michigan, Erie and Superior. An easy way to recall them all is to take the first letters from each of the lake names and form the word 'H-O-M-E-S.' Can all of you imagine a bunch of homes spread all over the lakes?" Something simple like this can give students confidence in their ability to learn and make the classroom process less stressful for them. In learning the Spanish word for horse, "caballo" ("kah-BYE-yoh"), note that the second syllable is pronounced in a way which rhymes with "eye." Simply imagine a horse kicking you in the eye (OUCH!). The kinesthetic and visual memory will create a life-long association, easy to recall. At first, give your students prepared images, then begin to let them create their own.

Indirect Self-Esteem and Confidence Builders

In general, people have difficulty with direct attempts to empower others. A solution is to use the indirect method. Not only tell your students they are important, treat them importantly. Increase the congruence of your presentation delivery. Make sure that your gestures say what your words say. Tape your class and listen to the tempo, tonality and volume of your voice. Then make corrections to insure that your voice is also giving the message to your students that they are valuable, trustworthy, unlimited and wise. Re-check the room arrangement. Make sure that the room says, "You are important." Make comments on your students' papers which give the message "I care." Be respectful of your student's time, and ask permission if you need to keep them later than agreed upon. Give more information than you think they can absorb; that says to your students, "I think you are unlimited and highly capable." Take time to listen to them. That says, "I respect you." Ask for input on your classes. That says, "Your thoughts are worthwhile." Tell the truth in class. That says, "You can trust me to be open, and you are a trustworthy person." Make references to their world. That says, "I respect you and who you are, and your world is worthwhile."

Use Linkage

Linkage is a language tool used to connect sensory-grounded experiences with externally-oriented experiences. The value of it is that it often bypasses the conscious mind and creates powerful behavior states. The simplest form is "A and B." An example is that "you are now hearing the sound of my voice and knowing that your confidence will grow." As you know, there's no actual relationship in real life between the sound of your voice and your student's confidence levels. However, the unconscious mind doesn't know that or care. It often links those two items together.

The strongest form of linkage is cause and effect. It can be symbolized by "A causes B." For example, you could say, "As you begin to pick up our pencil and write, you'll be feeling more confident." Or, "everyone take another deep breath . . . you're now a quicker learner."

Linkage as a Double Bind

Another form of linkage is the "if A, then B" format. It can be used many ways; one of the easiest is to give your students a suggestion of confidence which they must accept if they do what you ask of them. "Only quiet down if you're interested and curious about this next item from the upcoming test." "Stand up and stretch only if you're ready for a great weekend." "You may leave now only if you're more confident than ever before." Notice that you have given your students a small behavioral choice.

"As you get ready to learn, do you want to relax first or begin to think quickly?"
"Are you ready to absorb a lot while having fun or would you just as soon settle in and relax before learning?"
"Before you begin to learn easily, with more confidence, you can either get yourself centered and relaxed or we can do something else more fun?"

How to Use Quotes

Quoting is one of many ways to say something to your students that would be uncomfortable or ineffective if you told it to them directly. You already know about the traditional way of reading from a textbook, but you may be interested in a tool called "creative quoting." Say to your students, "This weekend I was talking to my friend about an idea I had and do you know what he said to me? He said, (look right at your students), 'You're brilliant. I've never met anyone who could pick up things as quickly as you. You're the greatest.' Now, I don't know if he was 100% accurate, but it felt great!" What you just did was to tell a story about your friend, but what was heard by the student's unconscious mind was a direct appreciation and acknowledgement about intelligence and worth as a person.

In the middle of a lecture you can use quoting to enlist the attention of your students. If you were about to present an important part of the lesson, you could say this to your students: "I remember when I was learning this material as a student and what the teacher said to me before he taught it. He said (raise your voice), 'PAY CLOSE ATTENTION with ann open mind, and you'll get it easily.' Now I'm not sure if THAT WAS THE REASON I UNDERSTOOD IT, but it sure helped." Then go right into your lecture as if you hadn't done anything differently. But your students will PAY CLOSE ATTENTION because they figure that later they might be thinking "THAT WAS THE REASON I UNDERSTOOD IT."

When Could You Use Metaphors?

Master therapist Milton Erickson used to tell about going to school for the first time and being faced with the alphabet. "At first it seemed like an overwhelming task. But now each letter has formed a permanent image in my brain and has become the basis for my reading and writing." Because learning the alphabet is a universal example in our culture, it's a perfect metaphor for something difficult becoming easy.

Another example Milton Erickson used is that of being a small child. He would say, "And when you were a very young child, and you first learned to crawl, you saw toes and table legs, and the world looked a certain way . . . and when you were able to stand up, the world looked different . . . and as you bent down to look through your legs, you gained a new perspective . . . then as you stood up you had even newer perspectives, each of which gave you additional knowledge and resources." In this case, the metaphor gives the message "grow and change your perspective and you'll be better off."

Successful use of metaphors requires these presuppositions: that an individual wanting to change has already attempted some kind of conscious effort; that most of our life's behaviors are controlled by our unconscious mind; that experiences (even if vicarious) are as, or more, powerful as an agent for change than didactic forms.

Basic steps in metaphor construction:

1. *Gather Information*
   identify key figures
   identify key interpersonal relationships
   identify key events of the problem situation
   identify how the problem progresses
   discover and specify outcome desired
   insure well-formedness
   utilize past coping strategies
2. *Build the Metaphor*
   select the context
   populate the plot with matches from above
   determine the resolution including
           a strategy
           the desired outcome
           reframing of the original problem
3. *Tell It*
   utilize additional resources
           nominalizations
           unspecified verbs
           lack of referential index
           embedded commands
           marking
4. *Move On and Be Patient*
   utilize trance state
   leave it alone
   results often take time

Using metaphors is a powerful way to evoke change in your students. They are easy to use, fun to listen to and often long-lasting. In the bibliography, read the books listed by David Gordon. He's a master of metaphors.

Respect Gradient Level

The dictionary defines 'gradient' as a rate of regular ascent or descent. This means that there is a smooth and predictable transition from one point to the next. You are 'out of gradient' when you simply do what's not appropriate for the moment in time of the class. How do you know what's appropriate? Use sensory acuity to check the responses of your audience. Be sensitive to both language and subtle facial and body clues. Move to each new activity only as your audience is ready for it.

For example, when you first meet students, a handshake or simple eye contact may be appropriate. After a strong bond of friendship has been established, it may be appropriate to hug them as part of a greeting ritual. But to do that your first time would be 'out of gradient.' In other words, the ascent to that point of intimacy has not been made gradually and predictably.

Certainty Affirmations

One tool that I have used that can work, depending on your audience, is the certainty affirmation. Tell your students with such a level of certainty that they will learn and remember the subject, that you are easily believed. It might be something as simple as: "I've taught this course hundreds of times and my students always get it. I am absolutely certain that each of you will totally master this subject." It's hard for your students not to feel that they'll succeed in the midst of such affirmations of confidence.

Time References

Time distortion is an important way of creating an environment of successful learning. One thing which is not useful is to tell students you are not sure that you'll get through all of the material that day. That creates anxiety. Are they missing anything? Must they rush and risk not understanding? Always let your students feel that there is sufficient time for what you need to do, or don't try to do it. Why would you want to tell them that they need to hurry to finish on time? Along the same lines, use time cues in your opening to let them know what's coming up and when. For example, "We have just three items to take care of before we start our main topic today." Or "In just a minute, when I start today's lecture. . ." "As soon as we have completed our daily stretching and preview, we'll be starting." Even if it seems as if you are running out of time, say "You have all the time in the world, three more minutes." This way the anxiety-producer of the second half of the statement is countered by the abundance of the first half.

Your timing could be as simple as, "Chances are, you'll find that next time will be easier than this one. And the time after will be even easier. In no time, you may know this stuff cold." Or, "Will you be suprised when this material suddenly all makes perfect sense to you!" Or, you could guide an extended visualization using full sensory responses to suggest a celebration of successful usage.

Female vs. Male Language Patterns

Woman often communicate differently than men. Men are often demanding, too-direct to the point and interrupt conversations often. Women have been brought up to be more polite, to give more parenting statements and to qualify what it said. "It sure is cold, don't you think?" "I'd really rather you not do that." Women often appear indecisive because they ask for permission or add questions to the end of their statements. "I presented that well, didn't I?" The effect is to soften the impact of their communications. Women often use words which reduce the impact of the content of their speech even though the intent is positive.

I'm *so* happy to see you all today and thank you *so much* for coming. It's *wonderful* to see your bright cheerful faces. We have a *terribly* important class today and I know you'll *really* like it."

While the above underlined words would be totally appropriate in pre-school through third grade, they may undermine the impact of your presentation for older students. In the classroom, those words can give messages such as "I want to be liked by you and I need your approval." Or, I want you to do something, but I'll change my mind if you don't really feel like doing it."

At the other end of the spectrum is the bossy and demanding teacher whose words and tonality say: "Do it now! I don't care about your feelings." There is a happy medium. In order to insure that your students know when you are asking (as a point of curiosity) and when you are telling (with no alternatives), simply change your tonality and be consistent with the tonality and the message.

Tell a Success Story

Select stories which have two key items. First, they must have a lesson or thought that gets triggered which supports the overall purpose and train of thought in your course. It's silly to tell a story which is simply funny when you could take the same time to tell a story which is funny, and has a message. The second thing is that the language, syntax and word patterns must all be favorable to, and consistent with your learning suggestions.

For example, if you were telling a story in a class about someone who eventually made good in school, but most of the story the person was not making it, check to see what the word choices are. If there is an excessive amount of words which have the words struggle, fail, problems, impossible, threats, etc., then I would change the story or forget it. Here's why: as soon as you start to tell a story, the conscious mind goes off for most people. Their mind wanders off because a trigger goes off in their head which says, "Here's a story, it's not important course content that I will be tested on, so I'll just think of something else for awhile." What that means is that the story is not usually received by the conscious mind. What's left is the unconscious mind, to which you are directing all those words such as struggle and problems. So guess what the student is left with? Only the thoughts from the unconscious! Here's a true story I tell in my reading class:

"A doctor who was one of my more easy-going students, turned out to be the best learner I have ever had. He got so good at reading quickly, that he used to confidently take lots of thick books along on leisurely pleasure trips, regardless of how short they were. Once, on a 20-minute plane flight, he started and easily completed James Michener's book *Centennial*. The person sitting next to him said, as the plane was coming in for a landing, "you should read that book sometime." The doctor smiled and said, "I just did, it was great! I especially liked the part when . . ." To which his fellow passenger exclaimed, "That's amazing, I took six months to read that book, and I don't even remember the part you just told me about." And the doctor casually tucked the book away and de-planed with a smile on his face."

Embedded Commands

You may have noticed the words that I include in the story allude to the fact that the experience was unstressful, easy, leisurely and creates a sense of satisfaction and pride. Nowhere do I come out and say to my students that they will all perform or learn just as the doctor did. What I do know is that there is a high likelihood that while they may be listening to the story line, they are consciously unaware of the adverbs which refer to confidence and success.

And that's exactly what I want to happen. As a result, the students don't know why, but they are more confident and quicker in their learning skills. In the field of therapy and hypnosis this is known as embedded commands. What is happening is that I am distracting the student with a story and the story may or may not be important. But it is a vehicle for letting my student's mind wander while I 'embed' commands to them about the course I am about to teach.

Embedded commands are simply messages woven within other messages which have a specific intended outcome. They can be used elegantly for behavior modification. To build confidence in your student's learning ability, you can "embed" suggestions of confidence to them in other statements. For example, "Make sure that when you're doing your homework successfully tonight you use our class handouts." Or, "Everybody who turns in their paper, whether they're confident of getting an A or not, should make sure they have their name on it." While the students were paying attention to the content of your message, their unconscious mind heard the affirmations of success you casually "dropped in."

You can use embedded commands in so many ways. As an example, you can ask your students to do something while also giving them 'suggestions' of confidence and resourcefulness. "While you are successfully and confidently putting your books away, remember that you have an assignment due on Friday." What students are paying attention to is that they have an assignment due on Friday. What they are actually hearing, even if it's subconscious, is that they are confident and resourceful.

If you wanted the students to quiet down one of many ways is to say: "Whether you still think you've learned this well or almost gagged on it is a moot issue. I'm sure that the material has quietly become a part of you and in fact, I may have to muffle your enthusiasm about it at a later time." Notice the references to silence: still, gagged, quietly and muffle. Each of those words is going into the unconscious of the students since it's unlikely all of your students will have their attention on all of your words. All that you know is that your class is much quieter!

Re-framing

Everything makes sense in its own context, so if you want to communicate more effectively, learn how to change the context, or the "frame" around the event. To "re-frame" means to give an idea or event, a different context. To most students, higher book costs are bad. But to re-frame it also means that the re-sale value might be high, or that they may not have to buy one at all, just borrow one. There are not only silver linings in every cloud; there are disadvantages inherent in every advantage. When you teach students to re-frame, you teach them to think. The best book on changing students' ability to see things differently is *Playful Perception* by Herbert Leff.

On a larger scale, to re-frame is to expand flexibility. If you are teaching a class and having difficulty explaining something, try another approach. How would a blind person explain it, how would a deaf person explain it? How would a foreigner explain it? What about a handicapped person, an athlete or movie star?

Use Presuppositions as a Double-bind

If you ask a student, "Would you give a presentation to the class?" You are open to getting a downright refusal. If you pre-suppose that the student will do it, then your question is "Would you rather give a short talk on Tuesday or a week from Tuesday?" This is the classic double-bind choice. It means that you have already decided on the 'what' of the outcome, it's merely a matter of taking care of the 'when.' You probably recall from your psychology classes the value of binds. They provide the illusion of choice—yet the options are actually very narrow.

"Would you rather relax now or in five minutes?"
"Do you want to learn 15 words now or 20 words later?"
"Do you think you might be ready to succeed on our first section or second one?"
"Would you like to breath slowly and allow your eyes to gently close or simply let all of yourself relax with your next breath?"

The double bind is a useful tool because it can allow you to give you what you want as a teacher, and the student what he wants as a learner. You want the learning objectives accomplished and the student wants some choice on how it happens. "Would you like to give your speech on a topic I choose or one that you choose?" "Would you like to write a paper or put your comments on cassette tape?" "I can pick a homework assignment, or you can. Which would you prefer?"

12 Active Teaching Tools

There are times when class seems to have ground to a halt. The students are bored, listless or concentration is low. What do you do when things seem stuck? Break the state with a pattern interrupt. You may recall that all behavior is related to the physiological state of the individual. In other words, if your head is hung low and you are crying, you will generate a different set of behaviors than if your eyes are up and a smile is on your face. In a classroom, anytime you are not getting the behavior you want, the first, easiest and best solution is to change the state of your students. This is also known as a pattern interrupt; it changes the existing state so that something better can follow. Either during or following the state change, you're likely to get the new behavior you're interested in.

The form of a state change or pattern interrupt could be nearly anything to break the routine. It could be as simple as you telling students: "Write this next idea down, it could be the most important point of the class." The simple act of writing can be state change. Ideal forms involve affecting the emotions and the body because usually the pattern you want to break is the classic non-participating "who cares" state. You may also want to include elements of surprise, humor or movement. Not only will the students like these, you're likely to have fun with them, too. All of these will break a static, stuck, non-resourceful slow-learning condition.

1. Get Physical

Students need and want physical movement to be at their best. They love to get up and move around: "the mind can only absorb what the seat can endure." Part of the reason many students don't participate is that they sit slouched over, with poor breathing, limited circulation in a stuffy room. Be responsive to your students! Watch them closely to see what they need. After 15 minutes or at most, a half hour, the best thing to give them may be a 60 second stretch break. You must monitor posture, breathing, and physiology to make sure that your students are in good shape to have the best possible experience.

What kind of physical break is appropriate? It depends on the room, the students, you, the context . . . one that's simple and that can be used easily is to do 30" of vigorous clapping while hopping or jumping in place. Or have everyone get up and walk or jog around the room three times for a break. Get a music system for your class and for half a minute play the kind of music your students like to listen to the most. If you aren't sure, ask around. There is hardly a more universal tool for creating movement and excitement than music. Even 30 seconds of music can create a whole new attitude in the classroom. For many students it works to have them stand up, raise both hands, stretch to the left, then the right, then forward, then back, take several deep breaths, then sit down. One that students like a lot is to have them invent new ways to shake hands with a partner. These and other kinds of simple physical breaks do miracles for a new frame of mind.

A simple and fun state changer is to have the students get up and change seats about every 20–30 minutes. Have them switch sides of the room on the first change, such as from left to right, then on the second change, switch from front to back. This will help the students see and hear the material better, break up lethargy and keep their circulation up. It also makes the class more interesting for the students and reduces disruptive talking.

Another simple physical strategy is this: Ask your students to stand up for a moment, then continue to give your presentation while they are standing up. This can be especially useful for about a minute, depending on the age of your audience. While standing up, students will see and hear things a bit differently, but most of all, it will be a simple way to get them out of a stuck condition. Just before they sit down, have them all give themselves a hand; the clapping will stimulate further circulation.

In other classes, it could be appropriate to have the students pair up and gently give back-pats or other circulation-inducing activity. You are the best judge. Many movement experts say the best kinds of movements are the cross-lateral ones which use the left side and the right side of the body working together. For example, doing 'apple-picking' with the alternating arms and bicycling with alternating legs is an excellent whole-brained exercise. Physical movement does two things. It increases breathing and circulation which gives more oxygen to the brain. And just as important, it creates a physiological state change so that any 'stuck patterns' are broken up.

2. Reach Out

Sometimes touching a student gently and respectfully on the shoulder or arm can bring about a state change. Usually, you'll know which students you can feel safe to touch, and in which manner. The classroom context you have developed should be your guide in this case. You can reach out in other ways, both with your face and body as offering visual triggers for a change and auditorily by changes in what you say or how you say it. Often a certain facial expression or gesture can change their state. This is especially true if you have previously used that expression as part of a funny, easily remembered experience.

3. Involve the Students

Stop what you're doing, and tell your students you had an idea. Switch roles with them; ask for a volunteer to present any part of your material, even if it's easy. Then have another get up and do some teaching. You could invite several students, one at a time to make brief presentations to the class. Students tend to pay great attention to their classmates.

Do market research and ask for your student's assistance. "This part seems a bit slow and we do need to cover it today. Who's got an off-the-wall idea on how to present this differently?" Or, tell them the truth; that you are frustrated and need some ideas. Simply stop the class and do a brief brainstorming session, collecting ideas to implement as soon as finished.

4. Change Your Own Routine

At times, teachers get themselves in a speaking routine which almost hypnotizes their own students. You could stop and change subjects, get personal or stop saying anything at all. Nearly any form of presentation becomes monotonous in time and therefore the secret becomes how to stay flexible. This could mean vary your volume; whisper for a moment, then raise your voice. Vary your rate; slow down, then for fun, talk at twice the rate. Change your pitch; first lower your voice, then talk higher. You could tell a riddle, a joke or speak a foreign language. Or, speak gibberish, a gobbledy-gook of nonsensical words. Better yet, have the students stand up and talk to the person next to them for one minute in total nonsense words. Its fun and it works!

5. Use Names

If you use names as a manipulative tool for pinpointing the culprits of unresourceful behavior, it breaks up rapport. If you use them as a way to appreciate and make your comments personal, it can build rapport. For example, when someone does something desirable, be sure to use his or her name at least once in your acknowledgement. To change individual states in your audience, simply be a name-dropper in the middle of sentences. For example, "There were five ways that the Vietnam War, Johnny, affected our economy."

6. Create Opportunities for Talking

Students often need to talk about what they are learning for maximum effectiveness. They need a 'reality feedback' not an 'authority feedback'. This means that students need to integrate and use the material they are learning with their peers in their own way, not in some structured class experience. Stop your class at any appropriate moment and provide your students with two or three minutes of time to talk about what they learned in the way they want to. For example, you might say, "Turn to your partner and talk for two minutes about the key points we've been discussing."

7. Ask For a State Change

Simply ask your students (as an experiment) to sit, look and listen to your lecture as if it was the most important, valuable interesting and funny lecture they have ever heard. Usually, their posture, breathing and attitude will change. Make sure that they are fully associated in that state, with a distinguishable physiological response. Then ask them to remember that ideal learning state. Even give it a name, so that they have an easy way to reference it. Maybe it becomes the "A-state" for attentiveness (the allusion to the letter grade may also be useful).

8. Use Props

Keep a supply of props in your classroom to break up student states which are not serving your class purposes. You might put them in a drawer or trunk near the front of the class and pull them out anytime you need to change the mood. Examples might include party noisemakers, hand puppets, Halloween masks or "Groucho" noses, a squirtgun, a jack-in-the box type surprise and as a last resort, a towel (if need be, you can always "throw in the towel").

9. Tell Stories

Stories by themselves are neither good nor bad—it depends on how they are used, for whom, and in what way. Stories have the magical quality of transference—your students might apply the lesson of the story to themselves. In general, the kind of stories that are most useful are the ones which have a specific and clear message which is right to the point of the discussion at hand. The ones that are rarely useful are those which are told because the teacher likes the story, it makes the teacher look good, or takes up time. In general, the stories that I find most useful are success stories of other students who had difficulties, yet overcame them and did well. I often use Sufi tales, with Nasrudin as the main character. Sufi tales meet most of my personal criteria: they are short, to the point, easily interpreted and timeless.

10. Use Humor

Researchers at Tel Aviv University demonstrated that students retained more information from lectures that have humor breaks interspersed. At Indiana University, researchers found that key learning points followed by a humorous story were remembered better than when they were not followed by a humorous story. One researcher believes humor stimulates the reticular formations in the brain, which bring out attentiveness, making the learner more receptive to information. Many teachers who use humor report that they do it to increase rapport with students, others say the laughter of the students decreases teacher stress and gives needed feedback.

When is humor appropriate? When it can make a particular point. When your students need a 'perk-up." When it's just the right tool to use to get a certain point across. When not to use it? When it is abusive, critical, or not empowering. Don't repeat a joke if it insults, damages or sets limits. You may have heard about the time a teacher said to the students: "If you get this information in your brain, you'll have it in a nutshell." Now that's an insult!

11. Breathing

The better the flow of oxygen to your student's brain, the better the ability to perform. Remind your students to take in a slow deep breath and exhale even slower many times an hour. Simply ask the whole group to do it together and you'll not only have a state-changer, but also put all of the students' breathing rates in rapport.

Useful state-changers and pattern interrupts involve the body, mind and the emotions. Ideally they shift the state from whatever mode they are in to another one: visual, auditory or kinesthetic. Many teachers find pattern interrupts to be as much fun as they are productive; it gets the energy up and students like the break. Even in the best teacher's classes, it's common to use five or ten state-changers per hour. You have got to monitor the state of your students and keep remembering that ALL behavior is state-related. If their state is not appropriate for the moment, change it!

12. The Power of Suggestion

Our brain is an associative mechanism which is constantly making connections. Think of black, your brain thinks white, think of up, your brain thinks of down, in and out, old and new, fresh and stale, small and big and so on. The point is this: for every thing you say in the classroom, your students will have an association to something else and will draw conclusions about themselves. Some of their conclusions may not be useful.

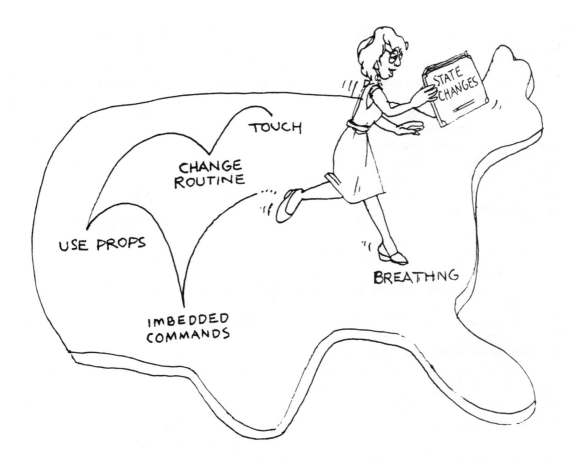

The upshot of this is simple. Put your language in the positive. Affirm what you want to have happen. Reduce classroom threats, demands and pressure. Avoid negations in your language. Present yourself, your office hours and your class with total positive feelings. Even the slightest hint of negativity or coldness can put off a student. Here are examples of statements and what might be implied by them:

1. "You are welcome to stay after class and visit with me anytime!"
(a great positive statement)
2. "While I do not expect to make scientists out of you, I do expect to provide you with the basics."
(reasonable, certainly a bit boring)
3. "If anything is unclear, please do not hesitate to call for help."
(remove the negations)
4. "It's Thanksgiving recess. Happy Turkey!"
(what about vegetarians?)
5. "Have a very Merry Christmas!"
(say "Happy Holidays" and include more religions)
6. "If the instructions are not clear to you listen more carefully."
(too hostile . . . lighten up)
7. "If you didn't get the assignment, ask another student for it."
(borderline . . . could be more positive)
8. "I hope you will gain an appreciation for the power and elegance of calculus."
(a beautiful way to put it)
9. "Don't forget to do your homework."
(remove the negation—say "remember your homework")
10. "Forget about Spanish and enjoy the holiday break."
(reword this—avoid telling them to forget the course)

11. "If these hours conflict with your schedule, leave your name and number and I'll call you for another appointment."
(this makes you sound too distant, like president of IBM)
12. "If you can't get this assignment done on time, call me and we'll work something else out."
(this implies that it's OK not to get it in on time—too dangerous)
13. "If you cannot see me during the regularly scheduled office hours, make an appointment for another time. I am more than willing to help."
(good, you come across as caring)
14. "Cut the chatter. We've got business to take care of."
(all depends on the situation and tonality of voice, body language)
15. "Ask any questions you may have, but don't expect me to outline your paper for you."
(just a bit cold—lighten up)
16. "The quality (or lack thereof) of your special projects will sway any borderline grades."
(remove what is in parentheses)
17. "If you fail to complete any of the four basic requirements, you can expect an F for the course."
(far too negative, reword this)
18. "Remember that we'll have our final examination on a week from Thursday."
(very neutral and safe)
19. "You may be able to slightly improve your score through good attendance, participation or attitudes. The opposite attributes could be detrimental."
(leave off the second sentence—it's implied)
20. I know you might be nervous or uptight about the upcoming test. Don't worry about how you'll do. You're not going to fail.
(reword all of it; turn it into positive statements)

This chapter has included some powerful tools on presentation skills. Again, the key is to practice just a few at a time until you have mastery of them. With practice, they will become a part of you and soon, they'll be automatic. The key ingredient is to first develop rapport. With rapport, nearly anything is possible. Use your feedback system, both conscious and non-conscious. Present your material with zest, commitment, flexibility and compassion. Use the tools in this chapter, along with your love and respect for students, to create understanding and enjoyment of your material.

☑ Check These Key Points

1. Communication consists of content, process and context.
2. To change the "state" of students, use physical movement, change the routine, use embedded commands, humor, props, breathing.
3. An accurate feedback system includes both conscious and non-conscious—it requires sensory acquity of both the verbal and non-verbal communication.
4. To get immediate feedback ask for a kinesthetic, auditory or visual response.
5. Use body gestures that are congruent with the verbal message.
6. Use sensory-rich language to activate the visual, auditory and tactile senses.
7. Use powerful words like "you, easy, safety, success, discover, guaranteed, free, save, results, new."
8. Anchoring is a stimulus-response system that can be used to associate a message with a location.
9. Tell success stories, use quotes and metaphors.
10. Music (60–80 beats per minute) can be used to induce a resourceful learning state.
11. Thinking skills can be described in many ways; recall, processing, application or as learning-to-learn, content thinking, basic reasoning.
12. Include the teaching of critical thinking by asking "why" and "how" questions.
13. The chalkboard, flip chart, posters, banners, guest speakers can enhance your teaching effectiveness.
14. Teach students to use mind mapping as a way to take notes.

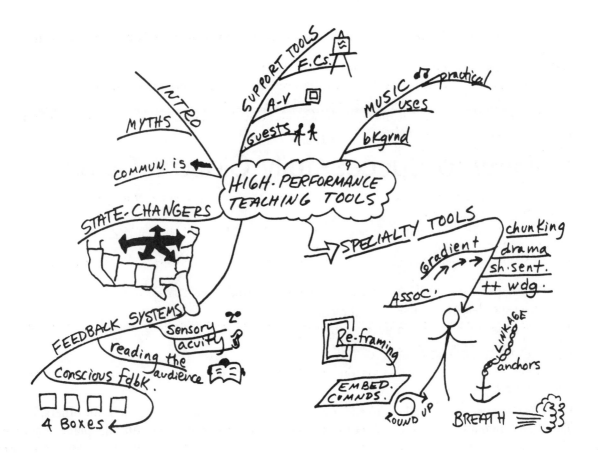

INTRO

MYTHS

COMMUN. is ←

STATE-CHANGERS

SUPPORT TOOLS
F.Cs.
A-V
Guests

MUSIC ♫ practical
uses
bKgrnd

HIGH-PERFORMANCE TEACHING TOOLS

SPECIALTY TOOLS
chunking
Gradient → →
drama
sh·sent.
Assoc.
++ wdg.

FEEDBACK SYSTEMS
Sensory acuity
reading the audience
Conscious fdbk.
4 Boxes

Re-framing
EMBED. COMNDS.
Round up

LINKAGE
anchors
BREATH

125

Chapter Ten

How to Successfully Close a Class

Objectives

- To identify misconceptions about closing a class
- To list the three keys to a successful closure
- To describe specific tools for closure

Many teachers are not sure how to end a class. For some, the bell does the job, for others, class is over when they run out of material. One of the best opportunities for learning can take place during the last few minutes of class. If you create your class with sufficient planning and attention, you'll look forward to those last few moments feeling complete and satisfied. This chapter is about ideas, tools and thoughts that can help give the entire class a sense of wholeness about your subject and, ideally, an inner sense of accomplishment. Here are myths that must be addressed:

Myth: Closures Are Not Critical for Success

Class closures belong in the category of completing unfinished business. A well-taught class needs an ending to tie pieces together and relate the parts to the whole. This simple act insures that the value students receive remains intact.

Myth: There's Not Time for a Closure

Even if you are rushed and running out of time, closures are well worth taking the time to do. If you are doing a ten minute class, do a closure during the last couple minutes. In a 50 minute class, do closure in the last five to eight minutes. In an all-day course, take 30–45 minutes for a closure. Closure is not part of the presentation, but allows the presentation to have an impact, to "settle in". Closure is the last word, the final thought, the ribbon around the package!

Myth: That Closures Aren't Meaningful

Closures offer time for students to integrate the course material in a way that truly adds to their resources. It can afford an opportunity to ask some important questions: What was the point? Did I learn anything? Have I enhanced my sense of myself? How can I grow from this experience? The closure will allow the student to make useful conclusions about what was just taught. Your job, as the master teacher, is to insure that the experiences in your class become an "added value" to your students.

Myth: The Timing Is Not Right for a Good Closure

At the close of class, are your students in the process of leaving? Leaving can be physical or mental. Most teachers feel as if the clock is like a burning fuse on a stick of dynamite during the last few minutes of class. Students seem compelled to be clock-watchers! Make it your personal challenge to create a kind of closure that will capture the attention and imagination of your students well enough to make it a memorable experience.

Three Keys to a Great Class Closure

A successful close to a class includes three things: a sense that something was accomplished (movement occurred), that it was worthwhile both internally and externally (validation) and that it is complete at least for now (wholeness).

KEY 1. It provides a sense of movement, meaning that progress was made and that we came a long way. This feeling can come from many sources including a review or test. It can come from the student's own discoveries during the class. Invite introspection and self-discovery. Ask students to ask themselves "what happened today, what did I learn, how does it affect me or how do I feel about it?" This is a great time for you to get some closing feedback on the effects or value of the class.

KEY 2. It provides a sense of validation, meaning that what occurred has been accepted and approved by the students as affirming, enhancing and real. It gets the stamp of approval and is labelled as worthwhile and beneficial to the students. This often takes the form of generalizing the experience to other areas of a student's life. It validates that each is a good person and enhances self-esteem. This can come from either you or the students or both.

KEY 3. It offers a sense of completion. Students like to know that a section or part of something is done. They need to feel everything has been taken care of, in their internal experience and in the external course material. Students need to have their questions answered, their upsets handled or excitement shared. Completion also means that you have led students into the future ("Future-pace") with the information—how will they use it and when? Plus, make sure you give students congruent congratulations for their attention and presence. The closure may also need to provide information for the student such as scheduling, announcements or assignments. And finally, students should leave your class with an excitement and curiosity to learn more.

A good closure is not something added on to your class *if* you have time. It deserves equal time, if not top billing, with the presentation and introduction. You must make the commitment (being willing to do whatever it takes to make it happen) to use a closure each and every time you teach a class.

The closure handles such questions as "Does anyone else feel the same way I do?" "Was this worth while for me?" "What do I do with what I've learned?" "What's next?" "How can I continue to learn more on this subject?" "Do I understand and remember what I got?" "How does this fit in with everything else I know?" "What if I can't use any of this information?" "What's coming up next?" Questions of these kind are on the minds of students as your course nears closing, and having answers adds to students' sense of wholeness and completion.

The actual strategies for closure are straightforward and simple. Use your sensory acuity to determine the closure most appropriate for your class. Try all of them so you have many choices! Here are over twenty ideas you can use to close your class skillfully.

Discovery

Find out how things went with your students by asking a few simple questions. First ask students to be truthful when answering. Then, simply state, "If you understood what we did today, please stand up." This will let you know immediately who "got it" and who needs help. You can also ask for a show of hands, "Who has gotten a lot out of our class today?" Another more kinesthetic option is to create groupings. Ask all the students to stand up. Then ask students to put themselves in three categories, moving to a specific part of the room for each group. The first group is for those who understood everything and could teach it to someone else. The second category is for those who understood but not well enough to explain it. The third group is for students who really didn't "get it" and want a clear understanding. This is a way for you to graphically and immediately get the results of your teaching.

Sharing

Sharing is the process of voluntary disclosure in the form of expressions, conclusions, discoveries or emotions. It's a moment when the student is validated merely by the acceptance and acknowledgement of others, not for the quality of what he or she had to say. When you make a space at the end of your class for voluntary sharing and let your students share a part of their lives with you, you allow them to complete, explore, express, and relish in being themselves. Some examples of the kinds of sharing that might go on in a class:

"I had a great time in class today."
"I discovered that I didn't work well with others."
"I found out that I like this subject more than I thought."
"I felt lost today."
"I really enjoy working with my partner."

Once the student has shared you have two options, depending on the amount of time you have left and the nature of what was shared. Your first choice is to accept, hear, and acknowledge what was said, adding nothing else:

"Thanks for sharing that David."
"I appreciate your sharing that, thank you."
"Great, thanks, John."
"Very good, thank you."

Notice that in each of the above expressions or responses, nothing was added to or taken from the experience that was shared. You simply let the person know that you appreciate him or her for sharing. This is the preferable response in most cases.

Discover the Conclusions Drawn

There's a saying that goes something like this: "It's not what happens, it's what you do about what happens." A variation is: "It's not what you learn, it's the conclusions about yourself that make the difference." Another possibility for closure is to respond to your students' sharings in such a way as to ensure positive conclusions have been formed. If a student has come to a potentially damaging conclusion about a just-completed activity, you'll want to lead him to a more resourceful one.

An example is in the quote, "I don't work well with others." Here's a person who has come up with a potentially disabling conclusion. If left alone, this could hamper progress in your class as well as in the rest of the student's life. In this case, ask some clarifying questions:

"I appreciate your sharing that. What do you think, specifically, causes you to not work well with others?"

"Thanks for letting me know. When you say others, I wondered if anyone, specifically, comes to mind?"

"I respect you for letting me know. Maybe you could you imagine what would it take for you to be able to work well with others"

"It's great you shared that with us, thanks. I was thinking, if you were to solve that, how would you go about it?"

With each question you ask, politely and respectfully you are helping that student reach inside himself to discover resources he doesn't know are there. You also have an obligation, as a learning coach, to make sure that any conclusions drawn are useful for the student's life. This intervention is not only preferred, it's the reason that you are in the classroom—to shape beliefs, attitudes and values.

You have the ability, as an outside observer, to notice patterns students might have that could hold them back. The gift you can offer is the gift of empowerment. No wisdom offered, no great lessons or experiences offered to them, just the gift of allowing them to learn the lesson on the spot. It can provide the three critical elements of a good closure: the sense of movement, validation and wholeness. In that, sharing can be one of the most powerful moments of your class.

Visualization

For many students, class goes quickly and for others, it lasts too long. In either case, there are few tools as useful for pulling it all together as a guided imagery. As with other closure tools, it provides a sense of movement, validation and wholeness. Leading a guided imagery is easy, leading one well is not so easy. It requires practical experience and a good way to begin is with relaxing, smooth paced background music. Use an imagery similar to this one:

Sample Guided Imagery

"Find a comfortable position . . . one where your hands and feet are uncrossed and your body is loose and limp . . . allow your eyes to close . . . take in a big breath and hold it for the count of 1–2, then exhale slowly and fully . . . take in another deep breath, even more air than before and hold it in for the count of 1–2–3–4, then slow——ly exhale as if you are blowing up the largest balloon in the world. As you continue to relax even more, you may be feeling more loose, more relaxed and open to learn . . . take in another deep breath, from the center of your body, and this time inhaling as much air as you possibly can and holding it for the count of 1–2–3–4–5–6–7–8, then exhale slow-ly . . . fully, and completely . . . relaxed and loose . . . you may notice that your breathing continues to be smooth, deep and relaxed. . . .

And as you continue to enjoy the relaxation, you find yourself on the seventh floor of a building, in a garden lobby . . . see a glass elevator and walk toward that glass elevator . . . step in and prepare for an exciting journey through the building . . . notice your favorite color on the walls as the elevator begins to descend so easily and quietly downward . . . as you pass the sixth floor you feel yourself becoming more and more confident, knowing that you fully understand the concept of (   ) that we began the class with . . . fortunately, your feelings of certainty and confidence are just beginning to grow . . . and, with another deep breath, you notice your continued feelings of relaxation and the elevator's arrival on the fifth floor where we have a chance to recall the concept of (   ) we studied so successfully earlier . . . continue your confident descent as you near the fourth floor and the concept of (   ). . . .

And the thoughts and images of (   ) surround you . . . comfortably and gently . . . with another deep breath, continue your descent to the third floor, so smoothly and full of energy, you easily and quickly review the concepts of (   ) and (   ) you know you understand them well and have total recall when necessary . . . now descend to the second floor, a calm and comfortable place of learning . . . a place where you recall that you learned about (   ) and (   ) as well as (   ) and (   ) . . . so easily and so confidently. . . .

Gently, you arrive on the first floor . . . step out of the elevator, into the future . . . notice how confident you feel at this time in the future . . . tell yourself how glad you are that you know this material . . . congratulate yourself on how well you remember and apply what you learned . . . take a moment to glance back at the elevator, remembering how far you've come . . . feel good knowing that knowledge stays with you . . . take another deep breath, feeling confident and prepared for your next step . . . and when you are ready, let your eyes open . . . feeling relaxed . . . complete . . . wonderful".

Notice that this particular imagery first puts the student in a very relaxed place, then constantly uses suggestions of things being easy, smooth, and simple. It makes continual reference to confidence. We want the student to feel competent, and able to master the material easily. By filling in your content where the brackets are, you personalize it for your class. Also be sure to pause frequently, especially

where the (. . .) appear. Be sure to evaluate your students to determine their readiness for an imagery. If you sense some students might be uncomfortable with doing an imagery, you may want to ask permission and do a shorter version at first. Here's one way to do it:

"How many of you would like to have less to review for homework tonight?"
(hands go up)
"There might be a way to do that, but I have a question first. Who in this class has heard of imagery?"
(Check response, if it's low, ask:)
"Who in this class has ever imagined in their mind something that they wanted to have happen?"
(hands go up)
"Has anyone here ever ended up with something that you dreamed about or imagined?"
(hands go up)
"How many of you would be interested in a way to use imagery with your classwork if it would cut down study time?"
(hands go up)
"Good. Then I'd like to do a short imagery with you in the next few minutes. In general, the students who do imagery find that they have better understanding of the subject and study for less time. But to get the results, you'll need to continue to stay very quiet. Are all of you willing to do that for a few short moments?" (If a student doesn't raise his hand, I ask individually if I have his permission. If he doesn't give it, I ask him to sit quietly while the rest of us follow along.)

How to Use an Open Review

One of the fun pieces of the closure process is the open oral recall drill. It can generate much energy and confidence within each student. To start an open review, begin with a sentence such as "Today we started with the concept of . . . and how it affects the _____ . Then we learned another form called _____ ." As you ask the question, the students answer orally in unison.

As you can tell, this kind of review requires mostly simple recall skills. Ask for items you are confident students know. The oral recall drill reinforces that they know the material, and they have a lot of fun doing it together. Most of this review is structured as a sentence completion. Make sure the answer is clear, singular and something discussed in class. For example, "There are three kinds of class closure we've mentioned so far. The first one is sharing, the second one visualization and the third one is the _____ ." (open review)

Using Mind-Mapping for Review

Mind mapping is an organizing tool used for note-taking and recall. Mind-maps can be used as a fabulous classroom tool during the closure process to review and test. Students have fun doing these in groups of 2–4. Have them create, as a team, one large mind map of the class's lesson. They will need to recall, organize, plan and think about the material once again and this process alone is worth the effort. In addition, students arrange the material in such a way, using visuals so their recall will be even greater. Usually a group can put together a quality mind-map in ten minutes or less. Put completed mindmaps on display around the room so each group's work can be admired. There are sample mind maps at the end of each chapter.

How to Remove Barriers

One process especially effective for coursework using psychomotor skills is called "removal of barriers". Developed by educator Vincent Peterson, this process provides an opportunity for review, for discovery of potential barriers to action, and for creation of solutions to barriers.

This exercise requires pencils and paper and can be used with students over 12 years old. Make sure the directions are clear and know that the process may take from 10–60 minutes depending on teacher experience, class size, student type, and course content.

1. On the first paper, write down all the useful ideas or tools that were learned in class.
2. Then start a second sheet titled "Barriers to Action." List all potential barriers to using the skills from the course or recalling the information later during an evaluation.
3. Have the students cross out any of the barriers which can be dealt with easily.
4. Remaining barriers are left open to the group to brainstorm for solutions. The goal is to find a possible solution for each barrier.
5. Then each student creates a personal action plan to initiate the solutions. They will share their action plan and affirmation of success with the group or the whole class. Class ends on an "I can do it" note.

There are many possibilities or variation on this activity, so improvise as needed. This type of closure activity is best used for psychomotor skills such as reading, writing, math, crafts, communication, art, physical education. It can also be done as a group oral activity to make it much quicker.

There are no failures
in the classroom. . . .
There are, however, often
unrecognized gifts

How to Create a Successful Partner Process

For this closure process each student needs a partner. Partners face one another for eye contact. The process begins with students receiving from you a list of self evaluation questions to prompt thinking about the coursework. Partner "A" reads the first question and gives an answer. That same person continues through the rest of the list until finished. Then partner "B" goes through the list, answering the questions. Be sure to give students some unstructured time just to chat. It's a great way to let the students say what they want and to assist them in gaining more clarity about your class. You might list questions like these:

1. What do I want to say about my progress?
2. Is there anything I would rather not say about my progress?
3. What did I want to get out of this class?
4. What is true right now about me getting my goals?
5. Is there a barrier between me and my goal?
6. What is my strategy or plan to handle that barrier?
7. How can I insure my success and what kind of support would I like?
8. What three things would I like to be acknowledged for?

When these are used, it's best to give each student a few minutes, then tell them to "switch." Once both partners have had a chance to share their thoughts with one another, you might open it up to the whole group by saying, "Who would like to share with the class something they felt or discovered?" This is a great way to reinforce the purposes of closure: to sense movement, completion and validation. In addition, this process supports each student's growth in being responsible for getting something valuable out of class.

Discussion

A common and useful form of closure can be discussion. Subjects that are excellent for the discussion are the three areas mentioned in the last chapter as part of the evaluation process: relationship, strategies and course material. Discussion also works well if you break the class up into small groups and have each group work with group leaders whom you have previously trained to lead discussions. Open the discussion with questions such as:

"How do you feel about this subject today compared to before?"
"What was the best way for you to learn this?"
"What points interested you the most?"
"What did you learn about yourself today?"
"How could what you learned, and how you learned it, affect your life?"
"Why do you think this was taught today?"

How to Get Immediate Feedback

The easiest way to get in-the-moment feedback is to ask for it. Say to your students:

"Raise your hand if you understood most everything today."
"Raise your hand if you're a little unsure of what we've covered."
"If you're glad class is over, stand up . . . then if you got a lot out of today, please have a seat. If you are just a bit confused, remain standing. Now, to those who are standing now, what can I help make more clear to you?"
"Raise your hand if you are so confused that you don't even know the questions to ask."

How to Use Written Evaluations

One of the most useful things a teacher can do is to secure the assistance of students in evaluating themselves. In this case, the ambiguity of the reference to 'themselves' is fortunate because it actually refers to both students and teacher. What's especially useful is for students to rate themselves at the same time they are rating the teacher. Even if you have just three minutes, you can get reasonably accurate and useful feedback on how they and you are doing. Try several different kinds of questions until you get the information you need for superior teaching.

Class Evaluation

Date:

Directions: No name, please. After each thought, please comment.

1. What I enjoyed about class was:

2. What I disliked about class was:

3. The most useful or valuable part of today's class was:

4. What I discovered about myself today is:

5. List attitudes or beliefs changed or new perspectives:

6. I describe my attitude toward this subject as:

7. How my learning strategies worked today:

8. Other comments:

Class Evaluation

Date:

1. When the subject of our class is mentioned, what words come to mind?

2. Which would you prefer more of: (1) _____ more visuals, pictures, charts, illustrations? (2) _____ more explanations and examples and analogies? (3) _____ more actual demonstrations where you can do it yourself?

3. What haven't you understood that you'd like to get cleared up?

4. What's made the biggest impact on you so far, something you liked, were impressed with, or affects you the most?

5. What suggestions do you have for making the class work better?

6. Other comments?

Class Evaluation

Date:

1. My intended results for the day: _____

2. My actual results: _____

3. What were my successes today?

4. What didn't work/what I am confused about/did not understand?

5. Suggestions for improvement:

6. At the end of this class, how do I feel about progress?

7. Further comments:

One of the most important parts of the student's evaluation process is that you must read and do something about them! Look for areas you need to improve, notice the feelings and moods of your students. If a student is exceptionally troubled, you might mention at the end of the next class that "some of you expressed some concern over how things are going, and I'd like to invite you to meet with me for a moment after class." This statement leaves it wide-open in case the student feels better or if the student just wants to be left alone. When you read the comments, make sure you don't read any more into them than is written. Any communication made about another person often says more about the sender than the receiver. In addition, be sure to mention to your class that you read the evaluations and you are attending to their comments. It is especially good if you mention specific suggestions.

Preview the Coming Attractions

One of the more important parts of a closure is the advertisement. Tantalize your students with interesting tidbits of learning coming next. Figure out what would be interesting to your students and turn it into a commercial for the next class. Use the form of a question, challenge or a muse. In a study skills class, you could say, "Next class we'll be learning how to reduce study time and increase reading comprehension. Anyone interested? . . . Great! See you next time!" Or, in other classes, it might be:

"Next class we'll learn ten new words in Spanish that could help you out of a jam."
"When we meet again, we'll find out how learning about rock formation has made millions of dollars for some enterprising persons."
"At our next meeting, we'll learn to use a power tool that can save you dozens of hours of valuable time."
"Next time, we'll discover who was the only president in our history to never marry and why."

Remember Your and Your Student's Vision

Everyone needs a reminder of vision, the main dream for his or her life. Use the end of class to be inspirational. Speak to students about the possibilities available and how things could be. One of the most inspirational presidential candidates was Robert F. Kennedy. He was famous for the quote, "Some people see things the way they are and ask 'why.' I see things the way they could be and ask 'why not'?" Many detail-oriented pragmatists or small thinkers call this "pipe-dreaming", but it is necessary for students to have dreams for their future, without them, there is no hope for tomorrow.

Handle Student Needs

Another necessary part of closure is the handling of student needs. There's a whole range of needs to meet so students feel good about the class being complete. Typical needs include:

1. *Weather.* Has it created any special needs? Do any of your students need special transportation because of it?
2. *Upcoming tests.* When is the next one, what's on it? What's the format?
3. *Homework or projects due.* Is there any deadline coming up? Remind the student of it at this time.
4. *Confusion or depression.* Is there any student who needs some special support after class? Simply notice your student's face and body language during class and at the end. Privately, call their names and ask to talk to them for a moment. You might say to them, "You seem a bit troubled. Is it anything you can talk to me about?"
5. *Organization.* There may be tools, papers or materials that need to be put away. Now is a good time to enlist the support of others to get things put away.
6. *Transportation.* Sometimes students need to carpool or have gotten stuck and need a ride. Now is a good time to ask if any students have travel needs.
7. *Handouts or materials.* Make a quick check to find out what materials student's need to take with them. Do they have all the necessary handouts? Where can they get extras?
8. *Next time.* Make sure the students know exactly what to bring to class next time. Whether it's an assignment, books, a project or a thought, let them know, and give them time to write it down.

Make Sure to Future Pace

Future pacing is a tool that allows the student to imagine a situation in the future where knowledge learned in class will be useful. There are a couple ways to empower students for future experiences. One is to lead a visualization, taking the students into the future where they can experience success. Have students close their eyes as they imagine their new skills or knowledge successfully at the next opportune time. Have them see, feel and hear others appreciating them and getting excited over their success. This can help create the future for your students by giving an experience from which they can draw confidence.

You may have heard a parent or teacher who says to a youngster, "You'll make a great doctor someday." Or, "With your creativity, you'll probably end up as some famous artist." Or, "That kid's got a mind for money, I'll bet he gets rich before he's 30." All of these are examples of future pacing, planting a thought for the future. Other ways are:

"Boy, will you be surprised when your grades jump up!"
"I have a feeling you'll be liking this subject soon."
"Somehow I just know you'll catch on any moment."
"Something tells me you're going to be able to understand this whole section once you open up your book at home!"
"You may surprise yourself with your well-done homework!"

Other times, you might plant the thought to look in their textbooks . . . "I wonder how many of you might find yourselves browsing through the textbook just as a review. . . ." (An ineffective teacher will say, "Don't forget to study or you might do poorly on the upcoming test." Students' minds access four experiences from your word choice and predicate usage: "Forget—study—poorly—test.") More effective is the statement, "Remember, the more fun you have studying, the better you'll do on the test." Now let's analyze the words most likely to be remembered: "Remember—fun—study—better—test." A teacher's success is partly dependent upon the ability and awareness to select careful words in classroom communications.

Congratulate with Congruency

The close of class is the perfect time to acknowledge and appreciate your students for their participation. For every single class, regardless of what was taught or how well the students learned, find something that you can sincerely appreciate or acknowledge. Make sure that your student congratulations are sincere and you demonstrate that sincerity with congruent posture, voice, words, tonality and gestures. Your student's self-esteem will be enhanced and they will appreciate your attention.

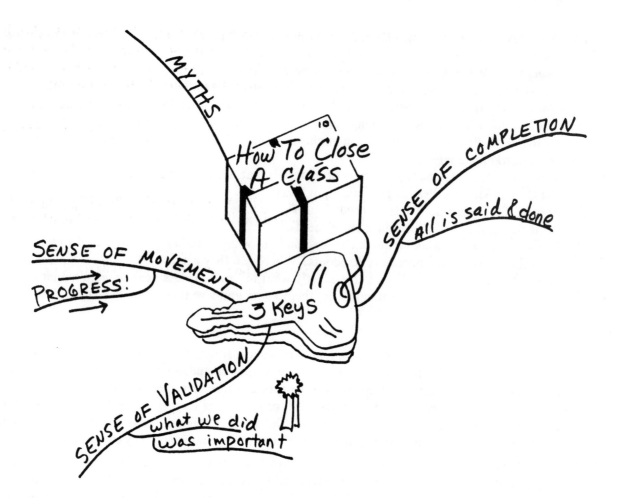

MYTHS

How To Close A Class

SENSE OF COMPLETION
All is said & done

SENSE OF MOVEMENT
PROGRESS!

3 Keys

SENSE OF VALIDATION
what we did was important

A Closing Ritual

Every teacher could add to their effectiveness by establishing a closing ritual to integrate the conscious content with the unconscious part of students' experiences. Some common rituals are:

1. Everybody repeats the class theme (it could be any one that you select, maybe the thought of the week such as "it's in every one of us)
2. Everyone sings a class song
3. Students give all the others a standing ovation
4. A simple closed-eye thought for the day
5. The use of a class mascot as a theme reminder
6. A student shares/the class philosopher
7. Clapping/a tai chi clap/dancing
8. Simply standing up and taking in a deep breath of energy
9. Pointing out or noticing the class accomplishments
10. A class cheer

Whatever the closing ritual, get class permission first or simply wait until the mood of the class is such that permission is already granted. Introduce the ritual with energy and enthusiasm. Be consistent and have fun with it. Some students may be slow to join in, be patient, they'll learn to enjoy the routine. The closing ritual is the final experience students have in your class so make it fun and upbeat!

☑ Check These Key Points

1. It is important to end class with a closure.
2. A good closure does three things: provides a sense of movement, confirms value and offers completion.
3. Specific techniques for closure are: sharing, visualization, do an open review, mind mapping, discussion, written evaluations.
4. For psychomotor skills, the process of "barrier removal" is an excellent review and closure.
5. Important parts of closure are previewing coming attractions and reminding students of their personal visions of life.
6. A closing "ritual" is an effective finale for your class.

Student Communication IV

Chapter Eleven

Relationships Make It Work

Objectives

- To establish the importance of relationship at school
- To list qualities of rapport between teacher and student
- To list qualities of relationship between student and subject matter
- To list qualities of relationship among students
- To offer ways the teacher can build students' self confidence.

By far, the best way you can reduce classroom problems and enhance the learning process is by making it a point to build strong relationships. The eminent educator, Robert Bills, did a survey of 124,000 students in 315 public and private schools. After gathering thousands of pages of research, his first and most critical recommendation was that the quality of relationships at school must be improved. This means primarily the relationships between students and teachers, though others are important, too. Improving the relationships you have is so important that it deserves headlines:

"Your success as an educator is more dependent on positive, caring, trustworthy, relationships than on any skill, idea, tip or tool in this book."

At school, students learn based on four relationships: (1) the relationship with the teacher, (2) the relationship with the subject matter (3) the relationship the students have with each other and (4) the one with themselves. The teacher needs to do whatever it takes to build relationships during the first weeks of school and then continue to maintain them on a daily basis. The easiest level at which to build relationships is in the elementary school. Here teachers spend an entire day with their students and can focus on building relationships as a source of support. At the secondary level, this is difficult because departmentalization robs the necessary time to daily build relationships. With 50–55 minutes per class and the pressure of teaching content, your relationship time is minimal. Every move must count. Each activity must serve as a vehicle for building a strong working rapport.

KEY 1: How to Establish Rapport with Your Students

There are many building blocks to a strong teacher-student relationship. Here they are:

1. *Love Yourself.* When you care about yourself and respect yourself, your students know that you consider yourself special and worthy of respect. This lets them know they are also worthy.
2. *Learn about Your Students.* Find out who your students really are. Have them fill out 3 × 5 cards on themselves telling where they were born, how many brothers and sisters, pets, and about their

mom and dad. What do they like? What do they dislike? What are their fears, concerns, and problems? What's important to them? Ask students what it is like being a student. (It's certainly different from when you and I were in school!)

3. *Appreciate Your Students.* Understand the pressures and difficulties of being a student. Know what kind of effort and courage it takes just to get through the day. Discover how much peer pressure is on your students. Know what kind of academic pressures they feel, too. To do this, it takes a special effort on your part to listen without judging.

4. *Acknowledge Your Students.* Thank them for little things. Thank them for big things. Thank them for being in your life. Appreciate every little thing they do. Give verbal praise, write notes, give hugs, smiles and warm gestures. Let them know that they are special to you and that you really like knowing them.

5. *Listen to Your Students.* Most students feel no one listens to them, not parents, not teachers and not even their friends. Open up class time to let students share about their lives, joys or problems. Even the seemingly little things are big things. If you can be a "no-particular-agenda" set of ears for your students, a real open-minded, open-hearted listener, you will be one of the greatest gifts in students' lives.

6. *Make Small Concessions.* Grant small favors. Bring their popular music to class. Do things that can make a big difference, even if it is letting class out 30 seconds early or giving no homework over the holidays, everything helps.

7. *Include and Empower Your Students.* Ask them what they think. Let them participate in decision-making. Give them options in how to do things as long as they are willing to produce the results. Actively solicit their advice. Have a class advisory board. Help students feel important.

8. *Respect Students.* Never, ever "put down" a student. Avoid all sarcasm. Honor their decisions. As soon as it is appropriate, treat them as adults by giving them more responsibility. Enforce rules, guidelines and agreements exactly as they were set up. Don't bend rules on key items where honesty or integrity is involved.

9. *Treat Students as a "Possibility."* This means that each student is treated as a potential success, not as a past record. Treat students as a possibility of their greatness and your job is to have greatness "show up" within the character of each student.

10. *Be Open with Students.* Share about yourself so students get to know you. Talk about your joys, successes and challenges. You provide a great opportunity for students to learn about adult life.

During the first few days of school you must establish the method, manner and structure of relationships that you want with your audience. Create the commonality of relationship that your students need to have in order to feel connected to you. How are you alike? What brings you together? What do you want and what do they want? Do you share common goals? How will you behave toward one another? This important piece of your presentation is the glue that keeps you together in the same room. Take the time to do this well.

How to Maintain On-going Rapport during Class

Once you have established initial relationships, you'll still need to maintain them on a minute-by-minute basis. You'll know what your level of rapport in the audience is by the amount of responsiveness to your presentation. Be aware constantly, using the information gathered to adjust what you're doing. At times, you'll need to make non-verbal changes, and at others, more direct verbal approaches will be necessary.

The most important clues you'll get from your students are non-verbal: posture, breathing, tonality, tempo, gestures, etc. These behaviors are critical to monitor because most persons are unaware of them—

meaning that they are the most accurate indicators of where you stand with another. Learn to make the following distinctions in your audience so that you'll know when you have the audience in the palm of your hand and when you need to make adjustments.

How to Monitor Rapport

1. *Auditory.* Listen to the questions and responses you are generating. Is the content of the question in line with what you've been saying or counter to it? Listen to the tonality and tempo. A faster paced, fluctuating or emphatic response could indicate you lack rapport unless that's how you speak. The tonality could be saying "Gee, I really like what I'm hearing." Or, it could tell you, "Why in the world are we even studying this?" When you are in total rapport, you may hear some of your pet words, phrases and ideas used. Listen for audience chatter—is the content and timing of it in line with your class purposes? If so, chatter could indicate rapport. Otherwise, it may indicate they're bored.

You can increase rapport with those students who are more auditorally inclined very easily. Vary your tonality. Let your tempo fluctuate, and change your volume often. Use other sounds to enhance what you're saying. Remember when you were two years old? You made playful sounds all day long. Sometimes it's just the variety needed to keep the students alert and interested. You may also want to use auditory verbs such as: "Things are clicking. How does this sound? Tune into this. That rings a bell. Here's music to your ears."

2. *Visual.* Wear colors which students can relate to while still dressing professionally. Notice what your students wear—many students will unconsciously begin to wear the same colors you wore the day before. If they do, compliment them. Look for facial expressions that say "I'm confused," or "I want to say something." Move around the class so you can keep taking in everyone in your field of vision from different angles.

Using visually-related verbs means that you'll gain rapport with those in your audience who are visually dominant. "I see what you mean. Take a look at this. From my perspective, you'll get a clearer picture of this." You can also talk more quickly if your usual pace is slower.

3. *Kinesthetic.* Get a sense of their posture. Is it leaning towards you? Do their heads tilt towards you as you speak? Are they nodding in agreement? Are they yawning or looking away? Are their legs or arms crossed? Is their breathing rate the same as yours? How about eye and mouth muscle movements? You've got many indicators, just be sure to check them out—not make assumptions about what they mean.

Those who have kinesthetic as their primary representational system will appreciate two things in your style. First, the pacing of your speech needs to be slower to appeal to the kinesthetic learner. This means . . . that you may have to . . . pause a bit . . . to let things "sit" with your students. The other rapport builder is use of verbs. Use expressions such as "How do you feel about this? What's your sense of this? Let me give you . . . a couple of concrete examples . . . so you can better get a handle on things."

Multiple Rapport Builders

You may be wondering how you could possibly maintain rapport with such varied factions in your audience. It would seem impossible to keep rapport with both the visual, auditory and kinesthetic learners. Yet, it's much easier than it may seem. Your presentation can be varied; speaking quickly, using auditory predicates and maintaining a kinesthetic posture is a simple way. Or, you can speak slowly, use kinesthetic verbs, use lots of visuals, and vary the tonality of your voice. Or, you can use one style for two minutes, then another for two minutes, then switch again. With a subtle "weave," all of your audience can constantly be included.

Every once in a great while
try to truly understand
what it must be like to be
a student in your own class. . . .
You might never teach the
same way again. . . .

If your students were randomly selected, approximately 40% of your audience will process information primarily visually, 40% auditorally, and 20% kinesthetically. This means that regardless of your preferred system, ("Do you see what I mean," or "How does this sound to you?" or "How do you feel about this?"), that if you are committed to reaching all of your students, you need to sprinkle diversity into your predicates.

You might also gauge the effects and responsiveness of your use of predicates by the audience you have. In a group of so-called "Special-Ed" or learning-impaired students, use predominantly kinesthetic predicates and metaphors. In addition, use them in courses where the dominant subject or activity is physical (crafts, sports, home economics, shop, etc), AND students chose to go on their own volition. In more visually-related courses (art, film, research-related, reading, etc.), use predominantly visual words. And of course, use auditorally-related words when your audience might indicate that as their preference (music, drama, speech, radio, sales, politics).

Be Responsive

If a student raises his hand, ALWAYS acknowledge it right away even if you cannot call on that person. Look at him and say, "I'll be right with you," or "I'll be ready for your question in just a moment." If a student asks you a question, be sure to answer it truthfully and briefly (more on this in an upcoming chapter). If students are restless, get them up for a stretch break. Be sure to use your fullest sensory acuity. It not only builds rapport with students because they feel noticed and heard, but it also makes smart teaching sense.

Incorporation

You gain rapport with students when you incorporate into your teaching that which goes on in the environment. Students want to know that you and they share the same world so when you include external and internal stimuli in your teachings, they feel closer to you. If an interruption occurs, use it as a positive example of something you are discussing. If a noisy truck or train goes by, use it to your advantage: "We're all on the right track, so let's stay with this." If a student yawns, include somehow: "You may have yawned if you feel that you already know this material well enough for a test." Or, if someone drops his books on the floor, say: "A question may have just dropped into your mind, does anyone have one they'd like to ask?"

Continual Acknowledgment

Learn to acknowledge; give credit to students even when it's marginal. Give it to them when they do what you ask. Thank them if they attempt to do it when you want them to, in the way you want them to. Appreciate all that they do. Respect that they are doing the best they can, given how they see the world. You can turn any situation into an opportunity to acknowledgement, if you are both flexible in your interpretations and committed to empowering others. For example, let's say a student responds to a question with an inaccurate answer. Say, "Thanks for having the courage to offer an answer, I like it when you are willing to go for it."

Devil's Advocate

When presenting information, be especially tuned in to the possibility of a negative or puzzled response. Then when you get one, USE IT! Change your strategies to either re-package what you just said or play the "devil's advocate" role. If you just said that the moon is made of green cheese and your students smirked, you could say, "now I know some of you may be thinking that's a crazy idea. And truthfully I thought it was, too. But when I heard such and such I changed my mind!" In other words, take the freedom to become the reactive mind of your audience, if need be.

Be flexible and be willing to change points of view as long as you can still get the desired outcome. You might say, "Let's have our class presentation next Friday." To which a student might reply, "Gee, I really couldn't get ready by then." To which you could reply, "On second thought, Friday isn't quite the right day of the week. Which other day did you have in mind?"

Use Names

If you use names as a manipulative tool for pinpointing the culprits of unresourceful behavior, it breaks up rapport. If you use them as a way to appreciate and make your comments personal, it can build rapport. For example, when someone does something desirable, be sure to use his or her name at least once in your acknowledgement. For example, "I like that idea, Kevin. We can implement that in our next project."

Be sure to refer to what students said before. A great way to build rapport is to use the comments and ideas of your students constantly in your material. For example, "As John mentioned earlier, our balance of trade deficit is getting worse." Or, refer to what the whole class said by taking a poll and using the results. "How many of you think memorizing answers is a key to school success?" Then, later on, "As you all said earlier, memory is important to school success, so let's learn how it works."

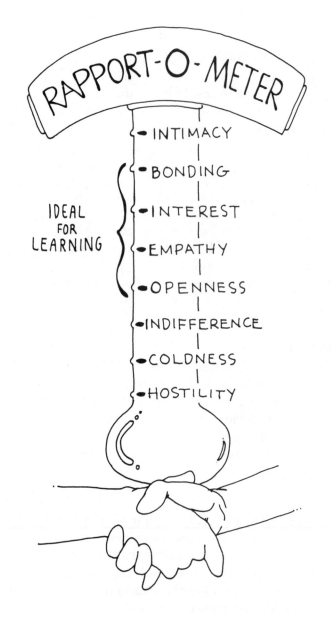

Use Agreement Frames

Differences lose rapport and similarities gain rapport. But what happens if a student is responding to you in a way you disagree with? The answer is to use the agreement frames to maintain rapport. Three magic phrases are "I agree, I respect and I appreciate." If you don't agree with someone, you can at least respect the opinion and the right to express it. If you don't agree with someone, you can at least appreciate their willingness to tell you. And if you don't respect someone, at least find a way to agree with the outcome. Here's an example:

STUDENT: "I hate this class, I can't learn anything."
TEACHER: "I certainly <u>appreciate</u> you telling me. What can I do to make it more interesting even if you don't (change your tone) LIKE THE CLASS?"

OR,

STUDENT: "I don't even care if I do well or not."
TEACHER: "Well, I <u>respect</u> your decision because you usually make good ones. I was wondering what things are important to you?"

OR

STUDENT: "Nothing's important to me except motorcycles."
TEACHER: "I <u>agree</u> motorcycles are well worth your time. If I could help you get a handle on your homework to get it done sooner, so you'd have more time for your motorcycle, would you be interested?"
STUDENT: "Yeah, I guess so. . . ."

Being "Real" with Your Students

One of the most simple and effective ways to maintain rapport is also one of the easiest to do. Be honest with your students. Tell them the truth about yourself, your world and how things are for you. Let your students know when you are happy, sad, frustrated, anxious or excited. Share your dreams, goals and disappointments. Tell the truth about what policies you have to enforce and which ones you don't. Explain why you do what you do and make sure that you include your students in as much decision-making as you can. Students who participate in creating and clarifying policies are more likely to carry them out. And last, do not lie. Even if it's a "white lie," it's never worth it. Your relationship with your students can take months to build and only seconds to destroy, so protect your investment and your integrity by being real and by telling the truth.

One thing about telling the truth is that it can always be "used" to hurt someone. For example, a poor way to reply is: "Your term paper was awful, I liked none of the ideas and it was sloppy, amateurish and lacked conviction." How much better to say, "Here's your paper back. To get a higher grade, I suggest you start with ideas we have talked about in class, rough draft it, write with more enthusiasm, then get someone to read it for you, type it, and proof it before turning it into me. By the way, things I liked were your determination to get it in on time and it was the perfect length. Let me know if I can help." Tell the truth, but be compassionate. Have an appreciation for the personal life of your students and especially for their self-esteem.

Key 2: The Student-Subject Matter Relationship

Critical to the success of your students is a positive attitude or relationship with the subject you are teaching. Most of the rest of this book is designed to build that attitude. Here's a summary of some of the points mentioned:

- ☑ Excite your students in a vision about learning
- ☑ Ask students to discover what the subject's possibilities are
- ☑ Have the students create some value or benefits in it
- ☑ Talk about the subject positively
- ☑ Role-model your own interest in the subject
- ☑ Make the subject matter more personal and relevant
- ☑ Make the subject closer to home
- ☑ Utilize a wider variety of learning styles: field trips/guest speakers/hands-on learning
- ☑ Bring humor, songs and games into the classroom
- ☑ Have students visualize liking the subject more
- ☑ Have the students work as a team
- ☑ Appeal to and reach more kinds of learners
- ☑ Create new associations to "re-anchor" the subject
- ☑ Link up the subject with positive emotions and music

Key 3: Building Student-to-Student Relationships

In order to develop powerful inter-student relationships, it will take an extraordinary amount of initial groundwork and constant coaching. Most students at the elementary level are taught to be kind and supportive to their neighbor and help out whenever necessary. Somehow, much of that spirit is usually

145

lost and by the time students are teens, the typical behavior is put-downs, sarcasms and indifference. There are many ways to alter this too-common pattern:

- ☑ Establish a definition and foundation of integrity
- ☑ Ask students to relate to each other in a supportive way
- ☑ Set up clear class guidelines for behavior
- ☑ Role-model: Relate to other teachers in a supportive way
- ☑ Express your relatedness and commonality to your students
  Have them do this to each other
- ☑ Declare to them you can be counted on—then role-model it
  Have your students do this to each other
- ☑ Have some out-of-class activities so students can see each other as people, not students
- ☑ Pick a class project that all students can get aligned on and excited about
- ☑ Develop student teams based on greatest diversity break up all cliques, split the sexes
  select team leaders who are most able to lead
- ☑ Have teams select their own name and team cheer
- ☑ Ask each person on the team to commit to the following:

> The success of the team
> The support of each member
> Being coached by the leader
> Promises of action and performance
> Specific lines of communication
> The team goal
> What the team goal can do for them

- ☑ Let the teams do activities together to build support
- ☑ Have your class teams meet often to:
  Discover what results they have produced
  Find out what's not working and make changes
  Celebrate their successes
- ☑ Give your teams a chance to do many projects
- ☑ Switch teams, leaders and projects to prevent cliques

Key 4: Building Student's Relationships with Themselves

Probably the best way to describe student relationships within themselves is self-esteem. A healthy self-concept means that you "relate" to yourself well. You think of others highly and yourself highly. All persons are of equal value, potential and deserving of respect and compassion. A later chapter describes in detail the conditions for establishing high self-esteem. As a brief preview, some ways for you to enhance student's self esteem are:

- ☑ You, the teacher can role model high self-esteem
- ☑ Let the students discover, list and share their own strengths
- ☑ Work with their integrity—it builds self-esteem
- ☑ Build a sense of "family" in the classroom
  Work with partners, teams and as a group
  Give a sense of belonging
  Call absent students, send get well cards to sick ones
- ☑ Honor the uniqueness of each student
  Extra attention, birthdays, compliments
- ☑ Listen to each student with your fullest attention
- ☑ Allow students to share about their family, pets, hobbies

☑ Give students more power and control over their life
Let them make decisions regarding the class
Teach them how to deal with criticism more resourcefully
Share with them options for dealing with problems
☑ Celebrate the joys and successes of:
Each individual student, their team, the whole class

In class or out of class, the only things that ultimately matter are relationships. Do what it takes to build relationships early and preserve them. Much of the problem teachers have with students arises from a lack of relationship or a poor relationship. Create an authentic, down-to-earth, honest, and caring relationship with each individual student and base that relationship on mutual respect, love and integrity. Because it's so important, here it is again:

"YOUR SUCCESS IS MORE DEPENDENT ON POSITIVE, CARING, TRUSTWORTHY RELATIONSHIPS THAN ANY OTHER SKILL, IDEA, TIP, TOOL OR TECHNIQUE IN THIS BOOK."

☑ Check These Key Points

1. There are 10 building blocks to establishing rapport between teacher and student, including love yourself, appreciate your students, listen to your students, be open, empower students.
2. Maintain constant rapport by using sensory acuity and then adjusting both verbal and non-verbal communication.
3. Monitor rapport using the three modes of visual, auditory and kinesthetic feedback.
4. For success, students must have a positive attitude about your subject.
5. Teach inter-student relationship skills by using teams.
6. Coach your students to high self-esteem by modeling high self-esteem.

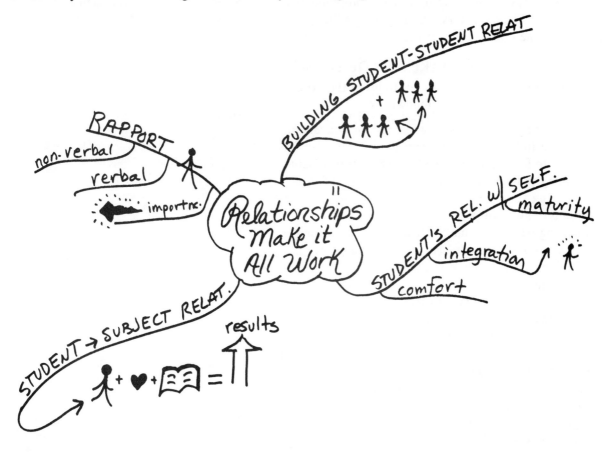

Chapter Twelve

The Lost Art of Listening

Objectives

- To identify types of listening
- To describe empathetic and precision listening
- To list specific ways to clarify communication

Regardless of the effectiveness of your presentation or teaching skills, you may be ineffective as a teacher unless you have strong listening skills. Quality listening is an information-gathering activity that requires commitment to live up to its possibility.

Potentially, listening inspires others, compliments them and has the capacity to enrich and nurture a relationship. The dictionary defines listen as "to hear with thoughtful attention." It also means "fully present with the intention to get the intended meaning of the communication."

DO YOU MAKE ANY OF THESE 20 LISTENING MISTAKES?

There are many more ways not to listen than there are ways to listen. What often occurs in a conversation is one or more of the following:

1. Trying to figure out a way of leaving the conversation
2. Wanting to be a nice polite person
3. Trying to find flaws in the other person's argument for your rebuttal
4. Forming judgements about them
5. Preparing your next statement
6. Trying to avoid or prevent rejection
7. Figuring out how to make the other person wrong
8. Trying to buy time until you have a cute retort
9. Checking your watch or the scenery
10. Pacifying the speaker
11. Thinking of what advice to give
12. Drifting off and daydreaming
13. Listening only to what applies to you
14. Pretending you know what the other person is thinking
15. Continually changing the subject or controlling it
16. Rebutting, arguing, and debating with the speaker
17. Constantly bringing your own story into it
18. Agreeing with the listener
19. Asking questions
20. Providing solutions

148

On the flip side, the only task you have while listening is to understand the speaker's world from his point of view. Receiving, understand and appreciate the communication, then acknowledge that fact by providing feedback to the speaker.

Myth: Listening Is a Natural Skill

Effective listening is a skill you must practice if you are to master speaking and presenting. Listening is a commitment to understand another's reality. It often requires detachment so you can hear without becoming personally engaged.

Unfortunately, our society offers few role models for effective listening. Master teacher Susan Kovalik suggests we actively question media's communication models. For an evening, listen to several television sitcoms. Notice how often the listener communicates with a put-down, then the canned laughter begins. Put-downs are a poor source of humor and should be banned from your classroom. Show a videotape of a typical program and ask your students for an analysis of the communication skills used. Each time a put-down is used, ask the questions:

What was the put-down?

Who laughed?

How did the listener feel?

How would you feel?

Does the put-down add to another's life?

Eventually, how might the listener feel about himself?

Could the speaker have said something funny and still be fair and respectful to the listener?

Myth: That the Speaker Wants a Response

A good listener knows that when the speaker is talking, the subject matter is often of secondary importance. Speaking is an act of personal disclosure and sharing. To the speaker, what's important is himself: needs, feelings, attitudes, observations and opinions. The topic of the conversation is simply a vehicle. Few speakers feel genuinely listened to and as a result, it is a rare honor for them when you are a good listener. To be listened to is to be validated. It says your thoughts, feelings, observations and needs are important to me. As a result, most of the time the speaker simply needs to know that his communication has been fairly and empathetically heard. One's actual response is secondary.

Myth: Either You're Listening or You're Not

Surprisingly, there are many kinds of listening styles. This means that people develop a filter through which messages are processed. Dr. John Geier and Dorothy Downey list six different kinds of listening styles.

1. The **leisure** listener has an acute ear for what pleases him, listens for the non-verbal messages, enjoys the stories, is present in body but often not mind, is seldom intense and listens as if it's a ride at an amusement park.
2. The **inclusive** listener has a wide listening band of interests, relies heavily on the key idea, is widely accepting, at times even gullible, and notices non-verbal messages well.
3. The **stylistic** listener evaluates the message by the medium, is fully tuned to the physical presentation of the speaker, watches for non-verbal messages, evaluates speakers for credentials, listens for style and flair, or gets bored.
4. The **technical** listener listens to those who have a track record or who are qualified to use up precious listening time. He is interested mostly in how and why something works, has a narrow listening band and is often a detached and unemotional listener.
5. The **empathetic** listener listens for the emotional state of the talker, detects voice fluctuations, tempo, tonality, etc., is sensitive to physical touch, and often becomes part of the drama of the conversations.

6. The **non-conforming** listener is most attentive to information which directly affects him, has a narrow band of listening interests, is excellent at sniffing out the story behind the story.

Did you identify yourself with a particular style? If so, you are "receiving" on only one "band" of a radio station. To be more effective, you'll need to learn which is your own style, then learn how to become a better listener by using the style that is most appropriate to the situation.

How to Listen Successfully

Quite simply, there are two important listening styles for teachers. One of them is empathetic listening which is a response to emotionally-loaded speaking and the other is precision listening, which is a response to content-oriented conversations. In both of them your outcome is discovery—you need to allow the speaker to become more visible with empathetic listening and to have the content become more clear in the precision listening mode. What works consistently is knowing which one to use and using it effectively.

Groundwork: How to Foster a Listening Environment

The pre-requisite for any tape of effective listening is the fostering of a safe listening environment in your classroom. The first condition is trust. Only after you have demonstrated consistently that your students can trust your responses and openness, will they feel safe and willing to take risks in seeking. To increase class trust among students, teach "respond with respect". More than teaching it, embody it. Never, ever put a student down, EVEN AS A JOKE. Never, ever be sarcastic to a student or belittle the remark. You must set the tone of love, safety and respect in the classroom.

If one of your students make a habit of responding with "put-downs", use a nonverbal signal as an alert. It may be some theatrical sign such as a line drawn across the throat with the wave of the finger. This signals an inappropriate response and requires a respectful one. With increased feedback, the quality of classroom communication will improve.

In addition, each person must agree that active listening requires commitment to the "work" of listening. This means more than silently pointing eyes and ears toward the speaker. To fully receive another's communication, give your fullest attention to the speaker. Actively hear all of what is being said. Be willing to ask questions if anything's unclear.

Your own mood is important to monitor as a way of preparing the listening environment. Before you put yourself in the position of listening, ask "What am I feeling right now?" If there's an unexpressed emotion inside you, it may create a distorting filter for the message. As an angry person, you hear differently than if you just won the lottery. Find a way to set aside your feelings so you can go about listening without the added filter.

Listening also requires a certain amount of clarity of intention. Do you need to be in a closer place to hear better? Are you willing to say, "I'm sorry, I didn't get that. Would you repeat it please?" Being ready to listen means that you are in a receptive state, committed to listening, and clear that you are ready to discover, not preach. The first of the two listening types is the empathetic style.

Empathetic Listening

This may be the most important listening style. It's for those moments when a student uses emotionally loaded speaking. Whenever you detect any emotion out of the ordinary from a speaking student, use this style. It is for the following circumstances:

When a student is:

1. Angry, frustrated or upset
2. Hurt, saddened or worried
3. Jealous, bitter or sarcastic

4. Excited, happy or enthused
5. Hopeful, uncertain or tense

Empathetic listening engages the listener very little in terms of auditory responses. It does engage the listener in the act of being right there in the shoes of the speaker. It's a way of listening that asks the listener to simply "be there" in partnership as a best friend. It is appropriate to listen this way when another would like to speak about something emotional. For example, "I am so sad . . . my best friend was hurt and is in the hospital." Your response would be "Oh . . . I'm so sorry . . . (or maybe: "It sounds like it's painful for you, too.") This style of listening goes after the speaker and tries to make the speaker more visible, not the content. Notice the listener did not say, "Which hospital" or "when are visiting hours?" For empathetic listening, here is the way to approach it with success:

1. Listen for the feelings behind the message.
2. Let the speaker know you are listening and care.
3. Avoid interruptions or lengthy comments
4. Listen for the relationships in the speaker's world
5. Be an "invisible" listener—make the speaker visible

Listen in silence with full attention on the speaker. Listen with an ear for the relationship of what they say to their own lives, not yours. Most listeners are so "into" their own world, they rarely experience the speaker's world. Untrained communicators have only one mode of communication—that of relating the message in terms of their own lives. Resist that temptation and listen to the speaker as if you were in his or her shoes living the experience yourself. Only then can you truly be empathetic.

The Indians were famous for the expression "To walk a mile in another's moccasins." It is difficult to over-emphasize the importance of learning to get the message from the speaker's point of view—his experiences, feelings and meaning. Yes, you may have your own point of view which filters the message, but to the extent that you can let it go and enter what's actually going on in the other's life at the time, you can better understand the message.

Listen with respect. Every person who communicates has a message to give you. They do not always know what their message is, and they do not always communicate their message well to you. But their communication to you is their way of including you in their world. In some way, the fact that you are there at the moment is a real blessing—to both of you.

Listen to what's not being said. Various percentages are bandied about from 50–90%, regarding the amount of communication which is non-verbal. As a listener, you can be assured that it is the majority of the message. The non-verbal is often the best clue to the full message—it will reveal things about the speaker that the voice will not.

Listen for feelings and voice changes. As valuable as the content of the message may be, learn to tune into the feelings of the sender. Often feelings are a more accurate clue to the meaning than the words. Emotions are not easily hidden and there are many ways to spot them. One of the clues that ranges from very subtle to very obvious in detecting emotions is voice. As children, we became very in tune with the differences in our parents' voices. There are obvious ranges of volume, but the most useful ones in listening for emotions are the cracking of the voice, the drop in energy level, and changing in tone—each of which may be a signal that an emotion has been triggered in the speaker.

Recover the generalization and deletion. What isn't said can be as important as what is said. Three ways to listen for what isn't said are generalization, deletion, and distortion. Speakers often generalize: this statement itself is a generalization. A typical generalization is making a blanket statement based upon a single incident. For example, after one upsetting incident at school, a student says, "School is stupid". A deletion is information left out so you get an inaccurate picture. Let's say that a student was doing well in a class until his last exam. Upon receiving a lower than normal grade, he might say: "I'm doing lousy in this class." The deletion was that all other times he was successful. In addition, he deleted his observations, needs and feelings.

Distortion is a change in the meaning of the information. For example, let's say a student is doing well in a class and the teacher makes a supportive comment. The student's distortion might be: "You are just saying that to be nice. I'll bet you say that to everyone." The student took the message and distorted the meaning to have it fit the meaning he wanted.

Listen for other messages. If we listen carefully, we can find that a speaker often has a strong bias in one direction or another. For example, if a speaker is continually saying what an awful job another teacher is doing, you may suspect some ulterior motives. If you hear a teacher complain about a fellow teacher, you may want to reply with, "I'm sorry to hear you're not happy with him (or her)."

Avoid These Listening Mistakes

A common listener reaction is to divert attention from the speaker or topic. This is frustrating to the speaker because it prevents him from truly being heard. The three most common mistakes of poor listeners are offering similar stories, solutions or taking the message personally.

Similar stories mean that you hear what is being said just long enough to think of one to tell back, a similar experience which happened to you. If the speaker is sharing about his troubles, DON'T jump in and try to make him feel better by telling about your own troubles. This tactic shifts the attention from the speaker to you, the listener. It doesn't allow the speaker to feel heard and understood.

Most people don't like to "be fixed." This means there's no need to start a "Dear Abby" in your mind where you are trying to fix, advise or correct the supposed ills of the speaker. If the speaker wants to know about your troubles, wait until you have given justice to his sharing. Just relax and be an empathetic and caring listener, giving the other the same attention and respect you'd like when you are speaking.

"Solution listening" means that you listen just long enough to discover the "problem" and then give advice on how to solve it. The mistake is in shifting the attention from the speaker to the problem. When a speaker shares his troubles, just listen. Do not offer solutions unless you are asked. Offering a solution shifts the attention from the speaker to the issue and at this stage of the conversation, the focus should be on the speaker.

The only thing you have
to justify an extraordinary commitment
to your students
is your integrity

The third mistake is engagement, taking a message personally. Receive the communication with disengagement. It is a rare speaker who can deliver a message from a perspective other than his own. Each message is colored by a lifetime of values, perceptions and personal experiences. For example, a student may say to you, "I don't like this class. You like the other students more than me." In fact, the student is really saying, "I don't experience feeling special, having self-worth or well-being in this class. I feel inadequate to other students and would at least like some more attention and recognition in class."

The only way to find out for sure is to ask. But the important thing is to detach yourself from the meaning and effect on yourself and focus on the meaning of the message to the speaker. This means do not start defending how you think your class is not awful after all, because that's not productive. One of the best analogies about remaining detached comes from author Stewart Emery:

"Most of the time we are no more than extras in other people's soap operas, in the scripting of which we had no part. They are simply using us so that they can continue with the production of the soap opera of their lives . . . anyone else in their life would have been given the same role. . . ."

Often, we are so busy reacting personally to a communication that we become entangled. Learn to listen without emotional involvement. Remember that compliments and criticisms reflect the tastes, values and attitudes of the speaker and probably have nothing to do with the listener.

Listen with easiness. This skill is contrasted to "listening on edge," where the listener is constantly ready to respond, either verbally or mentally. To listen at ease means to give the speaker "permission" to simply speak. It means that you don't need to placate the speaker by constantly saying, "I know what you mean . . . you're right as always." It does mean you can respond appropriately . . . "Hmmm . . . Yes . . . You bet. . . ." To listen at ease also means to accept what the speaker is saying without making judgments.

Your objective is usually to make the speaker more "visible," more complete in his sharing. Since much of a speaker's world is often masked, this tools serves to recover lost or deleted information. It is your role as listener to use the clarifying tools only as they are necessary to complete the communication.

To be a good listener means to stay out of the boxing ring and courtroom. The boxing ring occurs when the listener is constantly sparring with the speaker, either verbally or mentally. You may have met a person who constantly interrupts or argues with you, continually missing the meaning of the communication. Your comment might be: "Whew, it's hot. It must be over 90 today!" So the 'boxer' jumps in and says "Yeah? My uncle said it was only 86 at noontime!" That's an example of a chronic "communication boxer" who has no intention or commitment to get the meaning of the communication, but rather simply wants to fight.

Suppose a student says "I didn't do my homework because there's no place to study in my house." You could listen with the reaction of "That's just an excuse," or "Why don't you create a better place to study?" But to actually enter the student's reality would be to listen carefully to find out more of what's going on. And know that the student is making the best decision for the choices available to him at the moment. In other words, if the student avoids doing homework, it's not because the student is lazy or stupid. This doesn't mean that the act is justifiable—just that students are only going to do what they feel their best choice is, not what your best choice is for them.

PRECISION

ACTIVE

EMPATHY

For example, a student may say: "I feel like everyone in class is doing better than I." If you jump in and say, "No, that's not true. You did better than a third of the class on the last test," you have missed their communication. What the speaker is saying is that he is dissatisfied with his academic performance. He wants to be heard. Other conclusions you might draw from his statement are all your own opinions and should be checked out with the speaker.

Pay attention to body language and calibrate it! It's common to read gross generalizations about the meaning of body language. For example, "when your legs are uncrossed while sitting, you indicate openness." But, many times legs are crossed merely to rest one leg or foot. Below are some of the common gestures and the most commonly given explanations for them. You may feel discomfort knowing, after consulting several experts in the field of communication, that the explanations which emerged were often contradictory:

- Legs uncrossed—openness/receptiveness/macho/cool
- Scratch head—puzzled/nervous/impatient
- Tug on the ear—ready to interrupt/lending an ear
- Touch their nose or jawbone—doubt/contemplation
- Open extended palms—to explain/a generous offer/openness/disbelief
- Hands on lips—impatience/silence/deep thought
- Hands on knees, leaning forward—readiness/stretching/attention
- Clenched fist—power/anger/control
- Hands in pockets—hiding meaning/relaxed/cold atmosphere
- Shrugged shoulders—uncertainty/negative/tight neck
- Hands clasped behind back—authority/humility/service
- Looking downward—deep in thought/bored/feeling emotions
- Steepled fingers—confidence/boredom/scheming/a barrier

- Holding up objects—reaching out/hostility/distance
- Closed palms on the chest—struck by a thought/honesty/defensive
- Clasp both hands—grief/anticipation/confidence
- Eye contact—interest/anger/boredom/distrust

Use all of your sensory acuity skills to listen. Pick up on a flush in the face or the neck, or a dilation of pupils. It could be the texture of the skin changes, as in getting "goosebumps." The ear, nose, throat, hands or legs may twitch as a response to an emotion filling the body. An obvious visual clue is tears, which could actually be signalling sadness, anger, relief, frustration, or joy. The eyes may have an increased blink rate or twitch when the speaker moves into either highly emotional messages or they are re-living an experience, or even lying about it. The eyes may also squint when the intensity of the message goes up. The mouth gives excellent messages because it is also delivering the content. Watch for tightened lips, narrowed jaws, frowns, smiles, held-back laughs or lifted lips. An astute observer will also notice the breathing rate of the speaker. As the breathing rate quickens, you may guess the speaker is experiencing some anxiety, excitement, or other stimulating emotion.

The key to reading body language anytime is calibration. Observe, then check it out. Avoid assumptions, find out with questions—Avoid rules about what certain gestures or physiologies mean. Try something, check it out. Calibrate, calibrate calibrate.

Precision Listening

This is for information gathering. It engages the listener fully into the conversation. The listener asks questions such as "How specifically" or "who specifically" or "exactly when did you plan to do that?" It's a style of listening that goes after the content of the material to make the subject content more exposed and visible. It makes the content more real by engaging the speaker in defining the content and eliciting promises regarding what to do about what was said. For example: "Boy, am I in trouble; I'm flunking geometry." The listener would ask, "You mean you did poorly on the last test or you are likely to get an F in the class?" Then, once more information was elicited, the listener might ask questions such as "Well, what do you plan to do about it? When will you start?"

It is for the time when the emotions are calm and the content is the most important matter at hand. In this case, it's important to make the content more visible so that misunderstandings are reduced. Precision listening is really listening with a commitment to understand "and resolve" what the speaker is saying. It means that you become actively engaged in drawing out the details of the content in a way that insures you understand what the speaker is saying. The steps to follow are:

1. Listen fully without interrupting
2. Give feedback to the speaker on what was said
3. Ask for relevant details
4. Clarify, challenge, appreciate and respect elicit requests and promises retrieve deleted information
5. Ask if there's a next step to do

To make precision listening work, assist the speaker when necessary. Many speakers haven't the slightest idea what they really want to say—they talk around the subject or with it, but not directly to it. They mask or exaggerate their fears and often present to you an image of who they think you want to hear. For you to read through all of their distortions, deletions, and generalizations takes a real desire to get the intention and a willingness to respectfully question the obvious. Many speakers omit the obvious and it's your job to get the message as best as you can. Give speakers as much opportunity as possible to deliver the meaning without putting words in their mouth.

While precision listening is an active, challenging role, keep this in mind: It is unfair to others and is counterproductive to constantly monitor or challenge another's communications. If you do feel puzzled, unclear, or something doesn't sound right then ask for a clarification, but always with respect and politeness. You are doing both yourself and the other a real favor when you use these tools politely, as they are intended.

Understanding is important, so paraphrase if necessary. Re-state in your own words what you think someone just said. It is not repeating the exact same words like a pet shop parrot, but rather what you translate them into. Listen carefully to what has been said, then use the words and phrases you are comfortable with and restate as best you can the same statement. When you paraphrase correctly, you show that you really understood what was said and the speaker gets the real sense that you were 'with' him. Here's an example of paraphrasing:

Speaker—"This has been one of the longest weeks I've ever had in school." Listener—"Sounds like you've been through the wars, David."

Here's an example of how *NOT* to paraphrase.

This upcoming example is called parroting. It's a case of the listener being a tape recorder instead of a compassionate and empathetic human being.

Speaker—"I'm real happy with the score I just got on my test."
Listener—"So you're real happy with the score you just got on your test, huh?"

Complete communication provides the listener with "whole" information. It includes feelings, needs, thoughts and observations. When the listener gets incomplete communications, the mind has a tendency to "fill in" the missing information. And that can lead to inaccurate conclusions. Here's an example:

Speaker: "My notebook was stolen—I can't believe someone would do that!" (included an observation and a thought; it lacked a feeling and a need)
Listener: "Sounds like you're really upset . . . I'm sorry it happened. Do you need some help with your notes?" (listener tries to fill in missing items; the feeling and the need).
Speaker: "I'm so sad." (feeling expressed, what's missing is thoughts, needs and observation)
Listener. "I can tell it's really brought you down. Tell me what else has been going on. . . ." (listener asks for deleted information)

If you would like to encourage trust, safety and student rapport, make sure that you always acknowledge and appreciate the speaker for sharing. Say with sincerity, "Thank you for sharing that with me . . ." Or, "I really appreciate you being willing to share that with me—I feel honored and privileged." Or, in another example, you might say, "Thank you for letting me know that; it must have taken a lot of courage to share it with me." Notice that in each of the examples abouve the listener always acknowledges that he received the communication before addressing any of the issues.

One other thing—you may want to add something that lets the speaker know that you understood the essence of what was said. For example, "It sounds as if you've had a rough day. I sure hope things get better for you. Thanks for sharing that with me." There was a re-statement of what was understood as well as an acknowledgement.

Clarify if unclear. Most of what is understood is different from what is sent and we have become accustomed to living with the chaotic results. In order to communicate more successfully, you must train yourself to become more precise and insist on reciprocal clarity from the speaker. As you might guess, some tact is required to do it successfully. And when you ask for clarification, first acknowledge the speaker.

How do you clarify foggy conversations? By asking the right questions! Ask such questions as: Who specifically, what specifically, and how specifically. Clarify statements by asking, compared to what?, all?, every?, none?, never?, always? You can also ask, what would happen if . . . or would it be possible to. . . ? And since not everyone is ecstatic about having their communications dissected, you may want to soften up some of your clarifiers. Use phrases such as . . . "I'm wondering what specifically you mean by. . . ." Or, "I'm curious whether. . . ." "Here's an idea, tell me what you think. . . ." In each of the examples below, you'll note a student comment and a way for the teacher to clarify the question and stay in rapport with him or her.

Clarifications

Student—"I don't understand this."
Teacher—"I'm sorry I wasn't more clear for you. What specifically don't you understand?"

Student—"I don't want to do it."
Teacher—"I appreciate your telling me. Exactly what is it you don't want to do?"

Student—"I'll bring it by later."
Teacher—"Thanks for the offer. What time were you thinking of?

Generalizations Corrected

Student—"Geography is a pain in the neck."
Teacher—"I'm sorry it's not more fun for you. Specifically which part of it is tough?"

Student—"Teachers are really supportive here."
Teacher—"I appreciate your telling me. Which ones come to mind?"

Student—"Everybody knows it's a big waste."
Teacher—"Thanks for sharing that with me. Whom are you referring to specifically? And what do you mean by a waste?"

Unspecified Nouns, Pronouns and Verbs Exposed

Student: "I'm ecstatic."
Teacher: "That's great; tell me more."

Student: "He ripped me off."
Teacher: "What a bummer! Exactly what happened?"

Student—"I feel scared."
Teacher—"I appreciate your sharing that. What is it that you feel scared about?"

Limits Clarified and Exposed

Student—"I couldn't tell you that."
Teacher—"I appreciate your honesty. Have you thought about what would happen if you did?"

Student—"I can't do this."
Teacher—"Sounds like something's in the way. Could you imagine what would happen if you did?"

Student—"I have to be this way."
Teacher—"I respect your choice. You must have had a good reason for saying that. I was wondering what would happen if you changed it?"

Absolutes Exposed

Student—"I can never do anything right."
Teacher—"Thanks for telling me. What you said is possible, but can you think of a time when you did do one thing right?"

Student—"Nothing good ever happens to me."
Teacher—"Sounds like you're pretty down right now. Can you think of something good that you'd like to have happen today?"

Imposed Values Made Evident

Student: "Assignments are a waste."
Teacher: "I'm sorry. Is there any way I could make them more meaningful for you?"

Lost Performatives Retrieved

Student—"It's not good to keep us late."
Teacher—"I appreciate you keeping track of it. Whom do you think it's not good for?"

Student—"It's rude to say that."
Teacher—"I appreciate your sharing your thoughts. It's rude to say what, according to whom?"

Student—"That's a waste of time."
Teacher—"Sounds like you are frustrated or bummed. Anything you can do to make it worth your time?"

Distortions Challenged

Student—"I know you won't accept this paper."
Teacher—"You sound hesitant to turn it in . . . could I ask why?"

Student—"He should know better than to say that to me."
Teacher—"I respect your opinion. How would you guess he'd know?"

Distortions Clarified

Teacher: "You drive me crazy!"
Student: "I'm sorry. What specifically have I done, that you chose to get irritated about?"
Student: "If David hadn't had to go early, I would have had my assignment."
Teacher: "It sounds like you felt things were out of your control. How, specifically, did you put yourself in a position where David had control over your assignment?"

Next, discover if there are any additional steps to take. Most of the time, the listener is sharing more about himself than the issue or topic of the conversation. As soon as the sharing and disclosure is complete, the speaker usually is satisfied. Sometimes, he just had something to "get off his chest." In other cases, there's a legitimate interest in the topic. As a listener, you must check it out. The most appropriate action for the listener is to ask the speaker if there is anything that can be done. If, and only if, the speaker gives you permission, should you shift from being a listener of a real human being to a problem-solver.

Finally, acknowledge the communication and the speaker. The speaker deserves to know if you understand what is being said and if you can empathize with the sharing. There are two issues for the speaker: the primary one is self. He wants to feel listened to and to be worth paying attention to. The secondary issue is whether or not the meaning was understood.

Student—"I can't do anything right."
Teacher—"I appreciate your point of view, and it must be frustrating for you. I'd love for you to succeed. Would you like some additional choices?"

Student—"Geography is a pain in the neck."
Teacher—"Thanks for letting me know. I wish it was easier for you. You are important to me . . . can I assist you with any area of it in particular?"

Student—"I didn't get the assignment."
Teacher—"I'm glad you checked with me—it shows me you care about how you are doing. This assignment is important, here it is. . . ."

The key to empowering your speaker is simple: meet the speaker where he is "at". Accept his reality as true for him (it is!), then allow him to see, hear or feel his own inner beauty. Find a gift in every problem, a jewel in every situation and appreciate something sincerely about that person, regardless of what was discussed. You will excite, inspire and motivate your students and they will love it, too. Can you imagine how much more willing your students would be to communicate if you responded this way? Your students will feel so appreciated and noticed that their interest and motivation will go up dramatically. Wouldn't it be worth it to try?

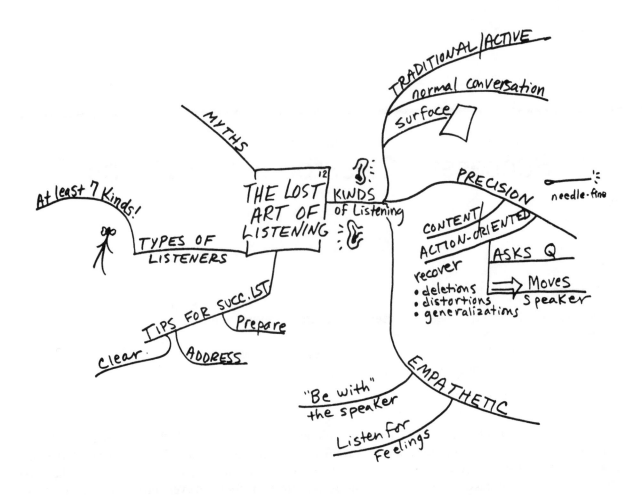

The Lost Art of Listening

12

- MYTHS
- TYPES OF LISTENERS
  - At least 7 kinds!
- TIPS FOR SUCC. LST
  - Prepare
  - ADDRESS
  - clear
- KINDS of Listening
  - TRADITIONAL / ACTIVE
    - normal conversation
    - surface
  - PRECISION
    - needle-fine
    - CONTENT / ACTION-ORIENTED
      - ASKS Q
      - Moves Speaker
      - recover
        - deletions
        - distortions
        - generalizations
  - EMPATHETIC
    - "Be with" the speaker
    - Listen for feelings

☑ **Check These Key Points**

1. Quality listening is an information gathering activity.
2. There are 6 types of listening styles: leisure, inclusive, stylistic, technical, empathetic, and non-conforming.
3. A pre-requisite to effective listening is a safe listening environment.
4. Empathetic listening asks the listener to "walk a mile in another's shoes"
5. For empathetic listening, hear the feelings behind the words, let the speaker know you care, avoid interrupting, listen for relationships in the listener's world, be an "invisible" listener.
6. Three common listening "mistakes" are: offering similar stories, solutions, or taking the message personally.
7. Precision listening engages the listener in drawing out the details of the content in a way that ensures you understand what is being said.
8. For clarity of communication ask "how?", "who?", "when?", "compared to what or whom?".
9. Acknowledge the speaker. Let him/her know you heard the communication and understand.

Chapter Thirteen
Successful Classroom Interactions

Objectives

- To identify key qualities of successful classroom interactions
- To specify pre-speaking steps
- To provide a framework for asking and answering questions
- To define a successful interaction

One of the most subtle parts of a teacher's job, and the part for which the teacher is usually the least trained is student-teacher interactions. Specifically, the moments when the teacher is talking one-on-one with a student. Those times could include when a student asks questions, when the teacher asks questions, inquiries, discussions, when ideas and feelings are expressed and even during the pre- and post-class interactions. All of these times can have a major impact on students' lives, and, often have more impact than the actual class itself.

It may not surprise you to know that classroom interactions can be some of the primary events in a person's life. Many students have made paralyzing or resourceful life decisions as a conclusion about, and in the aftermath of, classroom interactions. Many students will say things such as: "Oh, I could never do that. I don't have the talent." (Maybe in fourth grade a teacher said as much.) Or, "I was thinking about becoming an attorney." (Her tenth grade teacher may have said she had an aptitude for business, legal and communication work). When was the last time you heard a student talk about a lecture heard a year ago? They don't talk about lectures—or even classroom activities as much as they do about those moments of one-to-one interactions. Does each and every single interaction matter? Poet Hugh Prather says, "Are there any wholly useless encounters? I know this: there are no insignificant people. . . ." And yes, there are myths surrounding class interactions.

Myth: Interactions Are Not a Significant Part of the Class

The first erroneous assumption that arises out of this topic is the one that says momentary interactions, some of them merely seconds long, are not a critical part of the class. Some teachers don't encourage or even allow for questions or interactions. Yet it's been said that "we are all therapists, whether we know it or not." In other words, with each and every interaction, there is an opportunity to heal or damage. There is no middle ground—you cannot leave your students feeling neutral after an interaction because it's human nature to draw conclusions. Every interaction is initiated with the intention of accomplishing a result and of reaching an outcome. The outcome is important, but so is the vehicle for that outcome. When a student asks a question, he or she will either feel good for asking it or he or she will not.

Myth: The Key to Interaction Is the Answer

For example, if you say, "Who knows the answer to that question?" An erroneous assumption is that the answer is the most important part of the interaction. There are two items as important as the answer to the question: the process and the context. Process means how the student arrived at the answer, the way in which the question is asked and the way in which the teacher responds or acknowledges. Context means the circumstances surrounding the asking of the question. If you ask the question with an intention to empower and support, you will come across in a different way than if you ask the question to determine who has the correct answer.

Myth: Successful Interactions Are Just Common Sense

Unfortunately the meaning of the phrase 'common sense' is very different depending on who you talk to about it. Interactions that leave students and teachers feeling better, more knowledgeable and more resourceful are the result of being wide awake and clear on your outcomes as well as the result of having behavioral flexibility and sensory acuity. You've got to know what you want, know how to get it and know when you have achieved it.

Key Qualities

Successful interactions have three qualities. First, each person emerges as more resourceful. There are gains in self-confidence, knowledge, love, joy and well-being. Second, both people must get the outcome desired from the interaction. And third, they must each experience a sense of completion and closure. Successful interactions are not accidents. They are a result of your creation of classroom conditions which make it safe and worthwhile for students to interact openly with their teachers.

If your students don't participate, share, or ask questions, you can be sure that it's not that they have nothing to say. Classes naturally generate lots of questions and responses. Expression is a natural human trait and it is the unnatural circumstance which suppresses it. Here's how a classroom atmosphere can be created that encourages interaction and at the same time, structures it into appropriate formats:

1. The creation of class agreements for interactions—such as others must remain quiet while another is speaking. Encourage students to share from their own experiences or creations instead of telling others how "the world is." This allows students to learn to validate, honor and respect themselves as well as their thoughts and feelings because the teacher is placing a priority on what the sudent says, not what some textbook says. Of course this also means that an answer that the student came up with, or figured out is perfect for sharing, too.
2. Be sure to allow sufficient time for interactions, for they are a key part of the learning process. Class allotments may vary from as little as 10% of class time to as much as 80%, depending on the nature and circumstances of the course. If the teacher rushes them, students will withdraw from contributing.
3. Teachers need to share their own attitudes and thoughts about interactions. For example, students might be told that questions are appreciated and that it's safe to ask them. Tell them that you always support them, and you will not use interactions as a way to make them wrong or to pick on them. Let your students know that their questions don't have to be the 'question of the year' to be worthy to ask, and that it's better to ask it than to let it go unanswered. You also can open up sharing by self-disclosure.

You may not need to do this formally, though it's likely that some kind of initial discussion about class interactions would be useful. You are the one who creates the openness and the circumstances which can make successful interactions possible. It's not the students, the administration, or the outside world. You have the power and the ability to make your classroom perfectly safe and at the same time, a powerful learning experience.

First of all, develop a systematic procedure for scanning the room for raised hands, whether it's going row by row or section by section. One of the most frustrating experiences for students is to have something well up inside of such importance that he is willing to risk sharing it with the group, only to have a teacher miss his hand up in the air. Again, it's easy to blame the student who doesn't raise her hand high enough or wave it around, but the blaming doesn't serve you as a master teacher. Look, see, notice, scour, perceive and search the room constantly for cues that a student is ready to share something. Your students will give you non-verbal clues more readily than the verbal ones. But you have got to begin to notice the raised eyebrow, the shift in posture or breathing. For some students, it's very invalidating not to be recognized. In additon, to make it easier, you may want to set up some simple courtesy guidelines for listener behavior such as eyes on the speaker.

The next step to take is to move further from the person who is ready to ask the question. This makes him or her speak up and it includes the rest of the students in the interaction. Make eye contact, and before you indicate that it is time for them to speak, check your physiology. When you have students raising hands, ready to be recognized, it's a signal for you to shift your whole physiology into another role. You have a presenter role in which your body language, your tone, tempo and physiology is strong— you are putting out a lot of energy. But the moment that a student wants to contribute, share, or ask, you must make a shift internally from a visual mode to an auditory or kinesthetic mode. It's a softer, more receptive and open internal state.

Is it possible that you look bored, hostile, aggressive or close-minded? The proper physiology is the one that gives the message to the student, "I'm interested in you, your question, your well-being, and I respect you." This means an erect but not rigid posture, full face-to-face attention, with shoulders facing the student. It means both hands at your side or clasped behind you. Your physiology will be your key

to effective communications. Anytime your communications seem to be off, check your physiology. Then, indicate with a nod of the head or eye contact or with a motion of your hand that it is time for the student to speak. Instead of pointing, gesture towards the student with an open hand, palm up. This is usually accepted by questioners as less confronting and intimidating, thereby making them feel that their comments are more likely to be welcomed in the future.

How to Receive Questions Properly

So far, we have mentioned several pre-speaking steps for you to take: (1) keep your eyes open for signs of a question or comment (2) check your physiology before you recognize the speaker to speak (3) indicate with an outstretched arm and open palm gesture that it's appropriate to speak.

Next, make sure the speaker has the attention of the class before beginning. If not, have him wait a moment until the rest of the class is ready. Be sure each person has heard the question. If necessary, have it repeated. Be sure you ask in a tone that lets the class know that the question is worth hearing. For example, "John, that question is important, and I want everyone to hear it. Will you please repeat it?" Avoid blaming the class. Rapport is lost by stating, "The class was being rude, please ask the question again, John."

At this point, you might use your body to continue to regulate the volume of the question-asker. Be sure you move to the opposite side of the room to listen. This encourages them to speak up so others can hear and it puts enough space between you and them to include the rest of the audience. Also, make sure the speaker faces most of the class. If the speaker is up front, have him face the class. If he is on the side of the room, adjust the speaker's direction so he reaches the other students.

Or, you might use your hands as a movie director, raising them from a low to a high point to indicate that you wish the speaker to raise the volume. Of course, you can also cup your ear or lean towards the speaker to indicate your need for greater volume. Stay in rapport with the speaker, being ready to match tonality, tempo, volume, gestures, posture and breathing.

If you need responses such as to a question, outstretch your arms with open palms up and wait. If someone is talking, asking or sharing, be sure to thank and acknowledge them every single time. It's a way of creating more student respect and reinforcing the contribution.

Surprisingly, there are three instances during which you might interrupt. Ordinarily you'd let the response remain intact without corrections, changes or interruptions. The three exceptions are: (1) if it is extremely unclear, or dragging on when the attention of the class has disappeared, (2) if the question contains an initial premise which, as stated, makes the rest of the question invalid or inappropriate to answer, or (3) if the comment contains any damaging, profane, critical or hostile parts which you cannot, in good conscience, leave uncorrected. If you need to interrupt, do so respectfully, let the speaker know why and then have him continue.

While the question is being asked, quiet your mind. There's a tendency to do one of two things, neither of which is useful. First, one might 'check out', daydreaming in another world, not at all tuned into the question. Second, the opposite may occur. You might be overly engaged and reactive to the question so that while it is being asked, you are thinking of the answer, how to win, be right, dominate, or get control of the person. Let the student complete the question without being corrected for errors that don't affect the essence of the question. If the student asks a question to which your response is anger, pause for a moment, allow yourself to relax and get centered before answering.

Your students are more interested
in how much you care
than how much you know

How to Prepare to Answer Questions

It's important to give the framework in which you are able to answer or not answer. Here are some choices to make before you actually respond to the question:

1. Let the rest of the class know if the question is extra-important or critical to their success. It can serve as an attention getter.
2. Let the speaker know if you do not know the answer. Don't make it up, rather instead let the person know how to get the answer, when you will have the answer or how you both might come up with the answer.
3. If it's appropriate to not answer, there are several choices: invite the person to "stay with" the question and explore the nature of the question instead of giving a pat answer. Another possibility is that it's not the time to answer the question in which you should acknowledge the speaker for asking it and let him know that you can answer more fully at a later time.

Your Actual Response to the Question

First, acknowledge the student. It's a risk to be thought of as wrong, stupid or inadequate for asking a question. One of the biggest reasons students don't ask more questions in class is most have been embarrassed at one time or another. Reinforce the student by giving acknowledgement for asking the question or for asking a certain type of question. You might say, "Thanks for asking, Joe. The answer is . . .", or, "I'm glad you brought that up, Joe. . .". You may simply answer the question, thanking the student for asking. Once you've acknowledged the speaker, you have additional options. You might ask the speaker if he knows the answer to his own question. For example:

Student: "What's the real cause of a recession?"
Teacher: "I like your question, thanks for asking it. I suspect it's related to interest rates and a drop in the overseas value of the dollar. What are your thoughts?"

Notice that you have opened up the possibility that the student may already know the answer. It's a form of acknowledging the awareness and reservoir of information we all have. Another possibility is to turn to the group and ask, "Who would like to offer some possible answers to that question?" Here you'd be using the question as a way to empower others.

Here are a few additional suggestions for answering questions. Respect the student and the question. This means avoid jokes about it or making light of either the question or the student. Those can be trauma-inducing actions and thus dangerous. Stay with the sincerity and intent of the question. Avoid judgments about what the students should have known, studied or about the quality of the question. Use the student's name when responding. For example, "Good quality question, Johnny. I like questions that deal with central core issues."

An excellent way to encourage future questions is to make sure that the answer you give is brief. First, give the big picture overview, then the specifics. Students get turned off by long-winded answers. They're often boring and it takes the focus off the question putting attention on the teacher's answer. That's not the way to build rapport with students, nor is it a useful strategy for recognition of the student's contribution.

Also, be sure to respect the thinking style of your asker. The way some students learn is by mixing and contrasting. If you ask, "Why is the ocean blue?", you may have a student who says, "All oceans are not blue. What about the Red Sea?" Respect each person's style of thinking. The way some students learn best is to find exceptions to the rule. They are not being negative or sarcastic. Others, of course, will do the opposite. If you ask, "How are these cars different?", you may have a student who says, "They're not, they're practically the same." It's quite possible that each student learns best by matching and comparing. As you discover the thinking style of others, you stay in rapport with them and reach your outcome easier.

Finally, make sure that you create and continue the element of rapport in the conversation. Match predicates, adjectives and adverbs if mentioned in the conversation. It gains rapport and creates better communication. For example, a student might say: "I see what you're saying, but I have what I think is a good question. . ." To match it, use the same key words: "Johnny, you're right, that is a good question. Notice that the answer can be clearly seen from the perspective of. . ." (matching the descriptive words good and good, plus matching the visually-oriented words "see" with "notice, seen and clearly").

How to Respond to Hostile Questions

One of the primary jobs of a teacher is to maintain constant rapport with your students. When you get a hostile question, it is because the rapport has been broken. The moment you hear a hostile question, relax, "center" yourself, and re-establish rapport. Then discover the student's needs and do whatever necessary to re-create a new alliance.

One easy way to gain rapport is with non-verbal matching of physiology. If students are sitting, lower your eye level by leaning against a desk or sitting on it momentarily.

For verbal matching, listen to the content of the student's comments. Ask yourself what is going on in the student's world to cause such action. What does the student believe in order to ask that particular question? Place yourself in the student's shoes to understand it from his point of view. Listen for predicates such as "I feel that. . ." or "I hear that. . ." or "The way I see it. . ." Match the predicate in your answer. Match the tonality, tempo, and volume. If a student is aggressive, your response could be aggressive at first, leading to a softer more receptive way of speaking.

Open your response with one of these three rapport-builders, "I appreciate. . ." or "I agree. . ." or "I respect. . ." Complete the sentence as you and the student move towards co-creating a mutually satisfying solution. As an example:

STUDENT: "You don't know what you are talking about. This is really stupid!
TEACHER: "I agree it's possible I might not know what I'm talking about. But maybe you could help me out a little. What doesn't make any sense to you and what are some things we could do about it?

Listen, empathize and respect their point of view. Repeat back to them what you think their point is, so they know they have been understood. Always handle an irritated participant completely so that the rest of the group can relax and move on with the day. Even if you need more time with them later, ask for an appointment with the upset person from the front of the room so that they know you care and are willing to work things out. Never leave someone upset, hurt or brooding in your audience. Never, ever make fun of anyone except yourself from the front of the room. Never embarrass others or you risk shutting down the rest of the group and reducing their likely contributions.

When You Ask Questions

Check your intention when you ask questions of others. There are lots of reasons, purposes and potential outcomes and it's critical to have clarity on your intended outcome. An optimal outcome for each question that you ask is to empower the student who answers it.

Make sure that your questions are asked with compassion. There must be no intention to 'win' or 'make another wrong' by asking a question that cannot be easily answered. You must have the intention for students to be successful and feel greater self-worth. Eliminate trick questions unless used in the separate context as a learning tool.

Ask the question with full expectancy of getting an answer and engaging the entire class.

Old way: "Is there anyone who can answer the question of how the U.S. could decrease unemployment?"
New way: "Everyone get ready to answer this question: What are some of the ways that the U.S. could decrease unemployment?"

The new way engages the whole class in the learning, encourages the student to contribute, participating more than ever before. It's an old idea and a simple one. Involved students are more successful.

Whom Do You Call On?

The answer is difficult. How you decide depends on what you want to occur in the classroom. What's the outcome you want? Do you want everyone kept on his toes? Do you want to work with a few students who need extra help? There's no 'pat' answer. Successful teachers use many procedures. Try these suggestions:

1. Call on a volunteer. As you continue to create a more open class atomosphere, more and more hands will go up automatically. It's easier for the students this way, but there's always the possibility that the same ones may volunteer each time.
2. Call on students you feel could use the biggest boost in self-confidence. Of course, you must have the interest and skills to insure their success.
3. Call on randomly selected students. Use a system which is totally random for name selection. Put all the names on pieces of paper and put them into a hat. Draw a name each time you have a question to ask. Any similar method, such as a 'roulette wheel type' provides a vehicle for 'fairness' and also keeps more students alert, as they know that they may be called on at any time!
4. Call on the student you have selected as a class consultant for the day. Every student has some special or unique knowledge or talent. Make it your job to bring out the best in each.

Old way: "Today we'll be discussing history, so open your books to page twenty . . . Now, who has something they'd like to share about what they've learned?"

New Way: "Kevin, you know much about guns. Since weapons played a big part in history, I'd like you to be a class consultant in that area today. Just signal me when you have something you'd like to add."

166

Types of Questions

There are many types of questions that may be useful for you to ask in the classroom. Educator Arthur Costa identifies and makes distinctions for three types of question. The recall question is intended to elicit stored data from prior knowledge or experiences. The best description is that it's close to a stimulus response mechanism. The recall question draws from students the kind of information that a card file or computer might. Here are some examples of recall questions:

Identifying: "Which is your favorite book on teaching?"
Completing: "This chapter is on successful classroom _____ ."
Matching: "What other books is this one similar to?"
Listing: "Name all of the important chapters in this book."
Observing: "What subtitles do you see on this page?"
Reciting: "Earlier I said there are how many kinds of questions?"
Describing: "Describe the cover of this book?"
Defining: "What's the definition of a successful interaction?"
(Also included are questions which require counting, enumerating and selecting.)

The second kind of classroom question requires processing. It is the one designed to process information acquired and is usually associated with analyzing or cause and effect. It uses different skills than the recall question and requires more exact, detailed information. Some examples are:

Comparing: "What do you and your students have in common?"
Sequencing: "In what order should you call on your students?"
Analyzing: "Doing this is a lot like what?"
Inferring: "What can you infer from the first sentence on this page?"
Classifying: "How would you rate this book so far?"
Contrasting: "In what ways is this book different from the last one you read?"
Analyzing: "What could you say about that answer?"
Organizing: "How could you arrange this information better?"
(Also: Questions which require distinguishing, grouping, explaining and experimenting are considered processing)

The third category is the application question. The student is asked to move out of the immediate information to come up with new or hypothetical information. It's a creative state of make believe, construction, fantasy and invention. Examples are:

Applying: "What would happen if you learned all the tools in this book?"
Generalizing: "Now that you're a better teacher, what can you say about your self-esteem?"
Speculating: "What would happen if every teacher knew what you now know?"
Modifying: "How quickly can you adapt this book to your own classroom?"
Forecasting: "Based on last year's growth, how good will you be next year?"
Distorting: "After you teach one great class, are you the best teacher ever?"
Deleting: "What is it you want to ignore about this book?"
Inventing: "I wonder how many ways you could tell others about this book?"
(Also: questions which require theorizing, examples, judging, imagining and extrapolating)

What if the Answer Is Wrong?

A useful conceptual shift for American education would be the re-defining of failure and success. Many teachers and educators become dogmatic about the importance of the right answer, rewarding the students who know it and penalizing those who don't. The major argument suggested is that "either you know it or you don't—there's no in-between ground." In this age of computers and simple mass storage, ask yourself, "What's more useful, to teach students information or to teach them strategies to learn or create new information?" In other words, how your students came up with the answer provides the information necessary to become successful.

It's permissible for your students to fail momentarily with a wrong answer as long as you are using or learning a process that will eventually allow you to succeed. Failure is encouraged in the larger context of being successful, and in fact, failure is the information you need to become successful. Failure means you discovered that the content was not correct, and you had an opportunity to discover the process. Was your strategy useful? Would you use it again? If not, what's an alternative strategy? In that framework, could you ever call a wrong answer a failure?

Handle "Wrong" Answers This Way

J. W. Powell of the University of Windsor at Ontario says that our handling of wrong answers has led to an artificially low ceiling on performance. In a direct, single-answer recall situation, the student who offers the wrong answer may actually be using a higher order, more successful strategy for learning than the student who comes up with the correct answer. HIGHLY INFORMED STUDENTS READ MORE AMBIGUITY into a question than is usually intended, leading them to wrong answers.

Yet the strategy for most teachers is to encourage the simplest or most efficient path to the answer rather than stressing that there are many paths. The real problem is that you'll end up with inflexible learners. Powell says that "teachers listen for the expected answer rather than to the answer they get . . . and the student who cannot frame his ideas the way the teacher does quickly learns to be a failure." Increase awareness of multiple learning strategies and you'll discover that your students may show dramatic gains in test scores, enthusiasm and even IQ!

Given that wrong answers can be more useful than correct ones, what's the actual response to a student who has an "incorrect" answer? Here are some possibilities:

1. Acknowledge the student for contributing. "Thanks for contributing. . ." or, "thanks for adding that. . ." or, "I appreciate your answer. . ." Be sure to acknowledge any part of the answer that is accurate. Let the student know what part is in-accurate before you make any reaction to the rest of the answer.

2. Go right to the learning strategy of the student. Explore how he came up with that answer. "Let's check it out . . . what led you to that conclusion?" Or, "Let's explore that possibility—how did you come up with that answer?" Or, "That's not the answer I was thinking of, but I like it . . . tell me how you came up with it."

3. You can assume the student did come up with the right answer—to a different question. So you can simply ask him to come up with a different question which would make his answer accurate. If you ask "What's five times four" and you get the answer "twenty-five," you could say, "no" and go to another student. But it's much better to say, "You'd be right if I asked 'what's five times five?' Since there's one less five, the answer is actually _____ ?" What this does is two things: first it allows the student to be successful and it gives the chance to work with the student's own learning strategies.

4. Enlarge the context to make it into a learning situation. For example, let's say you ask a student to name three of the states that border New York. Say the answer you got was New Jersey, Delaware and Rhode Island. You might come back with a larger question from which the student can learn. "You gave different answers from what I expected, so let's learn from them. What do the states you mentioned have in common with Pennsylvania, Connecticut or Vermont that might cause confusion?"

5. You can rephrase the same question, knowing that sometimes words mean different things to different people. You may be surprised to discover that you have a style of phrasing questions that causes students to contribute inaccurate answers.

Use your senses to find out if the student feels complete with the interaction. Does he feel good about what he contributed or what he learned? You can tell by the physiology, posture, expressions and voice. If you were successful, the physiology will be confident, beaming self-worth. If the eyes are dropped, shoulders slumped and voice lowered, you can be sure the interaction did not achieve the intended result of empowering the student. If you are the least bit unsure, check with the student: "Jane, now that we've talked about this for a moment, what are you feeling, or what conclusion is on your mind?"

When Students Share Themselves

Sharing is just as important for tenth graders or college students as it is for second graders. It's valuable for many reasons. One is that everyone is on equal footing. If this activity is handled properly, it can be an opportunity for students in several ways: (1) to learn about other students by listening and watching others (2) to gain confidence through speaking to a group (3) to gain acceptance for being themselves (4) to learn and discover something about themselves (5) to gain self-worth.

Simple rules for sharing are that (1) you must speak from your own experience (2) that you be considerate and respectful; no put-downs, profanity or pre-judgments and (3) be respectful of the time available.

The moment of sharing time can, for each student, be a fabulous opportunity for acceptance of themselves and others. Therefore, be sure that students can hear and see one another well. If you notice others are losing attention while one is sharing, you may need to refocus the class, encourage the speaker to include classmates in the sharing process. You may also remind students that what's being shared might relate to them.

How to Respond to Your Students

The teacher's primary role during student sharing is to stay in rapport and receive the communication. Be sure you stand near the student, face him, provide eye contact and create rapport through either nodding or matching some of the gestures. The way to respond is to put yourself in his shoes for a moment, suspend judgment and join his reality without being caught up or paralyzed by it. When a student shares something, simply respond with comments such as, "I appreciate your sharing, thank you." Or, "I enjoyed what you had to say, thank you." Or, "Thank you very much for sharing yourself." Or, "Great, thank you." Or, "I respect what you have to say, thanks." In that way, the student knows that he is appreciated, heard and respected.

Building Thinking Skills

At times, each of us may have said about our students, "If only they would just THINK before answering!" After all, thinking skills are certainly valuable. The problem is, we have so much content, so much curriculum which seems to demand the piling up of more and more bits of information, that we never seem to get around to teaching HOW to think about WHAT we teach. It is how we teach, not what we teach that builds thinking skills. Students will grow more as thinkers by the way we interact with them on an on-going basis than by any special class or curriculum on "critical thinking."

It's become accepted knowledge that the acquisition and general usage of thinking skills are vital in this Information Age. And we have identified many kinds of thinking. We need only consult Arthur Costa, Bloom's taxonomy or Robert Marzano, Director of Research at the Mid-Continent Regional Educational Laboratory. Each describes three levels of thinking skills, each more complex than the previous one, although the descriptions are a bit different.

They can be discribed as direct recall (identifying, describing, completing, etc.), processing (inferring, contrasting, comparing, analyzing, etc.), and application skills (inventing, forecasting, generalizing, modifying, adapting, etc.). Or, they can be described as learning-to-learn skills, content thinking skills, and basic reasoning skills. The specific skills include everyday problem solving, memory aids for retention and recall, listening and concentration skills, goal setting, critical judgment and logical analysis skills.

But even with the need and identity established, can we really teach thinking? The evidence presents a definite "Yes!" Based on the results of some teachers, certain students are definitely better critical thinkers. The problem is that we don't know enough about how it happens, or when to teach it.

Some feel the skills must be taught as a separate curriculum first. As a subject matter, the evidence is weak that we can do this on a large scale. It seems to require extensive training to make it work well.

Others feel the skills are better taught by infusing them into the contents of courses regularly so that critical thinking becomes something "woven throughout" instead of an event—done once and forgotten. When taught as a by-product of another pertinent process, the evidence is very compelling that you can teach critical thinking skills—we have done it successfully (even unconsciously) many times.

This apparent contradiction makes perfect sense when viewed in the context of how we learn: Emanuel Donchin, director of the Laboratory for Cognitive Psychophysiology at the University of Illinois says that as much as 99% of cognitive activity (thinking) may be non-conscious. In other words, most of what we think and what we are learning is happening outside of our conscious awareness.

Regardless of the controversy, there are many things you can do in your classroom to enhance the critical thinking processes:

- Create a "brain-compatible" environment by reducing all threats or hints of threats for performance (right or wrong answers).
- Talk to students about real-life experiences, how you struggled with problems and how you came up with solutions.
- Stop to process answers given in class to ask the "why" and "how" questions. Find out how a student came up with an answer. Coach him to discover how he thinks and other choices.
- Bring in the works of the great philosophers as answers to important questions in the student's life. "What is our purpose on this planet?" "Why do people do what they do?" "Is human nature good or evil?" Get students to think about those things . . . and think about how they think about those things.

How to Validate Student Contributions

By validating student contributions you can foster an increase in classroom thinking skills. There are several ways to allow the students a chance to experience feelings of confidence and self-worth through a question-answer interaction. First, acknowledge the contribution. This can be easily done with the simple statement as above in item #1. Second, you can refer to a student's comment at a later time in class. For example, "As Johnny said earlier, . . ." It is a major boost for a student to be quoted by the teacher! Another tool for validation is to write student comments on a flip chart or the chalkboard, saving it for the whole class to see.

Responding to Creativity

Imagine a student coming saying, "I made up a new theory on why the Civil War happened." Or another student saying to the English teacher, "I have a new kind of poetry." Or a math student saying, "I am making up a new way to find square roots." While some teachers would respond receptively, others might raise eyebrows skeptically and ask for proof. If your outcome is to foster self-esteem and creativity in the thought process, you'll respond with enthusiasm and support. These brief moments can make a big difference in a student's life. Be ready for them.

How to Conduct Discussion and Inquiry

Teacher-led discussions have the capacity to enliven, inform, inspire and, perhaps most important, allow students to understand how others think. If done poorly, students will be resentful and unwilling to participate in the future. If you plan to have a discussion or inquiry process, first get clarity on your intended outcome. If your outcome is to pursue the truth, you are in trouble! After all, whose truth are you after, yours or a student's?

Nobel prize-winning physicists David Bohm, Niels Bohr and Albert Einstein have all said that there is 'no fixed reality.' It's all decided from the point of view of the observer. We each participate in the momentary creation of our own experiences, our truths and subsequently, our universe. Therefore each of us has a different, yet equally valid truth. The quest for a single "truth" in the classroom is not useful. It is useful to evaluate the relative merits of a point of view or a suggestion. Be open to ideas.

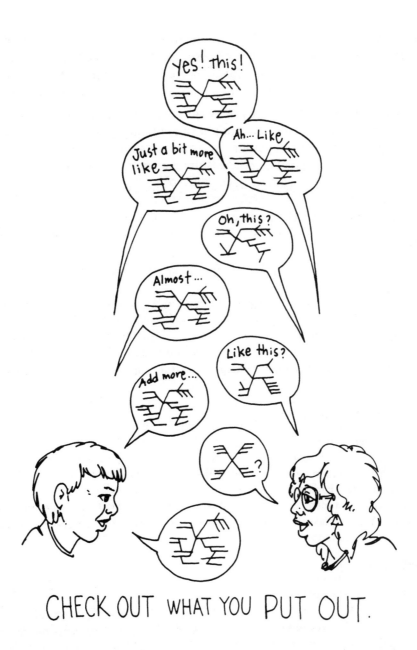

CHECK OUT WHAT YOU PUT OUT.

Create a Criteria for Evaluating Data

In the course of a discussion, much data will surface. What's needed are criteria for evaluating the data. Since searching for the truth often creates more disagreement and confusion, it's more appropriate for students to examine data in the context of usefulness. Is this important? Can I use this information? What does this mean to me? To others? To our world? How might my life be different now that I know this? What will this experience mean to me long-term? Questions such as these usually produce students with great resources and stronger reasoning skills.

Even your group discussions need closure. The all-important closure process can make a difference between whether your students succeed or not. During the closure process, ask what conclusions were drawn, both about the informational content of the discussion and about the process of the discussion.

Pre- and Post-Class Dialogues

The one-to-one contact is an important time for both the teacher and the student. If it's a positive sharing, just listen. If there's a problem, be extra alert. When a student talks to the teacher about something, you can be sure it is important to him or her. What you do or don't do in these moments is very important. Often when a student comes to you, he's feeling unresourceful and helpless. Your outcome must be to empower the student—to add to his resourcefulness so at the completion of your interaction, he will be stronger and more able than before. These times are prime opportunities for assisting the student to think! In other words, your interaction must add to the student's sense of his own ability, not further his sense of dependency and helplessness.

If the student's head is hung low, you've got two choices. One of them is to change his physiological state. Politely ask him to move his head more upright to eye level. This will immediately pull him out of the 'victim', or 'poor me' physiology and get him into another state, probably auditory or visual instead of kinesthetic. Another possibility is to match the posture momentarily so the student feels a commonality with you. Assume a posture that is similar, pace your voice tempo with him and match breathing, if possible. Immediately begin to match predicates, so that you can first, match the same state he is in, then lead him to a more resourceful one. Here's an example of a dialogue:

Do You Make This Mistake?

Student: "Look, I'm doing awful in this class. I don't see how I can get my grades up, and I just flashed on the final next week."
Teacher: "You sound real concerned. Thanks for talking to me about it, maybe you're right, our last class was an earful."
Student: Well, that's not exactly it . . ."
(Notice that in the first sentence, the student used visual words: look, see, flashed. The teacher responded with mis-matched auditory words: sound, talking and earful. That does not create rapport!)

Here's a Winner!

Student: "Get a load of this. I keep a stiff upper lip when studying, but it all boils down to the same old thing: I'm knee-deep in trouble."
Teacher: "Thanks for touching base with me. There's a couple of things that'll help you come to grips with this if you can just hang in there while we build a strong foundation."
Student: "Good idea, I can handle that."
(In the first sentence, the student used the kinesthetic mode: get a load, stiff upper lip, boils down to, knee-deep. The teacher matched the information modality and ended up with being able to offer some strong support. Find words in the teacher's response which show that she was able to gain rapport.)

The first thing you might say to a student who comes up to you is to acknowledge him. For example, "I appreciate you coming up to talk to me—you are important to me." The next step is to listen. Listen quietly, nodding and staying in rapport. Listen without judging, or trying to solve the problem for that person. Allow that student to be able to be himself without your additions or subtractions of advice or ideas. Allow any silence if it arises. Now, keep in mind what your intended outcome was: added resourcefulness and completion.

The next step is to help the student identify resources which are already there and could be of assistance. Do not offer advice, especially if the conversation is personal. For example:

Student: "I need some help . . . I just don't feel motivated to do my homework."
Teacher: "Thanks for coming to me, I'll do the best I can to help you handle it. As far as your homework situation, what do you feel is going on?"
Student: "Well, I'm not sure, I'm just not motivated."
Teacher: "What other possibilities are there?"
Student: "I guess I could (student names a choice)."
Teacher: "Which of those choices do you feel best about?"
Student: "I like the one that (student names a choice)."
Teacher: "Good, I'll do what I can to help you make it work. In fact, how about if you check with me in a week? However, I want you to know you did great at coming up with some solutions; you're pretty resourceful. As you continue to feel more confident, you'll find that you'll be able to easily come up with even more solutions in the future.
Student: "I hadn't really thought I knew my own answer."

Teacher: "Take a deep breath . . . how do you feel now? Is everything OK or is there anything else you'd like to talk about."

Student: "Actually, I feel pretty good."

Teacher: "Good . . . thanks for stopping by and good luck."

What If You Fail At It? What would you do if a student asked for help, then you in turn, asked him if he could come up with some solutions himself and he couldn't? Here's an example of two ways to draw out information:

1. If the student says "I don't know the answer." You might respond with "I appreciate you sharing that, but wonder, if you actually did know the answer, what would you say it is?"

2. You could say, "Do you know anyone in this class who might know the answer? . . . How do you think that he or she might answer that question? Just guess. . ."

One of the most useful ways to help students cut through problems is to help them cut through the vagueness to get at the core of the problem. Ask specific questions when needed and you'll get better quality answers.

Statements	Your Response
Something is "too much, too many, or too expensive"	compared to what?
nouns, pronouns (he, she, they, specifically? it,)	who or what
verbs (moved, asked, wrote, tried, hurt, inspired, etc.)	how specifically?
shouldn't, couldn't, can't, it?	what causes or prevents
must, have to, got to if . . . ?	what would happen
all, every, never, always, only	repeat, "every one . . . ?" "it always . . . ?"

Student: "This doesn't make any sense to me."

Teacher: "What specifically doesn't make sense?"

Student: "I've always disliked math."

Teacher: "Always? What about when you were in pre-school?"

Student: "I can't go through with this."

Teacher: "What would happen if you did?"

("What prevents you from following through?")

Student: "They don't let me ask questions."

Teacher: "Who specifically, won't let you ask questions?"

Student: "This is much too hard."

Teacher: "Compared to what?"

You can add 'softeners' in front of your questions to insure that the student receives your questions gently and respectfully. Before your question, add the phrases, "I'm wondering . . . (what specifically . . .)? Or you can say, "I'm curious. What prevents you from following through?" And, "Would you possibly be able to tell me how specifically . . . ?" These can make sure you get the outcome of clarity while still staying in rapport with the person. Once again, the secret is to use sensory acuity to determine the student's reaction to your questions.

Interactive Diversity

The multi-cultural influence on our educational system continues to build on two fronts. First, there's the increased awareness of our existing diversity of cultures. Only now are we beginning to acknowledge distinctive cultural patterns to be seriously dealt with in Black, Hispanic, Anglo and American Indian

173

cultures. These patterns significantly affect your student communications and learning styles. Although it's critical to avoid generalizations, you'll find that some background to fall back on is highly useful when a communication seems amiss or you get a response you're unprepared for. Use the following chart as a guide but use your own experience as a rule.

Examples of Cultural Diversity

	Blacks	Hispanic	Anglo	Am. Indian	Asian
Conversational Eye Contact	Low	Low	High	Med	High
Assertiveness	High	Low	Ave.	Low	Low
Ways to Align	Call for unified expression	Call for silence	Call for silence	Call for silence	Ask for silence
Conversation Style	Direct personal truth-issue oriented	Passive containment	Non-confrontive representative compromising peace-oriented	Direct combination issue/truth compromise	Casual calm historical
Use of Emotions	As a valid source of expression	To be held back until confront point	To be managed	To be contained as much as possible	To be avoided
Reaction to Heated Dialogues	As long as talking is going on, it's OK ventilaton verbal threats rarely serious	Extremes: withdrawal or high response to verbal can lead to pent-up violence	Discomfort; threats taken seriously	Discomfort; avoidance	Discomfort keeping emotion out

As always, ask, ask and ask. Check things out. Avoid assuming. The purpose of this is to stimulate some openness on the subject, not create stereotypes.

It's not what happens
that counts . . .
It's how I respond to what happens
that counts

In this chapter we've explored the classroom interactions such as the student question, the teacher question, sharing, discussion and personal meetings. The importance of clarity on your intended outcome is tantamount to success. With every interaction, reach for the goal of greater self-worth, greater resourcefulness and completion within the student. (Interactions are not the main course of the meal, but they are what holds it together). Good interactions make the class go better and ineffective ones can poison it. With the tools to make better interactions, you may notice some surprising changes in your students, and all of them good!

☑ Check These Key Points

1. A successful interaction has three components:
   - each person emerges more resourceful,
   - both people get their desired outcome
   - have a sense of completion/closure.
2. Keep your eyes open and scanning for signs of a question, check your physiology before speaking, use extended arm and open palm gesture to invite question.
3. The first response to a question is acknowledgement of the speaker.
4. Re-establish rapport before responding to a hostile question.
5. Clarify your intended outcome before asking a question.
6. The three types of questions are: recall, processing, and application.
7. An "incorrect" answer is an opportunity to acknowledge the student, learn the student's learning strategy, and empower the student.
8. Use one-to-one interactions to build the student's resourcefulness, thinking skills and self-esteem.
9. The diversity of cultural patterns can be used to enrich your communications with students.

Chapter Fourteen

Discipline and Class Management the Easy Way

Objectives

- To identify qualities of successful classroom management
- To describe rules, guidelines and agreements
- To list 10 tools useful in preventing discipline problems

For many teachers, this might be the most important chapter in the book. Yet, what's interesting is that the more you get out of the other chapters, the less you'll need this one! Therefore, it is strongly recommended that you read all of the other chapters first. As you'll be discovering, classroom management problems are usually symptoms of mis-management elsewhere. When the other parts of your teaching are done well, you'll have a bare minimum of discipline problems. In an area such as discipline, there are bound to be some myths to address and here they are:

Myth: Behavior Problems Are Other than Just Symptoms

Here's a surprise: discipline problems are not only NOT the real problem, but they are a gift to you. If you went to a physician to get a physical and your doctor said you have a calcium deficiency, would you be mad at the doctor? Of course not! In the same way, an undisciplined student is providing you with feedback essential for your success. Students who "act up" are not a problem. They are the reason you are there in class—the other students would do just fine without a teacher at all. What you call problems are the results of gaps in your teaching and give you important information that you can use to be a better teacher.

Have you ever watched a baby play? Learning and curiosity are natural human states. When curiosity is aroused, all our senses are attentive to the task at hand. We are absorbed and nothing else is important. Discipline is unnecessary. In an ideal classroom, discipline problems are minimal. If you do what is suggested in the other chapters in this book, your classroom management problems will virtually disappear. Guaranteed.

Myth: There's Such a Person as a Trouble-Maker

No student gets up in the morning thinking, "How can I be a real jerk today?" Each person makes the best possible choice, 100% of the time—given the context, the perceived choices available and the outcome desired. This means that our brain is constantly making choices. However, there are times when a student does make a choice that is not favorable or acceptable because the needs and conditions of others have not been considered.

You may recall, from an earlier chapter, a basic premise in learning: all behavior is state-related. Yet teachers often label something "problem behavior," or label the student as a "trouble-maker." Using a label to describe classroom behavior is an injustice to you as well as to the student. There are no un-resourceful people, only unresourceful behavioral states. To change the behavior, change their state. In other words, your students all have the capacity to act appropriately but they access an unresourceful behavioral state at times. Your job is to keep those states at a minimum.

Myth: A Quiet Class Is a Well-behaved One

During the industrial revolution, one of the primary roles of schools was to prepare our children for the workforce. In those days, that meant the factory world of promptness, repetition, neatness and compliance. Our schools did a superb job of turning out students who learned to shut up, form lines and do what is expected. As part of that line of thinking, classroom values emphasized silence and obedience. But, of course, times have changed dramatically.

Our information age requires greater levels of communication than ever before. The future of our country depends on sharing, cooperating, and thinking skills. To foster these in the classroom means that teachers will be encouraging their students to cooperate more in the learning process, talk over possible ideas and answers, and even take tests in teams. It means that the quiet lecture halls are fast-becoming a thing of the past and the noisy classroom, bustling with the activities of a pre-school are now becoming the standard. Classroom noise is now the pleasant side affect of a highly interactive and growing student body.

Myth: Tips and Tools Will Help Solve Behavior Problems

Another assumption is that all a teacher needs is a few tips, tools or techniques to manage the classroom better. They won't work. For things to change, you must change. If you have problems in your classroom the first thing you might want to consider is that you are a co-creator. Only from that context can you begin the learning process necessary to make your classroom work again. If the framework you operate from is that it's not you, but the students who are the cause of the problems, nothing will be resolved. This is not to say that the students don't have anything to do with it—of course they do. But, to mobilize your own resources to make the necessary changes, you must accept responsibility for what goes on in your classroom.

Myth: Some Students Are Out to Get You

In this case, "to get you" means to annoy, pester or foul up your class. This is absolutely false. Students are making the best choice they can for their level of awareness and personal growth. Unless you change their awareness, every conventional method of discipline will fail and fail consistently. Those methods will fail because, for the most part, they don't provide the student with additional resources or choices. In other words, telling a student to quit doing something does not empower him, it only frustrates and infuriates.

Classroom discipline must be done in a way that supports the dignity of the students. Keep their self-esteem intact or you will pay the price. Some students don't get mad; they get even by being a discipline problem as retribution for your damage to them. The theme of this chapter could as well be to discipline with dignity or to correct with compassion. Your job is to expand students' choices, not shut them down. To accomplish that goal you must be flexible and learn what unfulfilled needs students have. You must dovetail outcomes, find where you have common ground, then design a management strategy.

Myth: There Is One Single Best Way of Classroom Control

Another assumption is that there's a single tool or technique for classroom control. There are those who say the answer is to be strict—simply use strong punitive measures backed up by swift action, even physical/mental punishments if necessary. Others claim that harshness isn't the answer, that softness is.

Be warm and supportive, they say, and the students will respond. Neither is the answer at all times. Since people are so different, what works for one may fail with another. The best answer is have a clear outcome coupled with the flexibility to get you toward it and sensory acuity to know when you've been successful.

Three Steps to Successful Classroom Management

Teachers who have mastered the science and art of classroom management have done it many different ways. Some use sugar, some vinegar. Some follow a system, others say "do whatever works." What is most important when dealing with these issues is that you maintain an atmosphere of love, consistency and integrity. Students need to know they are still good people, it's their behavior that is unacceptable. Students need consistency so they know the framework and boundaries for behavior and don't need to keep testing them to find out how much you'll bend each day. And finally, students need to know that you will keep your word and honor your values. This sets the example for them to do the same and will reduce discipline problems long-term.

1. Prepare the Classroom Climate

One of the best ways to start reducing discipline problems is to change the way that you allow yourself to experience others. In other words, to reduce problems, change your point of view. Quit seeing students as a problem and start seeing your students as a possibility of greatness. Refuse to call anyone in your class a "trouble-maker" or "bad kid," he will prove you right every time. Instead, refer to the students as "pending miracles" (ones you haven't reached yet, but will). It will make all of the difference in the world.

- CENTER YOURSELF
- LISTEN FOR FEELINGS
- GATHER INFORMATION
- MAKE A DECISION
- RE·ALIGN WITH STUDENTS
- FOLLOW THROUGH AND SUPPORT

Here's an example. If I went up to one of your students and held my hand over his mouth and nose to stop his breathing, in a few seconds (if I kept it up), he would start kicking or elbowing me violently to get loose. If an observer could not see what I was doing to the student, he would only see the student acting violently. Naturally, judgements and labels would pop up like he's "rebellious, overly emotional, violent, has a short attention span and is certainly hyperactive." As ludricous as it sounds, those labels would make perfect sense if you could not see that I was suffocating the student. Now that's an example of an obvious "visible" form of damage to students. But what about the more "invisible" things we do?

When we break our word to our students, we damage them. When we are short or abrupt to them, we damage them. When we grade and evaluate them unfairly, we damage them. When we don't acknowledge or appreciate them enough, we damage them. When we fail to coach them on how to grow, we damage them. When we discourage divergent thinking and stifle creativity, we damage them. These invisible forms of "suffocation" are just as deadly as the real one. When our students are acting up, we are the ones who have often damaged them.

Another invisible quality of our student's lives is time. Each of your students is "referenced" to a primary time-status. It's either past, present or future. The decisions and behaviors of your students that you might call erratic, negative or undisciplined are often simply a reflection of living out a different time frame. Here's an example.

If your so-called "problem student" is constantly late for call, it may be because he is present referenced. That means that decisions are made which indicate a primary concern for "How am I feeling right now?" A present-referenced student might be out in the hallways or lockers talking to friends all the way up until the bell rings, then have to come to class late. If he was so "in the moment" of the present time, he's thinking about how much fun he's having, not what he SHOULD DO IN THE FUTURE (like get to class). This student is not motivated by future rewards (or punishments). He will do his homework if (at the moment he gets around to it), he feels like it. Hence this student is more fun, enjoys spontaneity, lives in the moment and is unpredictable. It would be a mistake to call him "unmotivated or "apathetic" because he turns his homework in late (if at all) or is late for class. He's simply not relating to the future and the consequences you may be wanting him to do.

Similarly, a more future-oriented student is motivated by getting good grades, scholarships and college. Or, he may be more paralyzed by fear of the unknown, pressure or uncertainty. A more past-oriented student is either motivated by past successes or paralyzed out of his past failures. So, instead of calling a future-oriented student "disinterested, short attention span and restless," you might understand a bit better that the present may both be real exciting for him now. So, he's had to go into the future. The time referencing is one of the most fascinating aspects of how we are all unique and different. Listen more closely about how you relate to your students and you may discover that who you were calling unmotivated was actually very motivated—in another time frame.

Even different learning styles that students have, or the teaching styles we use, can create discipline problems. If you relate to your students in a very abstract and sequential way, you'll lose the part of your audience that is more concrete and random. In fact, that's one of the most classic sources of behavior problems. A teacher who wants to emphasize ideas, theories and concepts in a logical and structured way will "suffocate" the student who learns from the random, nonlinear world of experience. It's almost guaranteed that you'll have discipline problems because you are trying to force a "square peg into a round hole." It won't work. Never has, never will. As you guessed, it takes a real diversity of teaching styles to be effective with your students.

How to Handle Minor Disruptions

Ninety percent of all classroom discipline can be solved easily with a few simple methods. First, and primary, your job of teaching and the student's job of learning are secondary to the creation of a classroom environment of mutual respect and trust. The chapter on introductions provides more detail.

The second key is what educator Madeline Hunter calls "discipline with dignity." To do that, keep the discipline action between you and the student or if you do need to be public about it, make it positive. Here are some of her suggestions:

1. *Vicinity.* If you are covering a topic and a student is misbehaving, most of the time you can deal with it by simply walking over and standing next to the student while you continue to teach.
2. *Inclusion.* You can use the student's name in a positive way. Say to the student, "Mark, I need your help. While everyone is thinking of the names of the countries which border France, be my assistant, please, and keep track of the ideas."
3. *Secret Signal.* Just walk by the student and touch the paper he's writing on or gently touch his shoulder.
4. *Private Choice.* Give all the students an assignment such as close your eyes and think of as many chapter titles from our textbook. Then walk over to the student who is misbehaving and talk to him. Say, "It seems like you're either bored or frustrated. Can you handle this or would you like some help from me?"
5. *Adjacent Student.* Avoid embarrassing the student at any cost. If a student is fidgeting or mildly disruptive, simply call on the person NEXT to them. This usually brings their attention back to the room.

There are many other ways to change a misbehaving student's actions. You can build rapport with him through "pacing" or subtly mimicking behaviors. Once you and he are in rhythm, change yours to the new desired one. If you have mirrored well, the student's behavior will follow perfectly in line.

You can give the students a stand-up stretch break and ask them to circle the chairs in the room twice. Use that time to say to the student, "I can tell it's not easy for you to STAY FOCUSED on what we're doing. Can you handle this on your own or would you like me to do something about it?"

In each of the above cases, the student was notified of your concern in a way that allowed him to maintain self-respect. When you help others keep that all-important dignity, you are serving both them long-term because they will grow and yourself because they'll be better students.

Your intention should always be to support, but there are times when you may slip. If you do, always talk to that student privately afterwards so that they know that it was you who ran out of choices in dealing with him or her. Tell him that you respect him as a human being and that you'd rather cooperate, but you simply don't know how to get results with him. Ask him what you could do differently next time so that you could handle it easier. And if he has publicly insulted you, abused you or threatened you in a way that backs you into a corner, you will make sure that he doesn't do it again.

Why Are There Behavior Problems?

The subject of "why" in behavior problems would fill several volumes. There are as many reasons as there are persons to come up with them and every reason is probably valid. The trouble is, reasons don't empower anyone. You as a teacher need tools, not psychological assessments. Yet, there's still one nagging question. When a person chooses to act, why isn't the choice made for good behavior instead of disruptive behavior?

One of the things to know is that since we are all humans, there are certain things we share in common. We all have a brain, a nervous system and an outcome that we want. Our brain is programmed to store information and to be able to compare and contrast data for decision-making purposes. It is an automatic process for our brain to be able to come up with the "best" choice.

In other words, your student's behavior makes perfect sense when looked at in the context of the choices that the brain made available to him. This doesn't mean that they're not responsible for their actions. It does mean that if you want to effect behavior on a long-term basis, one of your best options is to work at developing more choices within the brains of students who misbehave. Every piece of behavior seeks to accomplish a positive outcome (attention, safety, health, pleasure, etc.).

The problem is that many students don't have in their "options bank" a behavior that will get their positive outcome in a way acceptable to you. Unless you find a way to make your students more resourceful, you will continue to have behavior problems. Students need your support to help them discover that they can generate more behavior options in their life and that by using those new choices, they can still get the outcome that they wanted without being a discipline problem. And therein lies the key—provide new behavioral choices within a clear structure.

2. Provide Structure and Follow-Through

Rules, Guidelines or Agreements

For students to know what's acceptable in your class, set guidelines for specific behavior limitations. Studies show that setting limits and successfully enforcing them gives students a sense of stability, structure and self-esteem. Students with clear guidelines seem to develop greater self-esteem and confidence about the world. Be sure to make a clear distinction between rules, guidelines and agreements.

- Rules—"The exercise of authority or control . . . prescribed guides for conduct or action." Notice that Webster's says nothing about mutually agreed upon standards. Instead, it is the imposition of authority or control. These are to be put in practice for those actions which need a swift direct response regardless of the student's feelings about the matter. Examples include assault, property damage, theft, arson, truancy or substance abuse.
- Guidelines—"An indication of policy or conduct." Notice that a guideline itself is not a rule, it merely indicates a rule. This gives a lot of leeway in the interpretation and given teaching situations, a lot of leeway is needed in some areas. Examples might include seating areas, noise levels, profanity in class, or a dress code.
- Agreements—"A harmonious accord on a course of action." Notice that the key word in this definition is harmonious. It implies that both parties, on their own free will, and, in fact, with a spirited joyousness, agree upon a common code or plan of behavior. Examples are that you and students agree on a behavior code, homework or testing policy or class procedures.

Make sure you make distinctions for your students and tell why you have each of them. Once you have explained it, most students will know exactly where you are and will not test you continually (provided you enforce them consistently).

Here Are Some Sample Classrom Agreements

It doesn't make any sense to create agreements for a class if there's not even agreement on what they're doing there or why. May I suggest that you re-introduce the purpose of the course or of your purpose as a teacher. Let's say that your purpose is: "To create an environment which enables the participants to discover who they are and how to function successfully in the real world."

Next, translate that for your students. Tell them that you want them to discover more of themselves: their talent, resources and gifts. Then you want them to master the course material in a way that will assist them to function in the "real world." Then get agreement that they are willing to participate in your course now, knowing what the purpose is. You might say, "I propose that the purpose of this course be to. . . all in support and favor, say aye . . . all opposed, say nay." Then you might say: "Great! Next, let's create the agreements which will allow us to be able to have our purpose come true." In general, the fewer the agreements, the better; they are easier to remember and to refer to.

Proposed Agreements

1. *Time.* Each student agrees to be seated on time (as determined by the clock on the back wall) for the start of class or the resumption of class after a break. In other words, each student agrees to arrange his circumstances, take care of his needs, and do what has to be done in a way that allows him to be on time.

2. *Safety and Respect.* Students agree to listen while others are talking if the teacher has given permission. Each student agrees to treat other persons and all property safely and harmlessly. (Translated, it means you may not steal, harm, push, shove, destroy, insult, hit, deface, badger, name-call, tease or irritate another student or property.)

3. *Support of Learning.* Each student wil do what is necessary to accomplish the course purpose and allow others to learn successfully. (Translated: you may not block another's view, disrupt them, throw anything, talk while others are reading or writing).

4. *Respect the Learning Environment.* Keep your classroom clean. Pick up after yourself and keep your own desk area clean. No throwing of objects or tracking in dirt, mud or snow. Take pride in your whole learning environment.

5. *Speak from Your Own Experience.* Use "I" messages. This also means that you can't say, "That guy's a jerk," because the sentence must include the speaker's responsibility for the labelling: What you could say is that, "I didn't like him," or "I couldn't get along with him."

Next, Design Your Own Agreements

Create your own set of agreements. Those listed above are merely samples. The ones you design should be simple, to the point, explicit, and truly be necessary for the successful running of your class. At the elementary level, make your agreements simpler. Avoid creating rules which do not directly contribute to or facilitate the actual learning process. Those tend to be difficult to enforce because students sense the injustice of it. Once you have created a simple list of agreements, you have a proposal. Your suggested agreements need to be taken before the class and offered as just what they are, possible agreements, not rules you wish to manipulate them into accepting. If there's the least bit of coercion or manipulation, the students will be less likely to keep their word.

Steps To Follow

1. Present the course purpose and ask for support and agreement on that as an overall foundation. An example of the correct wording might be, "I propose that our course purpose be . . . all in favor, say aye, all oppose, say nay."

2. Next make the link between the course purpose and the suggested agreements. You might say, "In order to make the course purpose actually come about, we need a way to keep us on the path. I have five suggested agreements on which I'd like your approval."

3. Read the first one. Then read it again so everyone can be totally clear on it. Ask for questions, comments, suggestions. Most importantly, ask the students to come up with 'what ifs' and 'how about when . . .' and 'why this way?' The exploration of the agreement is a critical process and the more the questions arise, the greater the clarity you and the students will get on the agreement. Now's the time to re-word it.

4. Once they have asked all the questions and gotten all the answers they need, you are almost ready to ask for their support of and agreement on the proposed statement. But first, you might say, "Are there any more questions, comments, or possibilities that you think might come up or prevent you from being able to follow this statement if you approve it?"

5. Next, you might say, "All of you willing to agree to these and who give your word that you will do your best to follow fully, please say aye . . . all opposed, say nay."

6. Then, you can go on to the next agreement. What happens if someone does not want to agree to the statement? There are several possibilities. One of them is that there is a situation or example or question that arose that keeps the student from feeling confident that about the agreement. Or, the student may not have any questions, but feel as if he is being trapped, cornered or badgered into an agreement which might get him in trouble later. In this case, you need to spend some time with that student after class working it out.

7. Next, you need the evidence procedure and the consequences. The evidence procedure means that you need an agreed-upon method to know when there is a violation of the agreement. For example, what if one student says that another one broke agreement number two? Do you confront on circumstantial evidence? The answer is, it depends. You will have to be the judge in these gray areas.

The next part is the consequence. Each teacher has a different sense of what's appropriate for their age group of students and the kind of teacher they are. The actual consequences are up to you and the working environment you have. You may have the most success using peer pressure with some groups.

8. Finally, you need to have a talk about integrity. This is the point at which you need to introduce the promise as a powerful part of your class. Most students promise this and agree to that. But actually keeping the promise is different. Most of us are better at promising than we are fulfilling our promises. Unfortunately, the media reinforces this in too many ways. Invite your students to have their word, their promise become a powerful part of their lives. Remind them that keeping their word is the weight-lifting of character-building. Invite them to live up to the ideas of honesty they hold and become a count-on-able person. By doing this early in the course, you will have a foundation on which to build the rest of the course.

When an Infraction Occurs

First and foremost, when your classes are being taught well, discipline problems will be minimal. Your class needs to be active, fun, include participation, have clear rules, agreements, outlets for expression, a sense of 'family' and many other criteria to be immune from behavior problems. When a discipline problem does occur ask yourself, What's the outcome I want?" You must have, as your outcome, a more powerful and resourceful student. If you use your response to confront or take away power from the student, you will be challenged again in the future. If you can get the problem handled by empowering the student, you have made him a better person and you have lessened the likelihood of future problems.

When You Treat
Your students Special
They don't have to act special

This means that your ability to stay in rapport with the student during this interaction is important. It also means that you must stay clear on your outcome—to make the student a better and more resourceful student, not to destroy him or her. The next key after rapport and clear outcomes is behavioral flexibility. Be willing to change what you do until you find out what works best.

For mini-infractions, the ones that are more annoying than they are destructive, the easiest, most simple thing to do is to change the state of the student. When you change the state, you change the behavior. Ways to change state are listed in an earlier chapter and could vary from having the student stand up, move seats, go for a 30 second walk or a number of other state changers.

When larger infractions are broken, you have different issues involved. Keep in mind that the key item of importance is to enable the student to make better choices in the future. It doesn't serve either of you to lay blame, make them wrong, guilty, or resentful. It does serve you to find a way for the student to learn from the experience and be less likely to misbehave in the future. Here's one possibility:

Discipline Format: Beforehand

1. Tell students beforehand that you will let them know if they break an agreement and that you will make no concessions or compromises.
2. Be consistent and immediate in your communication to the student. Always let them know when they have broken an agreement and do it immediately. They must know that there is no 'safe time' unless specified.

3. Make sure that it's an agreement that was broken, not just something that you made up or something you just don't like. If you don't have the agreements memorized, you either have too many or haven't done your own homework.

Discipline Format: "In the Moment"

1. Get centered. Pause, take a breath and relax. Be calm both inside and outside. Anticipate a positive outcome and have a picture and feel for a successful result for both parties.
2. Get the attention of the student. This means that you would want to face him, no less than five feet away and no more than ten or fifteen. Do not stand face to face, inches away. Use this moment to really connect with the student.
3. Say the student's name (in a calm, respectful and polite tonality), what the agreement was and how it was just broken. For example, "David, you made an agreement to be in your seat on time. The clock says that it's two minutes past that time." Notice that you stated the facts, and you certainly made no judgement about him being bad, undependable or disrespectful.

You also did not tell how you feel. How you feel when a student is late is your business. To say that you are angry, upset, or disappointed because they were late, is wrong. It's wrong because first, you are responsible for your feelings, not them. They don't make YOU feel anything, ever. They can trigger a stimulus-response mechanism within you that allows that emotion to occur. But your internal mechanisms are not the creation nor the responsibility of the student. Second, expressing feelings to someone who doesn't know that your feelings are totally up to you is manipulative: it could make him feel guilty or badly about himself.

4. Let it sink in. Allow what you said simply to be absorbed for a moment. Just maintain eye contact after your first statement, saying nothing else. Five seconds of silence may be uncomfortable but it's important.
5. Next, listen and understand. Do some discovery to find out what went on in the student's world and ask what happened. You are there to hear his "case" and truly understand it from HIS point of view.
6. Next, go for accountability. Ask him or her to make a statement about being late. He might say, "I know, I was late. I'm sorry." In that case, your response would be, "David, I respect your integrity and I appreciate that you know you broke the agreement. Since you were not in your seat on time, something obviously got in the way. What I'd like you to do is to come up with two other ways that you could have handled the situation so you would get what you needed, and been in class on time. Do you have any ideas? (You now have a choice: you can let him come up with the ideas on the spot, or, if more appropriate, have him turn them into you at the end of the class.)

In either case, you might say next, "David, it's important for you to learn that you have within you the resources to be able to keep the agreements that you make. When you keep agreements, it's your reputation, your autograph and your mark in your life called honesty and integrity. It's what people know they can depend upon, it's how people choose friends and where they want to work. You can have that kind of reputation and I want you to have it. Could you come up with two other ways you could have handled the same situation better? (pause and wait for possible reply). I'd also like to see you after class for disciplinary action." (the displinary action is optional; it's whatever you set up prior) Then, wait for him to come up with two other choices. Usually, it's easy.

Another possibility, after you state the infraction, is that the student might come up with a story, explanation, justification, rationalization or excuse for his late arrival. If that happens, politely listen, then summarize the comment, "So, what you're saying is that blah, blah, blah happened, correct?" Then say, "I appreciate you telling me what happened. Now I understand why you were late for class." "There certainly are a lot of distractions, circumstances and ways to get delayed. No doubt about it. All I said was that you broke the agreement." Then you wait for the response. Either he will acknowledge that he broke the agreement ("Yeah, I was late.") or he will go right back into his story and excuses. If it's the story again, go right back into your polite interrupt again. You must stay with him until he understands what you are saying. You are saying the following:

- he is late
- he made an agreement to be on time

(and that's it!)

7. Be sure to acknowledge the student for accepting the truth (not blame!), for being willing to discover ways to be more resourceful in the future and for committing to the disciplinary action. You might say, "David, I appreciate the way you handled yourself in this conversation. I also think you'll be surprised at how much easier it'll be for you to be on time from now on." Ask for a re-commitment to the agreement. Once you have it, repeat it for clarity. Thank the student and move on.

Here's the Pattern All Spelled Out

Students aren't use to *not* getting blamed, so they may get defensive when you tell them what they did. That's OK and it's normal. Just be totally straight with them. The moment you try to act more powerful, they will try to take away your power. But the moment you demonstrate to them that you want them to be more resourceful, they'll respond. So here's the pattern once you have an agreement:

1. Tell them ahead of time you'll let them know if they break an agreement
2. Be consistent and immediate in enforcement
3. Make sure it's an agreement that was broken, not an informal guideline
4. Get the student's attention, keep your voice tone light
5. Use the student's name, state the agreement and the infraction
6. Pause, let it sink in for five seconds
7. Discover what happened and appreciate the student's position. Respond to them with #5 until they acknowledge infraction without excuses.
8. Explain importance of integrity and your support of the student's integrity
9. Have the student make a new commitment regarding creating new choices and disciplinary action
10. Acknowledge the student for handling it well

Notice that this entire process is designed to empower the student. There is no blaming, no feelings shared as a manipulation. There are no excuses, it's simply a way to get at the truth. Let the student know why the agreements were created to begin with and what integrity is, then allow him to come up with a better option for next time. Have you ever disciplined a student, then felt badly afterwards? At the end of this process, you will feel great! It's truly discipline with dignity. In fact, the student will feel better towards you because you added to his resources and did not make him a bad guy. Each time you do this for one student, will open up the resources for other students. One other thing that's surprising: this process will take less and less time to do. After a few, it could take 60 seconds or less.

The way to have classroom discipline work is two-fold. First, teach in a way that keeps students excited and interested so the attention is on learning. Second, set up rules and an integrity about following rules that provides a firm structure for dealing with occasional infractions. Remember the three qualities necessary for a well-managed classroom: love, consistency and integrity. Once you become a model for these three, the student's behavior will follow in line. In time, your whole class will get better and better!

3. An Ounce of Prevention

While the management of classroom behavior seems like a useful skill, it's purely band-aid work. Getting at the cause will serve you and the students much more. Learn to serve the needs behind the discipline problems and you'll discover that problems disappear quickly. There are so many ways to create successful classroom management that we'll concentrate on just the best ones. The best tools for your particular classroom are the ones you like and implement the best. You may have to try several to discover the ones you are most comfortable with but it's well worth it. It's also important to know that these tools are designed to be used only in conjunction with the other tools in the rest of the chapters in this book. An attempt to use them out of context will not create maximum results.

Idea 1: Create greater connectedness

Students who feel a part of what's going on are more likely to pay attention to what's being presented. To create greater feelings of belonging and connectedness, here are some possibilities:

1. Include individual students in more of your teachings . . . use their names in examples, point out things that they have done, refer to their part of the room.
2. Do something special for them . . . bring them a card, write them a note on their paper, or on a separate paper, offer them a special activity or privilege.
3. Listen without judging . . . allow them to be who they are without having suggestions for change.
4. Show more expressions . . . smile, laugh, wink, a touch of the hand on the shoulder, a pat, a hug.
5. Be specific in praise . . . tell them exactly what they did, what your reaction was, use clear words, and praise them for just being in your class.
6. Share personal thoughts . . . talk to them about your dreams, goals, interests, hobbies, encourage the same.
7. Let them know how the material relates to their world . . . make it relevant to their lives, constantly.
8. Allow them to have input on planning . . . or just simple ideas that you use. Let them know that they have a part of the show.

Idea 2: Create a sense of uniqueness

Students who feel special and unique usually do not need to get negative attention in the classroom. Everyone needs to feel special in some way and the more you can let students know just how important and special they are to you, the better they will feel about themselves. Senior counselor Linda Brown says that when students are made to feel special, they don't have to act special. Good advice for any teacher!

1. Encourage expression . . . let them have ways and outlets of self-expression. Allow the set-up of special projects and classroom activities.
2. Communicate acceptance to them. Make sure students know that you accept them for who they are. Use their names, refer to them specifically. Greet them with a big smile and hug at the door.
3. Notice your students, know who got a new dress, jacket, who got a haircut, earrings, etc. and be sure to let them know that you noticed.
4. Private time . . . be sure to make the time for private discussions with each student, even if it's just a few minutes after class.
5. Allow them to do special projects. Give them all the chances possible for creativity, let them make class announcements or share with the group.
6. Acknowledge special days. For example, always ask who has a birthday each day. If someone is sick for a week or more, send them a get-well card signed by the whole class.

Idea 3: Create greater personal power

As you've learned throughout this chapter, one of the secrets to better discipline is to give your students more power, not try to take it away. The more power they have, the happier, more confident, and more secure they'll be. Could you think of a better combination for a learner? Some options are:

1. Help them set their own limits . . . let them be responsible for their own behavior.
2. Show them ways to influence others . . . teach them communication tools that will increase their ability to get what they want.
3. Ask lots of probing questions . . . about how to solve problems instead of doing it for them. Let them learn to come up with answers. And listen carefully to what your students say.

4. Provide students with more choices. The process mentioned earlier in the chapter for broken agreements is an example of providing more choices.
5. Teach them how to make better decisions . . . give them tools for problem-solving and teach them how adults make decisions continually.
6. Confront cause and effect . . . give them lots of opportunities to see the cause and effect they generate. It begins the responsibility process.

Idea 4: Create better role models

One of the major problems for students is the lack of quality role models. Students have role model selections from magazines, television commercials, billboards and MTV. Where are they going to get the behavior model that you want in your classroom? From you! If you are committed to mastery in teaching and are on the path to mastery, you will be setting a good example for your students. There are some other ways to provide modeling for your students:

1. Understanding . . . help your students understand why they are doing what they are doing. It gives them a mechanism for re-creating success.
2. Share your philosophy . . . in this case, quality is better than quantity, let them know what moves you, and how you achieve the successes you have.
3. Set goals . . . help your students understand the power of setting goals, how to do it and the value in it.
4. Staying on purpose . . . .help your students see the cause and effects of behavior, being clear on the outcome you want.
5. Trigger their thinking . . . get your students to think about why they do things. Help them notice the discrepancies between what others say and what they do. Allow them to sort out false claims or other challenges.
6. Model-building. Talk to them about how people build models of their world in their mind by taking sensory input and generalizing, distorting and deleting. Show them how to do that more usefully.
7. Allow some of the better students do some sharing in the role of a student assistant.

Idea 5: Demonstrate sensory acuity

One of the ways to develop rapport and respect with your students is to use your senses to notice what's going on with your students. The periphery of your eye is physiologically built to detect movement far better than the foveal portion of your eye. The way it's constructed, you can gather most of the data you need between a forty-five and a ninety-degree angle. Surprising? You can detect movement, facial responses and changes in breathing on a non-conscious level if you'll just learn to trust that ability. That's one of many ways to begin to build rapport and respect with your students because they'll know you pay attention to all of them, not just a few. Use your sensory acuity in other ways, too.

1. While you are talking to one student, break eye contact, politely, so you can scan the room. Listen for unusual sounds and notice any new movements. These skills can provide you with the information you need to be successful in handling many persons and things at once. Teachers who demonstrate that they are in contact with every part of the room are letting the students know that there isn't any opportunity to elude your awareness.
2. Learn to use up what is called "dead time." All the transition time for collecting papers, starting or stopping activities or in between activities is usually a signal for students to begin disruptive activities. The solution? Fill that transitional time with questions or suggestions of a question. Say, "and while you're waiting for the handout to arrive, be thinking of three ways the American Civil Rights Movement has affected our economy."

GREATER CONNECTEDNESS

SENSE OF UNIQUENESS

GREATER PERSONAL POWER

BETTER ROLE MODELS

DEMONSTRATE SENSORY ACUITY

INCLUSION

INCREASE PREDICTABILITY

INCREASE RAPPORT

USE QUOTES

CREATE BEHAVIORAL ANCHORS

3. If students appear to be 'resistant,' remember that there are no resistant students. They are simply letting you know that you are on the wrong track. Be thankful that you noticed it. First, give them an immediate oxygen break. Have them stand up, inhale, hold their breath for a few seconds, then exhale. Then do some stretching or just a few quick movement exercises to get the circulation going again. Use that time to figure out how you can make the adjustments with that person or on that part of the lesson you are on. Then, when the oxygen break is over, go right into something more valuable, useful, fun or relevant.

Idea 6: Inclusion—include everyone in your class

Most teachers are actually, teaching to a minority of the students. Give your presentation three or four very different ways so that it reaches more kinds of learners.

1. You could explain things auditorally, then show visually, then demonstrate kinesthetically. It means that you give directions several different times, different ways, even with a higher or lower voice, so insure that you included everyone.
2. You should also include examples of what others have referred to and what you know about each person so that their personal life and history is included. If you are giving special help to one group of students, keep an eye on the rest of the groups, also.
3. Include others by occasionally breaking away from special groups and saying something applicable to the whole class.

Idea 7: Increase predictability

One of the ways for your students to access erratic behavior is through anxiety, confusion and lack of clarity. In earlier chapters, we mentioned the importance of structure and ritual. Students like to know that certain things will happen at certain times.

1. Build in your own ritual. For example, when you are giving directions, always give them with the same pattern. It might be that you first say, then show visually, then demonstrate, then say again, then post them up. This way, the students will learn quickly to pay extra attention during the style of the explanation they understand the best.
2. Post schedules, give schedules. It reduces classroom confusion because a surprising amount of noise and upsets occur over students not knowing what to do. The secret?
3. Have variety of options you can use within a predictable structure.

Idea 8: Create rapport

This tool is so important it was also mentioned in the chapters on introduction and presentation. Webster's defines rapport as "a relation marked by harmony, conformity, accord or affinity." Do you have that with your students? Only you would know. There are many methods of joining their world and building rapport. You need to choose the ones that are most comfortable for you.

2. Match language—use the same predicates. Listen to how each student represents experiences and match it.

Visual	Auditory	Kinesthetic
an eyeful	an earful	a pain in the neck
looks like	sounds like	it feels like
get the picture	pay attention	get the drift of
a dim view	unheard of	underhanded
perspective	an account of	get a handle on

Also match the superlatives that they use. For example, words such as "good, great, excellent, super, or fabulous," are all words which form parts of people's language patterns. Use the same words your students use.

The more power
you give to your students
the less they will try
to take it away from you

2. Match body movements—with whole body: adjust your body to match stance and posture; with gestures: carefully and subtly match gestures; with face: match their eyebrows, mouth, nose, smile; with their head: match the angle of leaning; with their voice: match tempo, tonality, intensity and volume. With breath: match the rate.

3. You may also increase rapport by discussing, referring to or simply mentioning things that are a large part of your student's world. It may be an upcoming exposition, a rock concert, a holiday, a symphony, a movie, the weather, clothing styles, movie or TV stars.

4. You may also do cross-over mirroring. This is when you use one activity to match a different activity with another. For example, pace a student's eye blinks with your finger tapping or foot tapping or pace the tempo of their voice by scratching or nodding.

Idea 9: Using quotes

The use of quotes as a tool for classroom management can be a powerful and effective tool. Quotes are a communication tool wherein you are giving a message to others in the form of quoted material. It's much easier and safer to say certain things that way. You can say almost anything you want, with impunity, if you use a quote (you, of course, can make it up) that someone else said. It's especially helpful if you change your tonality during a key part of your quote. The change will alert the listener to the special importance of that phrase. Here are some examples of how to use quotes in the classroom in your everyday presentation to your students:

1. "You know, I was talking to another teacher about his classroom and he was so pleased with his students, you know what he said to them? He shouted, 'You are the greatest group of students I've ever had! You really (raise your voice) *pay attention* well!' I thought that was pretty nice of him, what do you think?"

2. "Do any of you have a neighbor whose dog is constantly barking? My neighbor's dog really got to me last night so I went out in my yard and shouted over the fence, (raise your voice) SHUT UP! WILL YOU BE QUIET FOR A CHANGE?! And you know what? It worked and I felt much better."

3. You can also use quotes to release anger, frustration or edginess. Simply say what you want to say in quotes. For example: "I ran into someone today who was so angry, you know what he said? He said, 'I'm *furious*! I'm madder than heck and I can't take the noise any more. I'm so frustrated I could scream!' Boy, he must have been mad. Can you imagine someone being that mad?"

Idea 10: Create behavioral anchors

The anchoring process is one that is used all the time by most teachers. However, most don't know they do it, how to do it successfully or how valuable it is. An anchor is the process of using the association of one stimulus to trigger another stimulus in order to achieve a desired outcome. The most famous person for creating an anchor? Maybe Pavlov. He rang a bell when the dogs ate, so pretty soon he could just ring a bell and the dogs would salivate. The anchor was the bell and the outcome achieved was that the dogs salivated. Could you imagine how this same principle could be used for classroom management?

Anchoring is truly amazing because you can anchor anything. A mime anchors air by his movements defining space and objects. He then can go back to that space and you know exactly where all the boundaries are. Creating anchors is not new. Most teachers have them all over the room. Some teachers just look over at a corner of the room where the "isolation area" is and students know what's on the teacher's mind! That's how powerful an anchor is! The teacher had already created an experience of how awful it was to be in that corner. All she had to do was to look at the corner and it triggered a response.

Idea 11: When all else fails, do this

If you feel like you are at the end of your rope, here's another option.

1. First, do some research. Discover if something's going on that's making it difficult for students to pay close attention in class. Find out about the students you are having problems with. Call their parents and talk to them to get some personal history. You may discover something useful.

2. Next review the material in these earlier chapters—the key tools are rapport, participation and relevancy. If you have those three, you'll have a model well-managed class. If everything else fails, and it has to even the best among teachers, there's one last strategy.

3. First, tell the student you are drawing the line. On one side of it are a certain group of behaviors which you'll tolerate. Once the line is crossed, you will not tolerate any of the new behaviors. Tell them that if they cross the line, they are choosing to leave the class. Then, follow up on it. If you have to ask a student to leave your class, do so, with one hitch. Go up to the student after you expel him and tell him that you are sorry to have him leave. Tell him that you wish you knew of a way to help him stay resourceful and behave better in class, but you don't. Also say that you are having him leave because you were not flexible enough, NOT because he is a bad kid (because he's NOT a bad kid!). This way you can accept responsibility for it in a way which leaves the self-esteem and dignity of the student intact.

We started in this chapter talking about some of the underlying assumptions about classroom control. Important issues such as power, control, flexibility and outcomes were dealt with. You also learned ways to empower your students and make them even more resourceful. We saw that creating classroom agreements were important, and learned how to deal with those who break them. And finally, this last section is about how to maintain an atmosphere which will keep discipline problems to a minimum. Your classroom may not be perfect or have total learning, joy and bliss, but then again, its a lot more possible now than before. You now have the resources to create a well-balanced classroom where students feel safe and trust you. You have rapport with them and they are willing to abide by the agreements for no other reason than it's their word. Having students manage themselves is surely the key to a well disciplined class. Try it and let yourself be pleasantly surprised.

☑ **Check These Key Points**

1. Classroom management problems are usually a symptom of mis-management elsewhere.
2. Maintain an atmosphere of love, consistency, integrity, mutual respect and trust.
3. Keep your word and honor your values.
4. Help students to create more behavior options.
5. A rule is the imposition of authority or control and requires no mutual agreement.
6. A guideline is an indication of a policy or conduct and allows for leeway.
7. An agreement is a harmonious accord on a course of action.
8. Make certain that your students understand the differences between rules, guidelines and agreements.
9. Work with students to create agreements for each class.
10. Provide a firm structure for dealing with infractions.
11. Use preventive methods such as creating connection, a sense of uniqueness, greater personal power for students, include everyone.

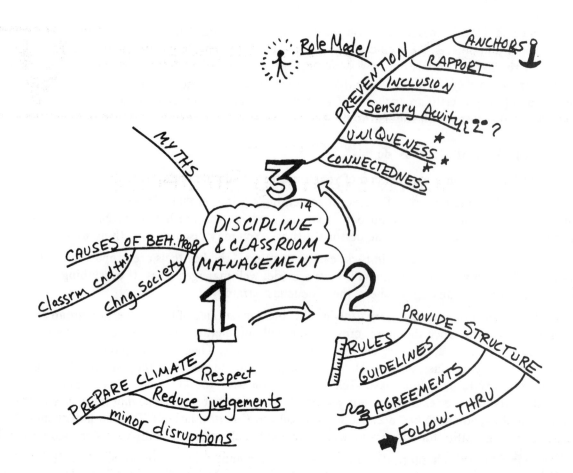

Role Model

PREVENTION — ANCHORS
RAPPORT
INCLUSION
Sensory Acuity [2°?] *
UNIQUENESS *
CONNECTEDNESS *

MYTHS

3

CAUSES OF BEH. PROB.
classrm cnd'ns
chng. Society

DISCIPLINE & CLASSROOM MANAGEMENT 14

1

2

PROVIDE STRUCTURE
RULES
GUIDELINES
AGREEMENTS
Follow-THRU

PREPARE CLIMATE — Respect
Reduce judgements
minor disruptions

The Discovery Process V

Chapter Fifteen

Active Learning Strategies

Objectives

- To describe the advantages of cooperative learning
- To identify the four parts of an activity
- To explain the seven types of activities

In the early 1900's, classrooms were primarily intellectually oriented. The goal was to train the cognitive mind and the lecture format was most common. In the early 1960's, the experiential format emerged and with it the whole genre of humanistic psychology applied to the classroom. In the early 70's research substantiated and validated the importance of teaching with far greater variety of strategies such as the use of humor, music, play, plays, games, puzzles and cooperative learning. This wider "band" of teaching came to be known as "whole-brain" learning. Good teachers have known this all along and eschew lecture when at all possible. The result is a new wave of classroom activities which make learning fast, fun and effective. This chapter offers both the framework and the tools to create the kinds of activities which embody, enliven, inspire, open up, and empower your students. But before the tools, let's look at some of the myths.

Myth: Classroom Activities Are Not Important

The first myth to challenge is that classroom activities are "down time" and that they are not serious learning. The truth of it is that any activity can be a waste of time and any activity can be useful—it all depends on the teacher, the context and the content of the activity. Teachers who consider that activities are not "on task" may be the same ones who have not observed or created successful ones themselves. Visit the classroom of teachers who use activities successfully, then decide.

One of the gifts that an activity provides is the opportunity for students to learn material in ways other than the standard traditional format. You may tap into the exact learning strategy necessary for understanding and excitement. The other gift is that activities have the potential to unite the conscious learning and thinking with the unconscious mind. Much of the material your students get is content-level rote learning. Yet activities can allow students to integrate that information into themselves in a more whole and complete way.

Myth: Activities Are Not Appropriate for Every Subject

Successful classroom activities have been used for every kind of class from algebra to zoology. And in each of those, the knowledge is useful and the experiences from activities is even more useful. One of the most successful accounting courses in the country is a completely play-oriented simulation by Nancy Maresh. A detail-oriented traditionally boring course is turned into an exciting, fast-moving, easily learned course with sound business principles. More input, more variety of input and more student-to-student interactions will increase student learning and enjoyment dramatically.

Myth: Activities Are a Time for the Teacher to Relax

Activities require that the teacher create them properly, monitor them closely and complete them judiciously. When activities are well-run, there may be no 'down time' at all. In general, activities require as much or more time than a presentation. Activities can produce tremendous value if there's a real commitment from the teacher to be fully present and alert throughout the entire activity. An "absent" teacher is one who is not able to be gathering information and providing feedback or support—two key roles for teachers.

Myth: There Isn't Enough Time for Activities

Many teachers argue that there's so much information to deliver that activities are a low priority. What about the possibility of changing your priorities? It is possible that one or more of the following is occurring: too much or too detailed information is being given. The material could be worded more concisely. Your lecture material could also be covered by activities.

Myth: Activities Create Discipline Problems

If you have problems with discipline during lectures, you may experience the same problems during activities—but then again, you may not. Often your students just need a change. The moving around, the talking, and freer schedule that goes with activities can give your students the classtime 'break' that leads to better concentration even during lecture. One of the most important things for your students to have is casual relaxed conversation about the subject matter. This casual interaction time is what shapes the perceptions, attitudes and memories of that subject in your student's mind. Activities can provide a unique open atmosphere of discussion and unstructured learning.

Advantages of Experiential and Cooperative

Learning

The group process may be the best means of promoting low-stress learning in or out of the classroom. As a child, your most fruitful learnings came as a result of actually "doing", either alone or in a group process, and by being with your family. With all the age diversity, you still managed to relate to and learn from everyone. You may have learned much from a grandmother or uncle and naturally passed on to a sibling all that you learned. The lecture format precludes student cooperation and teamplay. As a result, many students have learned to keep to themselves. Years of structured class discipline have made the whole notion of cooperation foreign to them. Cooperative class activities can break up unproductive cliques and can create new learning opportunities. It offers other important things to students:

- *Strategy:* The style of working together as a team means that students are offered information in different formats than a lecture. It often makes the difference between a student being successful in your subject or doing poorly in it.
- *State:* The casual relaxed format means that the physiological and emotional state of the student is often more conducive to learning. For many students, it's simply more fun.
- *Closeness:* The sense of "family" where you are supported, listened to and trusted. It can create a sense of belonging and reduce the psychological and emotional distance between classmates.
- *Influence:* The opportunity for sharing, persuading and self-disclosure on a regular basis. In a class of thirty, many students are not comfortable with contributing to the class. But in a group of three or four, it's quite safe.
- *Creativity:* A classroom activity is an opportunity to bring out the best in your students; the most fresh, valuable and useful ideas. It's an opportunity to break through stereotypes and self-limiting ideas about what can and cannot be done. It also can encourage critical thinking and problem-solving.

- *Excitement and Curiosity about Learning:* Activities re-capture those qualities that creative children express so well: a heightened sensitivity, a value of discovery, spontaneous behavior, wonderment, and strong desire to understand and learn. The adult world is a dull gray compared to the child's world of 3-D technicolor with sounds, smells and touch.
- *Opens Up the Learning Process:* There's an unlimited variety of ways to describe learners. You may have heard learners described as analytical or relational, left or right-brained, visual, tactile, or auditory. Canadian educator Gregorac has identified four types: the concrete sequential, abstract sequential, the abstract random and concrete random. John Geier identifies the dominant, steadfast, compliant and the influencer. Which one is the correct way of labelling a learner? Is there a single, right and correct way? Highly unlikely. That's the beauty of a variety of classroom activities: they provide alternative ways for students to learn how they learn and succeed.
- *Whole-course Content:* Activities which are chosen, planned, run and completed well have the capacity to encapsulate large bodies of knowledge and experience. They can give students a holographic sense of the entire course, thereby accomplishing something a lecture could not.
- *Tests and Evaluations:* Well-run activities can serve as vehicles for the teacher to gather information about who needs help, who's on schedule, and what needs to be done next. Sometimes evaluative information will surface that would never have surfaced otherwise.
- *Lightness:* For many students and teachers, activities provide a break that doesn't occur in other classroom methods. Students, as well as the teacher, appreciate a break from the routine.
- *Self-worth and Validation:* A successful activity can provide students with numerous opportunities to succeed as well as simply feel good about themselves.
- *Integration:* It's an opportunity for the student to become competent with and familiar with the material in the physical sense while the unconscious mind is integrating the experiences into the whole life-learning of that student.

The Four Part Activity Process

There are four parts to successful classroom activities: (1) selection and planning, (2) set up and introduction, (3) operation and maintenance, and (4) closure. Each of the parts are important and require careful attentiveness to achieve your desired result.

☑ 1. Selection and Planning

First thing to develop are criteria with which to evaluate activities. The key is to know the limitations and the possibilities of each so you can make an intelligent choice. Seven of the kinds of activities which meet most any teacher's needs are given, plus the criteria for choosing them.

Seven Criteria for Choosing Activities

1. *Intended Outcome.* What is the activity designed to do? What are the intended results? Are those the results you want?
2. *Numbers.* How many people is the activity designed for? Does it require groups or pairs? How will you divide students for maximum benefit?
3. *Interest.* Is the activity interesting? Is it new or thought-provoking? Is it relevant to the topic at hand? Can your students make the connection to the content in your course?
4. *Manageability.* Is it an activity that can be easily monitored? Can you set up others to act as monitors? Do you need training or a prior experience to run the activity successfully?
5. *Time and cost.* Can the activity be run successfully within the time frame you have available? Is there sufficient time for the introduction and the closure? Can you afford the activity? Are you distinguishing between the actual cost of the activity and the real value to your students?
6. *Simplicity.* Is it an activity that can be easily understood by your students? Is the intellectual level of the game appropriate for your students?
7. *Completion.* Do you know how to complete the activity with the students? Do you have the tools and abilities to confidently lead the closure and completion process to insure that the students get maximum value?

Activities are categorized many ways. This particular grouping is intended to give you three things: a description of the activity, how it's used and when it's appropriate, and the advantages and disadvantages. The seven major categories are: application, team play, games, song and dance, aids and tools, independent and fantasy.

1. Application. An activity in this category has a direct correlation between it and the classroom lecture material. Includes classroom demonstrations, discussions, guest speakers, hands-on practice, field trips, computers, classroom experiments, mechanical instruction and building models. In classroom discussions, conflict and controversy were found to be significant learning promoters when applied in a co-operative environment. Students learned more and remembered more with healthy conflict, concluded David Johnson, a University of Minnesota researcher.

This is the category from which is drawn most of the current classroom activities. Advantages are: easy to set-up, simple to maintain control, usually low cost and familiar to teacher. Disadvantages: lack of availability in some cases, lack of applicability or challenging thinking.

Note: The key in this category is advance preparation. Pay extra attention to the hands-on activities to insure that everyone can participate, not just one student in a group of five. If needed, borrow from other teachers to have enough models, objects or demonstration tools for your group. Make sure that you prepare your guest speaker well. Let students pair-up during the labs or experiments.

2. Team Play. This area specifically develops cooperation, harmony and group work. It includes co-operative learning, simulations, learning teams, memory games, debates, synergy games, drills and mind-mapping. Advantages: lots of variety, mental stimulation, usefulness, challenge and fun. Disadvantages: more difficult to set up, harder to run, tougher to complete, may be costly to get simulations.

Learning teams are groups which have a specific project such as to solve a riddle or class problem. Memory games have students use memory devices to memorize class material in a fun way—often under time pressure, in a games-like way. Debates are risky and boring for the participants. Synergy games are valuable for creating cooperation and team play. Drills can be direct-recall unison drills for review, vocabulary, facts, lists, etc. Mind-mapping can be done in groups: get a poster-sized sheet of paper, give it to groups of 2–4, then let them mind-map a previous class, guest speaker or text material as a review or new learning. Then either hang up the mindmap or have the group share it.

Notes: Anytime you create teams, you have a special dynamic going on. Here are some suggestions for cooperative learning:

1. Choose your groups based on likely synergy: age, diversity, behavior, common strengths and needs.
2. Allow time for team members to create rapport with each other through sharing personal information such as family background, key influences, behavior patterns or highs and lows.
3. Allow the group to create its own identity using a group name, a leader, a logo or a group cheer.
4. Make sure that each team as a whole and each individual team member has a vested interest in contributing. Create a win-win game with friendly competition or group cooperation games.
5. When the activity is over, make sure that each team is acknowledged—a different award to each team works well. Have the team members congratulate each other and give strokes to them yourself.

3. The Hollywood-Quiz Show. Whiz-Kid games and others are designed to make learning fun and competitive. They include quiz show formats, interviews of famous stars, TV shows, skits, or people's court. The advantages include high interest, fastpace, and lots of movement. Disadvantages are more set-up time needed, more planning, often rehearsals, requires more student support, may confront some students. Create a way for everyone to win. Use these activities for less actual learning and more for recall.

Notes: Quiz shows are much easier if given to the students to structure and run. Just make sure that you review it with the students before it's actually run. Interviews are a super learning device. First, put the students in pairs. One person is the reporter conducting an interview and the other is the supposed expert on the subject. You can also do courtroom trials and TV shows.

4. Song and Dance. This is the area of self-expression a la "Sesame Street." It includes plays, acts, puppet shows, magic acts, dances, talent show, skits, songs, Simon Says, poems and role-playing. It also includes ball-toss, New Games, hand-clapping, mime and learning games. Advantages: it engages the whole body, it's challenging, creative, satisfying and often a real personal triumph. Disadvantages: sometimes appears to be less related to course content, risk-taking, some may be hesitant to participate, variable results, unpredictable outcomes.

Notes: These are the highest quality activities for variety, fun and linking the conscious learning with the unconscious. They require planning, nerve to make happen and are well worth it!

We are all gifted . . .
only the context
determines the evidence

---

5. Teaching aids. These often do not fall into the category of activities but are included as a resource. Aids include: textbooks, booklets, handouts, brochures, flyers, magazines, newspapers, photos, pictures, paintings, slides, films, overhead projector, chalkboard, flipchart, bulletin board, cassettes, light shows, videos, holograms and sound displays. Advantages: they are simple, safe, low risk, inexpensive, predictable, and easy to obtain. Disadvantages: boring, lack of challenge, lack of cooperative possibilities, less feedback built in.

Notes: These kinds of contributors to the course can either be active or passive depending on how they're used. Make them active by giving students an assignment to do during the activity.

6. Independent activities. These are the solo ones; designed to encourage independence and stronger thinking skills. They include thinking, communication processes, creativity games, language games, self-processing, discovery processes, reading, creating tests, problem-solving, personal assessments and mind-mapping. Advantages: they are good for encouraging thinking, expanding intellectual confidence, easy to set-up, easy to run, safe, predictable, good for independent thinkers. Disadvantages: poor for those who need extra help or attention, slow or no energy, no movement, difficult to monitor for effectiveness, lack of feedback, less sense of accomplishment and cooperative effort.

Notes: This is, along with the category on team play, one of the most powerful areas for activity success. Thinking activities are those which ask a student simply think about something, think about the process of thinking, then have an inquiry or discussion about it. A perfect example for an activity is to have the students come up with a format for problem-solving. Then discuss and improve upon it. They usually come up with excellent answers such as: guess and check, make a table, find the pattern, elimination or to simplify.

7. Fantasy. This is the area in which the teacher, a guest or a tape uses a closed-eye process to create specific results. It includes visual imagery, early memory restimulation, trance induction and psycho-kinesthetics. Advantages: easy for students to participate, easy to do (once you've learned how), it can produce specific results effortlessly and is fun for students. Disadvantages: requires training of the teacher and lacks active student interaction.

Notes: This kind of material needs to be set-up well with a strong introduction. The group must feel much trust in you to make this type of activity successful. When done properly, it can be a most powerful experience.

The second part is to complete logistical preparation. There are physical pieces which need to come into play for the activity to be successful. For example, will your activity create any noise? Do nearby rooms or groups need to be notified? Can your activity be interrupted? If not, make some 'Do Not Disturb' signs and post them nearby. Is the room set up properly for the activity? If not, either enlist some support from other students, a set-up crew, a janitor. Do you have out all the materials for the activity? Have you made a head count and matched numbers to be sure that you have enough? Do you have extras or spares of everything needed? Is it in stacks or groups for easy dispersal?

☑ 2. Introduction

It's critical to allow students to reach into their own experiences and discover what your proposed activity could mean to them, based on their past. An easy way to do that is simply through asking questions. "How many of you remember learning how to ride a bicycle by reading a book?" "How many of you realize that you learn better by actually doing something?" "How many of you would rather go to the beach than read about it?" "Who in this group gets more enjoyment out of actually doing something than thinking about it?" "How many of you would like a break from our usual lecture routine?" As you continue to elicit a show of hands, you'll be allowing the students to create the value in themselves in the activity you are about to initiate.

Get the Students Physically Active

The opening of the activity is also an excellent time to get the students up to stretch and move around a bit. The brain weighs about three percent of the total body weight, but it consumes 20% of its oxygen. In order for your students to perform at their best give them oxygen! Create times for a few deep breaths or some stretching to awaken the body's senses and send extra oxygen to the brain. The more of those the better—you could have a oxygen break every 15 minutes.

Know the Outcome

Next, students need to know what, specifically, is the objective of the activity. The objective is very different from the purpose. The purpose is usually some open-ended statement such as "To expand. . ." "To increase. . ." But the objective, also known as the intended result or the outcome is a clearly defined goal that can be measured and described in sensory terms. For example, "The objective is to circle the gameboard with your gamepiece as many times as you can during the 20 minute game time while following the rules exactly." Once you have told the students the intended outcome, post it. Put it up on flip chart paper or on the chalkboard so students can refer to it easily.

Make the Directions Extra-Clear

One of the easiest ways to ruin a potentially successful activity is with poor directions. Most directions are 'C.I.P.U.' This means, "Clear if previously understood." With directions, avoid nominalizations such as "be fair, be responsible, stay honest, etc." Those are not specific enough to elicit equal behavior from all students. Describe the directions in clear specific language by continually asking for questions. "In this game, fairness means that you'll. . ." Wait until you have given directions verbally, visually, then have students actually try them out kinesthetically. Then write out the 3–5 basic steps and post them, pass them out or write them on the chalkboard. It's much more clear to use colors rather than numbers and terms such as "above" and "below" rather than "left" and "right."

Also include clear time references. If it's a timed activity, let the students know whether you are using your watch or the wall clock (advantages to each). Let them know what to do if they finish early or run out of anything—time, materials, people, etc. Explain to the students your policies on things such as noise (how much is OK?) and trash (what's messy and what's not?). Make sure students know what your role will be and if it will change throughout the activity. Also make sure they know what to do if they get lost, confused or need help.

Master teacher Susan Kovalik suggests a sociogram to aid in the selection process. First, have each student fill out a 3 × 5 card with their name at the top, underlined. Then have them add the names of five others they feel they can work with effectively. Next, decide how many groups you'll need to have: 4–6 students per group for elementary, three students for 6–12th grade. For example if your high school class has 36 students, you'll need 12 groups, if your elementary class has 24 students, you could have 4–6 groups. Collect the cards and sort them using your best-behaved class leaders as the nucleus for each group. Then add one student to each group who needs support for more appropriate behavior. With your "best" and "worst" behaved students as a core, add additional students to each group keeping in mind both the male/female and the student's preferences for group members. This sorting process can be done in less than an hour and can easily be done by one of your more responsible students. Plan on changing groups throughout the school year.

How else can you select groups, pairs or teams for activities? The first thing to do is to ask yourself what is the outcome you want. Do you want each person to have a personal breakthrough or solo experience? Do you want to open up any particular student? Do you want to break up any unproductive cliques or support any unresourceful students? The next question is what processes will go on as a result of the activity? Are any likely to cause a problem for some of your students? If so, you may need to arrange them differently. Can your students change groups, teams or partners during the activity? What will you do if you see a pair or team that is not working well together? What's your strategy? All of these questions need to be addressed in your mind before the activity even starts because something as simple as the pairings can make a difference between success and failure of the activity. Here are some possibilities for choosing groups:

1. Teacher subjectively selects. In this case, the teacher would say, "You go with him, you go with her, and you two go over here. . ."
2. Students subjectively select. Allow the students to get into groups on their own. Give them 60 seconds to break up into groups by finding their own team members or partners. If there are any who are left at the end who don't have partners, have them raise their hands, then let the extras pair up with each other.
3. Counting process. Have the students count off by ones, twos and threes (or whatever group size you want) then just say all the ones go over there, etc. This can, of course, be done with A-B-A-B.
4. Arbitrary differences. In this process, the teacher simply uses arbitrary criteria to determine groups. For example, "You and the person sitting next to you are partners, the one with the shortest hair is an 'A' and the one with the longer hair is a 'B.' Or, you could pick groups by birthdays, last names, street names, astrological signs, room location, clothing worn, etc.
5. Gaming process. This sets up a completely different context, depending on what you want. Bob McKim invented a game called 'barnyard' and it goes like this: have students count off A-B-C-D-E, in maybe five or ten groups, so that everyone has a letter. Then assign an animal to each letter such as all As are sheep, all Bs are pigs and all Cs are chickens, etc. Then make sure the students are all in the center of a large space, with the chairs cleared out. Then everyone closes their eyes and makes the sound of the animal that was assigned to them. Naturally, you'll have a room full of clucks, moos, baaahs, grunts, etc. The goal of the game is to find all the other members in your group by the sounds alone. Once they are all in clusters, the students can open their eyes and the game is over. It's a great way to break down some barriers, choose groups and have fun at the same time.

☑ **3. How to Maintain Successful Activities**

During the activities, it's important to monitor your own profile as well as the students. First, be sensitive to "group energy." Is the activity as a whole slow and boring? Then either do one of two things: quickly change the rules to enliven it or cut it short and keep your losses to a minimum. If the activity appears to be too lively ask yourself if the aliveness is creating a problem. Lots of noise and movement and fun is not a problem unless it's creating damage or students are being disrespectful of persons or property. Again, if the aliveness of the activity is a problem, you have the same two choices as above: change the rules or stop the activity.

Next, be extra sensitive to any individual situation developing such as detachment, hostility, anger or depression. This means that you must have your sensory acuity turned up to insure you catch things early and deal with it on the spot.

Another thing to be sensitive about is the ongoing process of the activity itself. Listen, watch and feel using your best sensory acuity to make sure the activity is meeting your goals. Use this time as a time to make personal contact with students who may need an extra smile, an encouraging word, a pep talk, or just a touch on the shoulder. In addition, be conscious of the time elapsed and make sure you give time signals so students are aware of the time. Also be sure to have allowed time for the completion process at the end of the activity. In a 50-minute activity hour, you might spend 10 minutes to set it up, 25 minutes to run it and 15 minutes for the closure.

☑ **4. How to Close Activities**

The closure is a time to let students surface with their joys, frustrations, conclusions, insights and expressions. But before they do that, be sure to clear off the tables or put all the materials to the side so the focus of the next few moments can be on the speaker, not any physical objects.

Often neglected, the closure is the most important part of the activity process. It's not what happens in life that counts, it's what you conclude and do about what happened that counts. During this time you are to assist the student in coming up with conclusions which will allow him to have more choices in the future. Herein lies the real value of the classroom activities.

During the completion or processing of the activity, stay focused on your intended outcome. Your intention is to have the students become more resourceful than ever before and to have greater self esteem. Ideally, the results and conclusions drawn by the student reflect an increased sense of power, confidence and well-being. This is the time for students to report or share the results of the activity just completed. You may either call on them or ask if anyone has anything they'd like to share about the just-completed activity. The kinds of responses useful to have expressed are the following:

1. What actually happened during the activity? What events happened in your group or team?
2. What went on for you, specifically? (describe your feelings, thoughts, judgements)
3. What did you learn, see, hear, do; about yourself, and the entire activity?
4. What conclusions can you draw about yourself and similar activities?
5. What other conclusions can you draw, true or not, that would add to your resourcefulness for the future?
6. What is it that you'd now do differently, given the same situation again?
7. How does this relate to your life?

After any of those questions, the reaction the student gives will be the most important part. Your goal in the closure process is to find a way to make sure that your students are able to leave the class with greater resources than they came in with. You'll need to listen carefully, giving full attention to each person who shares an experience of the activity. Make sure that your body is turned toward the speaker, with all your antenna out for maximum sensory acuity. Be sure to respond with an appreciative comment such as one of these:

"Thanks very much for sharing a part of yourself." "You've been great, thanks a lot." "I appreciate what you said and want to acknowledge you for sharing." "I respect what you've said, thank you." "Thank you for sharing yourself."

First, notice that each of the responses are designed to acknowledge the student for simply contributing. Your response says nothing about what was said. Simply acknowledge the student for sharing and participating. In addition, be sure to follow through each of the comments shared so that the student feels validated and more resourceful. It's also important to give students a holistic and global sense of what the activity was for and what it accomplished. When that occurs, your classroom activity will have accomplished all that you hoped it would. Specific activity resource books are listed in the bibliography.

☑ Check These Key Points

1. Cooperative learning offers a casual format, a situation of closeness to others, greater opportunity for sharing thus encouraging problem-solving and thinking skills.
2. The 4 parts of an activity are: selection/planning, introduction, operation/maintenance, and closure.
3. The 7 criteria for choosing an activity are: intended outcome, numbers, interest, manageability, time and cost, simplicity, and completion.
4. The 7 major categories of activities are application, team play, quiz shows, song and dance, teaching aids, independent activities, and fantasy.
5. Use a sociogram to select students for group activities.

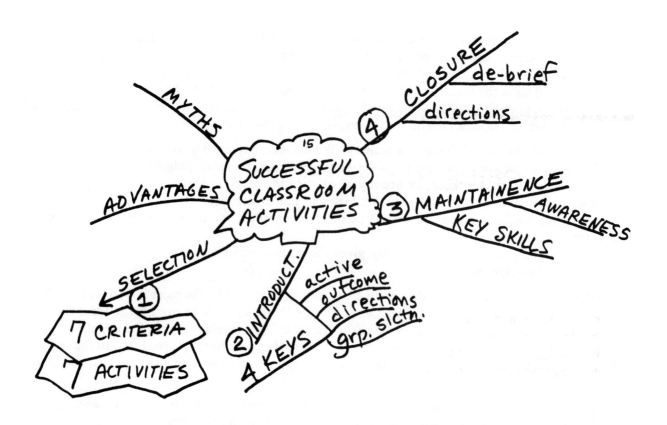

MYTHS

ADVANTAGES

SELECTION ①

⑦ CRITERIA

⑦ ACTIVITIES

15
SUCCESSFUL
CLASSROOM
ACTIVITIES

② INTRODUCT.

4 KEYS

active
outcome
directions
grp. slctn.

④ CLOSURE   de-brief
directions

③ MAINTAINENCE
KEY SKILLS
AWARENESS

Chapter Sixteen

Self-Esteem: A Way of Being

Objectives

- To define and describe self-esteem
- To list behaviors exemplifying high self-esteem
- To describe essentials of self-esteem
- To provide examples of acknowledgement and praise

If we took a cross-section of the students at risk in our society (substance abuse, teenage pregnancy, dropouts, low achievement scores, etc.) and compared it with successful students, one character trait would be dramatically different. It's not income, race, sex or geographical location. It's self-esteem. Students with low self-esteem have a difficult life and often become a burden on society. Those with a high level of self-esteem consistently make contributions to our society. In your classroom, students with high self-esteem participate more, achieve more, build friendships, complete assignments, score higher, stay in school and feel good about their future. Results of low self-esteem are lower grades, fear of participation, damaging relationships, trouble-making behavior and resignation to a dim future.

Self-esteem is made of two components: intellectual and emotional—that is, being capable and lovable. It is experiencing yourself as being "capable" as in "I am able to do many things now or at least have the capacity to learn them." It also means feeling loved as in "I know I am a unique, special and care-about-able person who is worthy of attention, affection and love." Research demonstrates that 80% of our children enter first grade with high self-esteem and 5% graduate from high school with high self-esteem. Something very damaging affects the well-being of most students between first and twelfth grade.

Self-esteem is really an attitude about yourself and attitudes are a critical part of the learning process. If your students believe they *can,* the job is half done. If you teach curriculum instead of people, you'll always have problems with motivation, self-esteem and performance. By teaching people, modeling and demonstrating useful positive life values becomes as important as the subject for the day. One of your on-going roles is to promote and enhance the self-esteem of your students. It's not a matter of, "Do I have the time?" Or, "Can I afford it?" You cannot afford NOT to do it.

Students who feel good about themselves, value who they are, what they do, and where they're going are a real joy to teach. These students generally contribute more, learn more, are better behaved and easier to get along with. They get along well with other students and they usually have more useful and fulfilling lives. Because you are an important person in each student's life, what you do can and will make a difference in his or her life. In this field, as in others, the myths are rampant.

Myth: You Already Do Enough

Some say, "I am already good at it" or "I already do it enought." If so, you're either the one in a thousand master teachers or you are simply unaware. Probably the best way to decide what's enough is to look at the results. Check your students' behavior, their language and attitudes. Most could use a major boost in self-esteem. In a 1985 nationwide survey of high school students, one of the two traits valued highest, by over 90% of them, was confidence and self-esteem. It is critical that we teachers learn to acknowledge more.

Myth: It's Not Important

Is your job to teach or give strokes? A master teacher's job is to produce results. Teachers who appreciate and acknowledge others usually produces greater results. How? The skills and abilities most necessary for academic competence thrive best in an environment of support and acknowledgement. The curriculum that you want so much to cover can wait. Make sure the students are growing as human beings first, the curriculum will take care of itself.

Myth: Not Every Student Deserves a Boost

Some teachers assume that students must earn self-esteem. There are three mistakes in that assumption. First, it falsely assumes that students must earn basic self-respect and dignity, as if it were a medal for performance. We all need it and sometimes we need it most when we are least able to perform for it.

The second mistake is presuming that teachers are innately capable of noticing what and when there is a need to build self-esteem.

The last mistake in the erroneous assumption that "not everyone deserves it" with is the issue of earned rewards. This is touchy because most of us are taught to reward the positive and punish the negative. As usual, there is a strong argument for each side.

Of major importance is to avoid a discussion about which side is right or wrong. Ask yourself a more important question, "Is acknowledgement, giving a stroke or self-esteem building useful?" Resounding evidence says that it is very useful! The founder of transactional analysis (TA), Eric Berne reminds us, " . . . I wish to restate the fact: strokes are as necessary to human life as are other primary biological needs such as the need for food, water, and shelter—needs which, if not satisfied, will lead to death."

Myth: Withholding Strokes Is Not Damaging

Teachers have used validation as a means of control over students. Eric Berne points out that the use of validation as a manipulation for behavior control is far more effective than brutality or punishment. Why would a teacher withhold strokes? Because teachers don't think they have the resources necessary to control the classroom otherwise. The tools in this book provide new resources so strokes can be given freely.

Myth: It's Not Okay to Give Strokes Freely

Our society has many taboos regarding the nature of compliments. For example it's uncomfortable for many of us, and especially so for men, to give strokes to members of the same sex. It is rare to hear one man say to another, "I like how you look today." When was the last time your associates gave you pat on the back or hug? And unfortunately, giving compliments to the opposite sex is often translated as flirting.

Myth: More Appreciating Might Cause Problems

You may be wondering if you'd come across as phony. Or, what if the students take it in a different way from how it's intended? You may be surprised to know that students are eager, even hungry for strokes. You may have fears about what would happen if you actually appreciated everyone who deserved it. You might be wondering if you'd end up acknowledging all day or if your students would get inflated egos. What if they start feeling more powerful? Relax. When you acknowledge others, a special magic occurs and students begin giving more and taking less.

Essentials of Self-Esteem

There's no secret formula to building self-esteem. Only you can build it for yourself. You cannot build another's self-esteem, you can only set up the conditions in which another is likely to build his own. Self-esteem is raised through a series of internal decisions made by the individual, not someone else for him. The student needs to come to the conclusion for himself that he is lovable and capable. That's why giving out "strokes" to students only leads to greater self-esteem IF the student is the one who makes the subsequent decision that HE did a great job and THEREFORE is capable. Regardless of what the praise was from another, it's always what we say to ourselves that ultimately determines self-esteem, not what others say.

If there was a secret to building self-esteem in others, it would be to start with yourself. Use everyday as an opportunity to set an example for your students. Be in the discovery process, be a learner and grower. Be the person you would like your students to emulate. Other qualities and behaviors that exemplify high self-esteem are:

1. *High Personal Integrity.* Tell the truth, always, and tell it with compassion. Keep your word and complete whatever agreements you make.
2. *Responsibility.* Speak the language of responsibility and be the embodiment of personal accountability. This results in greater personal power and a greater sense of your own ability to make things happen.
3. *Supporting Others.* Be a success by supporting the success of those around you. Speak supportively, praise often and back up other's ideas and work.
4. *Self-Discipline.* Do the things that others are unwilling to do. Follow through on promises and projects. Take care of details. Follow a schedule and complete lists. Be meticulous about quality and service.
5. *Build Relationships.* Show you care about others. Tell others you care about them. Do things for others; stick your neck out for others. Remember birthdays, anniversaries, special occasions.
6. *Know Yourself.* Know your own unique qualities. Know who you are and what you are strong at doing. Know what areas in which you need more work. Know that you are one-of-a-kind and unique in all the universe.
7. *Vision/Purpose.* Have a dream about what you want to do or have happen in life. Know your life purpose and your steps on its path. Have a grand vision or dream that inspires you and gets you up each morning. Share it with others and inspire them.
8. *Environment.* Create a specialized living and learning environment that reflects your highest thoughts about yourself and your students. Keep it spotless, up-to-date and rich in meaning.
9. *Excellence.* Give everything your best effort, even a seemingly small insignificant task. Do work with a song in your heart, knowing your purpose and how you fit into the plan.
10. *Health.* Take care of your emotional, mental and physical health. Be proud of your body and do what it takes to have it support your dreams and lifestyles.

Self-esteem takes many forms in the classroom. The least useful form is in *content* as in a self-esteem-building exercise. The most useful is to *live and embody it* so that it forms a weave or a thread throughout the entire school year. Self-esteem is so delicate that it can be damaged with just one off-purpose comment. Yet it may take many dozens of comments to raise it.

You want to build up a reserve of self-esteem feelings within each of your students. In the case of a mistake, you can simply apologize and move on without any permanent damage. That's why self-esteem needs to be your way of being, not a task you do to get it over with.

Classroom How To's for Building Self-Esteem

☑ 1. *Create a Sense of Purpose for Your Students.* Convey expectations, elicit student goals and assist them in setting realistic ones. Share your own goals. Build confidence and faith.
☑ 2. *Convey a Sense of Control.* Make sure that your students know they have a choice over their feelings; That others don't make them angry or upset or happy, that they can control feelings themselves.
☑ 3. *Establish a Sense of Security.* Develop self-respect through words and actions. Build trust, set realistic rules and limits. Enforce rules consistently.
☑ 4. *Create a Family Democratic Atmosphere.* When appropriate, allow students to make choices and feel more powerful. Give freedom when possible and allow students to participate in decisions.
☑ 5. *Create a Sense of Belonging.* Have students feel part of the family. Be warm, loving and accepting. Create responsibilities of group membership. Encourage the acceptance and inclusion of others.

☑ 6. *Create a Sense of Competence.* Have students learn and do tasks they consider important. Provide encouragement, strokes and support. Aid them in self-evaluation and provide recognition and rewards.

☑ 7. *Create a Sense of Identity.* Make sure that students know who they are, their strengths, their uniqueness and specialness. Aid them in assessing their qualities and provide unconditional acceptance and love.

Of all the things you can do in the classroom, one of the easiest and most powerful ways to weave in healthy self-esteem is with appreciation and acknowledgement.

Acknowledgment

Why acknowledgment? Quite simply, it works. No single tool in this entire book is as powerful as acknowledgment for raising self-esteem, creating more confident and resourceful students and boosting productivity. Yet, in spite of what it can do for others, acknowledgment is really about oneself. To notice the good in others is to notice the good in ourselves. Conversely, the better we feel about ourselves, the more good we'll notice in others. Our wants and needs are similar; our dreams and hopes, similar; our talents and abilities are similar. We all need reinforcement and approval for improvement as well as for just being ourselves.

With the apparent deficiency of strokes, approval and acknowledgment, there are superb opportunities for teachers to fill in the gaps. Teachers spend many hours with students and have the capacity to immerse them in an environment of support, acknowledgment and validation. Through so doing, teachers help make their students better human beings.

The first place to start is with you. Begin to acknowledge yourself for little things as well as the larger ones. Learn to acknowledge and love yourself for just being you. Appreciate yourself for being the courageous growing person you are. Appreciate yourself for just being alive. Embrace yourself and hold appreciative thoughts of yourself. Say to yourself, "I love you!" and mean it. Know that all love starts from within. You are the source of all good in your own world. And since you are the source of all good, that's a great reason to acknowledge yourself!

The next place to start acknowledging is with those closest to you. When was the last time you thanked or acknowledged your spouse or other family members? Do you recall the last time you appreciated the janitor, school secretary, other teachers or your supervisor? There have been dozens of persons who have contributed to your success as a teacher and to whom an acknowledgment would be immediately appropriate. And guess what? The more you acknowledge them for what they've done, the stronger you feel and the better they feel. How about the obvious . . . your students? There is no shortage of persons to acknowledge or places to start. Make it a goal to acknowledge ten people per day. The sooner you start, the easier it becomes.

How to Acknowledge Successfully

First, what makes one person have a better self concept might make no impression on another. Second, teachers must have the sensory acuity to be able to tell if an acknowledgment has "landed" and have the resources to change their behavior as needed. Third, there are those who try to deflect validation and the better prepared you are for that outcome, the better you can deal with it.

In one sense, there could hardly be anything simpler. However, as we found out earlier in the book, there are a lot of different kinds of people in this world and you can be sure you'll have diversity in your classroom. To be a master at delivering acknowledgments, you need just three things:

1. To be committed to the outcome that your acknowledgment will be received with the same meaning with which it is delivered.
2. To have the sensory acuity to know if it actually did "land" in the way you intended.
3. To have the behavioral flexibility to be able to make the necessary adjustments instantly so that the intended outcome is reached.

CONSCIOUS

CONSCIOUS

NON-
CONSCIOUS

NON-
CONSCIOUS

Individual Acknowledgments

1. Check your physiology. Hold the posture and breathing that could be labeled as "open, warm and safe" by others. It will vary. For some, the hands will be behind the back; for others, open palms extended; for all, a smile! You'll know what feels most comfortable.

2. Get the attention of the person. The most common ways are through eye contact, a hand on the shoulder, your position and posture or through a simple spoken word ("John . . . ?").

3. Say what you want to say. Be brief and to the point. Share feelings, observations or expressions with your energy and intention behind it. Say it without strings attached and use the person's name. ("John . . . it's been a real joy having you in class, thanks!") Use any gestures, eye movement, breathing and posture that corroborate the verbal message. Be sure that your non-verbal message matches your verbal message.

4. Pause. Let the message stay with the student for a moment by continuing to maintain some form of contact (eyes, hand, etc.) while keeping silent. Observe the reactions and quickly assess body language for signs that the message "landed" or did not.

5. Respond. At this time, you have two possibilities. If the acknowledgment did not "land", you'll need to develop a different approach for the next time. If it did land, continue with whatever feels appropriate. That may include more conversation, a hug, a smile, a handshake.

Group Acknowledgments

Nearly anytime is a great time to appreciate and acknowledge your students. Do it before class, "I love how all of you are dressed today—great flashy colors!" Do it at the start of class, "I consider it a privilege to be here in class with you—your time is valuable and I hope to do my best to make it worthwhile." Or, "Thanks for being on time. In fact, I'm glad just to have you all in my class. It makes me feel lucky!" Do it during the class, "Thanks for really participating today." Or, "You know what? Class is more fun with you in it!" At test time, "Thanks for staying quiet and respectful of your neighbor." In the middle of class, "Boy, I sure have a lot of fun with you!" As the class closes, "It's students like you

who make my job so great. Thanks for really participating and going for it!" There's no maximum or minimum, but you should be able to find ways to acknowledge your students dozens of times in every class. One of the best results is that students often begin to live up to our acknowledgements and standards of performance increase.

Teaching is not a job
or a duty to perform. . . .
It is a privilege to be accepted
by those able to be responsible and
with hearts big enough to love enough.

Each May Respond Differently

Some people need to have eye contact, to hear what you say, to repeat it to themselves and look at you again before the message is "received". Others need no eye contact, but may expect a hand on the shoulder, a handshake or a hug. That's the way they 'know' that they are validated. It's critical to know:

1. The way that you give out acknowledgements and validations is likely to be the way you like to receive them.
2. The way you give acknowledgements may not be the best way for the person to receive them.

Have You Made This Important Distinction?

Author Haim Ginott distinguishes between appreciative acknowledgements, descriptive praise and evaluative praise. The first two are healthy, the last is not. The first two are unconditional, the last is not. The first two are non-judgmental, the last is not. An evaluative praise is a performance-oriented judgment, the kind that an unaware boss (or teacher) gives an employee (or student). It consists of evaluating character traits or actions and often creates anxiety, defensiveness or dependency. For example, "You're a great student" is a performance-oriented remark which is vague. Better than nothing to be sure, but far from the optimum.

It is healthier to say, "You're a pleasure to have in class . . . and thanks for turning in your assignment on time." Instead of saying to a student, "You are so good," say, "Thank you for returning the lost wallet. I appreciate it very much." Don't say, "Good job, David. Keep up the good work." Instead, say, "I feel really blessed just to have you in my class. It's a great feeling!" Notice that there are no strings attached to an appreciative acknowledgement. It's just a straight-from-the-heart, "Thanks."

Praise

1. *Evaluative.* (Avoid this type!) It is judgmental. It is based on a powerful-powerless role of teacher-student. It is manipulative, stressful and often does NOT get the job done. By using this kind "praise" you plant conclusions in the student's mind about the quality of the job or the quality of the character. How much better to have the student come up with the conclusion for him or herself.

   EXAMPLES: "Good job, Johnny!"
   "Your homework was excellent, Susie."
   "You did great today, Jeff."

2. *Descriptive.* (Very useful) This is a statement in simple words that tells what occurred. It states the event, acknowledges it and affirms it. What's effective about this type of praise is that the student hears you state what occurred and can *conclude for himself* that he is a capable human being.

   EXAMPLES: "Your handwriting was perfectly within the lines, the letters were evenly formed and everything was capitalized exactly according to the rules we talked about."

   "Your skit was on exactly the subject matter requested. It brought up all the key points and was finished on time."
   "Your question is most relevant."

3. *Appreciative.* (most useful) This type of praise tells how you REACT to what was done. It's really your response to the event, rather than the event itself. It comes from the heart and lets the student know that he is special and makes a difference. But most importantly, after you make these statements to a student, HE or SHE can make conclusions such as, "I am lovable" or "I am capable." When the student arrives at those conclusions, it is much more powerful and likely to last as an acknowledgement and self-esteem builder.

   EXAMPLES: "I loved your skit, Ellen. I never laughed so hard."
   "I'm inspired by the last couple of questions you've asked."

   "I really appreciate the way you got your homework done. I am really proud for you and the progress you've made."

What If Your Acknowledgment Doesn't Land?

Students use three tools to form their internal "map" of the world: deletion, generalization and distortion. These tools may also prevent your acknowledgment from being received. A deletion is made when part of an experience is left out of the interaction. A generalization occurs when a student takes a conclusion which is true for a specific incident and assumes it can be applied to others. A distortion occurs when a speaker changes the content or meaning of the experience to make it say something different from what was intended. Redefining is a distortion method that people use to alter communications to fit their frame of reference. Here are examples of how an acknowledgment is not received and how to re-phrase, trying it again.

1. *Teacher:* "You're real special, thanks for being in my life."
   Student distortion: "What are you trying to get from me?"
   Solution: "You're right, I'm sorry. I guess sometimes I just don't know how to tell you how much you mean to me. Any suggestions?"
2. *Teacher:* "Wow, what a class we had and you really contributed!"
   Student redefining: "How do you expect me to believe that?"
   Solution: "Actually I don't. What I should have said was that I had a good time and felt good about having you as part of it."
3. *Teacher:* "Hey, David. Thanks for helping with the set-up before class."
   Student deletion: "You gotta be kidding, that was nothing. . ."
   Solution: "Have you ever had someone do a small favor to you, and yet it really meant a lot to you? I feel that same way. You did make things easier for me this morning and I just wanted you to know that, so thanks again."
4. *Teacher:* "I've felt great having you in my class."
   Student generalization: "But you say everything's great. Are you ever serious?"
   Solution: "You're right, I do use that word a lot. Guess I should have used a different way to let you know it's really made a positive difference having you in my class."

Another set of tools that prevent acknowledgments from "landing" are actually subtle variations on the ones mentioned earlier. They are discounts, denials, throwbacks, and "marshmallowing". Discounting is the process used to make a compliment worth less, hence to "dis-count" it. Denial is the method used to refute the validation, and throwback is the process of giving the compliment back to the sender. Marshmallowing is the apparency of support but is actually the subtle-message, "You're going to fail."

Discounts

Teacher: "Thanks for joining us today, you made real contributions and it felt great just having you around."
Student discount: "I actually didn't do that much at all. I just came and sat around."
Solution: "That's true and I agree that physically you didn't do a lot. I guess what made it worthwhile for me was just knowing you were in my class and enjoying your presence."

Denials

Teacher: "What a blessing to have you in class—you really got everyone participating!"
Student denial: "You're far too generous with your compliments—I couldn't take credit for what went on today."
Solution: "I respect your modesty and at the same time, I was just letting you know how much you mean to me. Thanks!"

Throwbacks

Teacher: "It's been a real joy to have you in class. Thanks."
Student distortion: "Hold it. You're the one who should get all the credit. It wasn't possible without all you did."
Solution: "I appreciate that you noticed what I contributed. Mostly I wanted you to know that it makes me feel good just having you in class. Thanks."

Marshmallowing (avoid this)

Teacher: "I know you're a good student. I called your folks to make sure you brought your homework because you're so important to me that I didn't want to take a chance that you'd forget it. I'll stay after class today to make sure that you understand today's assignment and help you all I can."
Student response: "I think I can handle it on my own."

Note: In the above comment the teacher is giving a "marshmallow" acknowledgement. Is not useful because it: 1) invites dependency 2) gives permission to be irresponsible 3) doesn't allow the student to learn the consequences of his own actions 4) implies that the student can't make it without you.

Other Ways to Know if Your Acknowledgment Has Landed

This is a critical part of the acknowledgment process because if you keep putting out validations that aren't received, you're in trouble. You need to know if your acknowledgments are getting through for two reasons. One, if the other person did not get the message, your appreciation wasn't felt so you must re-package it. And, you are speaking different languages and have poor rapport.

Most of the time, the body is a visible indicator of the subconscious. Body language will show you first, and most accurately, if the compliment is being received. If it's about to be turned away with one or more of the tools mentioned in this chapter, the body will show it even before the words do. Here's how to find out if your acknowledgment has been heard, felt and landed successfully:

Head—nodding in agreement. Eyes—opening wider and blinking less, perhaps looking from side-to-side or down. Facial tones—usually become fuller. Eyebrows—raised.
Shoulders—squared and fuller. Breathing—pauses, then becomes stronger, lower in the chest. Hands and arms—unfolded and still. Voice—varies, you must calibrate it with previous event.

We've seen how important acknowledgment is to the success of students and yourself. You can never sing the song of praise too often—if it's sincere. There are hundreds of other ideas and activities that can promote self-esteem. Some are listed in the bibliography and others are products of pioneers in the self-esteem field such as Jack Canfield, Frank Siccone, Helice Bridges, John Vasconcellos, Dr. Sidney Simon and Bob Reasoner.

Recommended resource books include Jack Canfield's *100 Ways to Enhance Self-Concept in the Classroom,* and *100 Ways to Promote Personal and Social Responsibility in Schools* with Frank Siccone. Canfield's Los Angeles organization and Frank Siccone's Foundation in San Francisco offer seminars, tapes, books and school programs. In addition, Helice Bridges in San Diego has a organization called Difference Makers which has superb programs and products for building self-esteem.

Certainly there's no shortage of people to acknowledge and you've always got yourself! Now that you know how to give acknowledgments successfully, to insure that they "land" and know how to make changes if they don't, start today! You can expect some positive, noticeable changes in your students and you'll enjoy teaching more yourself.

☑ Check These Key Points

1. Self-esteem is both intellectual and emotional, an experience of yourself as capable, lovable and worthy.
2. Build your own self-esteem and set up the conditions for students to build their own self-esteem.
3. Qualities of high self-esteem are personal integrity, responsibility, supporting others, self-discipline, strong relationships, knowing who you are, a vision of life, supportive environment, give best effort, health.
4. Essential for student's building of self-esteem is a sense of identity, belonging, lovableness, security and competence.

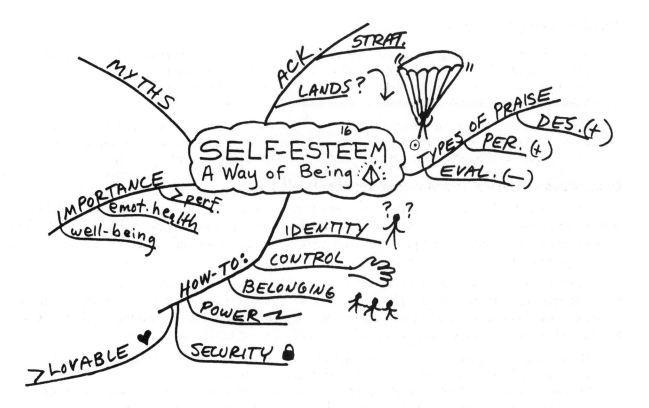

5. Assist students in setting goals for a sense of both control and purpose.
6. Acknowledge students as a group and as individuals.
7. Use appreciative acknowledgment or descriptive praise rather than evaluative praise.
8. If student responds with a discount, denial or throwback, re-package your acknowledgment until the student hears it the way you want him or her to.
9. Sing a sincere song of praise often!

Chapter Seventeen

Successful Evaluations Made Simple

Objectives

- To provide criteria for evaluation
- To identify the purpose and intended result for an evaluation
- To list qualities of testing procedures
- To describe specific test types

Evaluations and other forms of tests are designed to provide feedback on the progress of students. To evaluate and test your students successfully, ask yourself three questions. First, what's the outcome I want as a result of the test. Second, what information or experiences am I testing for and how is that best elicited? Finally, what constitutes a successful evaluation for the types of students and course material I have? There are, of course, some myths to be examined regarding testing.

Myth: There Is a Single Best Way to Evaluate

The first erroneous assumption is that there is a best way to evaluate your students. There isn't just one "best test." Given a specific outcome, there are some methods which are more successful than others. So, you must think about the outcome you want. For many teachers the outcome is to evaluate the understanding and recall of the course's content. You may be surprised to discover that there are other areas as important to master, such as discovery of individual learning strategies and the relationship and attitudes about a subject.

Myth: A Test Can Be Other Than Subjective

A second erroneous assumption is that the evaluation process can be separated from the evaluation. There is no such thing as an objective test. All tests are subjective, and all reflect the value judgments, priority systems, likes and dislikes. Choice of questions, wording of questions and even the format of the test are formed from the test maker's personal history. Even a test written by a committee brings to it the previous history, values and subjective background of individuals.

Myth: The Answers Are the Most Important Part

Another erroneous assumption is that the answers are more important than the questions. Most teachers make out an answer key to the test and score the student's responses. It's possible that the way a student got to the answer is more important than the answer.

Professor Dewey's slogan, "We learn by doing," could be amended to say "we learn by making mistakes", by trial and error, by finding out what works and what doesn't. The process of making mistakes has no end and the possibilities of learning are limitless if one's commitment is to learn from those mistakes.

Myth: The Results Reflect How the Students Are Doing

Another myth is that the primary result of the evaluation is how well the students learned. They do, partly. The result of an evaluation reflects primarily how the teacher is doing. The teacher is responsible to set up the class, teach the content, create the activities, determine the homework, write the test. Students' scores demonstrate how well your teaching met your stated objectives. When you teach well, the students do well. When you fail to communicate successfully, their scores drop.

Myth: Testing Will Uncover the Range of Abilities

Each student has a learning strategy that he uses to absorb and retain class material. The learning strategy is much like a combination lock—dial the wrong combination, and one might conclude you are ignorant. Dial the correct one and you are a genius. If it's true that each student has a unique 'combination', the whole question of which student has more ability or talent is irrelevant. Another, more important, question arises. How can I best dial each student's learning "combination"?

Many students don't test well because we don't know the exact process by which they learn. Students appear to have a wide range of abilities because of the various evaluation methods used. The student who appears dull, listless and unmotivated may be the same one who can assemble a motorcycle with no instruction manual or play an instrument well enough to join a band. If you changed the form of the evaluation, you might find the placement of students on the performance curve would reverse itself. Some students have simply: (1) Figured out their best way to learn—a personal learning strategy (2) Learned strategies which accidentally match the teaching strategy of the teacher (3) Developed good test-taking skills—they understand your "map" of that subject and prepare for it well at test time.

Myth: Testing Is the Main Way to Evaluate

Formalized testing is one of the least effective ways to evaluate student performance. It's ineffective because by the time you give your students a formal test, both you and they should already know how each of you are doing. You should know your weak and strong points so well and should have already begun to work on them. Most tests are a perfect example of too little, too late. Yet, you still need a solution and there is one.

Dr. Madeline Hunter of UCLA calls it "Dipsticking". You must get immediate and accurate feedback on your student's level of understanding at the moment of presentation. The way to do it is simple. Set up a system with your students of various hand signals which represent answers. You might have a sign for more, less, higher, lower, multiply, divide, useful, not, etc. Then you can use these immediate digital feedback signals during your presentation so that you know how much is being understood. It's a signal system which allows every teacher to get constant feedback on his or her presentation. Then, changes and corrections can be made right on the spot when they're needed, not at a test two weeks later.

Testing Background

One of the first things we might look at is what tests are used for and how we want to use them. In the past, tests have been used for many reasons and author Eugene Kim lists some of them:

1. To determine student progress and achievement
2. To provide information for grades, parent conferences, references, etc.
3. To motivate students to study or learn
4. To aid in the promotion and classification of students
5. To gauge teaching effectiveness
6. To provide a vehicle for instructional review
7. To evaluate the curriculum

Are these the only reasons to give tests? And what kind of tests are the most useful? As an example, let's say that your purpose in teaching is "to create an environment where your students gain the resources and commitment to expand the quality of their lives". Given this as a purpose, does the context of testing

3 KEY AREAS:
☑ SUBJECT RELATIONSHIP
☑ LEARNING STRATEGIES
☑ COURSE CONTENT

where a student can fail make any sense? Not really. But if everyone's going to succeed, why test? One reason might be to help students discover what they know and how they know it. Discovery learning through testing can make it even more valuable. In addition, it gives them a stronger sense of personal worth.

What Else Is There to Test?

In spite of the information explosion, many teachers focus on the content of information, even with the overwhelming evidence that content is expanding far faster than can be taught. Yet if you don't teach content, what is there? What you can do is teach and use, as the basis of your evaluation, two objectives:

☑ First, that the student develops a successful relationship with your subject, having appreciation for and interest in that subject. The "test" comes whenever new content in that subject is introduced in the future. Is the student excited about learning and "turned on" to the subject?

☑ Second, that the student develops, knows and uses a successful strategy for learning more in that subject. Many times different subjects require different strategies and students need to know the success process for themselves in a particular subject. In other words, these objectives are really an example of teaching students to love learning and teaching them how to learn successfully.

Should You Teach Content at All?

Does this mean that a teacher should not teach the content of the course itself? No, not at all. Teachers do need to teach content, and students do need to learn the essence of that subject. However, most subjects could have the essence of the content taught in much less time than thought possible. Some teachers may protest this point and say that their subject is different or that what they must teach is mandated. In many cases, they are right. Just do the best you can to include the teaching of learning strategies and relationship-building.

216

Students are usually tested on content because it's easy to measure, control and evaluate. But in order to master content, one must have a good relationship with it and have a successful strategy for learning it. Neither are usually taught. So, students are tested on something for which they may not have the tools to succeed.

The solution is simple. Tell students that your tests are only generalized indicators, merely your own personalized "shopping list" of facts and information. Have them relax about tests by repeating class affirmations such as, "Tests are easy for me." Then test, and test often. Use daily quizzes, where students can work in pairs as a team and share answers. This helps students learn information more quickly and gets them used to constant testing. Let students grade their own tests and test only when you're sure they will do well. Do not record these scores. After several weeks, you can test each individual more "formally". By then the student's confidence will be up, and he'll want to do the test by himself. At first, you require your students to cooperate by sharing answers. In time, they'll be protecting their privacy and will want to test themselves. It works. Try it.

What Can You Do about Cheating?

For many students, cheating is an often-used and best success strategy. To reduce this undesirable success strategy, the teacher must get at the cause.

One possible cause is that students don't have a learning strategy for your particular subject, so they are forced, because of the importance of grades, to be resourceful in scoring well. Students who cheat well are smart. They are more resourceful (and less honest!) than the ones who get poor grades and don't cheat. Dr. Wayne Dyer, author and teacher says:

> "How could anybody cheat? I saw a study in which tested chickens to see which ones were dumb and which ones were smart. A length of chicken wire was set up in front of their feed and the ones you eventually labeled dumb just sat and died of starvation. The chickens you labeled smart walked around the barrier and got at their food. Now when chickens go around barriers for rewards, they're labeled smart, but when students do the same thing, you label it cheating."

It's so curious in our culture that if a student gets answers from a teacher or a textbook, its OK. But when students get an answer from another student, we call it cheating! This is not to justify cheating. I am suggesting that with greater cooperative learning, more students would know the information and be less likely to cheat because they have a more desirable strategy that works easily and more consistently. When the conditions in your classroom for learning go up, cheating go down. It's simple cause and effect.

How Is Your Testing Environment?

Everard Blanchard of Villa Educational Research Associates has done some excellent work in the area of the actual testing environment. To put it briefly, environment matters. The tone of your voice, the tempo, the content, the expectations, all matter. Think carefully in terms of your purpose and intended result. In addition, Everhard confirmed that students who take exams with a light classical music background scored higher than those who took the exam in silence. The lesson? Improve the aesthetic and emotional atmosphere in your testing situations.

How to Present Your Evaluations

What you say and how you say it will determine students' test-taking attitudes. An evaluation is a feedback mechanism for the teacher. If the teacher designs it well, it can also serve as a feedback mechanism for the students. Simply tell your students that the tests will measure how well you taught instead of how much they learned. It takes the pressure off each student and reduces the incentive to use the success strategy called cheating. Turn evaluations into a game and make it fun—one that the students wanted to play. Re-name your tests. Call them "expansion exercises" or "loops".

Follow Up on Your Tests

One of the most difficult moments for a student is when a test result is below expectations. It is possible to reframe the student's experience. Find a different way of integrating the test experience so that each and every test causes the student to feel resourceful rather than a beaten down failure. What if you kept presenting to your students the following?:

- A low score indicates a gap in teaching effectiveness
- There's no such thing as a failure or a mistake
- What is called a failure is an outcome that we've prejudged as bad
- Every outcome gives the information you need to succeed next time
- Each experience is part of a larger success
- With every adversity comes the seed of an equal or greater benefit

These beliefs may or may not be true, but you'll produce more confident students by applying them. These new beliefs create the willingness to gain something from each setback. Imagine the change in feelings in your students when they call a test a result or a grade simply an outcome! Or, if each time you give test scores, your students were asked to come up with a decision about their results that would allow them to be even better learners. After all, one of the major differences between kinds of learners is the strategy used. Successful learners include, as part of their strategy, a decision about the learning event that makes them:

1. Have more resources, more choices for the next time
2. Feel stronger and better—it elicits positive emotions
3. Appreciate the valuable feedback
4. Re-evaluate ineffective strategies for next time

Another important role for teachers is to teach the necessary study skills. It's easy to assume that someone else has prepared your students for studying successfully, but that's usually not the case. Unless you are well-versed in the latest study strategies and have the time to teach them to your students, have your students get a copy of *Student Success Secrets*. It's listed in the bibliography and provides the fundamentals as well as the specifics for learning material better.

How to Create Successful Evaluations

Successful evaluations require that you do several things well. First, decide on the purpose of your evaluation, then the intended results. Next, prioritize the information or experiences that your test will elicit so that you can make sure that you get what you need. Then, prepare individual items, making sure you include both learning strategies and relationship questions.

Your purpose is a never-ending statement of policy, not an objective. It's the whole reason for undertaking the evaluation process. For many teachers, a purpose might read, "To evaluate the progress of my students". But may I suggest that you adopt a purpose which better serves you and the students? Here are some possibilities:

The Purpose of My Evaluation Process Is:

- "to create an empowering source of feedback for both students and myself"
- "to allow myself and my students to discover what we already know"
- "to add to the resources of all participants"

What's Your Intended Outcome?

Earlier we talked about the nature of a successful evaluation and were reminded that the meaning of 'successful' can only be evaluated in terms of "successful for which outcome?" If your outcome is that the students demonstrate a 75% or better score on a combination essay, oral and multiple choice test, here are some items you'll want to include:

1. *The highest priority is that students develop a favorable relationship with the subject.* This relationship means that they understand how they personally are related to the subject, how the subject

is related to the world in which they live, and the subject itself. It means students have a sense of 're-latedness' that can last a lifetime. It also means you have genuinely 'turned them on' to that subject.

Evidence procedure: Students can write or choose from options which describe a relationship with the material. They can demonstrate the relatedness by drawing from a prescribed range of possible diagrams showing who, how and why the relatedness exists or they may demonstrate orally. They may also show interest by volunteering for extra-curricular projects, organizing in-class projects, making a tape-cassette, by doing extra-credit work, by being in class. The quality or percentage rate of volunteering for projects could be noted.

2. *The second priority is that they understand and use the necessary learning strategies for that particular subject matter.* They should also have alternative strategies to use in case they get stumped.

Evidence procedure: That they can demonstrate their first choice for learning strategies in that subject by actually drawing a diagram or telling the teacher what it is. They should also be able to demonstrate to the teacher how they learned this subject and what alternative choices they would have to learn it. The format would be demonstrated by the teacher and made available on the test.

3. *The third priority is content.* Use several key ideas plus some related facts or relationships. The teacher can select the essence of the material and test for that, avoiding trivia questions which will only benefit the student on a quiz show.

Evidence procedure: true-false, turn in audio tape cassette, multiple choice, essay, fill-in, homework, mind-mapping . . . whichever the student is most comfortable with.

Qualities of Testing Procedures

☑ 1. *Test often!* Based on study results, direct observation and personal experience, it's been discovered that for feedback to be useful, it must be constant. Testing during every class is useful. The tests do not have to be written. It's just as easy to create class exercises in which students can respond orally, in unison drills or informal feedback systems. Probably the best "signal system" is a hand response or lap board. Set up a reply system so you get immediate answers from every student on every question. By using creative response-systems, you are constantly updated on how well each student is learning.

Avoid motivating your students
Instead, lead them to an addiction
of their own greatness

Students who get infrequent testing experience anxiety, disassociation, fears, lowered interest and participation levels. Daily testing creates more of a relationship with the subject matter, more interest in it and lowers stress about grades because each test is less significant.

☑ 2. *Keep them light!* Find ways to allow the students to devalue the test score, but still learn from the experience. Possible ways are including some questions which are silly or giveaways, making the test itself full of cartoons, allowing students to contribute questions, allowing them to take the test with partners, or to develop a new scoring system.

☑ 3. *Use a variety of testing methods.* You may recall from your own experience that some students best express themselves in writing, others talking, others by demonstrating, others on special projects, and others love a basic, standard written test. The greater the variety of testing forms you use, the greater the chances your students will have for success. That's why a hand or board signal system is an excellent quick feedback system for nearly any age student.

☑ 4. *Allow students to be successful.* Tell them ahead of time when you will test, what kinds of test methods you'll use, and the grading system. Many master teachers test only when they feel students are ready and likely to be high scorers.

☑ 5. *Score the tests immediately.* Scoring is what students and teachers need for feedback and course correction. The easiest way is to have students grade their own test as soon as they are completed. "What if they cheat?", you may ask. Somehow, when you do the things that this book talks about, kids don't cheat. If you make students more resourceful, and give them the learning strategies that they need to succeed, cheating becomes extinct. Correct tests in class with lightness and humor, then celebrate each right answer with group applause or cheers.

☑ 6. *Collect and record tests intermittently.* B. F. Skinner discovered that by far the most effective form of reinforcement was random because the consistent patterned ones became too ritualized and eventually ignored. Some teachers disagree and claim that reinforcement must be consistent to provide the information that both teacher and student need. Combine the best of both: test often, record scores less frequently.

Specific Test Varieties

To repeat something mentioned earlier, there isn't a single best kind of test because different students have different learning strategies. As a result, students test differently. If some of your students were color-blind and you gave them a test which asked them to distinguish colors, you might notice a high failure rate from that group. Does that mean that your students are stupid? Of course not. You simply tested something for which they didn't have a success strategy. However, with stronger sensory acuity on your part and by giving several varieties of tests, you'd quickly discover that they needed a different method of evaluation. This next section is about those different kinds of evaluation, a description of each, and their pros and cons.

Oral Testing and Evaluation

There is such a wide range of student responses to the thought of an oral exam. For some students, it's the greatest thing in the world, and for others, it's terrifying. Allow two purposes to work at the same time: make possible the success of your students and at the same time, add to their resources, empower them so that in the future they will be confident test-takers.

Dr. Jack Hill of San Diego County Schools, made it an option for students to do their work on a cassette tape. Many students took that option! Allow students who are already good at it to succeed and at the same time, don't let them use it as a reason not to learn any other testing strategy.

Demonstration Evaluations

This is the most varied category, using lap boards, songs, hand and body signals, skits, plays, work projects, demonstrations, mind maps, quiz shows and exhibits. All are fabulous types of tools to use as evaluations as long as you keep two things in mind. Some students will want this evaluation type all the time. Create a balance by teaching mastery of other test types. Also, you must give to the students a clear criterion for evaluation, not easy in some cases! Here are some examples:

1. Lap boards: small notebook-sized cardboards with a vinyl covering on them. They are cheap, easily used and effective. Basically, they are miniature chalkboards using quick-erase pens instead of chalk. You simply ask a question. Each student writes the answer and holds up the board for you to see. With these boards, students can give immediate, personal and private answers to any question you have. Plus, you can quickly scan the classroom to find students whose answer is different and follow up on them.
2. Skits. For a great deal of learning, use a skit to allow students to act out a particular event, and develop a positive and long-lasting relationship with the subject matter.
3. Plays require much planning and should be reserved for the student who volunteers for such a project as an out-of-class activity. It can be presented in class and should be limited to 3–5 minutes.

4. Songs. For students with even the mildest form of musical talent, let them compose a song about the subject content and sing it for their fellow students. It can be fun and a fabulous learning experience for them.

5. Work projects, demonstrations and exhibits. Students can turn in their final essay on tape cassette. It could be a science fair project, a term paper, a research project or class crafts project. Usually it's a great way for students to develop a positive relationship with the subject.

6. Quiz shows. These are an excellent opportunity for students to prepare course content with others and learn a lot. They can set up a quiz show like a "College Bowl" or "Jeopardy" format, entertaining others as well as learning much through the preparation of the questions.

7. Group, partner or individual mind maps. These can be produced in class or at home. They are a multi-colored pictorial and word-based representation of the course content. Students design colorful and creative ones.

8. Hand and Body Signals. This system is based on the old "thumbs up or thumbs down" signal as an answer to questions the teacher asks. Have students use dozens of different hand responses which include using different letters of the alphabet, pointing to different parts of the room, using body parts or partners. It's easy to imagine this working perfectly well in math classes, especially when students can make function signals easily such as add, subtract, multiply or divide. Yet, with some creativity, many other feedbacks can be developed. The desired outcome is to create a quick, easy, workable system to give immediate feedback. These signals have been described in detail in the chapter on presentation and evaluation.

Written Evaluations Part I: Homework

Probably the most common form of written evaluation is homework. First, consider the purpose in assigning homework. If it's busywork, don't assign it. If the assignment can be done in class just as well do it in class. Your classroom is a controlled environment. You can observe, support, give reinforcement and make the learning process more useful and fun for the student. Early steps in a learning process are like a cake making and you want to have the corrections made in the batter, not when it's in the oven!

Most students do homework because it's required and it affects their grade. Yet these are shallow and tenuous motivators because it's a case of "performing" for approval. There are other choices. If you have set up the structure of your class well from the start, you'll be able to create much more powerful incentives. If you have developed the theme of integrity, students will do homework because they gave their word. If you have developed the qualities of the joy of learning, they'll do it because it's fun. If you have developed a strong relationship with your students, they may do it out of the relationship you have with them—simply because you asked them to do and they respect you. These can create a powerful context for homework, ensuring it gets done and that it has some heart in it.

Each teacher must judge what form of homework is appropriate for his or her class. Find activities that students do anyway and turn them into a learning experience. For example, could students learn from television? From a phone call to their friends? A magazine? A computer? Design homework to be an integrating activity, such as a drawing, a mind-map or other whole-brained creation which embodies more of the course than random rote repetition. Chances are you will find it highly successful.

Minimize the homework, make it shorter, more meaningful. Have it be consistent, useful and fun. Let it increase fluency and proficiency of classwork. Vary it and involve as much creativity. Ask students to read a short synopsis just before going to sleep with a classical music concert as the background. This allows the mind to integrate and store the material for maximum usage. Be sure to follow through during the next class.

Consider the team approach to homework where students support each other instead of competing. Have them work on an assignment in teams of five which you have set up to have the greatest academic diversity. Use the group score as the score for each individual. Allow students to network with phone calls to learn the material. Have students bring homework into class early (or use the first five minutes), then work in groups to learn it. They can use synergy to come up with a "group version" of the homework which increases the understanding and interest. Peer pressure will cause students to prepare homework. If you do give larger chunks for homework, provide the tools needed for it. If students need it, teach memorization techniques or how to organize thoughts. This kind of support makes a big difference in student's attitude.

One of the best homework assignments is to create a format (such as the mind map introduced in the chapter on planning) to be used, then have students fill in what went on in class that day. It serves as a review, it increases recall, it may bring up questions that otherwise would not have risen and it's fun to do. Encourage students to share phone numbers and trade ideas for homework. Students should have every possible opportunity to learn. If they turn in something that has misspelled words on it, give them no grade until they find the words, re-spell them, and bring them back to you. Spelling strategies are in the appendix. Remind them that they can use anyone else's help to find the words. Other kinds of things that are useful for homework assignments are writing papers, doing reports and reading. The reading assigned should be short passages, not 20 or 50 page chunks to do overnight. Consistency is of more value than large chunks all at once.

Another success strategy for homework is to change the attitudes about it. For most students, it's drudgery and punishment. For a few, it's a useful chore. For pretty close to none, it's a joy. But what's the possibility that homework could actually be fun, be a joy to do? Ask your students to explore that possibility—that homework could be approached with the same opportunity as a journey or meeting new person. Just asking them what it would take for homework to be a joy may open up some possibilities for you in how you present it.

The most important part of homework is how you evaluate it. Evaluate the learning of the material, not the form or the content of it. Sometimes, you'll want to only evaluate the process, not the results. Other times, you'll want to stick with the results you wanted and let go the process. If you give ten problems as part of a math assignment, find out if they learned how to solve THAT kind of problem, not if they got right all of the ones you assigned. Be insistent and consistent with homework—and make it more meaningful.

Written Evaluations Part II: Classwork

In the category of written evaluation for testing purposes, there's plenty of variety—and controversy. All of this gets down to teaching philosophy, so here's mine: you have three priorities in testing—the relationship, the learning strategy and the content. Because the first two are highly important, always allow students to use their books or notes during test time, or work with a partner. That strategy allows the students to develop a relationship with that subject which is favorable and unstressed, and it stresses the understanding, analyzing and application instead of recall. You will be pleasantly surprised at the expanded thinking skills and learning strategies of your students as you allow open notes on your up-coming exams. And, as an added bonus, students will like the course more and have a good relationship with you and the course content. By the way, they'll also master the course content just as well or better.

How to Create Multiple Choice Questions

Multiple choice may be the most common category for evaluation. It is probably the most widely used because it is easy to create and simple to grade. It can be scored in a short time, by practically anyone, and there are few gripes or discussions about the answers. The effects of guessing add up to a relatively constant factor which is easily accountable for.

Its two major disadvantages are that first, it doesn't allow for a more qualitative and full expression of the subject matter or the relationship that the student has with that subject. What is occurring is more of the same; you come up with an "important" list of items, then ask the students to match it. This is what was described earlier as the 'game of matching grocery lists.' Secondly, multiple choice are usually simple and direct recall questions which do not ask more important questions such as "how does this apply. . ."

1. Make sure that not only is the answer clear, but that the other wrong answers are clearly wrong—if you know the correct answer. This doesn't mean that they must be ridiculous, but they should be distinctly wrong.
2. Keep answer grammatically correct and consistent.
3. Make sure that all the answers are of approximately the same length.
4. Be sure that the correct response is not the same letter answer for more than three times in a row, and check for other answer patterns.
5. Make sure that the answers do not contain any clues which might lead the person to the answer (such as in language classes, the cognates) or even just simple prefixes and suffixes. Use "all of the above" or "none of the above" only when it is a significant possibility.
6. Put your answers in the affirmative and positive form. Use four to five possible answer choices. For example:

Which of the following evaluation methods have not been mentioned so far:

A) Essay
B) Homework
C) Reports
D) Computers
E) Multiple choice

True-False Test Questions

Another category of evaluating testing is the true-false items. These are the simplest to construct and the easiest to score. They also do not lead to a great deal of thinking about something and are sometimes treated by the student more flippantly than the multiple choice. They are not very useful for getting either quantity or quality of data from the student. One of the most popular solutions is the modified true-false question. With this one, if it's true, the student marks it so, but if it's false, the student must re-write the question to make it true. For many students, this is not easy. An example:

"If the following statement is true, mark it true. If it is false, please rewrite it so that it becomes true."
The purpose of this chapter is to explain how to eliminate tests. (T)　(F)

This kind of question is as much a 'disguised' completion, fill-in question than a true-false. One other problem with true-false is that much of our information is contradictory. Is the earth round? Yes and no—it's actually oblong. Do humans have gills? Yes and no—in our earliest embryonic stages, we have gill vestiges! Is Mount Everest the highest mountain in the world? Yes and no—actually it's Mauna Kea on Hawaii (part of its elevation is under water!). Make sure that your questions have only one answer.

The Matching Format

The matching format is actually a modified multiple-choice and true-false. It consists of two columns of words or phrases: the one on the left is a list of phrases, the first half of a thought or word. The column on the right is another list of phrases, thoughts or words from which the student can choose a response to best complete the corresponding one on the left. Usually there are five to fifteen items in each column and the right or selection column is best made just a bit longer than the stem column on the left. It is often used to judge simple relationships, or for direct recall. It is easy to score, easy to make, and easy to make poorly! One should make sure that the items in the column on the right are very similar in nature so that it makes the choosing more valid.

For example:

Directions: Assign the letter from a choice on the right to the statement which best fits it on the left.

_____ Chapter title
_____ Testing purpose
_____ Why write your own

A. To evaluate & empower
B. Successful evaluations
C. Knowledge & power
D. Control & satisfaction

The Mastery Learning Concept

The mastery concept means that every student works towards successful completion of the unit of learning. Once mastered, he has earned an A. Either a student has an incomplete or an A, then he moves on. It's the simplest, makes the most sense, and avoids the entire issue of grouping and prescriptive labeling. It also allows students to learn at their own rates which is important for self-esteem and competency. It is, in the author's estimation, the best of available evaluation methods. Any way that a teacher can implement it is well worthwhile.

The mastery concept is brilliant—in concept. It takes good teaching to make it work, and fortunately you qualify! The mastery concept states that clear specific criteria be set for student competency in a subject area, and that each student is responsible for achieving mastery, at his own pace. To be fully effective, students need a full toolbag of resources for mastering the material, PLUS the commitment and drive to carry it out. Dr. Carlson tells the story of one of his students:

"A little girl came up to me one day and said, 'Dr. Carlson, Dr. Carlson, look at my paper.' She showed me her paper, and every single word on it was misspelled. I looked at her and said, 'Maureen, I really like your paper—the margins are nice and neat, and your printing is clean and readable.' And she said, 'Thank you, Dr. Carlson—I've really been working hard on it. Next, I'm going to work on my spelling.' "

How to Grade Successfully

The ways to grade successfully are: (1) set up a system that includes many kinds of input: attendance, class participation, daily sub-quizzes, weekly quizzes, monthly exams, projects or papers. (2) set up ways for students to make up absences or lower scores (3) tell students exactly how to get an A in your class, and remove the threat of failure—it's counter-productive to learning (4) give constant feedback to the students (5) grade sub-quizzes daily, but only record the weekly quiz scores. (6) treat the whole grading system lightly, and still respect its meaning to the students.

You may recall a statement that was made earlier along the lines of, "The better you do, the better your students do." With that in mind, you might already know what will be presented about grades: that it's not only possible, but desirable to be giving out all As in your class. All As would mean that you did a great job. Remember that as you continue to increase your ability to communicate effectively and bring out the best in your students (who are all of approximate equal ability), the results will be that their best is an 'A' and since they are all equal in ability, all of them will deserve one. If you are mandated to give out a certain number of Bs, Cs, Ds or Fs, or if you have been grading on the curve, you might want to re-examine that procedure and ask yourself why would you want to guarantee that a certain number of students do poorly?

The ultimate success as a teacher in the classroom is to have ALL of your students succeed. If half of them do well, you didn't reach the other half and that could be your goal next time. It should be the dream of every teacher—to have every student in your class succeed. If any of them don't, adjust the variables: your teaching, the tests, the grading system, etc. Behavioral flexibility, teaching skills, rapport, presentation methods all can bring you closer to the 100% goal.

---

1. Evaluations and tests are for the purpose of providing feedback.
2. Feedback includes information to determine a student's progress, to gauge teaching effectiveness, to determine a grade, to evaluate the curriculum.
3. Other "tests" are student attitudes about the subject and students' strategies for learning the material.
4. Light, classical music and an esthetic, comfortable environment will improve the testing environment.
5. Determine the purpose of your evaluation and the intended results.
6. Test often and use a variety of methods.
7. Make homework useful, meaningful and allow group efforts.
8. Use many kinds of input for evaluation: class participation, quizzes, projects, papers, exams, attendance.
9. Reduce student stress by telling them how to get an "A" in your class.
10. Provide continual feedback to your students.

The Vision VI

Chapter Eighteen

The Return to Aliveness

Objectives

- To establish ways to renew and refresh oneself
- To provide feedback mechanisms to allow for corrections and change

For most people, teaching is a combination of exhaustion, exhiliration, boredom, frustration and satisfaction. In teaching, just as in every other job, it is possible to experience many more highs and far fewer lows. The secret does not lay in the job, but in you. You have the capacity to experience teaching as satisfying if you so choose. To achieve that satisfaction, many things are needed including a broadening of vision and purpose about the future. You'll want to learn how to increase your level of satisfaction and decrease frustration dramatically. You must address both your personal and professional self, learning how to get excited and stay excited about your teaching as well as learn ways to renew and refresh, update and invigorate yourself. But first, the myths:

Myth: Teaching Has to Be a Burn-Out Profession

Is a teacher's job inherently tiring, exhausting, leading to burn-out? It doesn't have to be. It's certainly less physically challenging than some jobs. So what causes the exhaustion? What's exhausting is constantly trying to control discipline, suppressing student's classroom behavior, or teaching the same thing, day after day. Jumping on the bandwagon of every new fad and having to learn how to teach them is tiring. What's tiring is fighting with peers, the administration or other staff. Not growing personally is tiring—it keeps you in a rut. Boredom is tiring. Talking non-supportively about other teachers, students or yourself is also tiring. No wonder many teachers are tired. Certain actions use up your energy while others re-energize. The bottom line is that if you are worn out constantly or lack inspiration, you've got to make some changes within yourself or get out of the profession. Both you and your students deserve much better.

Inspiring others is not exhausting. Sharing love is not exhausting. Correcting brilliant homework or tests is not exhausting. Communicating openly is not exhausting. Enjoying your work and creating excellence is not exhausting. Having students call you or send appreciative letters is not tiring. Getting standing ovations is not tiring. Planning new and exciting classes is not exhausting and getting great feedback or changing lives is certainly revitalizing.

Myth: It's Going to Get Easier

One of the prevailing myths about teaching is that if you master it, it will become easier for you. The dominant theme of the universe is increasing complexity. It will only become more and more difficult to be a great teacher. However, although it will be difficult, it will be better. Our evolution as a human species is that as we become more adept at challenges, we become more willing to take on new ones. Expect your career to continue to be full of challenges. That's part of growing!

Myth: Teachers Can Be Lifetime Qualified

You may have undergone extensive training to become qualified to teach. At the rate things change, it's possible to become obsolete even more quickly than you got qualified! Students change, technology changes and most importantly, you change. To be continually effective, you must constantly update your ideas, discard old beliefs, and learn about yourself and your profession. In some way, a part of you must die each day for you to grow and personal growth is the key to significant reform, both in your classroom and in the entire educational system.

Myth: Teachers Are Becoming Less Important

Another erroneous assumption is that teachers are losing importance in this automated or computerized world of teaching machines and high-tech educational tools. False. Teachers have never been more important than they are today. Your role may change, but not your importance. The success of our future depends on you because the contributions you make in the classroom cannot be made by a machine. You can love, support, correct, inspire, excite and cooperate in a way that makes a real difference in the lives of your students. Former New York City principal and author of *Troubled Teachers,* Esther Rothman says, "Many teachers are already crusading rebels in the best sense of the word." She adds that, "If our schools are to change, teachers will have to change them."

Myth: You Are Teaching Only the Students in Your Class

You are an example of the multiplier effect. You affect dozens, maybe hundreds or thousands of students each year and they affect dozens, maybe hundreds or thousands of people each year. Each student in your class has, on the average, 3–5 close friends and 3–5 family members. Each student may also have 50 additional acquaintances and a dozen or two relatives. That's a sphere of influence of about a hundred people per single student in your class! From that viewpoint, the number of people you influence indirectly is:

1. Elementary school—2,500 per year (25 students × 100 influenced)
2. Junior and Senior High—20,000 per year (5 classes × 20 in each × two semesters × 100 influenced)
3. College—32,000–64,000 (4 classes × 40 in each × 2–4 quarters × 100)

What if you teach for ten years? Now the figures are:

1. Elementary—25,000 lives affected
2. Junior and Senior High—200,000 (a fifth of a million!)
3. College—320,000–640,000 (a third to two-thirds of a million!)

Myth: You Can't Teach an Old Dog New Tricks

One of the premises for this chapter is while you can't turn back the clock, you sure can wind it up again. You may be concerned about how long it will take to master the information in this book or to make other major changes in your teaching. Surprisingly, it takes little time to master new things. What does take time is preventing yourself, through old beliefs, from the new mastery. Do you recall how long you spent not being successful at something in life? Probably a long time, but at the moment of insight you learned it quickly. Learning takes no time at all.

Myth: The Changes Might Not Happen Overnight

One of the beliefs which has allowed transformation to take so long is the thought, belief, or opinion that change must take place over long periods of time. Change can occur slowly or quickly. When change has to do with people, the length of time is up to the people involved. If you've done one behavior all your life you still could change it at any moment, if you really want to. Werner Erhard says, "You and I possess within ourselves, at every moment of our lives, under all circumstances, the power to transform the quality of our lives." To me, this means that anybody, yes you or anyone else, can make a decision that will turn things around. That ability, that option is yours and no one can take it away.

Many things can make your role in education worth it. To experience aliveness and consistent joyfulness in your work, develop three things: a vision, so you become part of a larger plan; a path so that you can move towards making the vision happen; and a personal life that empowers your vision and path. Here's the six steps to be renewed and revitalized.

1. Develop a Compelling Vision and Grand Purpose

Nationwide surveys of satisfied persons indicate one common factor: a mission, purpose or chief aim in life. As a teacher, you have a choice. You can teach every day for a paycheck and be part of the "Thank-God-It's-Friday" group. Or, you can live your life for something larger, more grand and more important than the petty pace of those who are simply "putting in time." The real joy in life, at any job, is that of being used for a mighty purpose.

A story to further make my point: Two stonecutters were at work and were asked what they were doing. In a complaining voice one said, "I'm cutting stones." The other beamed and said, "I'm building a cathedral." Same job. One is part of a grand purpose, another is not. A vision without tasks is a pipedream. A task without vision is drudgery. A vision with tasks can move the world. Imagine the vision behind the pyramids of Egypt, the Taj Mahal or America's moon landing project. Here's how George Bernard Shaw said it:

This is the true joy in life
    the being used for a purpose
Recognized by yourself as a mighty one
    the being a force of nature
Instead of a feverish little clod of ailments
    and grievances complaining that the world
Will not devote itself to making you happy.
I am of the opinion that my life belongs to
    the whole community and as long as I live it is
My privilege to do forth whatever I can.
I want to be thoroughly used up when I die.
For the harder I work, the more I live.
I rejoice in life for it's own sake.
Life is no brief candle to me.
    It is a sort of splendid torch
Which I've got a hold of for the moment
    and I want to make it burn as brightly
As I can before handing it on to future generations.

Reprinted with permission of the Society of Authors, on behalf of the Bernard Shaw Estate.

Is it possible that you could live your life out of a grand mission? Maybe you want to impact the quality of education in your state. Maybe you want to eliminate all the labelling of students. Or maybe you want to make learning fun again. What dream could you have that is so big, it's a lifetime job? A job that you could not finish because it would always be expanding? Think about it. When you have decided on your dream, you are halfway to having it. The next step is commitment.

To commit to your dream is to say to yourself, "I will do whatever it takes to make it happen." Your commitment can be demonstrated in many ways: your thoughts, language and actions. And, usually, your commitment will require risking the status quo. The risk comes because we are conditioned to speak and act to protect our survival, our job, our beliefs, even if it means not telling the truth or not acting out of good faith. Risk also requires the sacrifice of some momentary personal comfort to make your dream come true.

Once your vision is established, determine the part you'll play in it. Usually a vision has enough breadth so you can do many things and still move towards it. But there's more satisfaction in designing a specific step-by-step plan and staying with it. For example:

VISION: That our school be selected as a nationwide example for excellence in education and that both the teachers feel important and acknowledged for their contributions."

This year:	take 2 acting and theater courses
	audiotape class 3 times and make changes
	apply to become mentor teacher
	Assist with ideas for staff development

Next year:	become expert in accelerated learning
	use it daily in my classes
	write and contribute 5 articles on it
	be part of the mentor teacher program
	contribute to staff development
	do fund-raising projects for extra money

Once you have your mission, you'll start discovering how many others do or don't share it. Since many will not share it, it's important to be accepting and compassionate. They may have their own, equally powerful, vision or no vision at all. In either case, share yours and avoid judgement of others. Simply communicate your vision and why it's important to you.

The nature of nature is change . . .
Become a natural success . . .
By changing yourself
You can change your world

---

2. Develop a Path and Sense of Journey

Once you have a vision, you'll want to put yourself on a path to make the vision come true. Your path will have a series of increasingly challenging tasks. These will likely include both professional and personal development. To make your vision happen, you'll need to be far more effective. This means you'll need to get more potent skills, tools and experiences—ones that you don't have right now. You need a coach or mentor.

Real mastery is made possible and is accelerated by coaching. Find someone qualified to coach you and study him or her. Visit his or her classroom. Take careful notes and analyze everything to find out how the results were produced. To learn from master teachers, you must become a master student. The more you love to learn, the more your students will love it, too. Your commitment must be to learn from others and be willing for others to give you coaching. In other words, your acceptance of the coaching is just as important as your seeking it.

Other sources of mentoring are videotapes, audio-cassettes, books and magazines. At the end of this book are some resources, including an excellent video cassette program. It is effective to get an experience of a master through a book because you can read it at your own pace, reread it or set it aside for days. In one respect, books are like people—you can often get more from them with each additional encounter. In the appendix, there's an extensive bibliography for the kind of source material that made this book possible. You will also find that the more books you read, the greater and more inspired your thinking becomes. Reading feeds thoughts to the mind, gives time for your subconscious to process and allows for creation of new ideas. Many of the most innovative ideas in teaching have come from materials outside the classroom.

3. Develop an Area of Expertise

To stay excited or to get excited about your profession, make it new. You can grow, learn and inspire yourself and others by becoming an expert on some facet of your teaching. Here are the steps:

1. Decide on a specialty. Match up two items—what's needed in the educational marketplace and what you want to do. Some of the greatest needs are: self-esteem building, parent support groups, thinking skills, memory, confidence-building, community involvement in education, teacher re-training, accelerated learning, neurolinguistic programming, and parent or peer counseling.
2. Decide the best way to learn the material. Choose from tapes, books, friends, peers, other masters, workshops, in-service programs, businesses, or extension courses.
3. Make a commitment to yourself about what you will learn and by when. Maybe your goal is one book a week for a year.
4. Take classroom risks daily. Try the different, the unusual. Follow through on the commitment and make corrections if necessary. The minute you feel mastery of the material, teach it. Teach your students, then pass it along to your fellow teachers. It is by teaching the material that you learn it and fully explore the possibilities.

4. Evaluations as Coach

The marvelous thing about human beings is that we possess the ability to adapt, change and grow. But most teachers lack the systems, forms or processes that can provide the coaching necessary for growth. To be the best that you can be, you must ask for and use feedback on your classes. Daily feedback is preferable, weekly is mandatory.

Through evaluations, you can get the feedback you need to make changes and corrections in your teaching. Many teachers who are resistant to the idea of evaluations are needlessly insecure about themselves. The better the teacher, the more interested they usually are in getting feedback. The way to excellence is through finding out what doesn't work and improving it. There are four basic ways to get evaluated. Use all four for maximum effects. They are self-evaluation, student evaluations, outside assessments and peer evaluations.

I. *Self-evaluation*. The simplest and easiest way is to keep a logbook or journal. Do self-evaluations after each class, each day or each week. Create the criteria for evaluation. My suggestion is to start with the students. Develop thermometers that you can use as a way of knowing how they are doing. You might include quantity and quality of homework, test scores, numbers of hands going up for class participation, comments after class, etc. Then decide on some of the other qualities you wish to evaluate. Suggestions are:

1. a reduction in the number of negations or sarcasm used
2. quantity and quality of acknowledgements
3. rating your preparation/intro/body/interactions/activities/evaluations/closure processes
4. rating your content for usefulness/interest
5. rating the atmosphere created/the environment/the emotions
6. most importantly, rating the outcomes
7. rating your relationships established and tools created

In your journal, stay focused on the outcome. How did things turn out? What were the final results? What would you do differently next time? All of those things should be put down, then thought about. What are some of the possible things that can be adjusted or varied next time? Do you have the resources to make the changes? If not, how can you get to those resources? Your journal can be an important tool for your growth because it helps you stay focused on the outcome.

BLUE PRINT FOR SUCCESS...

PURPOSE
JOURNEY
EXPERTISE
COACH
EVALUATION
PERSONAL
LIFE

II. *Student evaluations*. Many teachers claim that students cannot evaluate a teacher effectively. Many claim that students don't know what to look for and that they don't have all of the necessary tools to make their evaluations truthful or important. While that may be true, student evaluations are still a good source of information. Make sure you give them the opportunity to evaluate you anonymously. Even if a student isn't skilled enough to evaluate you, the fact that you allow them to participate and contribute in that manner is enough to make for a better teaching environment. Several student evaluation samples are included in the index. Try them all!

TEACHER'S REPORT CARD
Week #1

Directions: No name needed, please comment freely.

1. The best things in this class are:

2. What I have disliked or felt uncomfortable about:

3. What I still don't understand is:

4. Everyday in this class we:

5. In this class we always:

6. In this class we never:

7. What have I learned so far:

8. The teacher almost always:

9. The teacher almost never:

10. Overall, this class is:

Comments:

TEACHER'S REPORT CARD
Week #2

Directions: No name needed. Please comment freely.

1. What has the teacher done well?

2. Is class interesting/fun/lively?

3. When you talk to the teacher, do you feel heard and understood?

4. With the teacher, do you feel complimented and encouraged?

5. Is the teacher's voice, tone, and talking style ok?

6. Is the teacher clear to you in giving directions?

7. Do you understand the material the teacher presents?

8. What did you think about the handouts and textbooks?

9. Do you like the subject matter?

10. Do you feel like you have the skills and tools to learn it well?

11. If I were to give the teacher a grade, what would it be?

TEACHER'S REPORT CARD
Week #3

Directions: No name needed. Please comment freely.

1. What I enjoyed about class today was:

2. What I disliked about class today:

3. What was the most useful or valuable part:

4. What I discovered about myself today is:

5. Any changes, beliefs changed, new perspectives:

6. How would you describe your attitude about the subject:

7. How did your learning strategies work today:

8. Suggestions to make it better:

TEACHER'S REPORT CARD
Week #4

Directions: No name needed. Please comment freely.

1. When the subject of our class is mentioned, what words come to mind?

2. Which would you prefer? 1) more visuals, pictures, charts, illustrations? 2) more explanations and examples and analogies? 3) more actual demonstrations where you can do it yourself? _____

3. What haven't you understood that you'd like to get cleared up?

4. What's made the biggest impact on you so far, something you liked, were impressed with, or affects you the most?

5. Other comments?

TEACHER'S REPORT CARD
Week #5

Directions: No name needed. Please comment freely.

1. What I wanted to get out of class today:

2. What I ended up getting from class today:

3. What were my high points or successes?

4. What were the low points?

5. What I'm confused about/did not understand?

6. What would I like changed or done differently?

7. At the end of this class, how do I feel about progress?

Further comments:

TEACHER'S REPORT CARD
Week #6
(from Don Cosgrove)

Directions: Evaluate the teacher in terms of +, 0, −, then comment. After each item, please indicate your response with a plus sign (+) if you mostly agree, a zero sign (0) if you are uncertain or blah about it and a minus sign (−) if you mostly disagree. Then please make a comment afterwards.

1. On time for class _____ comment:

2. Pleasant personality in class _____ comment:

3. Sincere in communications _____ comment:

4. Knowledgeable and well-read _____ comment:

5. Enthusiastic about subject _____ comment:

6. Used relevant class material _____ comment:

7. Treated each student fairly _____ comment:

8. Made clear expectations _____ comment:

9. Kept classes orderly _____ comment:

10. Seemed to enjoy teaching _____ comment:

Reprinted with permission of MacMillan Publishing Company from *Resource Guide for Secondary School Teaching* by Eugene C. Kim and Richard D. Kellough. Copyright © 1983 by Eugene C. Kim and Richard D. Kellough.

TEACHER'S REPORT CARD
Week #7
(From Don Cosgrove)

Directions: Evaluate the teacher in terms of +, 0 or −, then comment. After each item, please indicate your response with a plus sign (+) if you mostly agree, a zero sign (0) if you are uncertain or blah about it and a minus sign (−) if you mostly disagree. Then, please make a comment afterwards.

1. Natural and easy friendliness ⎯⎯⎯⎯⎯ comment:

2. Clear understandable thinking ⎯⎯⎯⎯⎯ comment:

3. Encouraged creativity ⎯⎯⎯⎯⎯ comment:

4. Used up-to-date course material ⎯⎯⎯⎯⎯ comment:

5. Worked cooperatively with students ⎯⎯⎯⎯⎯ comment:

6. Procedures well thought out ⎯⎯⎯⎯⎯ comment:

7. Knew subject matter well ⎯⎯⎯⎯⎯ comment:

8. Friendly towards all students ⎯⎯⎯⎯⎯ comment:

9. Created and marked tests fairly ⎯⎯⎯⎯⎯ comment:

10. Corrected supportively ⎯⎯⎯⎯⎯ comment:

TEACHER'S REPORT CARD
Week #8
(From Don Cosgrove)

Directions: Evaluate the teacher in terms of a +, 0 or −, then comment. After each item, please indicate your response with a plus sign (+) if you mostly agree, a zero sign (0) if you are uncertain or blah about it and a minus sign (−) if you mostly disagree. Then, please make a comment afterwards.

1. Strong sense of humor ⎯⎯⎯⎯⎯ comment:

2. Planned assigned work well ⎯⎯⎯⎯⎯ comment:

3. Encouraged and supported class questions ⎯⎯⎯⎯⎯ comment:

4. Organized course material ⎯⎯⎯⎯⎯ comment:

5. Accepted and listened to student viewpoints ⎯⎯⎯⎯⎯ comment:

6. Used rich and exciting vocabulary words ⎯⎯⎯⎯⎯ comment:

7. Provided advance scheduling ⎯⎯⎯⎯⎯ comment:

8. Students willing to give 100% ⎯⎯⎯⎯⎯ comment:

9. Teacher was on top of things ⎯⎯⎯⎯⎯ comment:

10. Appreciated accomplishments ⎯⎯⎯⎯⎯ comment:

Reprinted with permission of MacMillan Publishing Company from *Resource Guide for Secondary School Teaching* by Eugene C. Kim and Richard D. Kellough. Copyright © 1983 by Eugene C. Kim and Richard D. Kellough.

TEACHER'S REPORT CARD
Week #9
(From Don Cosgrove)

Directions: Evaluate the teacher in terms of +, 0 or −, then comment. After each item, please indicate your response with a plus sign (+) if you mostly agree, a zero sign (0) if you are uncertain or blah about it and a minus sign (−) if you mostly disagree. Then, please make a comment afterwards.

1. Allowed and appreciated all kinds of answers _____ comment:

2. Is well-informed in other areas _____ comment:

3. Well-prepared with class material _____ comment:

4. Covered subject matter to your liking _____ comment:

5. Encouraged thinking and independent thought _____ comment:

6. Made guidelines and agreements _____ comment:

7. Completed activities on time _____ comment:

8. Course ran smoothly _____ comment:

9. Material was relevant and significant _____ comment:

10. Understood student problems, communicated well _____ comment:

TEACHER'S REPORT CARD
Week #10
(From Eugene Kim)

Directions: No name needed. Please comment freely.

1. Do you experience the lessons as being well-planned and well-thought-out?

2. Do you understand what the teacher expects from you on tests, class assignments and homework?

3. Do you feel free to ask questions?

4. Is there enough variety to keep you interested?

5. Is the printed material, homework, reading assignment, and text interesting?

6. Is there enough discussion on class topics?

7. Is your class participation welcomed and appreciated?

8. Is the teacher's voice clear, pleasant, varied?

9. Is the teacher's appearance acceptable?

10. How do you find the teacher's personality?

11. What kinds of materials have you enjoyed in this class and what would you like more of?

12. Other comments:

You now have evaluations for week one through ten. This will give you a balance of information and keep your students involved in the class more. These kind of evaluations have the potential to be most potent if, and it's a big "if," if three conditions are met:

1. Train your students in the areas of what to look for in your teaching so that they become trained observers. Teach students what to look for, listen to and experience. That way, they feel as if they are participating, contributing, and affecting others. It's very empowering.
2. READ the evaluations thoroughly and stay detached from them—don't take them personally. Keep a log or journal of the key areas you are working on to improve.
3. Make the necessary corrections. Tell students specifically what changes and corrections you are making as a result of the evaluations. If you do these on a Friday, tell your students on Monday what you are going to do differently that day. Prompt, clear feedback is important to establishing a partnership in learning.

By doing those three things, you have a fabulous, easy, inexpensive form of feedback. In the words of the Philosopher Ouspensky, "You can no longer deceive yourselves. You have had a taste of the truth."

III. *Outside evaluations.* Another possibility is to take courses or workshops that will evaluate your presentation. The best ones use video recording so that they can give you specified feedback. Other possibilities are Toastmasters or the Dale Carnegie course.

IV. *Peer evaluations.* Micro-peer teaching is one of several ways that you can be evaluated by your peers. This process involves having a teacher create and deliver a brief lesson to a few peers who provide immediate feedback. It utilizes a limited objective, short time period, and few students. It is most useful when videotaped so that each piece can be played back and there's certainty about what was said or done. The greatest single mistake made in peer evaluations is in the set-up. Three criteria must be met:

1. The safety level and support among peers must be high enough for each to be able to risk making comments about another's teaching.
2. There must be an expressed commitment to being coached and the coaching must be done with integrity. The only way coaching works is with peers who are willing to coach by telling the truth and telling it with compassion.
3. If the session will be videotaped, here's a suggestion. Nearly every peer evaluation is done by watching or taping or filming the teacher up in the front of the classroom. The most effective way, and the one that reduces evaluations to the simplest and purest unbiased elements, is to use two cameras: one on the group and one on the teacher. Review the teacher's performance on a split-screen so the teacher can see how techniques are received by students. Want to know how effective a speaker is? Watch the audience. Watch the expressions, the participation, the interest level. The key to a successful evaluation is having the focus on the student's response as well as on the teacher's presentation.

The final part of the sense of journey is contribution. Teaching is a partnership. It's about serving others in a way that empowers them for a better life. It's also about contribution, not just to the students in your class, but to the larger community as well. Find ways you can serve your community. Do a fundraiser, increase educational awareness or start a service group. If your time is already booked, support an existing organization. Call parents of students in your class. Have your students do a project for the homeless in your community. The more ways you can find to serve, the more value you'll find in your teaching. Why? Being a teacher is also being a role model. What better way to give your students a model than that of caring about the quality of life?

5. A Satisfying Personal Life

As a teacher, much of the process of feeling renewed and full of energy begins at home. One of the keys to being a master teacher is balance. Make sure that you get energized by your personal life rather than being drained by it. You will have to successfully handle four areas:

1. Economic security. Are you managing your money well? If not, it leads to stress that shows up in the classroom.

2. Relationships. What is the quality of your closest relationships? Unless it's great, you can be guaranteed that effects from it will show up in the classroom. When your relationships are great, you have greater aliveness, joy and love to share with your students. Take the courses, the time, the attention necessary to make your relationships successful, especially the ones with your parents and your children.

3. Control and management. Do you prioritize and plan both short and long term? Have you set goals and priorities in the dozen most important areas of your life? Do you have an organizing system for planning? Can you say "no" to unwanted requests for your time? Make or buy a personal organizer—the Personal Resource System of San Diego is an excellent one.

4. Self-esteem. Do you love yourself, others? Feel good about your work, the job you do? Do you continue your own learning and personal growth as a lifelong hobby?

Taking care of yourself is important—only when you are at your best can you give your best to your students. Be your own best friend. Cheer yourself up when you need it and give yourself compliments regardless of whether others do or not. There is no process of greater importance to your life than that of learning to recognize mistakes, continually forgive and love yourself, making necessary changes. If you miss a day of exercise, forgive and love yourself. If you get mad at a student, forgive and love yourself. If you don't teach a class as well as you know you can, forgive and love yourself. If you do anything that does not add to your resourcefulness or self-esteem, forgive yourself and love yourself. Nothing will provide more for you than the love you give to yourself.

6. You Get What You Really Want

There's a short chain reaction going on within each of us: first a thought, then the words, then an action. You can either choose to effect your actions, language or go right to the source, your thoughts. Thoughts are things. What you think about, comes about. To be a super-teacher, think like one. Read what they read, listen to the same speakers or tapes. Socialize with positive, uplifting and results-getting people. If teachers around you are bad-mouthing students, fellow teachers or administrators, refuse to participate. Either help change their attitudes or leave.

At Stanford, important research was done on amoebas. In one tank, the temperature, humidity, food, PH level and other conditions were adjusted for maximum comfort. In another tank, the organisms were exposed to alternating extremes of heat, cold, humidity, fluid levels and food supplements. To the researchers amazement, the organisms in the 'super-comfortable' tank died sooner than those exposed to extremes. The conclusion? Unlimited comfort promotes lethargy and decay while forced adaptation promotes growth and strength.

To teach at risk means that you will be authentic to the dreams and visions you have. You will be a part of the group of teachers who have taken that additional step of risk, the risk of failure. But the risk of failure, as you know, is nothing compared to the risk of being inauthentic or not being your best self or not doing what you know needs to be done. Teachers unwilling to put themselves out to teach 'at the level of risk' are not slowly dying, they are already dead. They have sold out their aliveness for a paycheck. They made the choice to play for survival and they are paying for it. Their lives lack the energy and aliveness and exuberance that you know is possible. They dread each day in front of the classroom, only heading towards that final pronouncement of retirement.

It's now up to you. You will no longer be sitting safely in your tree, you will now be moving out on the branches. It may be safer in your tree, but the fruit of the tree is out on the limb. To renew and revitalize yourself takes as much energy and commitment as it took to get trained originally for your first teaching assignment, maybe more. You have to be ruthless about your self-discipline. Get a partner to help you. With a vision, a path and a satisfying personal life, you can expect to stay refreshed and excited about teaching. But there's one more level. It's the level of making ALL of education work well. And that's in the next chapter.

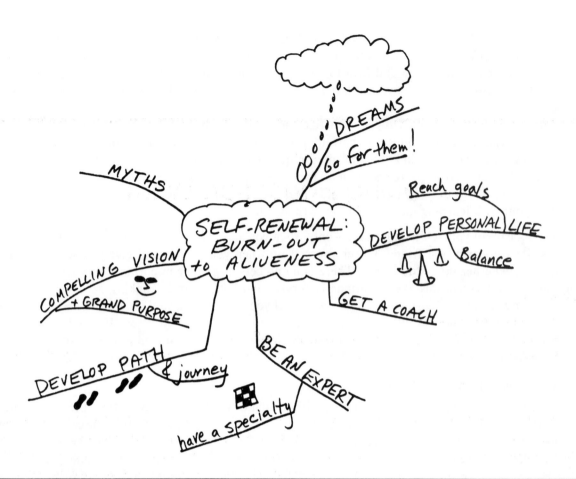

☑ **Check These Key Points**

1. Develop a compelling vision and plan for your role in education.
2. Be willing to become a student yourself.
3. Study a master teacher and be willing to be coached.
4. Become an expert on some facet of your teaching.
5. Be sure your personal life energizes you.
6. Determine what activities you love and do them!

Chapter Nineteen

Making Education Work

Objectives

- To inspire action
- To describe six steps to making education work
- To provide recommendations of ways to deal with the nine trends listed in chapter one

What will it take to make education work in the way we all know it can? A lot. It will take one of the most purposeful, courageous and sustained commitments ever made. It will take an unrivaled ability to bring forth your vision on a daily basis. It will require an relentless insistence on seeing beyond the problems, circumstances and complaints that make up much of the current conversation about education. It will take a whole new set of skills, many of which we haven't yet imagined. It will take stronger, new partnerships and relationships in every area of our professional and personal lives. It will take more focused planning and insightful thinking than ever done before. It will require a rediscovery and realigning of values and a certain ruthlessness to tell the truth. And finally, it will require that each individual teacher bring forth every last bit of integrity, personal power and ability to manage than ever before. It means being willing to live and teach only in its best and brightest vision. The job to take on education as a possibility and as something you are responsible for improving is quite a task. But it's worth it. Here are the words of philosopher De Ropp:

> "Seek, above all, a game worth playing . . . Having found the game, play it with intensity—play it as if your life and sanity depended upon it. (They do depend on it.) . . . Though nothing means anything and all roads are marked "No Exit", move as if your movements had some purpose . . . For it must be clear, even to the most clouded intelligence, that any game is better than no game . . .
>
> "But although it is safe to play the Master Game, this has not served to make it popular. It remains the most demanding and difficult of games, and in our society, there are few who play. . . . Once a person has . . . (decided to play), he is no longer able to sleep comfortably. A new appetite develops within him, the hunger for a real awakening . . .
>
> "Here it is sufficient to say that the Master Game can NEVER be made easy to play. It demands all that a man (or woman) has, all his feelings, all his thoughts, his entire resources, physical and spiritual. If he tries to play it in a halfhearted way or tries to get results by unlawful means, he runs the risk of destroying his own potential. For this reason it is better not to embark on the game at all than to play halfheartedly."

Choosing to make a difference, as you may have guessed, is metaphorically "the crossing of the Rubicon." It's a commitment on par with the most difficult on earth. And no awards are likely to be given. Expect no grand monument for all your efforts. Expect no hero's welcome for playing the game or even winning the game. Expect criticism, difficulty and unthinkable challenges. Your "prize", your reward and monument for all of your efforts is likely to be quite simple. Education will work. Our children

will be empowered, enriched and opened to the grand possibilities of who they truly are. Where do we begin? My first suggestion is that you read the excellent book by Leslie Hart called *Guide To School Change*. Next, here's the six key steps:

- Communicate Your Vision
- Become Part of the Planning Process
- Make a Commitment for Reform
- Build Partnerships
- Maintain Rapport
- Begin Now

Step 1—Communicate Your Vision

In the last chapter, we discussed the importance of having a compelling vision of education. If you haven't already done so, develop your vision. Do it right now. You will only be as powerful in life as that which you are willing to speak about and be responsible for. Your vision is necessary for others to take you more seriously and for you to excite them to become mobilized to support your dream.

A vision is two things—what you would like to have happen and your commitment in the face of that vision. In other words, the vision is a possibility of how things could be. What is also needed is your authorship of the vision and a relationship with that vision, making it powerful. You must take a stand for the vision. Then, communicate your vision to as many people as possible. Speak to individuals, groups, young and old. Bring forth a quality of vision that excites people and gets them thinking about possibilities, not complaints. Act as if you are the secretary of education and your actions alone determine the fate of education in this country. If you bring that quality of presence to your work, things will change. They have to change with that kind of momentum. Once you've done that, the wheels are set in motion for the next step.

Step 2—Become Part of the Planning Process

Once your vision for education is clear, your value as a contributor increases dramatically. Bring your vision to every group you join. Inspire others to share your vision. Assist in the planning for tomorrow's schools in any way you can. The changes are already beginning in many areas. Educator Dr. Jack Hill suggests some of the impending changes:

1. High technology mixing with greater humanism. A greater blending of the electronic education with the personal touch. More values and ethics conflicts will be arising.

2. Greater localized schooling. Fewer of the huge schools, more neighborhood schools called learning centers. We need more schools, but big schools cost too much and are inefficient. Instead of 2,000–5,000 students at a school, you'll begin to see more with 200–500.

3. Increased community input. Expect additional assistance from the two largest groups with vested interests: business, because it needs better educated graduates and senior citizens, because they'll want meaningful work. Excellent education will become everyone's business.

4. Increased attention on communication skills. The information age requires more people-to-people interaction than the industrial age. Schools will offer more skills such as listening, negotiating, planning, thinking, writing and information processing.

5. Greater career focus. The average American will be changing jobs five to seven times by the year 2025. Schools will focus on a "generalist" education with greater attention to how to search for work, interview and grow. We must teach our students how to learn, not what to learn.

6. Superior educational methodology. Schools will be learning how to reach more and more students. A change from sorting and tracking students to developing all human resources. Our national drop-out rates will decrease. In urban areas, the minorities will be the majority. We must become more sensitive to the needs of non-whites to insure their success.

7. Greater family roles played. With more parents working outside the home, schools will increase their roles in areas such as responsibility, substance abuse, values, ethics and career counseling.

8. Greater cooperative efforts. Schools will link up nationwide on satellite, video, computer and people-to-people. More shared ideas and contact with diverse individuals.

9. Greater global awareness. Schools will have more emphasis, especially in elementary and secondary, on the culture, religion, economics and politics of other countries. Massive student exchanges as well as general cultural expansion.

10. A broader-based curriculum. Liberal arts combined with technology. Theoretical and concrete. Historical-classical and contemporary-relevant. A mixing of analytical left-hemisphere with the more intuitive right hemisphere.

From Dr. Jack Hill: The Future of Education, private papers. Reprinted with permission, 1987.

To take part in the planning process means that you are taking on the role of responsibility. No one can assign that to you. No one can assign or "fix" responsibility to another. Responsibility is something that an individual "takes on" for him or herself. It always comes from within. It's a gift and best described as a privilege, not a weight. There's no guilt or burden in responsibility, only an opportunity to step out and be courageous. It allows you to be at the cause of things, not the effect. And best of all, it empowers you to be your best. You are only as "big" in life as the responsibilities you are willing to accept.

Step 3—Make a Commitment for Reform

One of the things that does not work in education (we've tried this one already . . .) is to give our opinions about how to fix it. Opinions are relatively useless in the face of what's required to make education work. Opinions come across like a cabbie's babble or the "guy in a diner" who has an opinion about everything. The problem with opinions is simple: they're vapid, cheap and irresponsible. What's needed is not some half-informed prognosis and dime-store conclusion, but rather some real honest-to-goodness commitments. We need educators to quit talking about what needs to be done and start committing to doing what needs to be done. Your commitment is the stand, the position you take and the place from which you can operate. You need that stand, that backdrop of grounding from which to express yourself. So the next time someone has a great idea about how to fix something in education, ask them what they personally would like to commit to to insure that the changes happen.

In addition to depth of commitment, it also takes depth. Start being committed to reform at every level until the vision becomes reality. Have a concrete plan, find those who will listen, speak about your plan with such a level of commitment and empowerment that others become excited about your vision, too. There will be many changes in education in the next few years and many of them are exciting!

Teachers will become co-explorers with students because no one person can know it all. It will be a high-tech and high-touch partnership with interchanging roles. Because so much learning will occur at home, it will become a new center of learning. In a curious reversal, younger students will come to school to play more than learn. Elementary students who will have already learned reading, writing and math on television or home computers, will need to interact with other students and play. School will become the place for social skills, field trips, experiments, plays, dance, music, and nurturing human contact.

It's clear that what we have done before will fail because we have been working on symptoms, not causes. Let's review what causal-level changes we are dealing with in our society. These are the underlying issues that, if left unattended, will result in behavior problems, low test scores or drug abuse. Unless we prepare our educators to deal with these, the money spent on symptomatic relief will continue to be wasted. These causal changes or trends must be addressed, for they are at the core of education's current difficulties.

The key is that *THE GAME HAS CHANGED*. To be effective, to be pro-active (as opposed to reactive), we must have some awareness of what's going on so we can begin to predict what's needed. Here are the same nine trends mentioned in Chapter One. Included, this time, are recommendations for the reform of education.

Change 1: Greater Velocity of Change

REFORMS: Prepare educators to become more flexible in their work. Increase training in flexibility, spontaneity, willingness to adapt. Reduce training of teachers in content or new curriculum. Instead, have preparation deal with more areas relative to students' lives. Have educators take time off to visit places like teen dances, other teachers' classes, concerts and travel study groups. Provide incentives for additional training.

Prepare students with more strategies and tools. Teach more HOW to learn, and less WHAT to learn. Work in class using a greater variety of learning styles. Teach students how they learn and how to become more accountable for their own learning process. Make high school mandatory only up to age 16. This will enhance the quality of learning for many of the students because many of the behavior problems or classroom energy drains are from students who don't want to be in school. These students should have the option to join the work force and they'll be literate because standards will have been raised.

Change 2: Information Age Impact Is Increasing

REFORMS: Ask teachers to relinquish the role as the only source of information. Have students take on additional roles, becoming more responsible for their learning. Use textbooks as reference books, not as standard issues for every student. Rely more on magazine subscriptions, computers, video and television.

Up the ante for students to learn the three fundamentals: reading, writing and speaking. Promote students from elementary school, junior high and high school only if they meet certain competency levels. In our democratic society, one goal education must achieve is to insure that every graduate speaks, writes and reads well.

Build schools, staffs and systems on relationships rather than curriculum. As more information becomes available, we need more caring, touching and quality in our relationships.

Change 3: Increasingly Advanced Technology

REFORMS: Train teachers to become better role models for students. Increase training in areas such as team-building, relationship-building, responsibility and vision.

Stress ideas, compassion and commitment as the source of classroom results. Channel monies toward teacher development of the qualities of being human: compassion, responsibility, communication, flexibility, self-esteem, curiosity, excellence and integrity.

Build a compelling vision that is exciting and real. Make it concrete through action steps and insure its continuation by providing sensitive and purposeful management. Most teachers have lost their vision and come to work each day as task-masters, rather than as partners in the vision or possibility that education could become.

Change secondary-level school schedules to match the elementary model of one-teacher, all-day. Rotate schedules so that students would have one class, such as history, with one teacher, all day. Schedule a physical education break each day. It refreshes students' brains and gives the teacher planning time. Students would have one subject one day, another the next. Same teacher all day. Have teachers stay with the same group of students all the way through schooling. In elementary, make it six years. In secondary, make it either three or six years depending on if there's a change in schools. This builds long term understanding and prevents a teacher from being sent someone else's "problem." This provides the opportunity for building better relationships between student and teacher—a significant step towards reducing absenteeism, discipline problems, improperly diagnosed learning problems, vandalism, alienation and dropouts.

Increase the amount of relevant coursework available for secondary students. Make the curriculum more applicable to student's lives. Offer courses in personal economics, relationships, communication skills and business.

Change 4: The "Provider-User" Relationship Has Changed

REFORMS: Change teacher role from being a subject matter specialist to a generalist. Train teachers to be learning coaches who assist in finding information. Increase the coaching role with each year of school. Change the system from a time-based educational system to a performance-based one. Greater interdisciplinary approaches with increased flexibility in learning methodology.

Minimize all lecture time, place a maximum of 20% of class time for teacher lecture time. Increase teacher listening and student talking time. Raise the status of the student. Ask for more accountability in learning. Develop "teacher teams." Have teachers trade ideas and work together as partners on their whole class grade level as a whole.

Reduce or eliminate lecturing or providing "truths." Increase flexible teaching methodologies. Develop and manage learning resources in addition to teacher. Train teachers to become communications specialists rather than just disciplinarians. Develop teacher self-concept, confidence, self-esteem. Provide training in human resources and values understanding. Increase the building of communication skills.

Re-structure the school's lines of communications, support and accountability for teachers. Create new positions for the coaching and support of teachers. (This role would be separate from a principal's role.) Teachers need constant, direct, qualified coaching on what they are doing and what can be improved. They also need daily, weekly and monthly systems set up to acknowledge and support that growth. There also needs to be greater measurable accountability on the part of teachers for the progress of their students. Not solely in the form of test scores, but also in the form of self-esteem, participation, breakthroughs and increases of growth.

Set up specific pathways and vehicles where teachers can have their concerns heard, acted upon and acknowledged. Create ways for teachers to fully participate in the processes affecting them the most, such as teacher-student ratio, class hours, curriculum and classroom design. Increase the salary incentives for mastery-level teaching.

Change 5: Restructuring of the Economic and Social Family

REFORMS: Prepare the teacher to provide more of the 'family' role. Increase the sense of belonging for students, provide better role modeling, emphasize uniqueness, give students more power and choices.

Train all teachers in listening, sharing and counseling skills. Train them in values, integrity and compassion. Teach teachers how to support others and how to reduce pre-judgments about kids.

Change 6: Drain of Leadership from Education to Business

REFORMS: Leaders in education need to spend time away from schools developing a vision. For those with an already defined vision, refreshment and renewal of commitment must continually occur. The power of a compelling vision will enable administrators to carry forth what is needed and relay that to teachers, staff and students.

Change 7: Increased Market-Driven Consumerism

REFORMS: Train teachers to help students feel more included, more important. Create classroom experiences to enhance students' self-esteem. Generate a real sense of uniqueness for each student. Share more about the influences of the media and how to deal with it. Train teachers to share more of their lives with students so they develop more realistic role models. Talk to the students about life purpose and money. Have students discover more about who they are, why are they here on earth and what the rest of their lives could mean for them.

Change 8: Growth to a Multi-Cultural Society

REFORMS: Train teachers in how to build student acceptance and self-esteem. Train teachers in more team building activities. Have qualified organizations train teachers in cultural similarities and differences. Contact San Diego City School's Race and Human Relations Department to learn how to raise cultural awareness.

Change 9: Lessened Predictability

REFORMS: Increase training of teacher and administrative flexibility. Reduce dependency on both stable and fluctuating budget monies. Reduce dependency on materials, supplies and administrative staffing. Increase dependency on peer level coaching. Encourage administrators to set an example in fiscal moderation. Change the topic of conversation from that of scarcity of money to that of abundance of ideas.

Train educators to hold a prevailing action plan that is visionary and pro-active. When led by a vision, conversation is usually about possibilities, rather than complaints. What's needed is the training of educators in three fundamental qualities: vision (the dream, the commitment to a plan), an accountability (which offers ways to be responsible, to be heard, acknowledged and have input in the decisions most affecting them) and humanity (the qualities of compassion, flexibility, and humor).

Change 10: Increased Fiscal Restraints

REFORMS: An increase in leveraged educational spending. This means spending money on areas which have a multiplier effect. Every dollar spent on teachers is multiplied in value because it affects many, many students. Every dollar spent on students is a "dead-end dollar," and the effects are less multiplied than with educators. Reduce spending on classroom materials, textbooks and supplies. Teacher salaries have dropped when measured as a percentage of the total educational dollar—that means we must reduce administrative overhead fast. Re-allocate monies for more effective teacher training.

Greater open-ness for sources of funding. Create better partnerships with the military or national service organizations for students who want to quit school. Create new, more effective partnerships created with business. Less regulation regarding private enterprise's relationships with schools.

Other Changes: Summary Statement

We must be clear that our profession is NOT about filling up students with facts, but rather about opening up people. It's really the business of creating environments in which exciting, fulfilling and empowering learning events can occur. We are in the service business and it is our job to make it work for the students. By recognizing that teaching is a service and healing profession, we'll accomplish much more. We'll have to re-educate others about our real purpose. This means that we need to begin other tasks as well as those done in the classroom.

Other activities needed are the following: your state legislators need to know what kinds of curriculum should be included or deleted to make things work. Your schools need to know the specific kinds of teacher training you need to make your school a total success. Parents must be included in many more ways. Your community needs to know that you would like to make a shift in the quality of education and you must invite citizens to give input. Your school board needs to re-prioritize teacher needs so that you can get the job done. This means less red-tape, more administrative support, less mandated curriculum, more acknowledgement for work well done and more 'say-so' in how the system is set up. School monies invested in teachers are better spent because the effect is multiplied: one teacher affects many students. Whereas monies spent on students are dead-end funds; the effect stops with the students.

You'll discover that there are both adapters and innovators. The adaptor is right at home in a bureaucracy and tends to try to make the existing system make do. The innovator sees that behavior as dogmatic and inflexible and wants to do things differently. The innovator breaks accepted patterns and the adaptor accepts the old framework. It will take both to make education work. As you find out who wants to join you, keep in mind that your game is not the only game in town. This means that when it's not right for others, don't force them into your game or get righteous about it. May I also recommend you read *The Diffusion of Innovation* by Peter Marris?

Step 4—Build Partnerships

We may think of ourselves as just one, but our effects move like the ripples on a pond. So what would happen if we began to work with other teachers and began networking? Do you wonder what's possible if we began to share ourselves and our mastery with other teachers and administrators? If we teachers are going to continue to grow, we have to do it together. There is little growth in isolation and the gifts you have must be distributed in order to have impact.

All you have to do is make a commitment. Tell the teachers around you what you intend to have happen. "I'm committed to making this system work for the students and me." Just by saying it, your words begin to make it happen.

Fortunately, there will be those teachers who immediately want to jump on the bandwagon to join you. Others may not be interested at all. Include those interested and allow the others to go their own way. Eventually, they may discover that what you've got provides fulfillment, joy and satisfaction.

The next step, once you have networked and gained supporters, is to create leaderships, agendas and items to do. Get parent support and community input. Choose a grand goal and make it happen. In Fort Collins, Colorado, School Board President David Neenan declared that their board goal was to win a Nobel Prize for Education. His vision and commitment started the wheels turning. That's the kind of optimism and vision education needs!

Once you have that grand goal as a beacon or mission, roll up your sleeves and start in on the little things. Concentrate on getting many small successes. This builds credibility, energy and elicits support for your work. Ideas for teacher network groups include: support meetings, acknowledgement ceremonies, a gala teacher barbecue or fund raisers for classroom supplies.

Include other teachers who want to get involved. The better you make the "game" of transforming education, the more others will want to join. Make it light, make it fun, and get things done! One of the things Walt Disney credited to his success was the notion that one must "do what you do so well that when people come to see you, they'll get excited and want to bring back their friends; and those people will get excited and bring their friends." That's how good you must make the game of transformation in education.

Step 5—Maintain Rapport with Others

The key to being successful at creating transformation is rapport. Rapport means that you make friends, not enemies. You will get nowhere if you start by making other teachers wrong or blaming them for not supporting you. Each person can accomplish what they do given their personal history, resources and intended outcome. Include everyone you can in your group because you need their support. Include parents, students, administrators, and anyone else who will listen. Include their ideas and find out how you can make the system work for everyone. Support others in helping them get what they want. A fundamental law of humanity is when you help others get what they need, they can better help you get what you need.

Even if you think someone is way off the track, you can appreciate their good intentions, respect their interest and agree with their need to live their own dreams. And, at the same time, you may feel that what they are doing is inappropriate for your needs. You will need a public relations person in your teacher's support group. Someone who will put out the news, create newsletters and let everyone know what you are doing. The more others know about what you are doing, the more support you'll receive. Be sensitive to the beliefs, positions and judgments of others—not in the form of taking them personally, but in the form of listening and understanding them. Then, if you need to take any corrective action, do it with the intention of keeping rapport in mind. Your path to mastery requires organization, involvement of others via networking, and the creation of support groups. It's much easier when we all pull from the same end of the rope!

Step 6—Start Now

If you were to get a closing homework assignment, it would be like this. Do what you do so well, set such a good example, that the enthusiasm, the shouts of aliveness and joy from your work area reaches out to others and wakes them up. Be so committed and so purposeful and so excited about what you do that others either want to join you or are embarrassed by the high standard you set and want to leave the profession for some other job more suited to their commitments. Go out and teach so well that you literally re-invent it. Re-create it the way that Elgin Baylor, Julius Erving and Michael Jordan re-invented the game of basketball. The way that Sandy Koufax, Roger Clemens and Dwight Gooden re-invented pitching a baseball. The way Casio re-invented the computerized wristwatch and Apple reinvented the computer with the MacIntosh. Be creative. Be outrageous. Somehow, get out the message about your commitment to make education work and most importantly, LIVE IT. Futurist Marilyn Ferguson says:

> "Our past is not our potential. In any hour, with all the stubborn teachers and healers of history who called us to our best selves, we can liberate the future. You are not just you. You are a seed, a silent promise. You are the conspiracy."

The end of this book is just the beginning for you. There is a new you who turned the last few pages of this book, far different from the one who opened it. May you grow and reach as you never previously thought possible. You have been an inspiration for me and you are the person from whom this book was written.

You have taught well
if ten years later
your students forgot who you were
and remember who they became
in your class

You knew there was more to education than showing up and waiting for the last bell. Teaching is so much more than that. It is discovery, sharing, growing, excitement and love. It's not a burden, it's a joy. And it's like a consuming, fulfilling bonfire that provides you with a glow of warmth and a blaze of passion. You've already demonstrated a commitment to education by reading this book. The intention to grow and willingness to improve sets you well above and beyond most other educators. Keep growing! There's no such thing as standing still; we are either expanding or contracting.

You must commit yourselves not only to your cause, crusade or mission, but to your own aliveness and self-expression. If you have a commitment to education with anything less than your life, it will be insufficient to the task at hand. Keep taking on more responsibility and more challenges. I know you might be tired. I know you have given a lot already. It's been great, but the results say that it's not enough. We must all re-commit to vision and the work that needs to be done.

It is you, and the choices you make in the classroom that will make a difference in this world. Each move you make, each class you give, and thought you think is shaping our tomorrows. So don't worry about how or why or when, begin now. Begin with your commitment. The possibilities are more grand than we have yet imagined. Take that first step now. There is a lot riding on our jobs as educators. If you stumble or fall, there are plenty of us who will reach to pull you up on your feet again. We know what kind of journey we are beginning and we are already taking the first and most important step. One last closing story for you:

> There was a wise old man who always knew the answers. People came from far and away to ask him things and he always knew the right answer. Then an envious village smart-aleck decided to trick him. He decided to hold a live butterfly in his hands behind his back and ask the wise man what was in his hands. When the wise man got that correct, the smart-aleck would then ask if the butterfly was alive or dead. If the wise man said dead, he would show the living butterfly, and if he said alive, he would kill the butterfly and show him the dead one.
>
> The day of the test came, and the smart-aleck went before the wise man with his plan, holding the butterfly behind his back. He then asked the old man what he was holding and the wise man answered, "a butterfly." Then the smart-aleck asked if it was alive or dead, and the wise man gave an answer which just might also apply to you right now in terms of education, "It is in your hands now."

☑ Check These Key Points

1. Making education work begins with each teacher choosing to make a difference.
2. Communicate your vision for education to everyone you know.
3. Take on a role of responsibility by becoming part of the planning process for the future of education.
4. Begin to create plans for solutions to education's problems.
5. Network and build partnerships with other teachers.
6. Remember, it's in your hands!

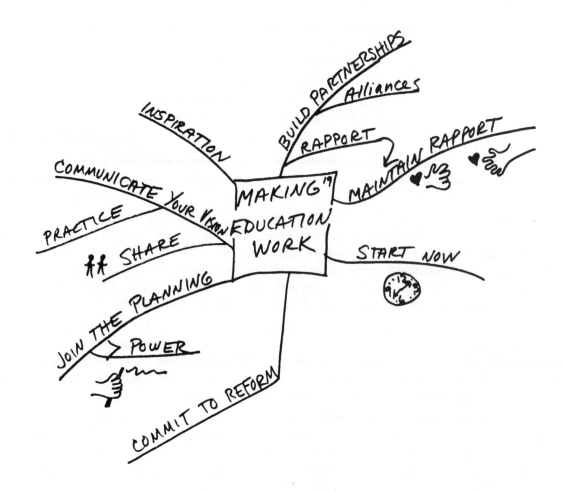

Appendix

Reader Evaluation

You are important to me and are the best qualified person to evaluate this book by completing the survey below. Your comments, new ideas, corrections, tools and other additions are read and appreciated. If used, they will be acknowledged in the upcoming revision.

1. *THIS BOOK:*
   a) What was the most useful part of this book?

   b) What was least valuable to you?

   c) What related subjects/topics would you also be interested in?

   d) What was the reason(s) that you bought this book?

   e) Where or how did you get this book?

2. OCCUPATION:
   a) teacher
   b) trainer
   c) principal
   d) student
   e) administrator
   f) parent
   g) other: _____

3. STUDENT LEVEL TAUGHT:
   a) elementary
   b) junior high
   c) senior high
   d) college
   e) other: _____

4. SUBJECT TAUGHT:
   a) English
   b) social studies
   c) science
   d) Foreign languages
   e) mathematics
   f) special ed
   g) other: _____

5. INFLUENCES:
   a) what magazines do you read?

   b) what person has influenced you the most in your teaching and why?

   c) what was the best book you've ever read on teaching?

6. *FURTHER SUGGESTIONS/COMMENTS:*

Once you've filled out this page, mail to me. The address to send to is: Eric Jensen/ Box 2011/ Del Mar, CA 92014. THANK YOU!

P.S. If you're interested in other products or trainings, please print your name and home address on the other side of this paper before mailing.

Resource Organizations

NOTE: This is a partial alphabetical listing of useful organizations, courses or workshops in or related to teaching. The address is usually the national office, so call or write for the one nearest you. No endorsement of any kind is implied by any of the listings here and if you know of one that should be listed, please write to me at Box 2551/ Del Mar, CA 92014.

* Aletheia Foundation
Jack Schwartz
515 NE 8th
Grants Pass, ORE 97526
(Biofeedback, learning, nutrition, auras, energy)

* Anderson Research Foundation
3960 Ingraham
Los Angeles, CA 90005
(mind expansion, research)

* Assn. for Humanistic Education
PO BOX 13042
Gainesville, FLA 32604
(information, courses)

* Assn. for Transpersonal Phych.
Box 3049
Stanford, CA 94305
(courses, newsletter)

* Assn. for Humanistic Psych.
325 Ninth St
San Francisco, CA 94103
(personal growth, psychology, various courses)

* Biofeedback Society of America
4200 East Ninth c268
Denver, Colorado 80262
(educational research, classroom methods and materials)

* Center for Accelerated Learning
David Meyer, Director
1103 Wisconsin St.
Lake Geneva, WI 53147
(courses, related materials in accelerated learning)

* Confluent Education
Box 30128
Santa Barbara, CA 93105

* Creative Education Foundation
State Univ. College
1300 Elmwood
Buffalo, NY 14222
(courses on creativity)

* Difference Makers
ATTN: Helice Bridges
Box 112415
San Diego, CA 92111
(acknowledging others, has excellent school programs)

* Education Network-
62. Firs t St.
San Francisco, CA 94103
(transpersonal humanistic teaching methods)

* The Forum/Education Network
61. First St.
San Francisco, CA 94105
(personal growth, dozens of related courses)

* Esalen Institute
Big Sur, CA 93920
(workshops in education, psychology, philosophy, body, etc)

* Frostig Center of Educational Therapy
5981 Venice Blvd.
Los Angeles, CA 90034
(materials, esp. on 'learning disabled')

* Human Brain and Human Learning
1560 Broadway
New York, NY 10036
(information, newsletter on 'brain compatible' schools)

* Insight Trainings
2101 Wilshire Blvd.
Santa Monica, CA 90403
(personal growth courses)

* Inner Dimension Research Foundation
Superlearning/(Don Lofland)
Box 496
Santa Cruz, CA 95060

* Interface
230 Central St.
Newton, MASS 02166
(education, new age courses)

* John Lilly
33307 Decker School Road
Malibu, CALIF 90265
(learning, research, memory, altered states, brain)

* Living TAO Foundation
Chungliang Al Huang
PO. Box 846
Urbana, ILL 61801
(t'ai chi courses, books, tapes)

* D.M.A
Box 571
Cambridge, MASS 02238
(workshop on personal power, effectiveness and
goals)

* Dr. Jean Houston
Box 600
Pomona, NY 10970
(workshops on human potential)

* National Assn of Humanistic Education
C/O Fred Richards
211 Bennett Circle
Carollton, GA 30117

* National Humanistic Ed. Center
Springfield Road
Upper Jay, NY 12987
(courses and networks in new age education)

N.L.P. (Neuro-linguistic Programming)
Grinder/ Laborde/ Hill
1433 Webster St.
Palo Alto, CA 94301

NLP Center for Advanced Studies
98 Main St.
Tiburon, CA 94920
(courses, books, tapes on NLP)

Earl Ogletree
Dept. of Curriculum and Instruction
Chicago State Univ.
95th & King Dr.
Chicago, ILL 60628

* Omega Institute
Lake Drive Rd 2
Box 377-c2
Rhinebeck, NY 12572
(personal, holistic, health, business, educational
programs)

* Learning to Learn
Stephanie Merritt
3768 Front Street, #10
San Diego, 92103

* Learning Resource Network
1221 Thurston
Manhattan, Kansas 66502
(National clearinghouse and support group for
learning centers)

* The Power of Knowing
Marilyn Ferguson
Box 42211
Los Angeles, CA 90042
(workshops on leadership, personal growth, future-
creating)

* Optimalearning
Barzak Educational Institute
88 Belvedere, Suite D
San Rafael, CA 94901

* Robbins Research Institute
3366 N. Torrey Pines Ct.
La Jolla, CA 92037
(NLP, rapid behavior change)

* S.A.L.T.
2740 Richmond Ave.
Des Moines, Iowa 50317
(accelerative teaching/learning)

* Siccone Foundation
2254 Union St. #1
San Francisco, CA 94123
(workshops, consulting, books)

* Self-Esteem Seminars
Jack Canfield
17156 Palisades Circle
Pacific Palisades, CA 90272
(workshops and tapes on raising self-esteem)

* Sound of Light
Don Campbell, Music
Box 835704
Richardson, Texas 75083
(excellent workshops, music, books)

* Summit
255 Harbor Way
So. San Francisco, CA 94080
(personal growth workshops)

* Supercamp
Box 500 #368
Del Mar, CA 92014
(10-day residential accelerated learning-how-to-learn programs for 8–12th graders)

Turning Point (Eric Jensen)
Teacher-training
Box 2551
Del Mar, CA 92104
(619) 481-6600
(staff development, books, tapes)

* University Associates
8517 Production Ave.
San Diego, CA 92121
(publishers of excellent sourcebooks for teachers, trainers)

** Voice Analysis
Dr. Sandra Seagal
1434 6th St. #1
Santa Monica, CA 90401
(research, personal growth, organizational development)

Waldorf Education
501 Berkley
Ann Arbor, MICH 48103
(whole-person educational processes)

* Whole-brain Learning
Dr. John-David
2441 Impala Drive
Carlsbad, CA 92109

Musical Resources

Guidelines: When building your classroom music library, be sure to include four basic types of music:

1. "Passive"—40–60 beats per minute/very slow excellent for relaxation, imagery, opening of class quiet time, review. Examples include artists such as Steven Halpern, George Winston, Kobialka, largo and pastorale baroque
2. "Active"—60–80 beats per minute/slow to moderate good as background for presentation of material, for students working together, stories, activities. Examples include Bach, Telemann Vivaldi, Mozart, Gluck, Corelli, Handel
3. "Movement"—80–100 beats per minute/moderate to brisk good for exit music, breaks, rituals, play, group songs. Examples include many current pop hits.
4. "Special Effects"—the fun-type of music which includes trumpet fanfare, applause, animal sounds, all which can add fun and fullness to the learning experience

* "How to Use music" tapes
Special Effects Tape
Turning Point
Box 2551
Del Mar, CA 92014
(619) 755-6670

* Baroque Music

* Health/Movement/Learning/Brain
Sound of Light, Don Campbell
P.O. Box 835704
Richardson, Texas, 75083

* Luramedia (Relaxation)
P.O. Box 261668
San Diego, CA 92126
1-800-FOR-LURA (outside CA)
1-619-578-1948 collect (inside CA)

How To Become a More Powerful Educator

Would you like to have 50–100 of this book's most powerful tools taught to you in a training program? *Turning Point* is a training organization (founded by the author) that teaches the skills and ideas of this book. Turning Point is also a state-of-the-art teacher effectiveness program and consulting organization. You or your staff can get trained on any of the material in this book in trainings of one to ten days. The trainings go beyond what's presented here by providing specific hands-on experience, concrete updated knowledge and unique networking opportunities.

The once-a-year full-length conference in Southern California is the most requested program. Long-term follow up studies demonstrate powerful results: 85% of the participants say that it has made a "substantial impact" on their lives. 93% of the graduates say that they use something from the program every day. In the six-month follow-up, 96% were still pleased or very impressed. You may call or write for graduate referrals.

You or your teachers can make dramatic shifts in the quality of education by improving the quality of teaching. Turning Point's program trains teachers in the specific skills needed to boost participation, test scores, student interest and motivation. You will learn how to set up a high performance learning classroom, how to open and close a class, plus, you will get specific feedback on your presentations. If you would like more information, call (619) 755–6670 or write today with your specific request:

MAIL TO: TURNING POINT FOR TEACHERS
P.O. BOX 2551
DEL MAR, CA 92014

Selected Resources: Journals and Materials

Included are possibilities that will support your path toward a new paradigm as well as a new level of mastery in the classroom. There are undoubtedly thousands of future-oriented educational journals and materials available, so just a sampling is included. If you know of one that should be included, please write to me.

* Brain/Mind Bulletin/Leading Edge
Box 42211
Los Angeles, CA 90042
(up-to-the-moment digest of discoveries, breakthroughs and insights into how we think and behave)

* Choices and Connections
The First Catalog of the Global Family
Human Potential Resources, Inc.
P.O. Box 1057
Boulder, CO 80306

* Dromenon
P.O. Box 2244
New York, NY 10001
(newsletter on personal growth, culture, heritage, education)

* Educational Kinesthetics
Box 5002
Glendale, CA 91201
(Materials and workshops on brain integration)

* Game Materials
Creative Publications, Inc.
Box 10328
Palo Alto, CA 95450

* The Movement
PO Box 19458
Los Angeles, CA 90019
(journal of inner change and personal awareness)

* New Age
32 Station St.
Brookline Village, Mass 02146
(monthly magazine on social changes and trends)

* New Realities
680 Beach St.
San Francisco, CA 94109
(journal on emerging trends in America, social, educational, business movements)

* Reading Research Council
1799 Old Bayshore Hwy.
Burlingame, CA 94010
(415) 692-8990
(Clinic for treating dyslexia)

* S.A.L.T. Journal
Box 1216 Welch Station
Ames, Iowa 50010
(suggestive, accelerated teaching techniques and ideas)

* Turning Point
Box 2551
Del Mar, CA 92014
(teacher training programs and workshops)

* Wholistic Education
Box 575
Amherst, Mass 01112
(sources of useful training materials, courses)

* Yellow Pages of Learning Resources
MIT Press
28 Carlton St.
Cambridge, Mass 02142
(community, govt. and private organization resources)

Publisher addresses for classroom simulations: (write for catalog and complete descriptions)

Houghton Mifflin, 110 Tremont, Boston, MA 02107
Nova Scientific Corp., 111 Tucker, Burlington, NC 27215
Psychology Today, Box 4523, Des Moines, IA, 50336
Social Studies School Serv., 10,000 Culver Blvd., Culver City, CA 90230
Urban Systems, 1033 Mass. Ave., Cambridge, Mass. 02138
Wiff'n Proof Games, 1490-yx South Blvd., Ann Arbor MI 48104

Supercamp—For the Best Summer of Your Life

Every summer thousands of students and some of the best teachers in the country participate in an experiment to push the outer limits of educational excellence. Students come from all over the world to attend SuperCamp, a 10-day residential program in accelerated learning skills and personal growth. The purpose of the camp is to provide an opportunity for students to experience the extraordinary in educational excellence. The students, all 8–12th graders are taught in three areas: academic, personal and physical.

The program offers no content; rather it builds the relationships and strategies for success. The curriculum includes innovative instruction in problem solving, rapid reading, accelerated study skills, test preparation strategies, advanced note-taking, memory, vocabulary, spelling, goals, writing, communication skills, responsibility, integrity, and authentic risk-taking.

The instruction is carefully monitored and accurately documented. Long-term results show dramatic and long-lasting increases in self-worth and academic excellence as well as autonomy, aliveness and confidence. The camp itself is held on college campuses across the country. If you are interested in participating in SuperCamp, there are two possible routes:

1. *As a faculty.* You must have an extraordinary expertise in one of the areas mentioned above working with teens. You must be willing to be coached and be available for 4–6 weeks of travel during the summer months. You must also embody the essence of this book in your teachings.
2. *As a support staff/internships.* You must be willing to do whatever needs to be done, work long hours, enjoy your work, and do it all as a volunteer. Every teacher who has gone has discovered a gold mine of ideas, tools and experiences to take back into their classroom. If either of these two positions interest you, or if you would like information on the program for a teen you know of, write today:

SUPERCAMP
BOX 5000 #368
DEL MAR, CA 92014

Eye Accessing Cues

To the untrained teacher, students are simply "thinking." Actually, you could break down what they are doing into many kinds of thinking processes. The two most dominant might be recall and creation; that is, you either already know it and are remembering it or you are constructing it in your mind. When we process information internally, we do it with any of our five senses: sight, sound, touch, smell or hearing. The founders of neurolinguistic programming, Richard Bandler and John Grinder, have observed that most people (especially right-handed ones) give clues through their eye movements as to which of the sensory modes they use.

The value of this information is enormous. If you know what mode a person uses you can better understand and communicate with them. For example, if a student's eyes are down and to the right, he may be experiencing some feelings. It's a cue for you to know that you may want to respect those sensations for a moment before you talk to him. Or, you may want to get him out of those feelings by asking him to look up. This will cause him to access the visual mode thus changing the kinesthetic sensations. Here's the specific breakdown and how to access the cues:

V.r . . . . . (up and to the left for normal right-handed persons) Visual Remembered: seeing images of the past. Simply ask a question such as, "What color is your living room rug?"

V.c . . . . . (up and to the right) Visual construct: seeing newly created images. Simply ask, "What would your brother look like if he dyed his hair green?"

A.r . . . . . (looking to the left) Auditory remembered: recalling sound heard in the past. Simply ask, "What was the last thing I said?"

A.c . . . . . (looking to the right) Auditory construct: creating new sounds in your mind. Simply ask, "What would your name sound like spelled backwards?"

A.i . . . . . (looking down to your left) Auditory internal: talking to yourself. Simply ask person to sing happy birthday to himself.

K.i . . . . . (looking down to your right) Kinesthetic: feelings and emotions. Simply ask, "How would you feel if you were sad?"

K.e . . . Kinesthetic external . . . touching and feeling anything real from the outside world, from the feel of clothes to the feeling of clapping your hands.

What are the implications in teaching? Infinite! Let's just take a couple of examples. When your students are taking a test, what would assist them in recalling prior visual information (what was on a handout, picture, drawing or in a text)? The answer is that they could recall it best by looking up and to the left. In order to construct an image of how something would look (such as if they were composing, writing, etc), they would look up and to the right to have the best access to that information. If a student wanted to recall what you said, he'd look to his left side. If he's composing and wants to 'hear' how something sounds, his eyes would go to his right.

Let's assume that a student is trying to do his best on an exam and is accessing his information. His eyes would need to move around a lot! And what do most teachers tell students to do? "Keep your eyes on your paper!" Guess what that does? By having to put the eyes down, it puts the student into either the kinesthetic mode (feelings of anxiety, fear, etc.) or in his auditory internal which means that he will be talking to himself about it (maybe telling himself how hard the test is). Many teachers inadvertently keep students from scoring well on tests because of where they tell their students to look while taking it.

How do you use accessing cues in conversations with students? If the eyes are down and to the right (student's right), it's likely that they are strongly into their feelings. If you want to communicate with them, you have some new choices: (1) gain rapport by matching their experience. Say, "You must be feeling low, David." This creates an immediate sense of rapport between you and the student. Or, (2) break the state by switching the state. Say, "David, just for a moment, could you please look up at this . . ."

258

ACCESSING CUES

**Up Right
Visual Constructed**

**Up Left
Visual Eidetic**

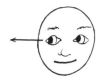

**Horizontal Right
Auditory Constructions**

**Horizontal Left
Auditory Tape Loops**

**Down Right
Kinesthetic**

**Down Left
Auditory Tonal**

This will pull the student out of his feelings and make it easier to present something that is visual. (3) Pace, then lead. You would also talk about feelings with him and begin to lead him out by slowly having him access sounds or visuals. The possibilities are endless and you'll be discovering more of them every day.

Spelling/Math Strategy Outline

A good speller (or a student recalling math formulas) uses a primarily visual strategy while a poor speller uses either an auditory (sounds the words or letters out) or kinesthetic (spells by how the word or letters feel) strategy. Here's an example of a primarily visual strategy:

1. For spelling: prepare a list of words to be learned or use the ones on a student's list.
2. Use the eye-accessing chart to determine the direction of the student's gaze while recalling visual-remembered material. For example, "What color are the curtains in your living room?"
3. Explain to the student that it is more useful to recall what something looks like when his or her eyes are pointed in the visual direction.
4. Ask the student what his or her favorite color is. Explain that it is easier to remember words in color.
5. Show the student the first word or formula on the list. Have the student glance at it, as if taking a snapshot.
6. Have the student look up to his or her best recalling direction and visualize a picture of that word in full color.
7. Ask the student, while looking at the word in his or her mind's eye, to read the letters backward to you. (This insures that the picture is in his or her mind). Make sure that the eyes stay up in the recall direction.

8. Next, ask the student to spell the word or formula forwards. Once again, make sure that the eyes stay up in the recalling mode.
9. Tell the student, "from now on, you will simply remember this picture in your mind and be able to recall it perfectly."
10. Repeat steps 5–9 for any new words, formulas or equations.

   Note: "Chunk down" longer words into 3-letter units. Make sure that this method is practiced until it becomes automatic. Make sure the student visualizes as directed. Make sure that each of the steps are followed explicitly and that the eyes are pointed in the correct direction at the proper time. If he or she has difficulty, have them create an imaginary tv set. Either way, this is a very powerful strategy when done properly.

the SUPER-TEACHING PROCESS

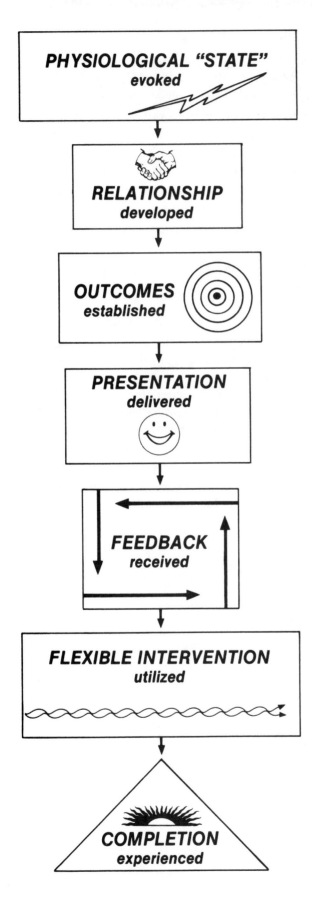

PHYSIOLOGICAL "STATE"
evoked

- Teacher state evoked
  (enthusiasm, excitement, flexible, loving, positive)
- Student state evoked
  (interested, confident, attentive, joyful, relaxed)

RELATIONSHIP
developed

- Teacher-student rapport
  (conscious/non-conscious)
- Student-subject affinity
  (global/relevant/curious)

OUTCOMES
established

- In behavioral terms
- Must have agreement on them
- Must be benefit oriented
- Specific, desirable and ecological

PRESENTATION
delivered

- To build and/or change internal representations
  in student with sufficient skill to elicit a
  corresponding behavior change
- With congruency, stay in ideal state, keep
  students in state

FEEDBACK
received

- Requires trained sensory acuity
- Know the unconscious responses
- Set up behavioral response system
- Includes signal system on-the-spot and visual,
  auditory and kinesthetic demonstration on
  quizzes and tests later

FLEXIBLE INTERVENTION
utilized

- Use tools of intervention
- Based on feedback received
- Re-group, re-package, re-format
- Use wide range of tools until successful
- Have more flexibility than students

COMPLETION
experienced

- Evaluation: teacher and student
- Q's, Review/Clarify/Affirm
- Generalize/Globalize
- Future pace
- Congratulate/appreciate

261

Accelerated Learning

Accelerated learning is a brain-compatible teaching methodology brought to the United States in the mid 1970's by a Bulgarian educator, Dr. Georgi Lozanov. This discipline describes the philosophy, skills and actions of the presenter as well as the processes and formatting of the lesson plans.

The phrase accelerated learning is a misnomer. You cannot accelerate the learning process except as compared to something else, such as traditional rates. And our traditional rates may be actually far LESS than our natural, normal or optimal rate. The brain's natural function is to learn quickly and easily.

Part of the discipline of accelerated learning consists of removing the barriers to learning and addressing the obsolete conditioning we've all been exposed to about learning as being difficult and slow. The other part of accelerated learning is to orchestrate the input in a way that is playful, multi-modal, relaxed, positive, consistent and congruent. Yet the real genius of the discipline is that it was the first to recognize and employ the power of the emotions and the non-conscious mind.

In the United States, the success rate of implementing accelerated learning has been less spectacular. Many teachers have reported significantly greater gains; but usually in the two to five times range. And that's certainly a breakthrough no matter how you measure it.

But while the cross-cultural transfer of methodology has certainly been inexact, something greater has come out of it. Lozanov brought more than a discipline; he brought a refreshing attitude about learning that has affected thousands of educators and their students. The attitude is "Let's see what high goals and really attainable" and "Let's break past old limiting thoughts and do the impossible." And it has.

This book has no special section on how to "do" accelerated learning. It is not the intention nor the scope of this book to present either of these disciplines in detail. What you will find is that this book includes and utilizes each of the disciplines in an integrated fashion. In chapter two, you'll find the beliefs of each of the disciplines. In chapter three, you'll discover how the latest brain research relates to each of them. Chapter four describes the skills necessary for both areas. Chapter five offers suggestions for lesson planning using both methodologies. And each of the remaining chapters offers insights and applications for practical implementation.

As you've probably discovered, being a "super-teacher" means using the eclectic approach, not being a crusader of zealot of any one particular method. So, instead of promoting any particular methodology, *Super-Teaching* is including them all and inviting you to use what's most useful in the moment.

There are many excellent books, tapes and courses which are specifically on the accelerated learning methods. A great starter book is *Accelerated Learning* by Colin Rose; it's listed in the bibliography as well as dozens of others.

NLP—Neurolinguistic Programming

NLP (Neurolinguistic Programming) is a term which describes a set of beliefs, distinctions and skills in communication. It was developed in the early 1970's by a Gestalt therapist and computer programmer, Richard Bandler and a linguist, John Grinder. Curious about the real nature of genius, both founders studied the super-achievers in many areas of life. They discovered a common set of operating beliefs, skills and distinctions which enabled the super-achievers to succeed. Once identified, categorized and taught, these became the foundation for NLP.

This technology offers extraordinary possibilities in education. It provides the necessary skills to determine more precise outcomes, develop strong relationships, draw out learning strategies and utilize with pinpoint accuracy the tools to build successful student experiences and resources.

As with accelerated learning, you'll find much of the science of NLP integrated into the "Super-Teaching" methodology. You'll find references and applications to representational systems, states, rapport, accessing cues, anchoring, sensory acuity, outcome determination, strategies and information gathering. The book also implores you to use behavioral flexibility and operate from personal power, two of the fundamentals of NLP.

For more detailed information, read *Magic Demystified,* by Lewis and Pucelik, *Influencing With Integrity* by Genie Laborde and *Master Teaching Techniques* by Bernard Cleveland. But just as importantly, use the skills and begin to experiment and generate your own. That's where the future of teaching is at—in your hands!

Bibliography and Suggested Reading

Adams, James. Conceptual Blockbusting. Standford, CA, Stanford Alumni Assoc. 1974.

Adler, Mortimer. The Paideia Proposal. New York, Macmillian 1982.

Al-Huang, Chungliang. Quantum Soup. New York, Dutton. 1983.

Anderson, U.S. Success-Cybernetics. No. Hollywood, CA, Wilshire. 1977.

Anthony, Dr. Robert. The Ultimate Secrets of Total Self-confidence. New York, Berkley. 1979.

Assagioli, R. Psychosynthesis. New York, Viking. 1965.

Bach, Richard. Illusions. New York, Dell. 1977.

Bandler, Richard & John Grinder. The Structure of Magic, Vol. I, Palo Alto, CA, Calif. Science & Behavior Books, Inc. 1975.

———. The Structure of Magic, Vol. II, Palo Alto, CA, Science & Behavior Books, Inc. 1976.

———. Trance-formations. Moab, UT, Real People Press, 1981.

———. Frogs Into Princes. Moab, UT, Real People Press, 1979.

———. Reframing, Moab, UT, Real People Press, 1982.

———. Using Your Brain—for a change. Moab, UT, Real People Press. 1986.

Bartley, William. Werner Erhard. New York, Clarkson, Potter, Inc. 1978.

Benson, Frank and Eran Zaidel. The Dual Brain. New York, Guilford Press, 1985.

Bentov, Itzhak. Stalking the Wild Pendulum. New York, Dutton, 1977.

Biehler, Robert & Jack Snowman. Psychology Applied to Teaching. Boston, Houghton-Mifflin, 1982.

Bills, Robert E. Education for Intelligence or Failure? Washington, DC Acropolis Books, 1982.

Blanchard, Kenneth & Spencer Johnson. The One-Minute Manager. New York, William Morrow & Co. 1982.

Bolles, Richard. The Three Boxes of Life. Los Angeles, Ten Speed Press 1978.

Botkin, James. No Limits to Learning. Elmsford, NY, Pergamon Press 1980.

Boyer, Ernest & the Carnegie Foundation. High School: A Report on Secondary Education in America. New York. Harper & Row, 1983.

Branden, Nathaniel. The Psychology of Self-Esteem. New York. Bantam, 1969.

———. Honoring the Self. Los Angeles. Tarcher, 1983.

Brown, Barbara. Supermind: The Ultimate Energy. New York. Harper & Row, 1979.

Brown, G. Human Teaching for Human Learning: An Introduction to Confluent Education. New York. Viking Press 1971.

Browne, Harry. How I Found Freedom in an Unfree World. New York. Avon. 1973.

Bry, Adelaide. Visualization: Directing the Movies of Your Mind. New York, N.Y. Barnes and Noble, 1976.

Bry, Adelaide. EST: 60 Hours that Transform Your Life. New York, NY. Avon. 1976.

Buscaglia, Leo. Living, Loving and Learning. Thorofare, New Jersey. Charles B. Slack, 1982.

———. Love. Greenwich, Conn. Fawcett Books, 1972.

Bunzel, John. The Challenge to American Schools. London, Eng. Oxford University Press. 1983.

Buzan, Tony & Terence Dixon. The Evolving Brain. Devon, U.K. Brunel House, 1979.

Buzan, Tony. Use Both Sides of Your Brain. New York, NY. Dutton, 1974.

———. Make the Most of Your Mind. New York, NY Linden Press 1984.

C.S. Lewis. The Abolition of Man. New York, NY. Macmillan Publishing, 1978.

Cameron-Bandler, Leslie with David Gordon & Michael Lebeau. Know-How. San Rafael, Calif. FuturePace, Inc. 1985.

————. The Emprint Method. San Rafael, Future Pace, Inc. Calif. 1985.

Campbell, Don. Introduction to the Musical Brain. Richardson, Texas, Sound of Light. 1982.

Canfield, Jack and Wells, Harold. 100 Ways to Enhance Self-Concept in the Classroom. Englewood Cliffs, New Jersey. Prentice-Hall. 1976.

Caples, John. Tested Advertising Methods. Englewood Cliffs, New Jersey. Prentice-Hall, 1974.

Capra, Fritjof. The Turning Point. New York. Simon & Schuster, 1982.

Carnegie, Dale. How to Win Friends and Influence People. New York, NY. Pocket Books, 1936.

Chall, Jeane & Allan Mirsky. Education and the Brain. Chicago, Ill, Univ. of Chicago Press 1976.

Cho, Emily. Looking Terrific. New York, NY. Ballantine, 1978.

Clark, Barbara. Growing up Gifted. Columbus, Ohio. Charles Merrill, 1979.

Clemes, Harris & Reynold Bean. How to Raise Children's Self-Esteem. San Jose, CA. Ohaus, 1978.

Cleveland, Dr. Bernard. Master Teaching Techniques. Stone Mountain, Ga. Connecting Link Press. 1984.

Dennison, Dr. Paul. E-K for Kids. Glendale, Calif. Edu-Kinesthetics, Inc. 1984.

Dhority, Lynn. Acquisition through Creative Teaching. Sharon, MA. Center for Continuing Development, 1984.

Dossey, Larry. Space, Time and Medicine. Boulder, Co. Shambhala Publications Inc. 1982.

Dyer, Wayne. Gifts from Ekyos. New York, NY. Simon & Schuster. 1983.

————. Sky's the Limit. New York, NY. Pocket Books. 1980.

Eble, Kenneth. The Craft of Teaching. San Francisco, CA. Jossey-Boss Publishers, 1976.

Elkins, Dov. Teaching People to Love Themselves. Rochester, NY. Growth Assoc. 1977.

Ellis, Albert & Robert Harper. A New Guide to Rational Living. No. Hollywood, CA. Wilshire, 1977.

Emery, Stewart. Actualizations. New York, NY. Doubleday, 1977.

Ferguson, Marilyn. The Aquarian Conspiracy. Los Angeles, CA., Tarcher. 1980.

Fluegelman, Andrew (ed.) The New Games Book. Garden City, NY. Dolphin Books/Doubleday & Company. 1976.

————. (ed.) More New Games! Garden City, NY. Dolphin Books/Doubleday & Co. 1981.

Fuller, Buckminster. On Education. Amherst, Mass. University of Massachusetts Press, 1979.

Furth, Hans & Harry Wachs. Thinking Goes to School. New York, NY. Oxford Univ. Press. 1974.

Gawain, Shakti. Creative Visualization. Berkley, CA. Whatever Publishing, 1978.

Gibran, Kahlil. Spiritual Sayings of Kahlil Gibran. New York, NY. Bantam, 1962.

Gibson, James & James Hall. Damn Reading! New York, Vantage, 1969.

Glasser, William. Schools Without Failure. New York, NY. Harper & Row, 1969.

Goodlad, John. A Place Called School. New York, NY. McGraw-Hill. 1984.

Golas, Thaddeus. The Lazy Man's Guide to Enlightenment. New York, NY. Bantam, 1971.

Gordon, David. Therapeutic Metaphors. Cupertino, Calif. Meta Publications, 1978.

Gordon, David & Maribeth Meyers-Anderson. Phoenix. Cupertino, Calif. Meta Publications, 1981.

Gross, Beatrice and Ronald. The Great School Debate: Which Way For American Education? New York, NY. Simon & Schuster. 1984.

Halpern, Steven. Sound Health. Harper & Row Publishers. New York, New York, 1985.

Hampden-Turner, Charles. Maps of the Mind. New York, NY. Collier Books, 1981.

Harrison, Alan. How to Teach Children Twice as Much. New Rochelle, NY. Arlington House, 1973.

Hart, Leslie. How the Brain Works. New York, N.Y. Basic Books, 1975.

————. Human Brain and Human Learning. New York, N.Y. Longman, 1983.

————, Guide To School Change. New York, N.Y. Longman, 1985.

Heider, John. The Tao of Leadership. Atlanta, Ga. Humanics Limited, 1985.

Highet, Gilbert. The Immortal Profession. New York, NY. Weybright & Talley, 1976.

Hill, Napoleon. Think and Grow Rich. New York, NY. Fawcett, 1937.

Holt, John. How Children Learn. New York, NY. Pitman Pub. Co., 1967.

————. The Underachieving School. New York, NY. Pitman/Dell 1969.

————. Instead of Education. New York, NY. E. P. Dutton & Co. 1976.

Houston, Jean. Life Force. New York, NY. Dell Pub. Co., 1980.

————. The Possible Human. Los Angeles, CA. Tarcher, 1982.

Howard, Vernon. Word Power. Englewood Cliffs, New Jersey. Prentice-Hall. 1958.

Hubbard, L. Ron. Dianetics. New York, NY. Grosset & Dunlap, 1950.

————. Fundamentals of Thought. Los Angeles, CA. American Saint Hill Organization, 1956.

Hutchison, Michael. MegaBrain. William Morrow. New York, NY, 1986.

Jacobson, Sid. Meta-Cation. Cupertino, CA. Meta Publications. 1983.

James, Muriel & Dorothy Jongewald. Born to Win. Reading, Mass. Addison-Wesley, 1971.

Jampolsky, Gerald. Love is Letting Go of Fear. Millbrae, Ca. Celestial Arts, 1979.

Jensen, Eric. Student Success Secrets. New York, NY. Barron's Educational Series. 1982.

Johnson, Eric. Teaching School. New York, NY. Walker & Co., 1981.

Jones, Russell. Self-Fulfilling Prophecies. New York, Wiley & Son 1976.

Keyes, Ken. A Conscious Person's Guide to Relationships. St. Mary, Ky. Living Love, Publications, 1979.

Kim, Eugene & Richard Kellough. A Resource Guide for Secondary School Teaching. New York, NY. Mcmillian, 1983.

Koberg, Don & Jim Bagnal. The Universal Traveler. A Soft-Systems Guidebook. Los Altos, Calif, William Kaufmann, Inc, 1974.

Koerner, James. The Miseducation of American Teachers. Baltimore, Md. Penguin, 1965.

Kohl, Herbert. On Teaching. New York, NY. Schocken Books, 1976.

————. Growing Minds: On Becoming a Teacher. New York, NY. Harper & Row. 1985.

Kovalik, Susan. Teachers Make the Difference. San Jose, Ca. Discovery Press. 1986.

Laborde, Genie. Influencing with Integrity. Science & Behavior Books, Palo Alto, Calif. 1983.

Lakein, Alan. How to Get Control of Your Time and Your Life. New York, NY. Signet, 1973.

Lande, Nathaniel. Mindstyles, Lifestyles. Los Angeles, Ca. Price/Stern/Sloan. 1976.

Lankton, Steve. Practical Magic. Cupertino, Calif. Meta Publications, 1980.

Leff, Herbert. Playful Perception. Burlington, Vermont. Waterfront Books. 1984.

Lembo, John. Why Teachers Fail. Columbus, Ohio. Charles Merrill Co. 1971.

Lewis, Byron & Frank Pucelik. Magic Demystified. Lake Oswego, Ore. Metamorphous Press, 1982.

Lemesurier, Peter. Beyond All Belief. Great Britian, Element Books, Ltd. 1983.

Leonard, George. The Transformation: A Guide to the Inevitable Changes in Mankind. Los Angeles, Tarcher, 1981.

Lewiton, Mina. Faces Looking Up. New York, NY. Harper & Bros. 1960.

Lieberman, Mendel & Hardie Marion. Resolving Family & Other Conflicts. Santa Cruz, Calif. Unity Press, 1981.

Lingerman, Hal. The Healing Energies of Music. Wheaton, Ill. Theosophical Publishing House, 1985.

Lozanov, Georgi. Suggestology and Outlines of Suggestopedia. New York, NY. Gordon & Breach, 1979.

Machado, Luis. The Right to be Intelligent. Elmsford, New York. Percamon Press, 1980.

Marris, Peter. The Diffusion of Innovation. New York. Pantheon Books. 1974.

Mckay, Matthew. Messages: The Communication Book. Oakland, Ca., New Harbinger Publications, 1983.

Macht, Joel. Teacher/Teachim. New York, John Wiley & Sons, 1975.

Malloy, John. Dress for Success. New York, Warner Books, 1975.

Maltz, Maxwell. Psycho-Cybernetics. New York, NY. Prentice-Hall, 1960.

Mandino, Og. The Greatest Miracle in the World. New York, NY. Bantam, 1975.

Marvell-Mell, Linnaea. Basic Techniques in Neurolinguistic Programming. Lake Oswego, Oregon, Metamorphous Press, 1982.

McKim, Robert. Experiences in Visual Thinking. Monterey, Calif. Brooks/Cole, 1972.

Miele, DM. Suggestopedia: Easier Learning the Natural Way. Box 264 Sandy Spring, MD 20860.

Nadzo, Stefan. Being Who You Are. Franklin, Maine. Eden's Work, 1983.

Naisbitt, John. Megatrends. New York, NY. Warner Books, 1982.

National Commission on Excellence in Education. A Nation at Risk: The Imperative for Educational Reform. Washington, D.C. U.S. Govt. Pres. 1984.

Novak, Joseph and Bob Gowin. Learning How to Learn. New York, NY. Cambridge Univ. Press, 1984.

Ornstein, Robert. The Psychology of Consciousness. New York, NY. Penguin 1972.

———— and Richard Thompson. The Amazing Brain. Boston, MA. Houghton-Mifflin, 1984.

Ostrander, Sheila & Lynn Schroeder. Superlearning. New York, NY. Delta, 1979.

Ouchi, William. Theory Z. Reading, Mass. Addison-Wesley Pub. Co., 1981.

Parnes, Sidney. The Magic of Your Mind. Buffalo, NY. Creative Educational Foundation Press. 1985.

Pearce, Joseph. The Crack in the Cosmic Egg. New York, NY. Pocket Books, 1971.

Perkins, D. N. The Mind's Best Work, Cambridge, Mass. 1981 Harvard Univ. Press.

Postman, Neil. Teaching as a Conserving Activity. New York, Delacorte Press, 1979.

Powell, John. Why Am I Afraid to Love? Niles, Ill. Argus Comm. 1967.

————. Why am I Afraid to Tell You Who I Am? Argus Comm. Niles, Ill., 1969.

————. The Secret of Staying in Love. Niles, Ill. Argus Comm. 1974.

————. Fully Human, Fully Alive. Niles, Ill., Argus Communications, 1976.

————. Unconditional Love. Niles, Ill., Argus Communications, 1978.

Prather, Hugh. Notes on Love and Courage. Carden City, NJ. Doubleday & Co., 1977.

Pritchard, Allyn and Jean Taylor. Accelerating Learning: The Use of Suggestion in the Classroom. Novato, CA, 1980.

Purser, Lee. Help Yourself. Del Mar, CA. Waterside Productions, 1982.

Ravitch, Diane. The Troubled Crusade: American Education 1945–1980. New York, NY. Basic Books, 1984.,

Ray, Sondra. Loving Relationships. Millbrae, CA. Celestial Arts, 1980.

Raudsepp, Eugene. Creative Growth Games. New York, NY. Perigee Books, 1977.

Richards, M. C. Toward Wholeness. Columbia U. Press, New York, 1980.

Robbins, Anthony. Unlimited Power. New York, NY. Simon & Schuster, 1986.

Roberts, Jane. The Nature of Personal Reality: A Seth Book. Englewood Cliffs, NJ. Prentice-Hall, 1974.

Rose, Colin. Accelerated Learning. New York, NY. Dell. 1985.

Russell, Peter. The Brain Book. New York. Hawthorne 1979.

———. The Global Brain. Los Angeles, Ca. Tarcher, 1983.

Rothman, Ester. Troubled Teachers. New York, NY. David McKay Company, 1977.

Samples, Bob. The Wholeschool Book. Reading, Mass. Wesley Pub. Co. 1976.

Satir, Virginia. Making Contact. Berkeley, Calif. Celestial Arts, 1976.

Schmid, Charles. Learning in New Dimensions. Sharon, MA. Center for Continuing Development. 1982.

Seabury, David. The Art of Selfishness. New York, NY. Pocket Books, 1964.

Silva, Jose. The Silva Mind Control Method. New York, NY. Pocket Books, 1977.

Sizer, Theodore. Horace's Compromise: The Dilemma of the American High School. Boston, Mass. Houghton-Mifflin. 1983.

Shah, Idres. The Sufis. New York, NY. Anchor Books, 1971.

Sheldrake, Rupert. A New Science of Life. Los Angeles, Tarcher, 1982.

Shuster, Donald. Suggestive-Accelerative Learning & Teaching. Ames, Iowa, S.A.L.T. 1976.

Shuster, Donald with Charles Gritton. S.A.L.T. Theory and Applications. Carlisle, Iowa. PhotoPrint. 1985.

Smotherton, Ron. Transforming #1. San Francisco, CA. Context Publications, 1982.

Smith, Adam. Powers of Mind. New York, NY. Ballantine, 1975.

Soloveichik, Simon. Soviet Life Magazine, "Odd Way to Teach, But It Works." May 1979.

Stein, Ben. Bunkhouse Logic. New York, NY. Avon, 1981.

Sternberg, Roger. Beyond I.Q. New York, NY. Cambridge Univ. Press, 1985.

Strauch, Ralph. The Reality Illusion. Wheaton, Ill. Theosophical Publishing House, 1982.

Toffler, Alvin. Learning for Tomorrow. New York, NY. Random House, 1974.

U.S. Dept. of Education. What Works: Research About Teaching and Learning. Pueblo, Colorado, Consumer Information Center, 1986.

Van Nagel. Megateaching and Learning. Indian Rock Beach, Fla., Southern Institute Press, Inc. 1985.

Viscott, David. Risking. New York, NY. Pocket Books, 1977.

———. The Language of Feelings. New York. NY. Pocket Books, 1976.

Watson, Lyall. Lifetide. London, Hodder & Stoughton, 1979.

Watts, Alan. Cloud-Hidden. New York, NY. Vintage Books. 1974.

Willett, Edward. Modernizing the Little Red Schoolhouse. Englewood Cliffs, New Jersey, Educational Technology Publications, 1979.   •

Wolf, Fred. Taking the Quantam Leap. New York, NY. Harper & Row, 1981.

Youngs, Bettie B. Stress in Children. New York, NY. Arbor House. 1985.

Index

Accelerated learning, 262
Acknowledgements, 77, 207–212
Affirmation, 85, 116
Agreement frames, 144
Analogy, 109
Anchors, 26, 111
Attention, How to get it, 72–75, 80
Audio-Visual aids, 103
Auditory, 21, 22, 36, 38, 46, 57, 110, 142, 189
Authenticity, 15
Authority, *see* credibility

Bachman, Jerald, 2
Bandler, Richard, 263
Barnard, Jack, 89
Bellamy, G. Thomas, 27
Berne, Eric, 204
Bills, Dr. Robert, 34, 139
Blanchard, Everard, 217
Bloom's Taxonomy, 169
Bohm, David, 170
Bohr, Niels, 170
Botkin, James, 18
Brain
    Structure, 24–25
    Triune, 24
Bridges, Helice, 212
Brown, Dr. Barbara, 91
Bryant, "Bear", 16
Butler, Susan, 23, 29
Buzan, Tony, 33

Campbell, Don, 105
Canfield, Jack, 212
Carlson, Dr., 224
Carnegie, Dale, 109
Chalkboard, 102
Challenges, 90
Change velocity, 1
Cho, Emily, 64
Chunking, 111
Churchill, Winston, 55
Classroom management, 178
Clives, Manfred, 105
Closure, 126–36
Coaching, 16, 231
Cognitive Dissonance, 12
Commitments
    Student, 84
Communication
    Content, 97
    Meaning, 10
    Myths, 95

Conditioning
    Beliefs, 12
Congruency, 108, 135
Contracts, oral, 82
Cosgrove, Don, 235–37
Costa, Arthur, 167, 169
Coupling, 33
Creativity, 170
Credibility, 79
Cultural Diversity, 28, 173–74
Curriculum, 42
    Thematic approach, 49

Dennison, Dr. Paul, 86
DeRopp, 241
Dialogue, pre and post, 171
Discipline, 176–91
Discussion, 132
Donchin, Emanuel, 35
Downey, Dorothy, 149
Drake, Dr. Roger, 69
Dress Standards, 63, 64
Dropout Rates, 2
Dyer, Dr. Wayne, 217

Educational Kinesiology, 86
Ego, 14
Einstein, Albert, 170
Electronic Authority, 2
Embedded commands, *see* language
Emery, Stewart, 153
Emotions, 86
Environments, 53–60
Erhard, Werner, 228
Evaluations, 132–34, 214–24, 232–37
Expectations, 81, 89

Fears
    Student, 79
Feedback, 98
    conscious, 99
    immediate, 132
    non-conscious, 99
Ferguson, Marilyn, 62, 248
Flip charts, 102
Free will, 8
Fuller, R. Buckminster, 32, 54
Future Pace, 127, 135

Gardner, Dr. Howard, 33
Geier, Dr. John, 149
Ghandi, Mahatma, 5

Ginott, Haim, 210
Gordon, David, 115
Gradient, 79, 116
Greetings, 73
Gregorac, 23
Grinder, John, 263
Guests, 81

Halo Effect, 12
Hargrove, Gail, 86
Hart, Leslie, 19, 53, 54
Heider, John, 15
Hemispheric Dominance, 23
Hermann, Ned, 23
Hill, Dr. Jack, 220, 243
Houston, Dr. Jean, 86, 100, 109
Humor, 122
Hunter, Dr. Madeline, 99, 100, 180, 215

Imagery, 91
Incorporation, 143
Information Age, 2
Interactions
    Receiving questions, 163
    Successful qualities, 161–63
Ishmael, Dr., 56

Kennedy, Robert F., 5, 134
Kinesthet, 21, 22, 37, 38, 46, 57, 142, 189
Kovalik, Susan, 49, 149, 199

LaBorde, Genie, 75
Lang, Eugene, 86
Language, its effects (*see also* communication)
    Body, 154–55
    Double bind, 114
    Embedded commands, 118
    Linkage, 114
    Metaphors, 115
    Most powerful words, 111
    Positive wording, 73, 112, 123–24
    Precision, 155–58
    Presuppositions, 119
    Quotes, 114
    Reframing, 118
    Sex-related patterns, 116
Lao Tzu, 15
Learning
    Active, 193–201
    Activities, 196
    Barriers, 131
    Disabled, 11, 22, 32
    Innovative, 18
    Maintenance, 18
    Multi-level, 19
    Non-conscious, 19
    Student specialists, 89
    Styles, 11, 25–28
    Transfer, 90
Leff, Herbert, 118
Lehrl, Siegfried, 111
Lesson Planning, 41–51
Listening, 148–59
    Empathetic, 150
    How to foster, 150
    Mistakes, 152
Logistics, 82
Lombardi, Vince, 16
Lorayne, Harry, 113
Lozanov, Dr. Georgi, 87, 105, 262
Lucas, Jerry, 113

MacLean, Paul, 24, 35
Malloy, John, 63, 64
Maresh, Nancy, 193
Market research, 66
Markoff, 113
Marris, Peter, 247
Marzano, Robert, 169
Maslow, Abraham, 68
McLuhan, Marshall, 62
Mehrabian, Albert, 61, 96, 98
Metaphors, *see* language
Meta-Teaching Model, 36
Mind-calming, 91–92
Mind-mapping, 51, 131
Miss "A", 7
Motivation
    tools, 79–93
Muller, Robert, 42
Music, 105–8

Nasrudin, Mulla, 34
Neenan, David, 247
Neurolinguistic Programming (NLP), 263
Note-taking, 104

Oh, Sadahara, 16
Outcomes, 44

Papez, Janes, 24
Participation, 102
Penfield, Dr. William, 86
Peterson, Vincent, 131
Powell, J. W., 168
Presentation
    Models, 46–49
Pre-testing, 81
Projection, 12
Provider-user relationship, 2
Purpose
    Course, 82
    Lesson planning, 43

Questions
    Preparation to answer, 164
    Responses, 164–66, 169
    Types, 167
    Who to call on, 166
    Wrong answers, 167–69

Race & Human Relations Dept., 4
Rapport
    Group, 75
    How to establish, 139
    Learning names, 92
    Monitor, 141
    Multiple ways to build, 141
    On-going, 140
    Verbal, 76
Reality
    Bridge, 93, 110
    Personal, 8
Reframing, *see* language
Rehearsals, 65, 66, 68
Representational systems, 22
Respect, 78
Review, 130
Riddles, 113
Robbins, Anthony, 32
Rothman, Esther, 228
Round-up, 110
Rosenthal, 12

Safety
    Emotional, 93
Self-Esteem, 114
Sensory Acuity, 98–99
Sharing, 128, 169
Shorbe, Dr., 56
Shula, Don, 16
Shuster, Don, 105
Siccone, 212
Skinner, B. F., 220
Sperry, Dr. Roger, 23, 35
Stable Datum, 77
States, Physiological
    As a Variable, 20
    Changing, 119–24
    Resourceful, 68, 74, 75
    Unresourceful, 13
Stories, *see also* metaphors, 122
Strategies, 20
    Learning, 25–33
Suggestion, the power and uses of, 122–24
Support Tools, 102–8

Tarkanian, Jerry, 16
Tasking, 113
Team Building, 85
    Classroom community, 92
Teen Suicides, 4
Testing, *see* evaluations
Thinking skills, 169–70
Time references, 26, 116
Trends, Nine Changing, 1–5
Turning Point for Teachers, 7

Vision, 85, 229–30
Visual, 21, 22, 37, 38, 46, 57, 142, 189
Visualization, *see also* imagery, 129

Wooden, John, 16
Wrong Answers, 101

Critical Thinking For Growing Minds

Fundamentals for Success

☑ Bolster important thinking skills
☑ Build self-confidence, self-esteem
☑ Learn how to "run your own brain"

Enjoy teaching and learning more. Boost achievement scores and instill a love of learning. Here's the program that deals with thinking from the brain's point of view—how we think, how we learn, thinking about thinking and growing. Learn how to infuse thinking, questioning and decision-making.

You'll learn:

☑ Why Bloom's Taxonomy is dangerous to your students

☑ What are the three thinking tools and how to improve them

☑ Five tools to run your own brain be more in control of your life

☑ The secrets to children who love to think and grow everyday

☑ How learning styles affect thinking

☑ Specific classroom examples given

3 Exciting Tapes (Regular Price) .. $39.50
Your Discount $29.50

How To Use Music in Teaching and Training

Insider's Guide to Success

☑ For both education and business
☑ Boost excitement of learning
☑ Control the environment

Enjoy your work and get top results! You get three specially-designed tapes. *Tape #1:* how to use music in the learning process. It's complete with music samples to make each of the points. *Tape #2:* is the most-requested special effects for both fun and results. *Tape #3:* is a specially selected and composed Baroque tape, perfect for the ideal learning state.

You'll learn:

☑ How to reduce stress and boost learning
☑ How to use all types of music and when to use it
☑ Musical secrets to motivation, excitement and fun
☑ Learn about concert reading and rap music
☑ Get the exact Baroque classics selected and re-composed for this tape set only
☑ How to use music to discipline and enhance memory
☑ The exciting special effects tape with all your favorites: Dragnet, screams, Jaws, fanfare and more

3 Exciting Tapes (Regular Price) .. $39.50
Your Discount Price $29.50

The Amazing Uses of NLP

Dozens of easy-to-use strategies

☑ Sky-rocket learning by 45-200%
☑ Gain greater poise, ease & effectiveness
☑ Boost excitement, participation & results

Get that success feeling! This tape is a beginner's guide to using NLP (neuro-linguistic programming) in teaching and training. NLP is a behavioral science developed in the mid-70's by John Grinder and Richard Bandler. It's a remarkable model of human engineering that allows for the duplication of human excellence. Learn how you can use this amazing tool in your teaching or training.

You'll learn:

☑ What is NLP and how can you use it daily
☑ Rapport – how to build it & keep it
☑ Reframing – the power of perspective
☑ Congruency – the value of single messages
☑ States – resource states and learning states
☑ Anchoring – does the name Pavlov ring a bell?
☑ Learning strategies – how learning happens
☑ Plus – specific examples of how to use each of these tools in your work

3 Exciting Tapes (Regular Price) .. $39.50
Your Discount Price $29.50

Mind Mapping: Your LearningTool

Best methods & Hot Tips

☑ Boost learning, comprehension & recall
☑ Build self-confidence and self-esteem
☑ Instill a real love of learning for all kids

You'll learn

☑ Learn how to boost recall, memory & motivation
☑ Find out WHY it works as well as how it works
☑ Discover how it's different from clustering, mapping or webbing
☑ Get the specifics of how to learn it and teach it
☑ Learn why colors and symbols are so important

See, hear and feel your kids succeed! Mind Mapping can make the difference between failure and success for many learners. It is a new brain-compatible form of note-taking and organizing information. The method is perfect for business, recreation and school—especially the "At-Risk" student.

3 Exciting Tapes (Regular Price) $39.50
Your Discount Price $29.50
30' Video Program $29.50
Audiotapes and Video $49.50

CALL 1-800-325-4769 OR 619-755-6670 TO ORDER TODAY!

Goal-Getting for Everyday Winning

- ☑ Boost performance without stress
- ☑ Start setting and reaching Goals
- ☑ Boost your self-esteem & satisfaction

Feel confident & boost self-esteem. Earn higher income and enjoy less stress. Goal-getting means that you actually GET your goals, not just set them. In these special tapes, you'll learn exactly how to set your goals so that you'll reach them. You'll learn how to run your own brain so that you are in control of your life. And best of all, this program works!

You'll learn:

- ☑ The ten amazing criteria for setting goals
- ☑ How to manage your goals like a project
- ☑ Why vision, purpose and mission affect goals
- ☑ How you've been sabotaging yourself & how to stop it
- ☑ How your personality & learning style affects goals
- ☑ How to get in touch with your beliefs, values & programming
- ☑ How to get massively motivated to reach goals

3 Exciting Tapes (Regular Price). .. $39.50
Your Discount Price $29.50

How to Use Accelerated Learning

Key Strategies for Teachers & Trainers

- ☑ Documented to boost learning 300% and more!
- ☑ Discover how to put more joy & motivation in learning
- ☑ Build self-esteem, confidence & boost performance

Your chance to boost self-esteem, build motivation and boost performance! Accelerated learning is a multi-disciplinary methodology of teaching and learning that was brought to the United States by Dr. Georgi Lozanov in the late 1970's. Key elements include using music, imagery, relaxation, lowering stress, high expectations and an orchestrated, activated lesson plan.

You'll learn:

- ☑ How to set up a special accelerated environment
- ☑ The ways to engage and activate learners
- ☑ From actual classroom demonstrations and recordings
- ☑ The secrets of activating the non-conscious brain
- ☑ The six stages of an accelerated learning lesson plan: environment, relaxation & conditioning, active presenting, passive learning, activation and verification
- ☑ The role of music, games and peripherals

3 Exciting Tapes (Regular Price) .. $39.50
Your Discount Price $29.50

"At-Risk" Students Success Tools

- ☑ Boost student motivation & interest
- ☑ Increase understanding, recall & test performance
- ☑ Get them to stay in school & graduate

Lower your stress and feel better about your work! The "At-Risk" student is defined as a student with high-risk factors in his life such as poverty, teen parenting, drugs, family violence, criminal conduct and poorly educated or single parents. These students have "the deck stacked against them" but can be successful in school and life with the proper educational environment. Learn what you can do to make sure that these students stay in school and feel optimistic about their future.

You'll learn:

- ☑ How to identify the "At-Risk" student
- ☑ How to create a more nurturing environment
- ☑ How recent brain research can help you reach them
- ☑ The power of teaching visualization & relaxation
- ☑ The tools to reach the "At-Risk" learning styles
- ☑ How to encourage expressing feelings, conflict resolution
- ☑ The power of rituals, affirmations & music
- ☑ Why give more control instead of taking it away!
- ☑ The secret of using teams to make a difference

3 Exciting Tapes (Regular Price) ... $39.50
Your Discount Price $29.50

Enjoy a Terrific Day Every Day

Ideas and Tools for Daily Joy

- ☑ Boost motivation, excitement and results!
- ☑ Gain valuable and permanent life skills
- ☑ Feel more confident, happy and joyful

Enjoy life and cut stress! It's not what happens to you that counts, it's how you respond. Living life well is a skill, not a matter of luck. There are things that happy people do every day that do make a difference. In these exciting tapes, you'll learn what it is that you can do to have a terrific day every day.

You'll learn:

- ☑ The real power of asking questions
- ☑ How to get in a positive frame of mind
- ☑ How to overcome obstacles and adversity
- ☑ How to get inspired to make every day better through goals, purpose, mission and planning
- ☑ How to deal with difficult people

3 Exciting Tapes (Regular Price) .. $39.50
Your Discount Price $29.50

CALL 1-800-325-4769 OR 619-755-6670 TO ORDER TODAY!

Classroom Interactions

Strategies & Tools for Success

☑ How to engage, excite and nurture learning
☑ Build self-esteem, confidence and motivation
☑ Learn the secrets to a great class session

Classroom Interactions are the one area that means the most to the learner. It's the area of asking questions, getting responses, handling wrong answers, handling "wisecrackers" and other student sharing. It's the interaction that students remember the most and teachers are often least prepared for to handle. It's time you got the specific interactive strategies to build a successful environment of learners.

You'll learn:

☑ How to build thinking skills and which ones are modality dependent (auditory, visual, kinesthetic)

☑ How to conduct discussion groups and inquiry

☑ How to ask questions that get answers

☑ Twenty five secrets to handling wrong answers

☑ How to respond to hostile questions

☑ How to respect cultural diversity

3 Exciting Tapes (Regular Price) ...$39.50
Your Discount Price $29.50

Introduction to Accelerated Learning

For first-time Presenters

☑ Put more fun in teaching & training
☑ Boost motivation and achievement in learning
☑ Build self-esteem & reduce discipline problems

Bring the joy back in learning! The accelerated learning approach was brought to the United States by Dr. Georgi Lozanov in the late 1970's. It's the original whole-brain, integrative teaching approach that gets students excited about learning! key elements include using music, imagery, relaxation, lowering stress, high expectations and an orchestrated, activated lesson plan.

You'll learn:

☑ How to get started and keep it going
☑ The real nuts and bolts of accelerated learning
☑ How to set up a special learning environment
☑ What are the key principles to make it work
☑ Classroom demonstrations and recordings
☑ The secrets of activating the non-conscious learner
☑ The six stages of an accelerated learning lesson plan: environment, relaxation & conditioning, active presenting, passive learning, activation and verification
☑ Learn the role of music, games and peripherals.

3 Exciting Tapes(Regular Price) $39.50
Your Discount Price $29.50

Restructuring A New School Climate

Strategies & Ideas for Success

☑ Build a model school you're proud of!
☑ Learn what other great schools are doing
☑ Get the skills,ideas and tools to succeed

Make it happen and feel great about it! Whether you're involved in improving school climate or fundamental restructuring, this is for you. Learn what other schools are doing and just as importantly, learn from their mistakes. Learn what improvements you can do with virtually no budget or the whole "ball of wax" with a larger budget. This is motivating, inspiring and the program that gets you going!

You'll learn:

☑ The types of educational reform & whats working
☑ Discover the ten issues of educational change
☑ Find out the REAL goal of educational change
☑ Learn to re-design education; a whole new paradigm
☑ Learn the four things it takes to be an effective change agent
☑ Find out more about the five areas of a restructured school management, relationships, systems, learning & people
☑ Learn 10 proven things you can do to change school culture.

3 Exciting Tapes(Regular Price) $39.50
Your Discount Price $29.50

Winning Time: Your Openings & Closings

Strategies for Teaching & Training

☑ Boost student motivation & interest
☑ Increase understanding & recall
☑ Make your sessions more memorable

You'll learn:

☑ The four key parts to a great opening
☑ How to set up a terrific environment
☑ How to get immediate attention AND keep it
☑ The secret of the first 60 seconds
☑ The four best motivators
☑ The three key parts to closure
☑ Secrets to long-term behavior change
☑ How to get your students excited and wanting more

Raise student success & boost learning! How you open and close a class is often more important than the class itself. Research shows that students remember the beginning and ending of activities more than the middle. Doesn't it make sense to find out how to make what you do MUCH more effective?

3 Exciting Tapes(Regular Price) $39.50
Your Discount Price $29.50

CALL 1-800-325-4769 OR 619-755-6670 TO ORDER TODAY!

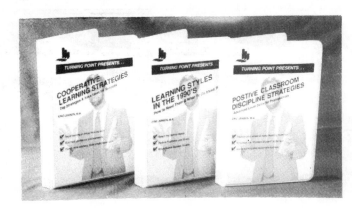
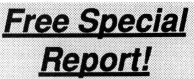

Presentation Success Skills Volume I

How to Successfully Present Nearly Anything

☑ Build self-confidence & reduce anxiety
☑ Reach your audience better-get results!
☑ Boost your career options

Get a boost of self-confidence and earn more money! This is a must for all teachers, trainers and administrators. Positive skill-building with interactive portions and special confidence-boosters. Get these fundamentals and feel the success!

You'll learn:

☑ How to open & close your presentation
☑ Massive self-confidence & poise
☑ How to build rapport and gain favor FAST
☑ Tools to engage, motivate and persuade
☑ How to respond to hecklers with poise
☑ Where to stand, move and look & why
☑ Why those first 60" are the most important
☑ How to get the all-critical feedback

3 Exciting Tapes (Regular Price) ... $39.50
Your Discount Price $29.50

Self Esteem Breakthroughs

How to Make it Happen

☑ For professionals and students
☑ Improve behavior, attitudes and satisfaction
☑ Boost learning and classroom success

Raise your own self-esteem and feel great! With your kids, expect it to boost academic success. Self esteem myths are exposed—what it is and what it isn't. This is an interactive tape where you get to do activities while listening. You'll learn how to build self-esteem plus get hot tips for quick results.

You'll learn:

☑ The three secrets to building self-esteem
☑ Find out why success is unrelated to self-esteem
☑ How to increase personal power
☑ Nineteen special specific to-dos including learning to support others, tell the truth, complete tasks, health, keep score, be responsible, enjoy uniqueness, etc.
☑ How to improve communications for better self-esteem
☑ 25 special bonus tips for classroom interactions

3 Exciting Tapes (Regular Price) ... $39.50
Your Discount Price $29.50

Learning Modalities: Visual, Auditory & Kinesthetic

How to Read Them & Succeed Daily

☑ Boost student performance 30-50%
☑ Reach the "Hard-to-Reach" Students
☑ Build communication, rapport & results

What a success and confidence booster! Read others and respond to them fast. You'll learn all you need to know about visual, auditory and kinesthetic learners. You also discover the world of the digital learner and the combination learners. The explanations are simple, easy-to-understand and next-day applicable.

You'll learn:

☑ What each learner likes & dislikes
☑ Who is good at spelling, reading & math
☑ The inside stories on how to get along with each
☑ The peculiarities of each and what to do about it
☑ How to identify each type within seconds
☑ The specific strategies for working with each of them
☑ The amazing folly of Bloom's Taxonomy

3 Exciting Tapes (Regular Price) ... $39.50
Your Discount Price $29.50

Presentation Success Skills, Vol. II

Advanced Level Skills Boost for Speaking Professionals

☑ Get greater self-confidence & respect
☑ Boost audience response & excitement
☑ Jump to "Star-level" presenter status

Boost that self-confidence sky-high! In this career-boosting sequel to Vol. 1, you'll learn all the inside secrets the pros use to build rapport, get attention and make your points heard.

You'll learn:

☑ How to build your self-image & self-esteem sky-high

☑ 10 Key state changes you MUST know about
☑ Inside tips on how to reach the unconscious mind
☑ How to reach the four primary audience needs
☑ Why you should have three or less goals each time
☑ How to develop "leverage" on the audience
☑ How to handle outside distractions with class
☑ The magic of unfinished sentences
☑ Purposeful metaphors and stories that change lives
☑ How to create a magical bonding-the "heartspace"

3 Exciting Tapes (Regular Price) $39.50
Your Discount Price $29.50

Motivation and Love of Learning

How to Boost Interest & Excitement in Learning

- ☑ How to "hook-in" Your Learners Better
- ☑ How to Boost Learning 20-45%
- ☑ Build self-confidence & self-esteem

Get this program and feel great! You'll be more confident in your work and enjoy less stress. This is the amazing program that tells you all you need to know about learning—how we get motivated, how we learn and how we know that we know it. You'll learn about "Optimal Learning States" and how to evoke them. You'll learn what causes slow learners and what creates gifted learners.

You'll learn:

- ☑ How to Motivate Nearly Any Learner
    Four Success Tools you can use everyday
- ☑ How to combat fear, frustration & apathy
    Which "states" are best & how to get them
- ☑ The magic of acquisition-Learning in Motion
    How to make it happen time & again
- ☑ The all-important Self-convincer
    Why reinforcement is not enough
    How to instill love of learning
- ☑ How to create gifted learners and heal
    the slow learner tendencies

3 Exciting Tapes (Regular Price) ... $39.50
Your Discount Price $29.50

Leadership in Action

Specific actions steps to be a top leader now!

- ☑ How to build confidence & charisma
- ☑ Get empowered to empower others
- ☑ Move to a higher professional level

Boost your self-confidence and self-respect. Make a difference in other's lives and feel terrific about it! Are you a leader now? Are you ready to be a leader? If so, this program is for you. It's got the 8 most important actions a leader can take and how to begin them now. It's inspiring and exciting to know you can be leader, but you've got to start now!

You'll learn:

- ☑ Vision – How to develop a compelling & inspiring one
- ☑ Integrity – How your actions speak louder than your words
- ☑ Commitments – How to make the type that leaders make
- ☑ Requests—Leaders ask a lot of others, do you know how to?
- ☑ Accountability – The buck stops here; or does it?
- ☑ Teamwork – How to create alliances and partnerships
- ☑ Outcome thinking – Thinking of outcomes instead of problems
- ☑ Listening – How to listen like a true leader

3 Exciting Tapes (Regular Price) ... $39.50
Your Discount Price $29.50

How to Teach or Train Using NLP

Strategies for Success

- ☑ Build your confidence & competence
- ☑ Reach more learners more often
- ☑ Reduce stress and frustration & have fun!

Learn the secrets of peak performance in learning. NLP is neuro-linguistic programming, a dynamic behavior model developed in the 1970's by John Grinder and Richard Bandler. You'll learn how to become more excellent by making finer distinctions, learning new skills and getting eye-opening ideas on how the brain and behaviors work. It's a terrific "upgrade" to your professional base and a real "toolbox" of goodies you can use with yourself, too!

You'll learn:

- ☑ Applications in your work for motivation, discipline, esteem, performance and rapport.
- ☑ Where to start, what to learn first in NLP
- ☑ How much you're already *now* doing without even knowing it & how to do it better
- ☑ How to positively "run your own brain"
- ☑ How to identify & work with your students better
- ☑ The real meaning behind all the jargon words like "rapport, state, representations, modalities, etc"
- ☑ Learn to create constant and consistent success

3 Exciting Tapes (Regular Price) ... $39.50
Your Discount Price $29.50

TeamBuilding: Top Performance Strategies

Skills for Success in the 90's

- ☑ For both education and business
- ☑ Boost motivation & peak performance
- ☑ Inspire quality work & participation

You'll learn:

- ☑ Learn how to engineer the team's make-up
- ☑ Uncover the secrets of building group bonding
- ☑ Find out how to develop team leadership & spirit
- ☑ Get the secrets to peak performance & accountability
- ☑ Plus – get 25 bonus tips on how to make teams excel
- ☑ How to deal with difficult people
- ☑ How to reduce stress and enjoy each day more
- ☑ The power of appreciation

Get results fast! Gain professional confidence. You get three tapes chock-full of the ten strategies for team success. These time-tested tools will get your teams built, developed and maintained. Learn the why as well as the how to do it. And learn this from an expert that DOES teambuilding, not just talks about it.

3 Exciting Tapes (Regular Price) ... $39.50
Your Discount Price $29.50

CALL 1-800-325-4769 OR 619-755-6670 TO ORDER TODAY!

ORDER HERE: ☎

1. <u>Choose: Phone/FAX or mail</u>

For faster service call 1-800-325-4769 or 619-755-6670. Have a credit card or purchase order ready. Or FAX us your order 24 hrs 619-792-2858 or complete order form below and mail to address listed on item #7.

2. <u>Tell us What You Want:</u>

	Product Name	Quantity	Unit Price	Total
1.				
2.				
3.				
4.				
5.				
6.				

3. <u>Total your Order:</u>

Subtotal: _____

UPS Shipping & Handling Charge: 10% U.S./$3 under $30 (20% Foreign): _____

(orders sent with insufficient shipping postage will be returned or delayed 4-8 weeks)

Calif. Residents Only Add 7% Tax: _____

Grand Total: _____

4. <u>Indicate Form of Payment</u>   MasterCard   VISA

☐ Visa/MC Card# _____ Exp. _____ Signature _____

☐ Purchase Order # _____ ☐ Personal Check OR Money Order (U.S. Funds only) ☐ Cash (At Conference Only)

5. <u>Tell Us Who You Are (or Where To Ship Your Order):</u>

Print Name _____ Street _____

City _____ State _____ Zip _____ Country _____ Phone( ) _____

6. <u>How To Qualify for a Free Gift:</u>

Print the names & addresses of 2 colleague(s) below & get a FREE Special Report: "Brain & Learning Research of the 80's & 90's."

Name _____ Name _____

Address _____ Address _____

City _____ State ____ Zip ____ City _____ State ____ Zip ____

7. <u>Mail or Fax Your Order Today To:</u>

Turning Point, P.O. Box 2551, Del Mar, CA 92014 • Toll Free 1-800-325-4769 or 619-755-6670/ FAX 619-792-2858

detach here